A WOMAN LIKE THAT

A WOMAN LIKE THAT

Lesbian and Bisexual Writers

Tell Their Coming Out Stories

Edited by

Joan Larkin

AVON BOOKS ◆ NEW YORK

"My Debut" by Blanche McCrary Boyd appeared in somewhat different form and under the title "Warpaint and Orchids" in the March-May 1999 issue of the *Oxford American*.

Lines from "Velvet Shoes" quoted in "The Secret Agent" are from *Collected Poems* by Elinor Wylie, copyright © 1921 by Alfred A. Knopf, Inc., renewed 1949 by William Rose Benet, reprinted by permission of the publisher.

Song lyrics quoted in "The Coming Out of a Gay Pride Child" are used by permission, as follows: "Goody Goody" by Johnny Mercer and Matty Malneck © 1935, 1936 by DeSylva, Brown & Henderson Inc. Copyrights renewed, assigned to WB Music Corp. and Malneck Music for USA. Chappell & Co. controls rights for the world excluding USA. All rights reserved. Used by permission of Warner Bros. Publications U.S. Inc., Miami, FL 33014; "I Just Fall In Love Again" by Stephen H. Dorff and Larry Herbstritt © 1977 BMG Songs, Inc. (ASCAP)/Careers-BMG Music Publishing, Inc. (BMI). Used by permission of BMG Music Publishing, Inc.

AVON BOOKS, INC.
1350 Avenue of the Americas
New York, New York 10019

Collection copyright © 1999 by Joan Larkin
Interior design by Kellan Peck
ISBN: 0-380-97698-6

Library of Congress Cataloging in Publication Data:

A woman like that : lesbian and bisexual writers tell their
coming out stories / edited by Joan Larkin. — 1st ed.
p.   cm.
"An Avon book."
1. Women authors, American—20th century Biography.
2. Bisexual women—United States Biography.   3. Lesbians—United States Biography.
4. Coming out (Sexual orientation)   I. Larkin, Joan.
PS153.L46W66   1999   99-35286
810.9'9206643—dc21   CIP

First Bard Printing: October 1999

BARD TRADEMARK REG. U.S. PAT. OFF. AND IN OTHER COUNTRIES, MARCA REGISTRADA,
HECHO EN U.S.A.

Printed in the U.S.A.

FIRST EDITION

QPM   10   9   8   7   6   5   4   3   2   1

for Martha Shelley

ACKNOWLEDGMENTS

Creating an anthology is a complex collaborative effort, and I owe thanks to the many people who contributed to the shaping of *A Woman Like That:* my extraordinary agent Sydelle Kramer and the staff of the Frances Goldin Literary Agency; my gifted and supportive editors, Charlotte Abbott, Rachel Klayman, and Tia Maggini; my generous friend Steve Turtell, who loves clarity and who took time to read and offer excellent advice; Linsey Abrams, Bea Gates, Gerry Gomez Pearlberg, and the volunteer archivists at the Lesbian Herstory Archives, who helped me think about lesbian history and literature; and, once again, Kate Larkin, for lending her always trustworthy ear and eye. Work became pleasure thanks to Kate Clinton and Urvashi Vaid, who offered a room with a view, and to Michael Bronski, Blanche Wiesen Cook, Karin Cook, and Michelle Crone, who steered me to contributors I hadn't previously known. I am indebted to numerous artists, photographers, and writers whose work, though it does not appear here, helped shape my vision of this book, especially Electa

Arenal, Jana Brenning, Toi Derricotte, Louise Fishman, Katherine V. Forrest, Morgan Gwenwald, Marilyn Hacker, Ann McDonald, Cherríe Moraga, Esther Newton, Sarah Schulman, and Carmelita Tropicana. I am grateful to Stanley Siegel, rare witness, for illuminating the originality and courage of gay lives. I owe deep thanks, always, to Eileen Myles and to all the friends who listened lovingly and patiently, who reminded me to rest and laugh and write, especially Doug Atwood, Jill Bosworth, Naomi Bushman, Edith Chevat, Fletcher Copp, John Masterson, Honor Moore, Paul Selig, and Bill Sullivan. My greatest debt of all is to the thirty-one contributors, all of whom wrote new, truthful, and eloquent stories for this collection. These writers have added immeasurably to my knowledge of and joy in lesbian life and writing. Working with them has been an immense privilege.

CONTENTS

CONTENTS

x

INTRODUCTION

Coming out:

First desire. First awareness that desire may not be told. First awareness that another is gay or lesbian, perhaps without having words for this yet. First time being called a lesbian—or *lezzie* or *dyke* or *queer*. First time naming oneself lesbian—or femme or butch, bisexual or transgender, outlaw or "not sure, but . . ." First kiss with a woman. First time making love with a woman. First time getting caught. First affirmation by another.

"Coming out" is shorthand for countless passages, chosen and forced, welcome and unwelcome. The same phrase can mean a long struggle to let go of sexual conformity or a single moment of remembering early stirrings, before they were labeled and censored. And coming out means the necessary, ongoing courage to be visible. To risk ostracism, violence, and loss. To embrace one's core sense of self—whether through rebellion, defiance, mourning, laughter, relief, or tenderness.

★　　★　　★

When I began editing *A Woman Like That,* I invited lesbian and bisexual writers of various ages and backgrounds to write their coming-out stories. I didn't anticipate the rich complexity of experience these memoirs would encompass, nor did I begin to suspect the powerful impact they would have on me personally. These stories illuminated experiences that years of "living out" had blurred. I recognized feelings I thought no longer lived inside me. Reading this book, I encountered my vulnerability, anger, and optimism, my core of emotional strength.

Having read lesbian writing for twenty-five years and coedited three anthologies of lesbian and gay poetry, I thought I already knew the full spectrum of experiences we call "coming out." I loved the range and variety of lesbian voices: I cannot forget the "open mike" night in the mid-seventies at which a lesbian ex-nun told bawdy stories of sex in the convent; the crackling intelligence of Martha Shelley's WBAI-FM radio show "Lesbian Nation" (the fan letter I wrote her was part of my own coming-out process: it led to our meeting and my initiation into the mysteries of lesbian bars, politics, and sex); critic Jill Johnston's original, idiosyncratic voice in the *Village Voice* dance column she had transformed with revelatory autobiographical writing and queer cultural commentary; and poet Adrienne Rich's thrilling voice at a New York City Pride rally urging us to expand what we meant by our love for women. Unlike the previous generation of writers, who had discreetly downplayed or concealed their lesbian themes, my generation seemed to be coming out together.

Poet Muriel Rukeyser first articulated the startling idea that the core of a woman's writing must be her own vision and experience:

What would happen if one woman told the truth about her life?
The world would split open.

As woman-owned presses, bookstores, magazines, and distribution networks proliferated in the seventies and eighties, women found courage to break lifetimes of silence. The feminist movement that inspired us was fueled and shaped by writers—most eloquently by lesbian poets such as Judy Grahn, Adrienne Rich, and Audre Lorde, who insisted on the power of language to transform our vision, our selves, and our world. Lesbian writers, working perhaps for the first time within a responsive community, began producing a vital body of work—work by women speaking to other women of experiences that pertained directly to our own memories and moral lives. And still, in a culture that continued to judge love between women degenerate and dangerous, coming out in print meant breaking a taboo. Judy Grahn, who had witnessed the McCarthy era's vilification of "perverts" and "subversives," and who had directly experienced the military's witch-hunting of lesbians, kept *The Psychoanalysis of Edward the Dyke* in notebooks for seven years before publishing it in 1971. What would in time become the title poem of Fran Winant's *Dyke Jacket* was first published with the less in-your-face title "My New Jacket." Elly Bulkin and I called our 1975 anthology *Amazon Poetry;* the more explicitly titled *Lesbian Poetry* came six years later.

Today, coming out has supposedly gone "mainstream." TV shows have their requisite gay characters, and the places where the word "lesbian" can be uttered without a blush or an angry stance have increased dramatically. The past few years have seen the publication of numerous lesbian anthologies, most by large commercial presses. Clare Coss' *The Arc of Love,* Beatrix Gates' *The Wild Good,* Lisa Moore's *Does Your Mama Know?,* Eileen Myles and Liz Kotz' *The New Fuck You,* Lesléa Newman's *My Lover Is a Woman,* and Gerry Gomez Pearlberg's *The Key to Everything* are only a few. This wealth of books suggests that coming out in print in the tolerant, tell-all times we inhabit is no longer a challenge. But the prominence of the homophobic Christian Right, the continuing violence against us, from gay-bashing to gay murder, the absence—still—of human rights protection for lesbian and gay people throughout much of the country are harsh reminders that, for most, there is still a price for coming out.

Several contributors to *A Woman Like That* acknowledged that exploring the territory of their own coming out in writing was unexpectedly difficult. Seasoned writers told me how arduous, even painful, it was to explore coming-out memories that had long been held under pressure at a depth. One novelist said that her family's rejection of her as an open lesbian had been too agonizing to revisit; she was unable to complete her story. Another, author of a soul-searching memoir and surely no coward, wrote a haunting piece about her first erotic experience with a woman, but withdrew it when she remembered that the words "lesbian and bisexual" would appear in the book's subtitle. These are indeed powerful words. I am deeply indebted to the writers who are free to embrace them.

Many writers in this collection recall childhood desire, embryonic lesbian hunger, and the innocence and mystery of those feelings on the brink of collision with the straight world. One writer asserts that she was "born queer," while another confesses to the sin of "converting"—implying that, contrary to current rules of political correctness, some feel they have *chosen* to be lesbians. Some write with youthful ebullience and wit of adventures as "sex-positive" lesbians, with almost a gasp of surprise at the seeming absence of oppression in their lives. A handful write of uncommonly loyal families that nurtured independence in childhood and remain a source of strength to their unconventional daughters.

Some contributors write of harsh punishment rendered for sexual nonconformity and of the survival skills and moral intelligence they have wrested from their experiences. Two write of their incarceration in mental institutions as young gay women, and of the exhilaration of release. Another, stunned by the abrupt firing of teachers rumored to be lesbians, learns that even a "progressive" environment may be unapologetically homophobic; her knowledge of danger ultimately empowers her to speak against injustice. One writer, who tells of coming out to the sons of whom she has lost custody, speaks of having cracked open their small universe—a shattering, but one that allows light and the possibility of new knowledge and connection.

A number of writers in this collection tell coming-out stories that are not about a single defining moment but rather about a continuum of experience. They recall many passages—a gradual shedding of false selves, an ongoing process of self-discovery and self-naming. One writer, nearly deported from the U.S. for her outspoken political writing, equates coming out with the freedom to explore deeper places in her own psyche. A writer in her seventies tells movingly of her failure to name herself a lesbian at a reunion of those who as children were transported to safety in England to escape the Nazi death camps. Next year, she resolves, she will come out to them. Another, in the form of a diary of a week in the present year, reminds us that, regardless of how secure our identities, we are forced to come out as lesbians each time we intersect with the heterosexual world, or remain invisible as we have been for centuries.

The writers whose stories are collected here range in age from their twenties to their seventies, are of all classes and races, and come from various parts of the United States. They inhabit many different places on the continuum of sexuality. Their voices are intelligent, sad, funny, and searingly honest—as diverse and untamed and idiosyncratic as their coming-out memories.

I see them as a bouquet of unique blooms in dark and light shades, wild and familiar, each speaking to me poignantly of my own experience. Together, they offer a vision of coming out that is richer, more witty and courageous, more telling and memorable, than I could have predicted.

All of them move me.

Joan Larkin
January 1999
Brooklyn, New York

A WOMAN LIKE THAT

THIS SONG IS DEDICATED TO THE ONE I LOVE

Bertha Harris

PRETTY girls deserve more of the things of this world than the rest of us. They shouldn't have to do the dirty work, they shouldn't have to work hard for a living; instead, they deserve to marry up, then get treated right when they do. Sometimes, though, pretty girls are so hot they can't think straight; their brains are lodged up there between their thighs, tucked in out of sight in the tail-end of their torsos. Mary Zuleika cloaked hers in peach silk panties that were tight in the crotch, loose in the leg. Tap pants.

I lived with Mary Zuleika for only sixteen years, but we lived up close against one another. It was as if a heavy-duty band of ecto-plasm—that fleshy emanation from the entranced medium to the par-ticipant in her séance, the one who wants to know why—roped us together. She used it to impress, wordlessly, certain words on me: on the *tabula rasa* which was my mind. She also used it like a leash; I might as well have been her dog, slavering for handouts one minute, cringing in submission at her feet the next—or going barking mad

1

when she denied me any attention at all. Mary Zuleika was my mother. I suppose she was. I have only her word for it. The words she taught me were dirty words: fuck, pussy, cunt, etc. I overheard them; she was talking to herself. But in the spirit of "waste not, want not," I wrote the words down.

I was in the second grade at St. Patrick's. I was six. One day a little girl named Lucy, to whom I'd given my heart, my love and devotion, wasn't there. "She ain't sick," said Mary Zuleika; "her mama and daddy got killed in a wreck. Now she's an orphan in the orphanage. You want to go see her?" John and Mary Zuleika never took me anywhere they could help not to. The Catholic orphanage was fifty miles from their front door, which was 603 Pilot Avenue, Fayetteville, North Carolina. Its parlor was paneled in golden oak; its scent was furniture polish and bouquets of flowers. It was spacious and peaceful. I thought that Lucy must like it there.

"You watch that door over yonder," Mary Zuleika told me. "Lucy's going to come through that door."

"I don't know about this, Zeke," John said. I hated how he called her "Zeke." They followed a nun out the other door, then she shut it behind them.

Lucy never appeared. John and Mary Zuleika were angry when they reappeared. They wanted to have a fight on the way back to 603 Pilot, but John had to keep his hands on the wheel and his eyes on the road; and to make things worse, he had to pull over and change a tire, then drink from the pint of gin in the glove compartment. It was his nerves.

The visit to Lucy was, I've lately decided, a mind fuck: they either tried to get the orphanage to take me—or to take me back, and the nuns had told them to fuck off. No wonder they felt like hell.

I didn't decide that Lucy was dead. I kept on waiting for her.

It's not so much that pretty girls deserve to get fucked—although they're asking for it—while they're young and still pretty and tremendously hot enough to burn with the desire to get fucked: it's that if they don't, they'll never get fucked at all, the same as—to be fair—un-pretty girls. I'm nothing if not fair when it comes to pretty girls.

Mary Zuleika Jones was a pretty girl who was hot and let it show. She had a sense of humor—that is, she made fun of females who had to make do with nothing but other females, and she made fun of genuine old maids, especially the ones who had to work hard for their livings but then spent every last cent, selfishly, on themselves. She made fun of old maids because they were selfish. They didn't know the meaning of having to make sacrifices the way she wound up having to do. Every time she whipped me, she spoke from her heart: "I cain't have nothing," she cried out to the beat of the switch against my legs; "why cain't I have nothing and you think you got a right to anything you want?"

In the summer of 1949, the polio epidemic happened. I was eleven. The Health Department warned everybody to keep their children in their own yards or in the house. No going swimming at the town pool or going to the picture show or church or having any contact with any other children unless they belonged to the family. This was something new. Usually, it was a typhoid epidemic; the Cape Fear River would overflow and get inside the drinking water, so we got painful inoculations that made us feverish. Just a sandy driveway separated Mary Zuleika's house from the house next door where the girl next door lived. I did what I usually did during the long, humid summers: I squatted down in the sandy driveway and used a stick to divert or destroy the industrious ants laboring to perfect their ant-hill homes.

One afternoon, John's cousin Frances Catherine drove in the driveway. Fanny was that particular selfish old maid Mary Zuleika made fun of. Fanny was a treasured bookkeeper for a plumbing supplier. She drove her fine car fast; she bought herself diamond rings and brooches, and she lived in a big two-story white house by herself. She was always in a thrilling state of happiness. Fanny had brought me a present. To get me through the epidemic, she said. It was a book. It was *Mistress Masham's Repose* by T. H. White. There wasn't a single book in Mary Zuleika's house; I had never had any books but school books, which were strictly on loan and had to be turned back in to Sister at the end of the school year without a single mark or break in the spine.

Mistress Masham's Repose was about an orphaned little girl who's bespectacled, gawky, lonely, scared. She's captured by the tiny, almost invisible, descendants of Gulliver's Lilliputians, who become her loving friends and transform her fear into happiness. I already needed glasses; the world was a blur. "We need a lot of other things around here besides glasses that make you look ugly," said Mary Zuleika. And Lucy was the orphan, not me. Fanny was my godmother. "You're going to turn her into a bookworm and drive her blind," Mary Zuleika told Fanny, "and you spoil her." Fanny didn't take offense. I kept on tending to my tiny, almost invisible ants in the sandy driveway. My nose was to the ground, so I could see them.

The girl next door leaned on her windowsill and told me that when the polio was over her mother was going to give her toe dance lessons. Doris Lee's mother went to business with her father every morning and had a cute little colored woman, Rosa, to clean and cook and look after Doris Lee Mendenhall. When there wasn't an epidemic of any kind, the neighbor women—Rosa included—pitched in to give Mary Zuleika some relief from me. Rosa would invite me to eat supper with Doris Lee. Rosa served us supper in the dining room where the table was covered with white linen and the plates were china and we used silver to eat with. That's how I found out that I ate wrong. You were supposed to hold the meat down with your fork, cut a piece with your knife, then lay your knife down and transfer the fork to your right hand before you put the piece of meat in your mouth. Doris Lee had my best interests at heart; she was benign, she'd been taught to feel sorry for me. It was Rosa who discovered Doris and me having the girls' sex ring we devised behind the flowered chintz skirt of Mrs. Mendenhall's dressing table. Rosa walked in and caught us stroking one another's slippery little cunts and breathing in the heady smells while we sat cross-legged on the floor, knees touching, behind the flowered skirt. The first things Rosa saw were our underpants. We stripped, then tossed our underpants on Mr. and Mrs. Mendenhall's double bed. We didn't use their bed. Doris Lee had said: "It's more fun playing when it's a secret." Rosa was friendly. She just laughed, then walked out again and shut the door.

Mary Zuleika had a big crush on girls who took toe dance. She took me to their spring dance recitals to teach me how pretty a girl could be if she only smiled and tried to make people happy. Mary Zuleika had done her level best by me, but I stayed in the audience. The toe-dance teacher told Mary Zuleika she couldn't afford to have girls in her class who looked scared. Scared girls made mistakes; they ruined it for the rest. Her girls had to appear before the public confident and serene.

When the dreadful event, menstruation, got me, I searched through my bag of tricks till I came up with a more suitable explanation for the blood pouring down my legs. "I've got a condition known as amnesia," I told the nun who, rag in hand, was hurrying me from her classroom to the Girls' Room. "Mary Zuleika had to whip me till I bled, but I forgot till just now." Sister Mary Joseph, who was herself a pretty girl, said, "No. You've got the curse."

So I've cultivated the curse of amnesia ever since. My ability to forget has been essential to reinventing myself. I was ashamed of myself. Mary Zuleika made it plain how I ought to be ashamed of myself. I became fiction. My secret life has always been memory in infinite detail, and its reworking. It's more fun playing when it's a secret.

I must have been six or seven when Mary Zuleika brought me out, although the process began, in tiny increments, before then. Her erotic technique was rejection. She avoided touching me; she turned her head and laughed at me when I tried to kiss her. She told jokes and riddles rife with sexual innuendo in my presence to her best friend, Sally Maloney, and to her sisters. I had my first drink when I was six; I was five when I heard her tell the peach riddle, so I practiced self-control for nearly a year afterward.

Mary Zuleika believed, till she stopped believing, that she had married up. John was twenty years older than she was when they met and started double-dating with Sally and Frank Maloney. John had the look—long, lean, with mother-haunted eyes—of James Joyce, so he looked intriguing; and drink still worked for him; and he behaved as if he were rich. Mary Zuleika and Sally were living at the Ivy Inn, a respectable boardinghouse for unmarried girls who had to work till they married up when, in the slaphappy reasoning of the times, they would be granted a home of their own and everything else their hearts desired.

Sally married up. Frank Maloney was in fact rich, the owner of a Chevrolet and Cadillac dealership, and the home that Frank built for Sally was a grand one, and it was enviably childless. It was pointless having a daughter, Sally once told Mary Zuleika, when you could afford hired help.

John and Mary Zuleika eloped one night by driving across the state line, from Fayetteville, North Carolina, into Dillon, South Carolina, where marriages didn't require any previous paperwork. John told her they had to elope, but he didn't tell her why. Mary Zuleika, who had been buying her trousseau bit by bit while she worked for the telephone company, took her suitcase to Dillon with her. It held thirteen pairs of peach-colored silk panties, with two slips and two brassieres to match; pairs of peach-colored satin bedroom wedgies and black leather pumps (she was wearing the red open-toed cuban slingbacks on her way to Dillon); three still-new dresses which were cut on the bias, and as á la Joan Crawford the Young as Sears & Roebuck could make them, and the red one had a peplum—a little flourish that called attention to feminine buttocks. Five pairs of seamed silk stockings were in the suitcase. She was wearing the blue garters her best friend Sally had given her (something blue), and the four-teenth pair of peach silk panties, the third peach slip and third brassiere, and she was anxious about whether the seams were still running straight up behind her legs on her sixth pair of new stockings. Her Coty powder and lipstick were in her navy blue pocketbook, which almost exactly matched the navy blue suit and the little veiled hat she was wearing. She had chosen the navy blue suit because it would set off the white orchid he would give her.

John didn't go to the florist and buy her the white orchid, or any other flower. His mother, Bertha—Miss Bert, they called her—might find out. And then she would know.

I'm making this up. I questioned her about every instance of her life before John, and then before me. "You hush," she always an-swered. I wasn't supposed to talk; it made John nervous.

All immigrants to America are nervous. Their nerves are hard on their children; we were born here, so even if we didn't know the score, we absorbed the nature of the scoreboard to some extent. Miss Bert had immigrated from County Kilkenny with a husband from Dublin who died young and was never mentioned, at least in my presence. Miss Bert had been a servant in an Anglo-Irish household. I know what a consommé spoon looks like; I know how to relieve a fish of its skeleton in one piece. I know the difference between the glass for claret and the glass for port. John didn't remember the voyage in steerage to the new country; he was a babe in arms, but some old thing who drank and sang with John in the front office of Frank Maloney's dealership mentioned, at John's wake, that John—who'd been christened Sean—had been the best little baby on board the worst of boats. Then the old thing promptly vomited all over his rosary, and I finished my pint of gin, then told the priest to go fuck himself.

After I was born, John had to tell his mother. I can't imagine where he'd stashed his wife after the trip to Dillon or hid her out during her pregnancy—if there was a pregnancy. The Ivy Inn took in virgins only, and John continued living with his mother the way a bachelor son ought to, and he couldn't contemplate any other way to live. He and his younger brothers had sworn an oath to Miss Bert that since they weren't smart enough to enter the priesthood, they would do her the favor of at least practicing abstinence. He moved

Mary Zuleika and my infant self into his mother's house by the railroad tracks; he had to, there was a baby.

Miss Bert's house was big enough to hold everybody: John and his brothers, Jimmy and Jesse; my gay cousin George and his boyfriend, Mac; my gay cousin Mary Catherine and her series of girlfriends; my godmother, Frances Catherine, a lively old maid; then, my mother and I. My purpose was to soften Miss Bert's heart toward Mary Zuleika and so let John have sex with his wife in a bed of their own behind a closed door. Miss Bert never had anything to do with either of us. The Immaculate Conception and the Virgin Birth were good enough for her—unlike some people. During their life together under Miss Bert's roof, they continued to consummate their unhappy Dillon folly—who was it making happy? nobody—with hasty, dressed fucks in the tool shed in the dark of night, with Mary Zuleika's peach silk panties down in the dark on the dirty, greasy rough floorboards. Or draped on the blades of the lawnmower. It wasn't more fun playing when it was a secret. Fanny went out and hired an elderly black couple, Percy and Elizabeth, to look after me. Percy also polished Miss Bert's brass and mowed her lawn.

Mary Zuleika drove John to drink (he always said so, those times he was beating her) by nagging him, nagging and nagging, for a home of her own. It was an ugly little box on an ugly rectangle of backyard and front yard. Oil heat cost money; the living room and the dining room had to be shut off during the cold months. The oil burner stood alone in the little hall that had doors to the two bedrooms and bathroom and kitchen. It was five feet tall and made out of squared-off brown-colored tin. The cold months smelled like fuel even when we ran out of fuel. Its flames showed through its tiny glass porthole when the bill got paid. I cost money, too. Mary Zuleika, lover of new clothes and shoes, had to go without because of me. He got to fuck her, but who he loved was his mother. Somebody had to love Mary Zuleika. There wasn't anybody but me.

I made my move the summer I was four. We were walking up the railroad tracks away from Frank Maloney's dealership where we'd gone looking for John to get some money. We were heading for the bus stop. Mary Zuleika was walking her fearsome walk; it was a stomp, a coming down heavy on first one high heel, then the other. She was stuck with me, day in, day out; the neighbors would think she was trash if she left me alone by myself so she could get some time. She was going to get plenty of time if she could get her hands on him, then use the money—it was tuition—to get them to take me at the

Catholic school, St. Patrick's, in the first grade. Then, in September, all she had to do was pack me a lunch, dress me, and make John get me in the car and get me to St. Patrick's Church, which was just around the corner from the school, for 7:30 Mass. Then, after Mass, the sisters would walk us to school and we'd have to stay there until 3:30 when John would have to pick me up and take me home to her.

Frank Maloney had told Mary Zuleika that John wasn't there, he hadn't seen him all day. I could see him. I was too short for my age, so I could see the toes of his wingtips sticking out from behind the black curtains that divided the front office from the mechanical side of the dealership with its ramps and new tires. I didn't tell on him. Sometimes, for no reason whatsoever, John would put me in the car with him and drive me way out in the country. I could remember holding on hard to the door handle on my side of the front seat because I was scared to death, every time, that why he was taking the trouble to drive me out to the country with him was to kill me. My plan was to jump out of the car door and run and hide behind the pine trees. I knew what happened to rivals for the love of a woman; I'd read about that in *True Detective* magazine. Somebody got killed was what happened.

John was the one who'd found out that I could read when he started looking for his new issue of *True Detective*, but couldn't find it till he finally yanked open my closet door and caught me sitting on the floor reading it. A gorgeous blonde who was no better than she ought to be had got herself murdered in Los Angeles because she was fooling around with more than one man at a time. The rest of the story was about how the true detectives were tracking the killer and would bring him in, and a jury of twelve honest men would make sure he got the chair because bad girls deserve justice no less than good girls. John made me stand up and read the rest of that story out loud to him. He took me in the car to his mother's house and made me read some of the *Fayetteville Observer* to her.

"If she can read, she ought to be at school," John said.

"If she can read, she has no need of any school," Miss Bert said. "She can stay home and help with the work."

"The idea being," said John, "is put her in school so as to give Zeke some relief."

I hated it, how he called her Zeke. I knocked over the shot glass Miss Bert had there on an end table and it broke. Miss Bert had a shot glass and a bottle in every room in her house so that when she needed to take a drink for her heart trouble she needn't go to any trouble.

"That painted whore," said Miss Bert. "What is it she needs relief about?"

John then got down on his knees and held on to Miss Bert's skirt.
Miss Bert listened to what the St. Patrick's tuition was. It was five
dollars a month. She said she'd contribute one dollar a month. But
only because I favored her, nose and eyes in particular.

I did not favor her. She had the looks of an Edwardian beauty,
her neck especially. It was long, swanlike, as cheap novelists put it. It
was swanlike. She contributed her dollar a month because John (to
win favor) had forced her name, Bertha, onto me with the result that
I've gone through life often being mistaken, by those who haven't
met me, for a black woman. "Bertha Harris" is not an unusual name
for black women of my generation: I read about one last week in *The
New York Daily News*. That Bertha Harris was news because her son,
Darrel, had gone berserk and murdered three people in a Brooklyn
social club.

John found a way to get the four dollars. Every night before he
got drunk enough to beat up Mary Zuleika for luring him from his
mother, the three of us would sit at the kitchen table in front of packs
of different brands of cigarettes and rolls of pennies and slip one cent
between the cellophane and the pack. Cigarettes out of vending ma-
chines cost twenty-four cents. People dropped in quarters; they expected change back with their smokes.

Mary Zuleika was an immigrant to the town of Fayetteville from
the flat tobacco-growing part of North Carolina very close to the farm
town where (legend has it) boys could get the pre-movie Ava Gardner
to do it in a ditch for the price of an ice cream cone. Indoor plumbing
was important to Mary Zuleika; so was wearing shoes and dresses that
weren't made out of feed sacks.

I want you to look at her while I do. She made sure I'd salvage
a few things out of the ashes, and the things included a snapshot of
her before John, before me, when she was a teenager. They didn't let
me know that Mary Zuleika had died and that they'd given her a
funeral with lots of flowers till she'd been dead and buried three
months. "The upshot is, Bertha Anne" (the man in charge told me
over the phone) "is she didn't want your kind of person, you, coming
for this occasion, and the truth of the matter is, Bertha Anne, neither
did any of the rest of us."

She's sitting on a park bench beside Sally (who blinked). Sally has
her hands tucked under skirted thighs. Mary Zuleika is giving the

photographer that movie-star gaze she learned at Joan Crawford movies, and her eyes are deeply set behind their dark lids. Her lips are closed, their corners touch her cheekbones. She's wearing a necklace and a tam. Her flowered blouse is cut low, her shoes are open-toed. Her dark skirt is covering her legs to just below her knees, but her right hand fans out its fingers in a gesture that suggests to all but the pure in heart that in the next instant they will snatch the skirt up and bare a glimpse of peach silk. The girls' feet don't seem to be touching the ground the bench stands on. They're levitating; they're waiting for the guys who'll get them down to earth.

After the polio epidemic was done—the cold months seemed to kill the bug—Mary Zuleika escorted me to the hospital to visit a girl from school who was living in an iron lung because her mother hadn't been as careful as mine was. "And maybe she'll turn out to be that Lucy you write all those letters to," Mary Zuleika teased. I burned inside the cold white-tiled room at the hospital. I thought I'd hidden those letters, which increasingly had dwelt graphically on the passions of the body. I didn't even know the girl in the iron lung. It wheezed; the girl's head stuck out of it through a rubber ruffle. There was a mirror affixed to the thing that she could look into if she wanted to see who was sneaking up behind her. I wondered if she was naked inside the iron lung.

When I made my move, it went like this. I decided to take her away from John. He had beat her the night before and, as always, she was flushed and grinning when she emerged from their bedroom the next morning. She was putting a brave face on her torment, I mistakenly believed: one book to own and read had led to the public library where a multitude of cheap novelists were represented. I sat down by her on the couch. I pulled her face to mine (*"Roger pulled Jean's face to his . . ."*) and I said, "Let's leave him. Marry me!" (*"Marry me, my darling!"* blurted Frank Yerby's hero.) I tried to take her wedding ring off and put it on my finger. Mary Zuleika laughed. She said, "I wish Sally was here to see this." She deftly avoided my kiss. She said, "That kind of thing makes me sick."

I woke up one cold morning. It was still dark, but it was time to get up and go to St. Patrick's second grade. The electric light was burning, and the flames were burning in the oil heater out in the little hallway. I was the audience in the dark watching the performance. She was warming my underclothes by the heater. They were warming by themselves. She was grinning—a full-teeth appearance—at me. Her lips were wet. Her pink rayon nightgown had been ripped from stem to stern. It was soaked in bright red blood. She was happy about that; wild sex with John and getting her period always delighted her. But I chose to believe that she was grinning because she had murdered John in the night; in *True Detective* stories, the blood flowed and stuck and dried.

She said, arising from her perch by the stove, "I got to get under the covers and get warm with you. It's cold out here."

She got under the covers with me, flat on her back. She used her right arm to hold me tight against her side. She opened her legs and put my hand down there. "Down there" was the first name of cunt. "I didn't come last night," she said. She gripped my wrist and put my thumb and fingers where she wanted them down there, and she moved until she heaved a huge sigh, and then she got up and went back to the oil stove.

She said, "You want to hear a riddle? It goes like this. What's wet and juicy on the inside and hairy on the outside?"

I don't remember what I answered, or if I answered. So at last she said, very impatiently: "A *peach*. That's the answer. Just a peach. You've eaten plenty peaches. Wet and juicy on the inside, hairy on the outside. Sometimes I think you're slow."

Mary Zuleika Harris

With borrowed chihuahua

WIDOWS

Judy Grahn

1953

I was at that stage of early adolescence when the possibility that the shining black widow spider hovering near the faucet would actually bite me was grounds for a deep and thrilling meditation on the nearness of my stilled hand upon the spigot to the glistening mandibles of her impressive lower face. I was a child of the high desert of southern New Mexico, in a small town strung between the thin line of silver Rio Grande River marking the west side of town and the living wall of purple Organ Mountains majestically and moodily guarding the east.

This was the year that the sexual doings of our neighbor, Byrel, excited talk among women sipping iced tea in late afternoon lawn chairs pressed together in the scanty elm tree shade against the last scorching rays of early summer sun. His scandal and impending divorce—for he had taken up with another woman and was leaving his wife and two toddlers—was heightened in intensity by the enormity

12

of the social illusion he was shattering. The son of a school teacher who had long watched out for me, Byrel had married his high school sweetheart in what was written in the high school annual as the world's most perfect marriage. Around the kitchen table at his mother Jewel's house, where I frequently went to hang about as if it were a social center, being a latch-key kid (though without a key, as no one locked their doors in small towns in 1953), the women's talk filled the air with a combination of outrage and musky sexual innuendo. The scandal lay all the more thick in throats for the fact that the bereft wife was a perfectly-formed blonde, well-behaved Mormon who did not even smoke or drink coffee (rules I found incomprehensible), while wayward Byrel had taken up with a tall, dark-haired woman who drank liquor and lived in a trailer up on the high breast of the Organ Mountains near St. Augustine Pass. "She's fat and old, too, nearly forty," the gossiper added, as though to cinch the young man's madness and the devilish power of lust.

The upshot of the scandal was to be to my advantage, as Jewel's house, where her errant married son had been sleeping in the porch bedroom for months, now had some empty space. He moved into the tiny trailer with the new woman and the divorce moved into the court. My parents, who had difficulty providing material comforts and frequently seemed to forget that I had a body, had been promising to provide me with a full-sized bed for months. The rose couch given to them at their marriage thirty years before was now six inches shorter than I had become by this my twelfth year, and puffy in the springs, so even they noticed it was affecting my posture. The invitation came as a wondrous surprise. I was to move into an area of phenomenal luxury: my own private room, the porch bedroom at Jewel's house. In exchange, the adults informed me, I was expected to be the gardener of the yard around the place. Hence my new relationship with black widow spiders. Though I had seen them in the open adobe brick garages attached to my parents' apartment, I had never stopped to examine one up close. My new "job" gave me this opportunity, and I took advantage.

Jewel, widow of a cotton farmer from West Texas, and who now taught junior high school English, had raised her three children in this three-bedroom house. From the time my parents had moved to New Mexico when I was eight, the place and people had been my refuge— as this whole family took me under their wings. The son, Byrel, would get me my first job when I was seventeen, ensuring I could go to the local college. Older sister Leela sang marvelously to me as I sat in her kitchen window every morning the year I was nine, and as her babies arrived nearly one a year, she turned her young boys over to my care. Even when she and her husband moved seventy miles away to the east to Alamagordo, various members of the family drove me over the Organ Mountains and across the Sonora Desert to visit for weeks on end. Even recently at the opening of summer, Darnelle, the youngest, who was eighteen and in college, had driven me back from Methodist summer camp on a long Sunday night. The camp was in pine-covered mountains near Alamagordo, lush rain-fed mountains with wild strawberries rousing sudden red thumbs of desire from their hiding places in the pine needle mulch. These soft mountains were a contrast to the powerful rock steepness of the Organ peaks. I still recall the mystery of that June night ride between Cloudcroft and Las Cruces, as we crossed the flat sagebrush-smelling land, tall jackrabbits slowly turning their backs to safety from our deadly headlights as we tore through the tunnel carved by their piercing yellow glow.

Trembling with the intimacy of the experience, I crouched knee to knee in the backseat of Darnelle's car with two other girls my age. We were telling stories, secret never-before shared stories, especially about our fathers. I told about my father's drunkenness, his inability to bring money home. (I did not tell, since I wasn't aware of it, of our family's excruciating isolation, or anything about my mother. We did not speak of our mothers.) Annie Ruth told a worse story, about her father breaking horses by beating them with chains. . . . We felt united in our understanding of our mutual horror at this bad behavior. Alone in the front seat behind the driver's wheel, Darnelle covered our whispers with clear Country Western, song after poignant song delivered in her generous, bold voice. Though I loved the entire family, I felt especially privileged to be in Darnelle's company. A redhead with freckles, she was athletic and interesting and going to college. She had always kept a distance from me, but now this nighttime over the desert car ride told me that she would be someone I could confide in, a longed-for older sister type. A guidance of some sort in the increasing mysteries of adult life.

At night now as my hormonal pulses quickened I watched the blood-red moon with a secret piercing long eye extending mournfully and erotically into the suggestions of English romantic poetry about a highwayman in black who was repeatedly riding riding riding to the very door of a lass with a white bosom, "Bess, the landlord's daughter," whose parameters had leapt into my imagination as the most luscious of all possible fruits. This even though I hadn't the vaguest notion how anyone went about eating such a dish, or even that anyone went about eating such a dish. My idea of what to do with billowy bosoms was to attempt to lay my head on them. Even I did not yet notice that it was the highwayman, and not buxom Bess, whose image caught in the mirror of my identification.

The narrow porch bedroom became a place of burgeoning if unbordered dreams, as it had my first real bed and a lamp, and a little blue record player my father got me at the end of July when I turned thirteen. My first album was of Harry Belafonte singing folk songs, joyfully played over and over, especially a song called "The Fox." In exchange for all this richness, all I had to do was "be the gardener" and "keep the yard." That sounded easy enough, though I had witnessed almost none of this activity in my parents' rented lives. Jewel provided me with some tools and general instructions. Unable to imagine what gardeners, exactly, do, I stood for long minutes with the indecisive brittle sheers drooping at my side ready to weep over the very thorny bristles and runaway dandelions that the family expected me to decimate in their behalf. I had no idea which were the "plants" and which the "weeds," as I loved them all equally. Everything in the yards around here had thorns—the delicate mimosa tree and the rosebush no less than the tall thistles and spreading goat's head grasses that filled my bicycle tires with hundreds of stop signals. In this land of sparsity, the lovely spiky yellow flowers of the dandelions were surely a beautiful lushness, surely as desirable as the thin wisps of bluegrass that struggled so incompetently against the dryness of the light brown adobe dust. With growing consternation I realized that gardening was escaping me, and so was keeping up my end of the bargain that had been struck between the families.

But now with summer vacation Darnelle was home for weeks from her first year at college, and had brought a sturdy-looking friend with her. The scandal around Byrel had settled down, and a slow July pace had settled in. Cumulus clouds stacked up in the afternoon sky, precursors of the August monsoon and more plant life requiring more choices. But I still had options. I remembered how Darnelle had been, driving the car that night—competent, present, protective, accessible. Next time I saw her I would ask her how to keep the yard, how to have the proper discernment, and what motions to make thereafter— how to dispose of the bodies of the unwanted weeds.

Late one hot Saturday afternoon, in keeping with the intense stillness of the air, I had closed the screen door silently and then instead of going into my narrow bedroom sanctuary to listen fifty more times to Harry Belafonte's song about the fox going out on a moonless night, praying to the stars to give him light, I unexpectedly turned right and padded on my perpetually bare feet across the kitchen linoleum. I was six steps into the living room before even seeing them. They were lying together on the couch.

They had half risen up, their trunks twisted like young athletic trees that had grown together, and as if only one face, their two faces stared at me with identical blankness. Darnelle's friend, stockier, had been on her back, and Darnelle had been lying on her side and half on top of her. They were wearing white blouses and shorts like the phys ed teachers they intended to become. I was struck by how clean they looked, and how frozen in place—an ice sculpture puts out more resonance than they did.

No one was breathing. Our stillness created negative space, which drew our attention into a monstrous force-field.

They two seemed to be in a deep meditative state, long rays emanating from their intertwined and stilted lower bodies to the iris of my eye, along which their feelings ran back and forth in miniature like panicky young horses. We held ourselves within the glacier paint-ing while my girl-self, suddenly overly important, figured out what to do with the icicle tension in the room.

The mortification, I saw, was all mine. I had made them insane and paralytic. A thirteen-year-old had frozen the two eighteen-year-olds as a black widow might have frozen me, but with mysterious potential I had not known I owned. The two did not take charge. No one spoke, the breath and need for air had vanished. We might have hung in space this way till nightfall if some highwayman inside had not ridden me to action. Placing a foot in back and then another, I attempted to erase the scene for their sakes, and in slow motion. Like a movie running backward I unraveled it for them, going back-wards into nothingness with intent to leave no shadow of imprint on the floor of their fears. Screen door did not creak or slam, floor boards did not interact with each other. No one's breath got hot or sweated, no voice croaked any passionate outbreak across the slate-gray sea that suddenly united us. Screen door did not creak or slam and I was gone with never a peep to anyone, till now.

Grief married silence the next day when I arrived at the family lawn chair gathering and saw her, and was ready to accept a new status toward adulthood: I can keep secrets even without knowing what or why they are. Darnelle's eyes flew away; she shifted her gaze, and left. Never spoke nor sang nor showed herself to me again.

Following this was when I began taking off the heavy protective gloves Jewel had loaned me along with the hoe and sheers of order and selection. Now I craved the nearness of my hand to the glisten of the shining black spider, whose innocence of discernment matched my own. Companionable though this friendship may have become, it was broken by my first firing and eviction. "She isn't doing the job to our satisfaction," Jewel told my mother in an understatement that didn't even flicker my mother's conviction that I could accomplish "anything in life you put your mind to." My parents took up again their own job, buying me a splendid fold-up rollaway bed which, when I lay on my stomach with my chin on the pillow, turned into a downward spiraling World War II twin engine fighter plane, and me a kamikaze pilot, nightly wiping out all foes in behalf of everyone I loved.

Vera Grahn, NM 1952

Ready to roll

MAD FOR HER

Jill Johnston

IN 1944–45 I was a sophomore at Saint Mary's School—a boarding/ prep school for eighty-five girls max in Peekskill, New York. Nuns of the Sisters of Saint Mary's, a High Episcopalian order, ran the school, aided by a cadre of lay teachers, unmarried women all, "old maids" of various ages. I had entered this glorified orphanage when eleven, a seventh grader with one other classmate. By sophomore year, our class numbered fourteen, and in 1947 we would graduate sixteen strong. At least half the school was in a nubile state, with raging adolescent hormones, but no one would ever have known it. Unless it could be deduced from the group who pined conspicuously over boyfriends at home or at boys' schools. My own pubescent changes were absorbed completely by the school's intense athletic program, participation in which held more status than academic achievement. During my sophomore year, aged fifteen, with no diminished zeal for athletic excellence, I became possessed by a junior called Katherine Cheshire—my first infatuation.

Newly arrived as a junior, and unlike most girls at the school who were northeastern seaboard products, she came from the exotic city of Charleston, South Carolina. She had a thrilling Southern accent, and a bubbly winning personality to go with it. She and her roommate Constance—a new kid at school too, with a precociously developed woman's body not so hidden within her plain uniform school jumper, and an exciting life at home (an affair already under her belt with a man more than twice her age—no doubt a reason for her having been sent away to a religious school)—had taken an interest in me, as a sort of mascot or adoptee. I suppose it was Katherine's manner of addressing me by my nickname William—"Will-*yam*" she pronounced with teasing intimacy—that tipped me over the edge. Certainly sex was not on my mind, since I had no idea what sex was or probably even how I got here. In my case, "raging hormones" did not translate to arousal. But oh, I was in love. All I needed, as I can determine in retrospect, was the right degree of physical proximity and suggestiveness to spring my arousal mechanism. I stalked Katherine unashamedly through the corridors and school grounds, and contrived whenever possible to sit next to her at morning chapel services, to be close to her on the many lines created every day for marching into chapel or refectory, to visit the room she shared with Constance, to see her between classes in the Quad, and most promisingly to join her and Constance in the Music Room where under cover of Constance's tutelage in the matter of my introduction to classical music I was able somehow to improvise my best opportunity for expressing my powerful emotions and inchoate intentions. To the romantic strains of Rachmaninoff's Second Piano Concerto, Tchaikovsky's Fifth and Sixth Symphonies and the like, I would curl up or stretch out on the couch next to Katherine and boldly lay my head in her lap. Despite her failure to reciprocate by touching me or anything (she politely never protested either), I experienced the height of ecstasy—all mental to be sure. And I never got any closer, except for the occasional goodnight kiss—the slightest pressure of my cheek against hers managed on her corridor or mine outside our doors before lights out, executed with the correct measure of unthreatening flippancy.

Whether sex would have transpired had Katherine's interest approximated mine in any way remains of course a mystery. As does the question of whether she knew just how interested I was. But these were endemic mysteries at Saint Mary's. During my six years at the school, unless I was unusually dense and unobservant, there was no sign whatsoever of any heavy breathing by one girl for another or for a teacher or a nun. For all I knew I was the only one. To this day,

I remain none the wiser. My schoolmates generally were headed for the "finishing schools" and debutante circuits in preparation for very proper Republican marriages. Recently I learned that one of my fifteen classmates, the daughter of an Episcopal priest, became a lesbian during the 1970s, following a marriage that produced a daughter. After Katherine graduated in 1946, and I acceded to my own senior year, I can deduce by how things went that I felt bereft: I succumbed to the required boyfriend; there are photos of me in our yearbook looking uncharacteristically glum or cynical. Also I had a permanent, the first and last of my life—sure sign of a major capitulation to girl training.

I had to wait three years for my next infatuation with someone of my own gender. I was a junior in college in Boston, and my quarry, my dance teacher, had, not unlike Katherine and Constance earlier, taken an interest in me as a kind of "pet." But here was a worldly experienced woman, a Brahmin of fifty-three, with power and elegance. A dark brunette, built like Isadora Duncan, in gabardine skirt suits, black or beige, she was ravishing. I stalked her everywhere; I knew instinctively the proper covert style for that kind of pursuit. I shone to a prodigious degree in her classes—not an inconsiderable feat for a confirmed athlete, particularly in the modern dance specialty. Then suddenly something happened that upped the ante of her interest. I learned that a close relative of mine whom I had always thought to be dead had really been alive, and had only now just died, causing such mental confusion and disorder that I sought her counsel. I cannot say that from then on she found me fascinating—I was still a mere schoolgirl, a pretty blank canvas—but my story apparently turned her on, or commanded her attention in a way that made her notice me differently; and before long I would experience for the first time, aged twenty, the stirrings of that high-premium human commodity: a mutual attraction.

My erotic transmission system was still not activated. The obligatory necking and petting with prep school boyfriend had not sprung the works. Now I would be launched by the mere touch of my inamorata's hand in mine. I suppose the buildup had been so lengthy and intense that a brushed knuckle would have had the inevitable electrifying effect. Key to my new state was her initiative, and my amazed surprise. It was evening, late in May. She had been sitting quietly in her armchair; I had been pacing about mouthing off on some subject of agitated postadolescent interest to me (perhaps the world, as I had begun reading the newspapers then), and had stopped close to her, silenced, having run out of gas. I was looking away, into the middle distance of the room. An eternal moment fluttered by, as we were fixed in this pose, when she made the slightest move, placing her warm pithy hand inside mine in a firm yet light grasp that could not be mistaken for simple friendliness. Lingering, motionless, in this juncture, another eternal moment, ignition for lift-off took place. Soon I fell to my knees more or less and kissed her face passionately and professed my great love for her. How we got from there to her bed I have no memory. But once in the site for understood serious action, I know I did not become an instant lover or anything. Arousal did not translate to appropriate activity. I had no idea what was appropriate. Anyway my awe kept me in abeyance. And I must have believed that any initiatives in her own bed had to be hers. But either she did not know what to do herself, or she expected from my tall lean athleticism and youth that I would spring into action as a butch. At the time, not knowing any better, what actually happened—an extensive kind of pre-foreplay—was galvanically satisfying. And it set the tone for the whole affair.

The other condition defining the affair was of course its secrecy. Here, on the holy ground of the illicit, I was not altogether inexperienced, having known as a teenager at Saint Mary's that my strong feeling for a schoolmate was strictly classified information, even to the schoolmate. Ignorant though I was of sex, I did know that my *feelings* were misdirected. Now almost a seasoned initiate to an ancient form of government control, I would have to wait two decades before I was able to question this censorship of my emotional life. Until then, I played out recognizably familiar variations on the theme of a hidden existence. The effort to pervert oneself by looking and/or acting proper female parts had to be the standard ploy. But in believing that one was really straight, hardly difficult after growing up surrounded by the all-pervading obvious or insidious directives to be so, preemptive commands confirming that one already was what one was supposed to be, the ground rules were set for carrying out roles or behaviors contrary to self. Classically, one would be having an affair with a woman, all the while convinced that it was an interim exceptional thing, an aberration soon to be forgotten when the "right man" came along. Typically, these vital abridgments of self could not be articulated. They tend to come to light only under revolutionary conditions, when the state at last can be held responsible for the schizoid lives its policies and directives breed. Before such a time, the strategies developed to survive a seriously contradictory existence can form a fascinating kind of archaeology. A prerevolutionary state of antiquated being. Coming out then meant nothing more than the covert or chance discovery of a "true" love or sex object.

Love and sex did not in my case happen at once, if by sex we mean the fully genitalized orgasmic experience. I had to go far away to the Midwest to be introduced to the positively libidinous.

Wrenched away from my real love by the itinerant peculiarities of youth in preparing for life by graduating from one place to another, I found myself in an instructorship at a liberal arts college in Minnesota, now aged twenty-one. I lived in a stone gothic U-shaped faculty house. A most handsome and zesty woman of thirty by name Polly Hunter, resident across the way, lost little time in identifying me as a sapphic possibility, bedding me down within a week of my arrival. I must have been drunk on two martinis. Ms. Hunter, who had already undertaken to initiate me to the mandatory ritual of imbibing this powerful before-dinner cocktail, never rested at one. I had no tolerance at all, but doubt that even sober I would have resisted the confident advances of this attractive experienced virago, ushering me into an intimacy that immediately stanched my forsaken state, marooned in friendless middle America. Still in love with my lady in Boston, I simply partitioned her, going on to create another compartment in which sex, make it SEX, reigned by itself. With all erogenous zones and the miracle of orgasm on go—this latter an earthshaking surprise, having never *heard* of it before—the purpose of that icy cold year in Minnesota would seem to have been complete. But not quite.

Immersed in my second affair, it did not escape me that once again the liaison was of a high order of secrecy, due obviously to its contract with my own gender. Though still too young to think or imagine clearly that my abnormality or "phase" would evaporate once I took proper note of the opposite sex, my partner in crime assumed the responsibility of articulating this essential belief in any sexual pervert's scheme of things. Staying in a motel en route east by car (Ms. Hunter also taught me to drive that year), we were lounging in the tub, when she remarked on the few stray hairs lying around my areola, startling me out of my unversed slumber by saying that I might want to shave them in order to be alluring to some man. A diminutive feature I took for granted, like an indistinct mole on my chin, clearly it was no deterrent for her. But there it was. I was being delivered up to "some man." I heard the message. And within no time, preparing to go east for another school break, I telephoned a young man my age named Will who had been a student at Brown, and who had sent me reams of letters with love poems enclosed, asking him (more like ordering I think) to meet me in New York at a certain hotel at a certain appointed time. He responded with alacrity and punctuality. With no preliminary ado, we undressed completely, and lay down naked side by side on the hotel bed. Then waited for a *deus ex machina* or something to propel us into action. I suppose he was a virgin to women as I was a virgin to men. After a while, when it became obvious that nothing whatsoever was going to happen, we got up, donned clothes, took the elevator downstairs, paid at the desk, and went out to eat and take in a movie. I wonder if he continued writing to me after that. I don't have to wonder if he held any attraction for me beyond his letters. No sooner did I see him at the hotel, even before undressing, than I knew he did not. But in only a matter of months, "deliverance" was at hand.

Still on the move, graduating from here to there, my next stop was North Carolina, where I was now a candidate for a masters in fine arts. Landing in Greensboro by bus, a stranger to the South, knowing nobody, shocked by the "whites only" signs I saw every-where, and two intimacies behind—women of high significance to me, whom, it was understood somehow, I would never see again—I felt stranded for the first time in my life to a shipwrecked degree. I was hardly unpacked when a college-mate called Ann, an art student and native North Carolinian, signaled her verboten interest in me. Our first sexual encounter would become our last. With her sad ap-peal, interesting creativity, hourglass sensual body, I might have found her perfectly worthy for a new venture in the "love that dare not speak its name." But I had precedents, and now I had fears as well. Now at last in fact, noticing that I was veering off course for the third year in a row, I was *properly* fearful.

So just around the time of my brief stand with Ann, I succumbed to another signal from the land of sex. This one, from the impeccably appropriate gender, also fit in with my previous choice of objects: older women to whom I had played novitiate, protégé, inductee. My Boston lady had awakened me culturally—giving me Dickinson, Whitman, Sir James Frazer to read, taking me to concerts, introducing me to cultivated friends, in the end to her famous intimates—the leading dancers and choreographers in the modern dance field of her time. My Minnesota connection had taken me in hand for drinking, driving, and the fullness of sex. Now, in North Carolina, I got another teacher—he was a visiting professor of philosophy—and to boot some-one who could screw me into a seemly female submission. There was actually an understanding—given a confession I made when first he invited me to tea—that he was saving me from certain lesbian perdi-tion. For the privilege of sitting at his feet osmosing Plato and Socrates, Whitehead and Russell, I endured a year of missionary sex, indoctrina-tion that this was what sex with men was about, utter forgetfulness of orgasm and the splendors of polymorphism, and the terrible suspicion that the professor's devoted wife, who would sit with us at teatime knitting and chattering and had once been lobotomized (a popular operation performed particularly on women, if emotionally over-wrought by anything, in the forties and fifties), was living with her husband under false pretenses.

Coming out in those days was not a once-for-all-time experience, unless by chance or unusual persuasion the first time stuck, over-whelming the general certitude that by nature we all loved men, and that we must make every effort to prove it. With North Carolina behind me (a fine college try indeed), I relapsed badly, as if on the rebound, falling quite madly for a dancer called Ruth Currier. I had moved on again, now to New York City to further the powerful legacy of my dance teacher, my first consummated amour, throwing my still incompletely broken athlete's body onto the dance studio boards for additional instruction—to what exact end it was unclear—in the traditional female art of being sexy and decorative. Ruth, a leading dancer in the José Limon company, in whose studio I had practically taken up residence, was adorable and beautiful at once, with the dancer's approved ideal body, trained to sleek definitions. And she was older, perhaps by ten years, the established condition for my inti-macies to date. She was also unequivocally straight, or so it seemed, never without the pleased attentions of one adoring boyfriend or an-other. In pursuing an interest bound to be unrequited, with no open-ing even for a testimonial of love (though I believe she was fully aware of my hopeless feelings), I seem to have been recycling my original unilateral infatuation for Katherine at Saint Mary's. As if in order to come out again, I had to play my tunes in the sequence they first occurred.

Alas, it was not so easy this time. I was at large in New York City, no longer under institutional, largely female protection. All the while I pined for Ruth, I would let an occasional man have his way with me. This led to two pregnancies and two abortions (dire, danger-ous, and of course illegal procedures in the 1950s) which in turn led to my marriage, in 1958, to a man—the culmination and apotheosis, one could say, of the predicted sacrificial course for a woman. Not until 1964, when spewed out the other end as a single divorced mother of two, lo, thirteen years after my last personally authentic relationship, was I brought out again. But coming out now was much complicated by the presence of my two children. The sexual connect was made actually while they were away for the summer with my mother. Upon return, they helped form a *ménage á quatre,* their mother having cohabited instantly with the body she had waked up in bed with one morning in August (after the immediate and drunken romantic revelation of eternal love). This of course was an unworkable unacceptable arrangement. A lesbian mother was an oxymoron. I did not need to know this consciously. It was vastly assumed, insinuated already for centuries. In any event, the newness of my situation was shocking. I had never lived with a woman before. Nor been involved with one younger than myself. Suddenly an old lady at thirty-something, I had become the one looked up to for guidance and mentorship, a role for which I had no aptitude or inclination.

One familiar thing about our relationship was its utter secrecy, even to ourselves. But now for the first time in my clandestine history, I was under surveillance. For all the privacy we had, we might as well have been conducting our affair under some familial roof. We lived and played complementary roles (she a dancer, me a critic), in the small claustrophobic art world of the 1960s. Everyone knew or guessed everything. And since this was a very very macho little world (male artists more tarzan than thou in an underdog profession for males), and my paramour had been viewed as a reigning virginal beauty, practically Greta Garbo incarnate, we were under siege the moment an artist with knightly credentials (rich, prodigious, admired, aggressive, hungry, etc.) had been identified for a rescue mission. It took a year to pry her loose. But his attentions compromised our relationship considerably. She was flattered, I knew I was condemned. Whether or not this particular pursuit would succeed, its implications were clear: the male species awaited her as surely as does a spider a fly in his web. Having crash-landed into a couple of websites myself, my recent extrication did nothing to convince me that I had the right to try to save another woman from a similar fate. Anyway, there were dividends for me in the tragic ending of our consortium. Now a failed dyke and cradle-snatcher, I was no longer under surveillance. In fact, because our ending found me in big trouble, under institutional lockup for having gone mad, putting my career as critic at risk (a role the art world had loved me in), I aroused quite a bit of unexpected sympathy. The problem of motherhood vs. lesbianism was also resolved—if not exactly the way it was supposed to be. Even before my unlawful relationship was seriously threatened by the male advance, I let my children go to their father and his new wife. Then when I looked "legal" again, ready perhaps to resume life as an impoverished single mother, an understanding developed, with my newly acquired ex-mental credentials, that I was now "unfit." I became free therefore to be a proper lesbian (another oxymoron, I realize), and since the world was fast unraveling—when I got done lying in bed depressed after two major breakdowns it was 1968—with a gay revolution looming, a movement tumbling like jack after jill or vice versa in the wake of feminism, I was ready at last to see another woman as in some way marriageable.

I made this easy for myself by falling for an heiress. Instinctively I realized that security and protection were things I needed. I did not therefore go and seek out an heiress. I just happened to stumble into bed with one, drunk and nearly insensate—the normal state for illicit beginnings. We had met one night on the street outside the artists' mecca, Max's Kansas City, collapsed into a taxi together, and headed for my shabby loft on the Bowery. In the morning, over coffee and toast, getting a good look at her, and even before she opened her mouth to tell me about herself, I could see that a kind of Saint Mary's girl, purebred and genteel, athletic and preppie, had made her way into my ungilded cage. She even wore a navy blue school-type blazer, much like the one I had once spent six years in. However, at twenty-one she was no sexual naïf. I had just had the best sex since Minnesota, by now a piece of ancient history. And whether or not the sex had been tops for her, and/or for whatever other reason (she did say "a writer was perfect" for her), she left forthwith to go to her Gramercy Park apartment, shut it down, and return to live with me in my inferior but romantic downwardly mobile quarters.

With my star in the art world rising again, my new Polly (yes, another Minnesota reminder) was the perfect asset. Unlike my Garbo dancer, she took the scene by surprise—an outsider, a different order of threat. But by the time a charge might have been mounted against us, once it had fully sunk in that a most desirable female—rich, young, nubile—had become an ornament to the wrong sex, we had left town, practically in a cloud of dust. It was January 1969. I had lost my mind again, and my youthful mate, precociously understanding the need for escape, the necessity of eluding any authorities who might once again throw me in the bins, had bought a brand-new VW hatchback and made all due preparations for a long cooling-out trip around the United States. Now a columnist, I sent touring reports home every week, sort of on the order of "travels with Polly," heraldically if obscurely coming out—readable no doubt to the tight little art world that knew me well, but also to elements of a world that would soon be my own new totality. The Stonewall Riots were virtually upon us. My readership would cross over to some insurgent lesbians of the Gay Liberation Front. And soon I would have the perfect personal motivation for rising up in rage myself and joining them at the barricades.

Home again after several months on the road, my young savior and heiress, lover of my dreams, decamped suddenly for Europe where her sophisticated mother had been waiting patiently at one of the family estates for her errant daughter to come to her senses. Oh, I tried to get her back. I made an extraordinary trip to Spain, locating her deep in Mediterranean seclusion, holed up with her triumphant mother, who would graciously drive me up the coast to Malaga in her XE6 Jag and buy me a first-class ticket home. And although I did not run straightaway out of the plane in New York into the arms of the revolution, I know this was my watershed moment.

Coming out would now become a political matter, a means of establishing identity, of challenging the status quo, no longer simply a private venture in sex and bed. But eventually it would become clear that the political act of coming out was no more a once-for-all-time thing than the purely personal had ever proved to be. And that "going back in" would be as endemic as "coming out" to the besieged estate of the queer. There is, sadly, no end to coming out in a society that still makes secrecy a rigorous condition for same-sexuality, and refuses to admit same-sex couples and their children to the community of family, to bring them into the fold of the state that collects their taxes.

Should it ever cease to be necessary to come out, a lesbian or gay identity would itself cease to exist. Nobody speaks of a "heterosexual identity." It's just assumed and understood, a legal mode of being, as acceptable as a taste for Dickinson or Rachmaninoff.

Al Giese

FIRST LOVE

Karla Jay

I suppose my parents tried to raise me just like other little girls, but it was soon apparent that I was different. Even at two, when the other little girls in Flatbush, Brooklyn, posed in pink lace crinoline dresses and white patent leather shoes, I stood ready for the reflex lens Kodak in my black cowboy hat, boots, floral Western shirt, and holster complete with shiny metal gun. I threw my dolls into the corner of the room and played only with a teddy bear I'd named Corey because he was the color of an apple core that had sat on the table for a long time. I put Corey in the doll carriage my mother had purchased for me, while my brother made off with the dolls and performed major surgery on them. They returned, if at all, as amputees, their heads literally on backwards or their hands gone. Occasionally, a blue eye drooped disgustingly out of a bashed-in porcelain face. Meanwhile, Corey and I paraded up and down St. Paul's Place with the doll carriage. When I got tired, I pushed Corey to one side and crawled into the carriage with him. Still in a crib at home, I was good at sleeping in tight places.

My mother wanted a clean, pink, passive child, one who adored her sterilized apartment and pretty clothes, but I adored chocolate, which made lots of lovely splotches on anything pink. My mother tried hard to keep the world pale velour and crinoline for me, but I was always brown as ice cream and dirt and red as cut knees and elbows. She soon gave up trying to keep me pink; instead, she created a totally pink room for me, with pink French Provincial furniture, hand-made pink beds with posters and canopies, and a pink high-gloss toy cabinet built by one of the carpenters who worked with my father.

The beds came at the same time as our housekeeper Nene, when I was four. Nene was brown like me, but a lot darker. Even though she tried to toilet train me and teach me to sleep in a bed—which my mother had not bothered to do—I loved her dearly. I was a failure at both and wound up black and blue: every night I rolled out of bed as I tried to curl against the crib bars I dreamed were still there.

Summer was my favorite time, when I could play unencumbered by snowsuits, mittens, and, worst of all, hats. And summer was when Nene and I took the BMT to Ebbetts Field to see the Brooklyn Dodgers play. Her passion for the team was undiminished by their losses but ultimately destroyed by their treacherous abandonment of the East Coast for Los Angeles. We never forgave them.

My daily trips to Ebbetts Field ended when I was five. My mother needed intestinal surgery, so my parents sent me to Camp Swatonah. It was there that I had my first love affair.

The camp was in Pennsylvania, just across the border from Calicoon, New York. The bus snaked up Route 17, the so-called "Quick Way," but the trip was long and miserable because the kids my age kept throwing candy and gum at me, or vomiting up their lunch, while the older girls sang a bunch of songs I had never heard before: "R-A-T-T-L-E-S-N-A-K-E spells rattlesnake." I couldn't spell, but if this was what camp held in store, I didn't like the sound of the whole thing. I held onto Corey and told myself that we were going to be brave in the woods. I prayed someone would be in the woods to tie my shoes for me.

The ride seemed to take days. I was the only one in the Junior group not crying, throwing up, or both, maybe because I didn't know I was supposed to be sad. We finally reached the camp and rushed out of the gum-bedecked bus.

Camp Swatonah lay in a valley between two hills. In the very center was a small lake, supposedly formed when the mythical Indian

Princess Summer-Spring-Winter-Fall sacrificed herself for her people, who were threatened by neighboring tribes, probably the Cohens and the Levites. But, thank God, the bunk—made of crude wooden logs sealed with mud, cement, and straw—wasn't pink. The bathrooms were primitive but working, and there was one shower for all fourteen of us.

Mick greeted us at the door. She had a short d.a. ("duck's ass") haircut, slicked to a perfect point in the back. She was lean, with sharp features; a slow smile lurked on one side of her mouth. She wasn't like my mother, Nene, my grandmother, or my mother's friends. She spoke in a deep, soft, lilting voice, and when she lifted my duffel bag, hauled it over to my locker, and gave me a long hug, I was instantly in love.

Mick loved me too, or so she soon said, because I was just like her. I wondered what she meant. From the moment I arrived in camp I was always having accidents; maybe she was a clod, too. The first week, I slipped on the swimming crib stairs and skinned half my leg. No one understood how I'd done that in the "safety crib," and Mick said she wouldn't mention it in the weekly letter she wrote home for me since I couldn't write at all myself. The second week, I got a huge splinter under a fingernail when I was playing jacks. The doctor had to remove the nail to get it out, and he asked me why I didn't cry.

"Little girls are allowed to cry," he said.

"I'm not really a little girl," I replied.

He picked out the remaining splinters and gave me a candy bar for my bravery.

Maybe Mick had always been in trouble, too, as I always was. I had a talent for catching frogs and toads, and when I couldn't find a place to keep them, I placed them in someone else's bed. I also kept a good supply of crickets and salamanders ready to launch at any older girl who threatened me with force. Though I hated to start a fight, I didn't hesitate once someone else threw a punch. Somehow, I usually wound up tangling with the older girls. They had long arms and would grab my hands, but I butted them with my head until they let go. Mick nicknamed me "Billy the Goat," a name everyone at camp called me for years—without the goat part, of course.

Maybe Mick and I were alike, I reasoned, because we were both unafraid. Mick was the only person who didn't scream when I appeared armed with frogs or snakes. She laughed when I led a fawn into the bunk one night and fed it peanut butter sandwiches, which it ate with gusto, smacking its lips when they got stuck on the gooey concoction. The only girl in the junior group who rode horses instead of ponies, I would gallop after Mick into town, about two miles away, buy Cokes for a nickel each, and then head back.

I was also the only one unafraid of the water: I followed Mick into the crib, hesitating at first only because the water seemed oddly nonsaline to someone like me, who had spent the first two summers of her life playing in the Atlantic Ocean. I would have followed her anywhere. She taught me how to swim, holding me in her strong, well-muscled arms. I became nothing; I floated without weight. The liquid of the crib joined us; I was no longer sure where I left off and she began. With such a teacher, how could I be afraid?

It was bad enough when I got into fights with the older girls, but when I started butting around my peers, the camp owners got worried. The one we called "Uncle Eddie," a kindly, lean man with a stubbly face, took me aside and gave me a long lecture on being nice to small kids. Since I was one of the youngest campers, it was hard to take him seriously. It was hard to take *adults* seriously. Despite my immediate positive response to anyone who was affectionate, I felt I couldn't let myself be bullied by an adult. As the toughest kid in the junior group, I had my reputation to protect. I continued fighting until Mick made me "hold boots" to punish me. Standing in the middle of the bunk, I held out her riding boots, stretching out my arms until I felt they would drop off from the searing pain and fatigue. Worse than this was the thought that Mick was punishing me, that she would no longer love me because I was such a monster.

One day, while Uncle Eddie was busy reprimanding another kid at the waterfront for swimming without her "strong buddy," I pushed him into the lake, clothes and all. He pretended to be terrified of coming back onto the shore. He swam out to the raft and tossed his waterlogged shoes onto it before hauling his dripping body out of the water. He made faces at me from afar. He made my reputation.

Finally, he came back to shore and gave me a soggy hug. Then he realized everyone was laughing, and knew that we had set a bad precedent for the camp. I was sorry that I had made him wet. He stood there like a drenched hen as he decided what to do with me. After a moment, he announced, "I'm going to hang you!"

My execution was set for dinner the next night. Mick told him not to go ahead with it, but the kids in my bunk pleaded against a stay of execution, reminding him that he had to keep his word. I was that popular.

Somehow, I wasn't worried: I tended not to take things seriously. Death itself was unreal to me: the only time I had seen someone die was in *Bambi*. When Bambi's mother was destroyed in the forest fire, Nene had to take me from the theater. I'd had no idea mothers could die. And my mother was clearly unwell.

That night, however, my main thought when I walked into the dining room was whether the meal would be any good. It was usually chewy meat, overcooked vegetables, and the most disgusting thing of all—milk. I hadn't seen other movies besides *Bambi,* and the only television I had watched was *Howdy Doody* and *Captain Kangaroo*. I had no idea that I was supposed to relish my last meal or make a request.

When the meal ended, Uncle Eddie called me up to the front of the dining room. He read off my offenses and my sentence. Everyone cheered, and I began to feel a bit queasy. I think Uncle Eddie did, too; we had both gone too far. He slowly finished his reading and then swung a rope over one of the huge rafters. Finally, he put the noose around my neck. This was going to be a hard one for either of us to get out of gracefully. Fortunately or unfortunately, at that moment my mother chose to make her one visit of the summer— maybe (it's hard to remember) her only visit during all the years I was at camp.

"It's all a joke," Uncle Eddie said to my mother.

Mother was not amused. She carried on so much that the camp instituted regular assigned visiting days, limiting them to only twice a summer. Despite my mother's threat to bring a lawsuit, I somehow managed to stay at camp that summer. I was more willing to risk my neck than my relationship with Mick, and I felt that had my mother failed to appear (and who knew she would?), Mick would have saved me. I pictured her riding up on Sunshine or one of her other favorite horses and whisking me, noose and all, off the table and into the saddle, even though horses weren't allowed in the dining room. I was a tough kid, but my fantasies were all femme.

Next summer, I returned to Camp Swatonah. As the bus pulled up the red clay road and parked in the hillside lot overlooking the camp, I felt as if the winter had just been some hazy and prolonged dream which filled the gap between last summer and this one.

Of course, Mick was there. She was no longer my counselor, since she had been promoted to group leader of the entire Junior contingent. This meant that I would have to share her attentions with a large group of girls, but it also meant that she had more power.

Unfortunately, authority didn't sit well on Mick. Everything she planned turned out wrong, starting with the first cookout of the season. Cookouts were held every Thursday night so the kitchen staff could have a night off. We trudged up to a cleared field on which were scattered lots of open stone pits covered with grills. Hamburgers were cooked on top and ears of corn were tossed, husks and all, into the ashes.

The dinner bugle sounded. Bugles rang out for every conceivable occasion—reveille in the morning, flag-raising before breakfast, the beginning and end of all group activities, and then taps at night. By the end of the summer, the bugler was blue in the face. She was replaced every year by a fresher, younger mouth, until finally a phonograph record banished those strained notes once and for all. When the cookout bugle call rang out, the older girls bolted up the hill. Since they had longer legs and could run faster, they always got the best pits at the best locations in the middle of the hayfield. We younger girls were stuck on the periphery, where, if you took one wrong step, you were attacked simultaneously by wild raspberry bushes and the poison ivy lurking under them. It was a camp axiom that the younger you were, the itchier you were.

Mick always grumbled when we got the worst pit in the field, but she never made nasty comments about our unbearably short legs or deserted us on the path to run ahead and claim squatter's rights to a better pit. For one thing, she had been the counselor to some of the older girls during their first years at camp. She simply pretended that even though we were farthest from the place where the truck dropped off the food, we really had the best pit and could eat as well as the others.

Of course, her version was never true. We always got the last box of food. Although the older girls had left our corn untouched—they were either on diets or had braces on their teeth—they had already swiped half of our hamburgers.

Since Mick was the group leader, she had to cook our food. Mick was no Julia Child. She could never get the hamburgers to stay on the grill: they either slid into the ashes when she wasn't looking or flew into the poison ivy when she tried to flip them. All twenty-four girls in the group screaming "Rare! Medium! Well-done!" didn't help her concentration much, either. She would threaten us with her spatula and try to coax the mutilated hamburgers into their buns. The corn refused to come out of the ashes when it was done, and by the time she got the ears out, the kernels looked like blacked-out teeth. She didn't have a good sense of which way the wind was going to blow, either: The smoke always got into her face so that at the end of dinner she looked like a leftover hamburger.

One Thursday, Mick was given frozen veal cutlets by mistake. Instead of returning them to the kitchen, she assumed they were breaded hamburgers and tried to cook them. Barbecued veal cutlets were not very popular that night, and neither was Mick.

If Mick's cooking had been the only thing that went wrong, the rest of the group might have forgiven her. Unluckily, everything else she touched went wrong, too. One day she planned a boating trip down the Delaware River. She arranged weeks in advance for the rowboats to be trucked to a spot she had chosen for its gentle currents and scenic beauty. She hand-picked the best counselors to row and, auspiciously, a day on which the sun shone brilliantly. There was, however, something she hadn't counted on: drought. When we arrived at the Delaware, the river was bone dry, and the only way to get a rowboat across the river was to carry it across the stony bottom, now occupied by a group of contented rattlesnakes sunning themselves.

Mick was not discouraged. Instead of a rowing expedition, she proposed a long nature hike which would end in a campout on top of a nearby mountain. She chose a sheltered spot and instructed the truck drivers to deliver our sleeping bags and food (precertified as veal free).

After a long trek, we arrived at the campsite. We were all nearly starving, so we urged Mick to make dinner as soon as possible. She went over to a pile of cinder blocks left over from last year's campouts, but the blocks were filled with hornets' nests. Mick was less afraid of hornets than of twenty-four screaming, hungry girls, so she heroically took several rolls of toilet paper, draped them over the nests, and lit them. Naturally, Mick had misplanned the assault. We were upwind from the smoke but downwind from the hornets, who flew at us in a rage. We stampeded down the hill, but not in time. We were all bitten, and Janet, who was allergic to insect bites, had to be rushed to the infirmary.

Finally, we crawled back to the campsite. Mick was standing there covered with hornet bites, making hamburgers with her usual lack of grace. We were so hungry that as soon as the meat hit our mouths we forgave her. Less forgivable was her burning the S'mores—a magical concoction of Hershey's chocolate, marshmallows, and graham crackers. Mick somehow got herself covered with the melted marshmallows, and her body looked as if she had been attacked by web-weaving spiders.

After dinner, we looked for the outhouse. When we found there was none, we were not amused. Mick directed us to the trees. "Over there, girls. And, uh, I used the toilet paper for the hornets. Use some leaves, and make sure they ain't poison ivy." We shrieked and protested about lurking bears and snakes, but Mick and Jean, another counselor, accompanied us. Afterwards, we were all too glad to crawl into our sleeping bags and go to sleep.

I awoke in the middle of the night, feeling very cold. I had been told there were a million stars in the sky, but I was too near-sighted to see any of them, and anyway they clearly weren't much good at keeping people warm. Finally, I decided I was blue enough to arouse sympathy, so I got out of my sleeping bag and crawled over to where Mick was lying. She wasn't asleep. Maybe she was counting stars . . . or sheep. Maybe she was secretly afraid that bears would come to eat us all in the middle of the night.

"I'm cold!" I whispered desperately and shivered to give emphasis to my statement.

"Go back to your sleeping bag and you'll warm up," Mick growled.

"That's where it's really cold."

Mick unzipped her sleeping bag and gestured for me to climb in. I tucked my head between her two small, hard breasts and breathed in the musky smell of her body and dead smoke from the campfire. I put one arm around her neck and, as I moved up to try to kiss her, I fell asleep.

I was ready to take my first swimming test. The best swimmer in the crib, I wanted to swim in the lake. To be allowed to do this, you had to swim to the raft and back without any help.

Brenda, though she wasn't as good a swimmer as I was, was also ready to take her test and insisted on going first. She jumped in the water after Mick, who went along as a "strong buddy" to guard us. Brenda swam really fast for about a hundred yards and then announced, "I'm tired!" She clutched Mick around the neck and started to sink, taking Mick with her. Mick came up choking and spitting water, but quickly loosened Brenda's grip and pulled Brenda, one hand cupped under her chin, to shore. Another counselor plucked poor Brenda, now sobbing hysterically, out of the water. When Mick got out of the water, Brenda collapsed in her arms. Mick held her and tried to comfort her.

I was furious. Couldn't Mick see that Brenda was a jerk and just wanted Mick to hold her? If Mick didn't like "scardey cats," she sure wasn't acting like it.

I told Brenda to hurry up and stop crying—I wanted to take my test. Brenda sobbed even more loudly, but eventually Mick turned her over to another counselor and climbed back into the water.

I climbed in after her. The water felt much colder than the crib, especially when I put my feet down. I couldn't see the bottom, except for some vague, mossy shadows that looked like rocks. I was afraid the fish would bite my toes when I swam, but I was determined to do better than Brenda.

I swam slowly. Mick was a few feet in front of me. With her there, I could have swum the ocean! I made it easily to the raft and swam back almost as easily.

Shivering, I strutted up the ladder and onto the deck. All the counselors congratulated me, and Mick hugged me and crowed, "You're another Esther Williams!"

"Who's Esther Williams?" I asked.

Mick laughed and pinned a small gold star on my swimsuit.

"I guarantee it will work, Billy," Andi assured me. Believe me, it's foolproof."

She had to be right. After all, Andi wasn't in the older group for nothing: she had to know by now all the tricks which were best for total revenge. Besides, I was mad enough now at Mick to try anything. After all, Mick had been showing Beth an awful lot of favor lately. She had even let Beth fold the flag when it was our group's turn. I would teach her a lesson.

I did just what Andi said. I got up before the bugle one morning and checked to make sure that Mick was sound asleep. Then I went into the bathroom and got some cold water, which I heated up with some matches I swiped from another counselor. When it was body temperature, I took it to Mick's bed and poured it into her out-stretched palm. This was supposed to make her pee in her bed, but something went wrong. Mick woke up.

"What the hell, Billy!" she screamed, shaking her hand.

I tried to look innocent. "Your hand was dirty. I decided to wash it."

"Like hell you were. I know that trick. Why did you do it? You've turned on me."

"More like you turned on me—letting Beth fold the flag."

"So that's it!" Mick smiled. "You can't do everything, you know.

There are twenty-four girls in the Junior group, and you ain't them. Next time, maybe Terry or Randy will fold the flag. You've got to learn to share things with them. You know I love you best. I'm not sharing *that.*"

This was Andi's fault. I, who never cried, was about to burst into tears, but Mick wasn't going to let me wet her shoulder, too.

"Hey, I get enough tears from Brenda every day. Cut that stuff and shine my shoes for what you done."

I polished Mick's saddle shoes with joy, trying not to get black polish on the white parts. It was challenging—like a coloring book; I liked to work on things that I could look at very closely. Yes, I felt better, and I knew that I would feel even better once I had stuffed some green apples down Andi's lying throat. I contemplated the idea and waved the shoe brush menacingly.

"What are you planning now?" asked Mick.

"Oh, nothing. Just admiring this brush."

"Sure."

When I had graduated to the last bunk in the Junior group, we were allowed to go with the Middies to a social at the boys' camp. Without my bunk, there would be too few girls. The ratio of boys to girls, it seemed, had to be equal.

"What's a social?" I asked Mick.

"Well," said Mick, blushing and drawling, "it's a party where you'll get to meet the boys from the other side of the lake, and you'll get to dance with them."

I was suspicious. *"Dance* with them? Who wants to dance with them? Who wants to dance, period? Why can't we challenge them to a game of newcomb, instead?"

"Uncle Eddie thinks that a dance will be fun for a change."

She wasn't convincing. Square dancing couldn't be much fun if we had to take baths first.

Cleaned up and miserable, we were all dressed in stiffly starched skirts or shirts and then marched around the lake to the boys' camp.

We were put into squares and assigned partners. I got stuck with Tim, a little boy with a blond buzz cut. He said that he hated all this dosie-do stuff (he was an older Middie and had been to one social already) and that he'd give me a piece of gum if I'd sneak out with him. He knew a place where they'd never find us.

I liked Tim immediately. At last I knew that some boys could think as well as I could. I told him to wait until old eagle-eyed Jean went for a glass of punch, and then we could sneak out. We pretended to dance, while the counselors stood by, explaining the calls on the scratchy square-dance records. It was going to be hard to get out of there: one counselor was watching every square of eight kids. But the hope of escaping kept me doing all those silly motions.

Intermission came, and while Jean was getting some punch and Mick was talking to Tad—another female counselor who was always hanging around when Mick wasn't on duty—Tim and I headed out the door. We stuck close to the walls and scampered over his bunk—the last place, he said, that his counselor would look for him.

He showed me the bunk, which was exactly like ours, except that the boys already had indoor plumbing—bathrooms as well as running water. Then he showed me his cubby. He took out two pairs of white socks and stuck them under his tee shirt. He said that that was what his sister looked like, adding "And you're going to look like that too in a few years."

I knew that he was lying—Mick was older than his sister, and *she* didn't look like she had two socks stuck under her shirt, and neither did my mother—so I punched him. Tim said, "I never hit girls," so I punched him again. Then I knew that Tim was a down-and-out liar, because he punched me back.

"I thought you don't hit girls," I said, wiping blood from my nose.

"You're an exception."

"Good. In that case, we can be friends."

We shook hands, and I wiped the rest of the blood onto my shorts.

Mick spotted us as we came back into the social hall. "Where were y'all?"

"Oh, we were just out on the porch getting some fresh air." I hoped my nose had stopped bleeding.

"Well you must have tripped down the stairs then, 'cause your pants are covered with blood," she laughed, and then added, "I can see you've had a good time at your first social."

I had. If this was what socials were about, I could hardly wait for the next one.

Tad didn't like me because Mick was so fond of me. One day when Mick wasn't around, she told me that Mick was dead. I shook my head in disbelief: though *Bambi* had shown me that mothers could die, I refused to believe that counselors, too, were mortal.

I ran wildly around the camp looking for Mick. I asked several counselors where she was, but they didn't know. I was in despair. I moped in the bunk, saying I was too sick to go to group activities. I refused to go to the infirmary.

I sat in the bunk until it was time for dinner, and I sat there while the rest of the bunk went off to eat. It was rare for me to miss anything involving food. Corey tried to comfort me, to no avail.

Suddenly, Mick walked in. By this time, I really believed that she was dead, so I screamed, "It's a ghost!" and ran like hell out of the bunk. Mick saw how white with fear I was, but she thought I might be up to another one of my pranks, so she laughed and gave chase.

Finally, she caught up to me and grabbed me by the arm. "What the heck is going down here?"

"You're dead. Let me go!"

"Why do you think I'm dead?"

"You're a ghost! Don't haunt me! Tad said you're dead. She even showed me the rock they're going to bury you under." Despite my frantic explanations, I was beginning to calm down.

"Now who are ya going to believe, her or me? I say that I'm alive and that Tad is a doggoned liar. Now ya got to believe me. Y'hear?"

I saw for myself that Mick was alive and unchanged. She was in the dark blue denims she wore on her day off, so she must have been in town while I ran all over the camp looking for her. I grew quiet.

"Then why'd she say that?"

"She was just joshin' you. But it was mean, and I'm going to tell her so."

"Are you going to beat her up?"

"No."

Mick didn't beat Tad up, but I noticed that Tad didn't hang around Mick so much anymore, and I was glad.

The last day of camp, we all had a skinny dip—a tradition supposedly due to the fact that our bathing suits were already packed, along with everything else that was going home, in the trunk. Some wise girl in the Inter group, however, suggested that the skinny dip tradition had originated in Uncle Eddie's dirty mind. That story was followed by another suggesting that our entire skinny dip was being observed by telescopes strategically placed in the boys' camp. I countered that no boy could see *that* far, no matter what he was looking through, and even if they could see, I, for one, was not going to be deprived of a last swim.

My reasoning made sense to the juniors, who unanimously threw off their shorts and T-shirts and jumped into the water. The seniors were not so sure, or maybe they just had more to hide, so they sat miserably on the shore while we swam around in the buff. The counselors also had their clothes on and had to be rowed out to the rafts. Several juniors pretended they were drowning so that counselors would have to jump into the water and get their clothes wet, but the counselors weren't having any of it. "Go ahead and drown," said Jean. "It will be one less trunk to pack." We stuck out our tongues at her and went to annoy another counselor.

Mick stood on the shore with a safety pole. She was in shorts like the other counselors, and I remembered that last summer, too, she had refused to go skinny-dipping. I dog-paddled over and tried to taunt her into getting undressed.

"How come you ain't skinny-dipping like the rest of us? Are you chicken?"

"Nope. Don't feel like it."

"Come on. Admit it. You're scared like the seniors."

"Nope."

Mick was getting monosyllabic, and that was a sure sign that she was pissed off.

"Spoil sport!" I called and swam off before she could reply.

The night before we left, the harvest moon was shining bright and orange in my window, and that brought home to me the contrast between camp and the life I would be returning to. I was sad and hugged Corey closer. He was never sad. I held him tight and fell asleep.

The next day we ate a quick breakfast and were packed into the waiting buses. Mick rode back to the city in my bus, and she said that in the city she had to get on another bus which would take her home to Virginia. I asked her why she came so far every summer, and she said that she didn't like the ways of the South, even though she lived and went to school there.

The ride home always seemed faster than the ride up to camp, maybe because I never wanted to go home to the gray city. The others, too, were less boisterous than on the trip up to camp, even though they still sang color war songs and other camp ditties.

Soon we arrived in New York City. I saw Nene and my father in the crowd ready to pick me up; as usual, my mother wasn't there. Mick and I were the last ones to get off the bus. She took my hand

and helped me down. Then she leaned over and kissed me gently on the forehead.

"So long, sport," she said, and then she disappeared into the crowd.

I had lots of friends at camp, but my heart belonged to an older woman.
That's me, standing third from left.

Collection of Karla Jay; © Karla Jay

NOVELTIES

Joan Nestle

LONG, old wood counters filled with the needs of every day—pins, threads, candies, buttons, rubber bands, socks, zippers. Counters filled with the needs of vanity—small gold earrings on square white cards, plastic barrettes, lipsticks in pinks and tangerine, thin neon orange and green neck scarves, often used by us high school girls to cover our first hickeys. Hiding something is often the best way to reveal it.

The year is 1956. I am sixteen, and my responsibility in this Bayside, Queens, five-and-dime is the pet department. In the morning, I review the mayhem in the goldfish tank, scooping out the dead and terribly maimed; carefully clean the parakeet cages, knowing that if I am careless, the evidence of my failure will be in the air for the whole day, letting out tropical screeches as the customers swivel their heads to catch sight of the blue-and-yellow fugitive. I have learned how to keep the fish alive in small amounts of water collected at the bottom of plastic bags so small children can carry them home, how to seduce the budgies into delicatessen containers, and how to handle the small painted turtles so their heads and feet splay out as if they are swimming in air.

In 1953, when I was thirteen and living in a basement off the Grand Concourse with my mother, I secured those documents called working papers that allowed young men and women from working-class families to bring in some kind of income. I remember joining a long line of teenagers in a street shadowed by the El, waiting our turn to enter the public health center, where we would be given a vague health exam to make sure we were fit for work. Like young soldiers, we stood on line until we were told by a public nurse to step up to the white mark on the linoleum. Stripped to the waist, I stood in front of her. "Turn your head to the left," she said "and look at the potted plant." I did and felt her hands squeezing my breasts. "You got a nice pair," she said. Thus I was launched into the work force.

For the next two years, I "worked retail," as we said. After school, during the weekends, through the summers. Picking up the dresses that fell off the hangers, sheepishly following the assistant buyer—a title exalted beyond my wildest dreams—as she indicated to me where I should put the new winter lines. At holidays, I filled in at the wrapping desk and took returns, but was never allowed near the cash register. By then I had moved from the Bronx into Bayside to live with my aunt and uncle, my mother lost in her own struggles to find sex and money at the racetrack. In the coat department of May's Department store, my education continued. There I learned how the salesmen made their days more interesting. At the end of the day, they would gather behind the racks of car coats, boasting of how many wives they had managed to feel up as they helped the women try on the merchandise. "Did you see that? Right in front of her goddam husband."

These hours of work were for the most part deadly tedious. Walking the aisles, pushing at the clock to move along, taking the ten-minute break, running downstairs to the filthy employees' lounge and sitting numb on the torn, stained couch. This, I decided, could not be my life. But then one summer, along those same aisles, amid the dragging hours, I fell in love. A love so marked by want that all the years have not worn down its teeth.

The men who managed the five-and-dime stores of the chain I worked for all knew each other, like coaches of minor league teams. I knew more about their cultural habits than most, because my uncle had worked his way up to being manager of one. Mr. B., as my uncle was called—all the managers were known by the initials of their last names—was not a nice man, but at least he helped me get a job after

I flunked the arithmetic test that applicants to Macy's had to pass: I was caught counting on my fingers. Mr. T., a burly man with a thick mustache and a kind heart, was the manager I had to charm. The two brothers who were his assistants I knew from my uncle's days. One was Fred, a sallow, thin man with a strong German accent, whose main job was to try to keep his younger brother, a round short man in his forties, out of trouble. Wally had already caused the firm some problems. He could not keep his hands to himself. But unlike the joking salesmen in the coat department, Wally was driven by his compulsions to risk all for a touch. He would squeeze past us behind the narrow counters and caress our backsides, he would sit on his haunches beside the couch in the women's lounge, hoping that Irene, who was slow and had large breasts, would allow him to stroke her on her break. He had been transferred to this store, way out in Queens, to escape several charges of indecent exposure by irate customers. Like a hapless Laurel and Hardy, these two brothers tormented each other. All of this in a neighborhood five-and-dime, where notions and novelties vied for the small change of working people.

My immediate peers in the store were the other clerks. Mrs. Kamato, a widowed Japanese woman, who showed me the ropes of the pet department and whose pink smock was always spotless, Irene, who had been working at the store for ages even though she was in her thirties, Sophie Beck, who ruled the fabrics department and kept sadnesses in her pocket. And there was Joseph, the stock "boy," a tall, sturdy black man in his twenties whose muscles threatened to break out of his blue T-shirts. He ruled the nether world, the unending basement below the store, the storehouse which replenished the counters. Our anthem, "I'll see if we have it in stock," was a quiet prayer to Joseph. This was my work family; we punched the time clock together, our cards sitting in their slots instantly telling us who was on what shift.

One summer afternoon I noticed a new card, another part-timer like me. Sheila was a year younger than me, and as physically different from me as she could be. Slim, with sharp, clear features, honey-touched hair drawn tightly back in a ponytail—she was half cheerleader, half ballerina. Athletic and seductive in her white blouse and slim black-and-white-checked skirt cinched at the waist with one of the wide elastic belts that were so popular at the time, she bounced through the aisles, flirting with us all. I took her up on it, at first wanting only her friendship and enjoying so much the girlish horsing around we did, wrestling behind our counters, stretching our breaks together, me being the lookout while she sneaked a smoke. We laughed so hard our stomachs hurt. I went home each night tired in a new way, tired with the joy of her physical challenges. We started to have late-night telephone talks; it must have been from these that she discovered I had "ideas," and that she too wanted to talk about love and loneliness and freedom. She told me all about her boyfriends, and there were many, and never asked about mine. Then, one lunch break, I was lying on the bench with my head in her lap, the whole expanse of the parking lot stretching out in front of us, looking up at her as she stroked my hair. The sun was hot, but I was in heaven. "Joan, I don't think you will ever marry," she said right into my eyes, all the wisdom of our play in her fifteen-year-old heart. Here in mid-fifties America, where marriage was a national edict, two young women looked into another world.

I spent that summer holding on to Sheila's presence. I have no memory of her parents. We would sit in the living room of her family's garden apartment, talking, talking, that delirious communication of youth on the verge of adult life, I in a big chair and Sheila hunched over, her knees drawn up, at my feet. I had been transformed into a philosopher, and I even believed I knew about the big things. This Socratic time would eventually end with the arrival of Sheila's boyfriends—she usually had two or three at a time—and we reverted to a teenage gang. Usually the most unattractive of the boys would attach himself to me. Together we would watch Sheila play her court.

One afternoon, before the boys arrived, Sheila went into her bedroom and took off her blouse. She called to me, wanting to carry on with our conversation; I had never been in her bedroom before. I felt as if I were swimming underwater, moving toward a bit of land I could only vaguely see. I paused in the doorway. Sheila was pulling off her top, her arms raised, her head half hidden. I know words were coming out of my mouth, but it was my eyes that were most alive, my eyes telling me that what I was seeing would become a lasting part of my memory of what was sacred about life. Sheila so flat and real in that fifteen-year-old body. Crossed by the white bands of her cotton bra, her chest was a secret, but I did not need to know any more. A longing arose in me so huge that even then I knew it would last a lifetime. To hold her in my arms, to touch that body so contained in its neatness, to stop the flow of time that would carry us both away. Shaken and hidden, I turned and left her.

By the end of the summer, Sheila had discovered the Village scene. She would beg me to go with her, keep her company on the long subway ride from the outskirts to the center of all things, where the action was. Washington Square with its arch and sunken circle was a throbbing dance of cool older men putting the make on naïve outer-borough girls. Sheila was ready for bigger conquests, and she found what she was looking for in the whispered adorations of the young street men of the Village. One night as we were walking down Sixth Avenue, she linked her arm in mine and my whole body went tight. I knew where I was, in the home of the freaks. Sheila pushed against me and said in her playful voice, "Come on, Joan. Lez be friends." I pushed her away from me with such force that she staggered into a plate-glass window of one of the small head shops that lined the avenue.

Once school started, we cut back our hours at the five-and-dime. I seldom saw Sheila in the halls of my high school—I was a year ahead. The nights we did work together were more constrained, and the late-night telephone calls had stopped. Then one night I walked Sheila home. She went up the four steps that led to her apartment. I waited below her. She turned, her face taut with her beauty, and looking down, she said with a certainty that changed my world, "You know, my boyfriend said I'm the kind of girl lesbians really go for." I knew then that I would never see her again.

Two years later, I entered the public lesbian bar world of Greenwich Village; by then I had faced my terror and willingly, in full face of the freak-hating fifties, pursued the touches that brought me life. But now in my later years, with a body devastated by cancer, Sheila appears to me again; again I see those white bands of desire, so fresh, so perfumed with the body's perfection, my icon of want. "Crush" they call it, those who have no idea of the mystery of our desire and how like a god it stays with us through all the years, how its remembered perfection, no matter how false, keeps kindness alive.

Martin Van Buren High School yearbook, 1957

THE SECRET AGENT

Jane DeLynn

CRUSHES

I'LL start here, in the fall of 1958, because this is where "love" begins, though by love I mean what the straight world would probably call a "crush." It was "love," however, in its seriousness and persistence— or, let us say, for I am one who dwells in fantasy and conversations that often take place only in my head—that it was comparable to the state which I still refer to as "love," though others around me may use another word. No matter. What is love is love, and back then, when everything was unspeakable, a "crush" on someone of one's own sex—semilegitimized by Freud as an adolescent stepping-stone along the way to "mature" heterosexual love—was an acceptable term for a form of emotion otherwise unspeakable.

And it was love that burst into my heart when Mrs. P, my seventh-grade English teacher, stood in front of our class on a snowy afternoon and recited Elinor Wylie's poem "Velvet Shoes" ("We shall walk in velvet shoes/ Wherever we go/ Silence will fall like dews/ On white silence below/ We shall walk in the snow"). Mrs. P had the prim, scrubbed-clean quality of the young Julie Andrews, and these words vaulted me into a world where people actively valued cleanness, calmness, tranci-ness, qualities I had never before heard extolled, but spoke to some hidden, quiet space within me. I loved both the messenger and the message, not just Mrs. P, but words and the transcendent states they could bring you to, plus a feeling of utter peace that still descends upon me on gray winter days when snowflakes fill the air like static on a black-and-white TV.

I was not the only one of my classmates to fall in love with Mrs. P. I was attending a most peculiar school, a public school that was free but which you had to take a test to get into, a school for precocious girls of the five boroughs of New York City who could not afford, in those days where quotas operated against rather than for such things as economic disadvantage and religious and cultural diversity, the more secure private-school path to attendance at the better colleges. And we knew, for we were told from the first week of seventh grade, that our classmates would be our adversaries in our attempt to get past the barriers placed against NYC public school kids, in general, and Jewish kids (as most of us were) in particular. So we're competitive, to the point all of us can recite each other's grade-point averages to the decimal place (and, later on, our PSAT and SAT scores), and all the intensity and pressure and praise of us for our superior intelligence creates, for those on the edge of puberty, a supercharged sexual atmosphere that, in the absence of the opposite sex, must emerge in some other way.

I guess this is a long way of saying we were the kind of school that, if you were going to develop a crush on a teacher, it would more likely be one who recited "Velvet Shoes" on a winter afternoon than one who made you vault a pommel horse in gym class. So my friends "fell in love" too, and others as well, and in our lack of sophistication we did things it is impossible to imagine anyone doing today—at least without being immediately summoned to the school psychologist—such as writing in chalk on the blackboard of Mrs. P's room statements such as "Jane (or Cathy or Barbara or Ruth) has a crush on Mrs. P." But there was no school psychologist then, only "guidance counselors," and Mrs. P. would erase the offending statements, usually without comment, but sometimes with the kind of ironic quip ("you would think, if someone 'loved' me, she wouldn't be so anxious to force me into unnecessary manual labor") that ever since has seemed the height of verbal sophistication, accompanied by a smirk that to this day still hints for me at pleasures to come.

Cathy and Barbara and Rena and Rhoda called it a "crush," but I knew it was "love," at least in the sense that it was not in the nature of something temporary and adolescent that would pass once I learned to appreciate the phallus, but a place in which I would emotionally reside for the rest of my life. (By this I mean—alas!—not just the gender of the object of my affections, but the childish, infatuated nature of my passions, which flourish so much better in absence than presence.) Almost surely my friends did not go home after school and call up Mrs. P on the phone every day, merely to hear the sound of her exasperated voice (or, sometimes, if I waited too long, her husband's) inquiring who the silent speaker was on the other end of the phone. Certainly, if my friends did this perhaps once or twice, they did not do this for the next several years! It's decades late to tender an apology; I only hope that, having been a student in the same school not all that many years previously to me, Mrs. P knew whereof such calls came, and did not let them disturb her unduly.

There was no goal to such telephoning, other than a desire to hear the sound of her voice. I was under no illusion that anything could come of my feelings. The furthest extent of my fantasies was a kind of friendship (to be formulated only after I myself graduated from high school and college and came back to teach in the same school) in which Mrs. P and I would walk through Central Park discussing poems and books, and perhaps, after a long period of time, a confession of my feelings, to which she, in her infinite kindness, would listen calmly and sympathetically (albeit without reciprocity), and without banishing me permanently from her company.

At camp that summer, desire further ensnares me, as well as a pain I came to associate with these feelings. For I, who had always been so popular, suddenly find the world arrayed against me. My bunkmates tease me mercilessly, and for a peculiar variety of reasons: because I don't have a bra, because I don't shave under my arms, because I have no boyfriend sending me letters, because my athletic knees have constant scabs on them. All these reasons have something in common, and it seems to have something to do with them becoming "women" in a way I have not. Not that they all had their periods, or boyfriends, or breasts (and certainly no one "needed" to shave under their arms), but they were mimicking, in the ways of cargo cults, what they wanted to be and have, and in justice I found myself forced to admit that they were right—I was *not* like them, having spent seventh grade not in the pursuit of boys or elucidating the intricacies of lipstick application, but in arguing World History and disputing New Math. What I want is not to put curlers in my hair every night (for what purpose? we were an all-girls camp), but to do the same things I did every summer: play various games with balls and sticks and be cheered for my prowess in these areas. But time is passing me by, and my bunkmates sit around in rest period oohing over Vicky's biweekly letter from her boyfriend, and helping her compose the letters she writes back, while I lie on my cot and read *The Count of Monte Cristo* and *Jane Eyre*—something that also irritates them, for I am a "snobby New York intellectual." Yes, they were the Great Unwashed—the Great Upper-Middle-Class Unwashed—from the Five Towns of Long Island and the Jewish suburbs of New Jersey (*Goodbye, Columbus* country), and part of the great torment of the summer was that my contempt for them went hand in hand with my envy and my desire for them to love or at least like me. They seemed to have access to a simplicity of thought and action and emotion I could only aspire to.

I am quite conscious, as I lie on my bed reading during rest period, that I want the world to stand still, I who began the first draft of my sixth-grade valedictorian speech with a reference to our time in elementary school as being "the best years of our lives" (everyone looked at me aghast, my teacher rewrote the speech). But I had known something bad was coming, even if I hadn't known what it was. Now I begin to realize this was it. Something is separating me from others, something deep and unspeakable and shameful, and though at times I had felt this way before, there was something in me that hoped perhaps it would change. But I know now it will not change; it's way deep in my soul. Perhaps even today queer teens regret the coming of adolescence, with some kind of inchoate awareness of the disjunction about to occur between them and the rest of the world; certainly we did back then. But I'm a tough motherfucker, and if the world will not stand still, I will damn well catch up with it. I insist my mother send me a bra (she sends a training bra, almost worse than none at all) and razor, but it's no use: my bunkmates sense, in a visceral way, that there's something wrong with me, and all summer long the torment continues. One night, in unconscious prescience, they even strip off my underpants. It's humiliating, of course, but also exciting, and for all I know it is there that a strange erotic begins to formulate itself.

I have only one friend. Well, perhaps two—the "fat girl" in the bunk (also picked on, but not stripped), and my camp counselor Margie. Margie had been a leader of one of the "color war" groups a year or two before, and back then I had had the standard kind of crush on her that one gets for older campers. But Mrs. P had taught me to take my crushes seriously, and I was ecstatic when I found out Margie was my counselor.

Because Margie was not my teacher, because she was so much nearer my age, because she slept in the same room I did and was in some way at least partly in charge of my welfare, I was able to torture her in a way I never could with Mrs. P. Was it because Margie actually liked me, or because she took pity for the torments being inflicted on me, or merely because she graciously accepted the impossibility of discouraging me, that she put up with me as I hung about her all summer like a mosquito, sitting on her bed as she got ready before dinner, trailing her back and forth from the dining hall, talking to her on the bunk steps before turning off the lights, buying her stuffed animals and other tokens of affection which I left on her bed? (Girls do this all the time in this camp—it's an utter hotbed of unacknowledged perversity—but somehow everyone also knows that I'm the only one who takes it seriously!) At times Margie tries to rid herself of me by telling me to go find someone else to pester, that she's got better stuff to do with her time than sit around having conversations with a *thirteen-year-old,* but I decide, perhaps incorrectly (and I have been known to make similar mistakes up to this very day—but I have also had such persistence rewarded!), that she is teasing me, that where there's banter there's affection (for the kind of love that can't speak its name only banter will do), and if I keep it up, who knows?

Once, near the seats by the softball field, after a particularly brutal day of insults and snidenesses, she initiates a discussion of my bunkmates' hostility. It's the first time we've actually gone into (as opposed to merely "mentioning") the subject, and, as I still do when someone blindsides me in an area that will cause pain, I try to avoid it. But this doesn't work, and Margie's words—"It's because they know you're different"—seem to hang in the air like a banner trailed by a low-flying airplane. In the immense confusion of having been caught, words—my weapons—desert me, so, blushing, my heart racing, I lamely stammer out that I don't know what she means.

"You know," she replies, and though I am petrified she will continue, and delineate all the ways in which I am different from my bunkmates (including but not limited to my reading of *Jane Eyre*), I also yearn for her to do just that, to push through my barriers of embarrassment and shame so that at last who I am and what I am will be said in the open air: spoken and therefore, somehow, accepted.

But discretion prevails. Perhaps she's afraid of the doors she may open, perhaps she decides (in the face of my obtuseness) she was wrong; perhaps she's worried about what these thoughts about me indicate about her. (I remembered being surprised—and disappointed—when on a day off a boyfriend picks her up, though I also wondered—never having heard of the word "beard"—if it was a kind of subterfuge similar to what I myself will shortly practice.) Several times during the summer I try to resurrect this conversation, but as I speak with an obliqueness impenetrable to those of normal temperaments ("What you were talking about last week." What?" "*You know,*" etc.), it's perhaps not surprising Margie doesn't pick up on it—especially if she *is* of normal temperament.

The combo of emotions aroused by Margie—shame for what I am, and relief and fear that it may be discovered—remains, for decades, a potent source of arousal: either in fantasies of "confession" to which I masturbate (they result in acceptance and unspeakable acts), or, later, in that eroticized ritual known as "coming out."

Meanwhile, back in the city, even as I write the occasional letter to Margie (ecstasy when she writes back!) and resume my anonymous phone calls to Mrs. P, I commence my life not just as a hidden *subversive-in-place* but as an active *counterintelligence* agent. For the lessons of the summer must be actively implemented: reply with vicious sarcasm when attacked, and lead a double life in which what I am is regularly concealed. It's not a problem, exactly, for we begin to have dances with our "brother school"; as a "cover," I begin to date. And because I'm a bad actor, I know instinctively not just to *play* a role but to actually *live* it. It isn't even that hard, for, though I know I like girls better, I know there's no way I'll ever get to be with them, and I like boys well enough. At least my body does, for it gets wet on cue.

Of course, when you're overcompensating, everything you do is a *little too much*. So if my friends date, I date *more*. If my friends get felt up *on top of* the bra, I'll let myself get felt up *under* the bra. When you don't like anyone in particular, it's harder to say no to anyone, and easier to say yes to everyone. Check out the class sluts at your next high school reunion, and do not be surprised if nowadays they turn out to be sleeping with girls.

WRONG

Although the summer I turned thirteen begins to make clear what it is that is "wrong" with me, the fact that there was something wrong was not much of a surprise. I had felt it on and off (at least so I tell myself, in the myth we construct to make sense of our lives), always, from the first awareness of my self "as" a self (before memory, before language). And, though I didn't know what it was, I knew it was dangerous, and that I had to hide it. The best way I can describe it is as a kind of distaste, or at least lack of enthusiasm, for the kinds of objects and experiences that other people seemed to get pleasure from: not just dolls and dresses and behaving the way girls (as opposed to boys) were supposed to, but something about the very nature of life itself—talking, eating, getting dressed, washing one's face—struck me as unbearably tedious.

Perhaps, as with so much of queer life, it simply came down to a matter of *taste*.

Every once in a while, of course, I had moments of enjoyment (with friends, with sports) but until I learned to read I found life much of a chore. (Afterwards, I would have been happy to gaze at a book every waking hour, including at the dinner table, in the bathtub, walking down the street. . . .) I thought the people around me stupid and dull, their relationships—on the surface full of affection and kindness, but underlain by boredom and hatred—false, their jobs and amusements a sham. This is the kind of insight people tend to have on LSD—often to the detriment of their later success—and this kind of distaste for ordinary pleasures has always left me just a bit removed from the center of life. I fake it, of course (even to this day), but that's not the same thing. I could not be certain that others weren't feeling this same way, also hiding their disaffections and boredoms, but this concealment was such a struggle that I, in my vanity, didn't believe other people were capable of enduring it. All I had, I felt, to see me through, was my power of endurance; and if I am proud of anything in my life, it is this. Such endurance, on the other hand, exacts a terrible price: it makes one put up with things one could not put up with if one were only weaker. (The immense promiscuity of gay men in the seventies is no surprise to me; it was the joy of being released from the terrible bonds of endurance. Gay women took longer to achieve their own—albeit lesser—degrees of promiscuity, having also to overcome feminist dictates against casual sex and role-playing.)

The most obtuse of all grownups, of course, were my parents, who did not even recognize the stranger who was living under their roof, contemptuous but also protective of them, in their unbearable stupidity and blindness.

Why do I associate these feelings of wrongness and insufficiency with queerness? Because the embarrassment and shame evoked by my feelings for Mrs. P and Margie and various others connected with these feelings in a way that somehow made sense of them. I've met many queers who have had such feelings all their lives—which bolsters my belief that at least some queerness is "innate." (I've also met heterosexuals who felt similarly, but they were writers, with another kind of displacement from the "normal" world.)

Being an outsider was something I didn't like. I still don't like it, though I feel it in relation to almost every group I am supposed to be considered a part of, *including* queers. (Indeed, at this point in time, there is no group I feel so much an outsider with *as* queers—though perhaps this is because my fantasies of being "inside" are so much stronger, and my habits of accommodation to this kind of outsiderness more recent.) Certainly all I wanted back then was to be "in"—by which I mean "normal," like everyone around me—but would I even recognize it if I got there? (To me, it seems, there is no "there" there). And how to do this? Well, since what is "off" are my feelings and my preferences, I will try to change them—or, rather, as taste is an inoperable condition, I will *pretend* to change them. The way to do this, naturally, is to try and figure out what others ("normals") will do or feel or say in a certain circumstance, and imitate this. Questions of authenticity go off the chart: I will do what I have to to survive, and if this includes lying, deceiving, living a life that is not mine—a spy from another country passing as one of the local populace—I will.

No wonder queers have always been fascinated by lives of double agents, undercover police, and members of the acting profession: all those who pretend to be what they are not.

But there's a problem. Because "normal" people don't have to think about being normal, they don't shirk from evincing the occasional bit of "abnormalcy" (odd opinions and behavioral quirks) that, to a person like me, seem a dead giveaway. So I experience less freedom and act even more rigidly than the average "normal" person. In addition, the effort to mimic normalcy distorts it, if only by the self-consciousness one brings to what should happen effortlessly, as when one tries to feign "sincerity" by gazing into someone's eyes. So when I evince enthusiasm for something I feel no enthusiasm for, I may exaggerate (I am, after all, an actor mouthing words that are not mine), or pick the "wrong" aspects of an experience to become enthused about, or something else will give me away—so that the falseness of the entire enterprise is quickly exposed.

Example: I am forced, sometime in high school, to go to a shrink. The shrink asks me to draw a picture of a person. "Male or female?" I inquire. "It's up to you." My initial impulse is to draw a woman, but, fearful of this trap which will reveal me as homosexual who desires to sleep with women, I draw a male. "That's very unusual," says the shrink. "People usually draw the sex they are."

These efforts, nerve-wracking and exhausting as they were, forced me to sharpen my powers of observation and interpretation (always useful for a writer), as well as helped ease me into the stance of preternatural alertness and savviness (and contempt for our more obtuse hetero brethren) so common among gays. To us, so used to disguise and concealment, heteros seem so astonishingly unseeing, not even noticing the coded language and behavior going on all about them, a universe within a universe of activities and flirtations oddly invisible to them, though their world is almost frighteningly visible—indeed, transparent—to us. With the increasing acceptance of "gayness"—perhaps as opposed to "queer"ness—in America, such deconstruction of ordinary behavior is increasingly unnecessary, to what I am sure will be (if it not already is) the detriment of our art, our insights, and culture; an unpopular position, certainly, but this is what happens when repressive regimes disappear.

Because decoding and hermeneutics requires constant vigilance and anxiety, not to mention overarousal of the adrenal and perhaps other systems, I devise a strategy to make it easier. Instead of psyching out others, I'll use myself as the "standard"—not a standard to follow, however, but a standard to do the *opposite* of. It's a simplistic and mechanistic, but rather effective, solution. So I profess to like what I do not, I profess indifference to that which I care for, I buy clothing in colors I do not fancy and order foods I do not wish to eat. When asked who I love more, my grandmother or my aunt, I say "my aunt," because if it is not true it can't be wrong and I cannot be killed for it.

Years later, when I am trying to overcome this habit of reflexive self-annihilation, I torture eating companions and waitresses (I cannot afford, back then, the kind of restaurants that require *waiters*) as I painstakingly try to figure out what I *want* to eat, as opposed to what my self-reflexive noninstinct tells me to eat (e.g. "I had chicken yesterday, so I shouldn't today"; "this restaurant specializes in seafood, so I should have some, even though I'm in the mood for lamb chops," etc.). My initial tendency, at that point, was to indulge in some *further* reflexive self-annihilation—by which I would automatically reverse whatever choice came to me as a result of the initial self-annihilation (so automatically that it felt "natural"—but of course that would mean still going by rules, and systems, and self-annihilation, when the whole point is to get to a place where I recognize—simply, instinctively, without reference to prior decisions, actions, thoughts, and strategies—what it is I actually desire).

But this is not simple. If it were, would it have taken me until my forties to recognize that perhaps what I want after all is not the golden-haired femme but the truckdriver butch?

1964: THE SUBVERSIVE, THE SPY

I am a senior in high school, seventeen, routinely "finger-fucked" by my boyfriends but technically a virgin (I check off everything up to "69" and "Around the World" on the "Purity Test"—does anyone really *lick* someone's genitals? *Why? Ugh!),* still getting the occasional mild crush on older females around me. But then, in my senior year, in Advanced Placement English Class, Love strikes again, in the shape of my thirty-seven-year-old teacher "Miss Maxfeld." By ordinary standards Miss Maxfeld is not attractive; she's overweight, horrendously dressed (less a sin in those days than it is in ours), poor (teachers' salaries hadn't yet been raised by the Great Strike), not to mention twenty years older than I am, but she is also a great talker, a *schmoozer,* a charmer, not to mention extraordinarily perceptive and intelligent.

Although I am still a secret operative, a subversive, one who consciously conceals her preferences and desires by misleading words and actions, I am a spy who has trouble keeping her secrets, and soon all my friends know about my crush. Nor are my actions very spylike. As it happens, Miss Maxfeld is not just my English teacher but also the guidance counselor for the twelfth grade, so anyone who has questions about which college to apply to has an excuse for a *tête-à-tête* with her. I am not alone in my affliction; intelligence and wit are still prized in my high school, even by heterosexuals, and the line outside that guidance office grows day after day.

But it soon becomes clear it is me she particularly likes. She saunters over to me in the lunchroom to make jokes; she brushes the hair out of my eyes in a way I still associate with secrets being unmasked. Then, for an essay about "the Tragic Hero," I pick not Agamemnon or Achilles or Odysseus to write about, but myself. This clinches it; I'm clearly a neurotic, and we neurotics can smell each other. I begin to see her every day; we talk about books, and myself, and eventually even *her*self. I am in thrall to her words, long self-reflexive sentences full of humor and irony ("I doubt even God could come up to your high standards of perfection") and a way of looking at the world ("the terrible tyranny parents exert over their children") that is anything but philistine or "bourgie"—in other words, the opposite of my parents and their friends. Even then I know I want to be a writer, and for the first time someone I personally know is giving shape to words like a craftsperson.

Later on, when I am having anxiety attacks, she will soothe me with stories: not made-up ones, but ones about her life. It will not be the content that soothes me (for her life, at least up till that point, was not very happy), but the telling.

Eventually, I am invited to her apartment. The invitation astonishes me, as does the apartment itself, which I describe to my eager friends. No matching upholstered sofa and chairs, no polished walnut dining table and paintings on bark brought home from Mexico, no wall-to-wall beige carpeting, but a walk-up railroad flat, a country-style old oak table, unmatched armchairs around an old wooden trunk used as a coffee table. Not even a sofa, but something more like a daybed, a padded bench, not the plush overstuffed thing in my parents' living room. A row of old bottles balanced on a shelf, art posters on the wall. To today's sophisticated eyes the whole apartment is a cliché of a certain kind of educated lower-middle-class slightly "downtown" lifestyle, but back then it was like nothing I had ever seen, and original enough for its time. It smacked of poverty, bohemianism, Paris in the twenties, a kind of unmarried sex life that we joked about and read about and saw in the movies, but that I, at least, was never quite sure people actually led. But there it was, here I was, and there were poetry books, and the new *New York Review of Books,* and flowers my mother would never have thought to have paid for (not roses or tulips, but *daisies*). I am given odd foods to eat and drink—artichokes, some Italian syrup that goes in seltzer, even, on occasion, Dubonnet or Lillet. I feel sophisticated, worldly, charming, and my narcissism flourishes in the immense attention paid to my every word.

A comedown, after this, to go out into the twilight and take the bus uptown to my parents', where over dinner we discuss my father's business and my mother's canasta game, then on the weekends out with my boyfriend, whose penis I have to jerk up and down until some white stuff comes out (impossible to understand why anyone would like this, but he seems to). It is true, his fingers go in my body and I get wet, but after awhile the fact that he gets me wet begins to bother me, so that I'd rather not feel anything at all. . . .

Although I tell my parents about my visits to Miss Maxfeld, which please them (teacher taking interest in precocious student), I never tell them what the apartment looks like. My mother, the Queen of Bourge, will turn up her nose, and although I have nothing but contempt for every single notion that crosses her lips, I am by this time such a reflexive self-annihilator that I will annihilate even my own contempt, just enough to end up in a place where I reflexively and compulsively disagree with almost everything and everyone—including myself. (I'm still in this place today, although by now I realize distrust is not such a bad lens through which to see the world.) Anyway, either because of reflexive self-annihilation, or because there really is a part of me that agrees with her, I hide Miss Maxfeld's vulnerabilities from my mother, lest her judgments contaminate my feelings.

What was going through my mind in regard to Miss Maxfeld, during these months I visit her two or three times a week after classes? Contradictory things, to be sure. Well, of course she's a "lezbo"—a word, with its male equivalent, "homo," my friends and I use with blithe casualness in relation to almost all the unmarrieds in the school (and which I later learn, when I am sleeping with Miss Maxfeld and hear the secrets of the school, we mostly used correctly). But if she's a "lezbo," then I must be a "lezbo," too. But this is impossible (though my friends sometimes tease that I am), because if I was, my friends would no longer be friends with me. On a more philosophical level, I cannot bring myself to actually believe there really *are* "lezbos" in the world—or, if there are, that there could be more than *one* in such a limited environment as a NYC high school (pop. approx. 1,000, not including teachers)—and if there's *one* of course that one was *me*. Also, if Miss Maxfeld is one, then *surely* Mr. Pauley is, and Miss X and Madame Y (who live together) and Mr. Z, etc.—but there is scarcely such perversity in the entire city of NY! Or, if there is, why are they exposing us—innocent schoolchildren!—to this?

Who can I ask about this? Not my friends, who (I assume) would have shunned me, and discussed such things only in jokes. Not my parents, who, when I float the topic of "homosexuality" at the dining-room table, tell me not to bring up such nauseating topics. Certainly not my 6' 2" male shrink, who later will refuse any discussion of my affair (save ordering me to end it) on the grounds that it is "too disgusting" to talk about.

I consult books. There are not many, back in 1964 (when paperbacks were mostly genre novels or out-of-copyright "classics"), and these are mostly about men, and all are hardback and expensive. I buy them at bookstores down by Times Square, far from where I live (so no one can recognize me), and which I read behind false covers at home, till I throw them down the incinerator (not yet "garbage compactor"). Others I read in the public library. I would never check these books out, because, being a spy, I know how spies work, and take-out slips on books about homosexuality are sent to some central authority which in turn reports you to the police, your school, and your parents. (As they *should,* for after all are we not *criminals?*).

What I learn is this: lezbos (at least, butch lezbos) are creatures with elongated clitorises that resemble penises and bind their breasts and cut their hair and pretend they're men and take jobs as truck drivers. Although the image is horrific, the result is reassuring: my clitoris—whatever that is—cannot be especially long (or I *would* know what it is), and I don't bind my breasts—or need to (I wear a double A bra). And I'm a Jew, and Jews are not truck drivers, quite the opposite—we grow up and live with our husbands in Scarsdale and join a (Jews only) golf club. Or at least we aspire to. Or at least we aspire to aspire to.

So I'm not a butch.

Of course, there are "femmes" too, girls who look like normal girls who the bulldyke lezbos get to sleep with them. (Sometimes the femmes don't even know—but how is this possible?—that the bull-dykes are not men!) But I know in my soul I'm not a femme—both because I'm a tomboy and because if I desire any woman it's not a truck driver but the same blond actress every guy in the movie theater wants to boff. (But I *also*—don't I?—desire to have sex with Miss Maxfeld. Confusing.)

And what about Miss Maxfeld? Her large breasts are clearly un-bound, her hair isn't short like Miss X and Madame Y, and everything I've heard makes me think she doesn't spend her nights in bars trying to seduce girls who look like girls. On the other hand, she's *clearly* not a femme.

But if we're not butches or femmes, how can we be lezbos?

On the other hand, if Miss Maxfeld was *not* a lezbo, what was she doing with me?

To today's ears, this must sound insane, impossibly naïve, but, although I am a well-read, devious, curious, shrink-trained, psycholog-ically aware, moderately cool teenager brought up in the most sophisti-cated borough of the most sophisticated city in the United States, a National Merit Finalist, a member of the National Honors Society, an A student in an elite (albeit public) New York High School—this is the information that was available to me back then, and this is how I thought.

Then, one day, late in March or early April, as I am standing at Miss Maxfeld's door, thinking (I remember this clearly), "I better not come back here any more," Miss Maxfeld kisses me good-bye. On the lips.

Oh. This settles the question. I *am* a lezbo—even if the question of butches and femmes is still up in the air.

And though in retrospect the Kiss seems utterly inevitable, what the months of friendship with Miss Maxfeld have inexorably led up to, it also seems utterly implausible, as if the government were suddenly to reveal that yes, aliens did land in Roswell, New Mexico, in 1951, and everything you have feared and hoped and been lied to about for all these years is true.

Then another kind of lying begins. I no longer boast to my friends or my parents of my visits to Miss Maxfeld, but conceal them. One afternoon after school, when I say I am going home, a friend suspects me, and insists on accompanying me to the bus stop and seeing me get on the appropriate bus. (I get off a few stops later and circle back.) The weekends are long and free, but how can I ask, say, Rena, to provide an alibi unless I provide her with an explanation I am unwilling to give? On occasion I tell my parents I am going to a library, or a museum. ("But not with your friends?" asks my mother, who finds pleasure only with others.) My mother is so naïve she even arranges a blind date for Miss Maxfeld with an intelligent, divorced male cousin of ours. I think this is a wonderful idea, as they can get married and Miss Maxfeld can be part of my family. (They like each other, but when they try to sleep together, she "can't." What does it mean, this "can't"? You just spread your legs and—she cannot explain this to my mechanistic satisfaction.) One time she formally invites me to the theater. She'll buy the ticket, but I should buy her flowers. I have never bought flowers for anyone in my life, and let my mother do the choosing. Miss Maxfeld hates the flowers: "Gladiolas—why would you choose such a thing?" She buys me a little book of poetry; I do not know how to reciprocate, so I go out and buy her the *same* book. This is how crazy people act, suddenly adrift in a world whose rules they do not know. I am adrift in the world.

Sexually, what we do is . . . pretty tame. No oral sex (I still have trouble believing people put their lips *there*), and although on occasion I have the desire to suck her huge ungainly breasts, I resist this because I am Freudian-savvy, and it is too much: this *sucking my mother's breasts.* (Once, in Bloomingdale's, with her, I run into an old camp tormentor, polite enough now, who makes some remark about "my mother." No more public appearances!) Mostly we put fingers in each other's orifices, and to be honest, though I do get highly aroused, I am also, somewhat, disgusted. Too smelly, too wet: my boyfriends come in a spurt, at which point they immediately go to the bathroom: with Miss Maxfeld it just goes on and on, and my hand stays wet. We kiss, of course, and engage in a lot of what with boys is called "dry humping," but in the books is referred to as *tribadism*—lying on top of one another simulating intercourse. An ugly word.

I am not even sure what orgasms are, or whether Miss Maxfeld and I have them. There is noise and increase of activity, then a kind of cessation, which seems to indicate the above. But I also feel I am doing something that imitates the rhythms I see in a movie, and when, years later I ask her, she tells me no, she did not come. (It takes me several more years of high-level hermeneutics to figure out this question regarding myself!)

In general, we speak very little about such matters. Although Miss Maxfeld is thirty-seven, I am only the fourth person she has ever had sex with, and the first person in four or five (or is it six or seven?) years. Two of the others were students, like me. She does tell me, however, about Mr. Pauley, and Miss X and Madame Y, and Mr. Z, and a host of others about whom I and my friends guessed right. Of the women's lives I learn nothing, but I know that Mr. Pauley, her best friend, goes to bars and cruises in the then–unfashionable neighborhood around Bloomingdale's. A breach of confidence, surely—but how else can knowledge be transmitted in societies that have no official history?

Years later, when I see her again, in the summer of 1981, she is living with my former art teacher in a big house in a fashionable part of Long Island. (Smart buying at the right time.) There are two bedrooms in the house, as there are two bedrooms in their apartment, and they pretend to everyone that they are "just friends." By then, I have learned how to sleep with women (even to put my lips "there"), and I have spent what is surely the equivalent of weeks of my life in bars, where I try to decipher what to me are the still strange codes of women, and I am of course very strongly "pro Gay Lib." I ask Miss Maxfeld if she and my former art teacher have been to the bars, or gone on marches. They look at me in astonishment: *What for? We have nothing in common with people like that!*

They still don't. Or didn't. Years later when I speak to Mr. Pauley, he tells me he's no longer friends with Miss Maxfeld. Because he insisted on referring to her and my former art teacher as *lovers,* and they could not handle that.

When, the following fall, around the start of college, my parents find out about my relationship with Miss Maxfeld (a letter I thought destroyed, written to me that summer in Europe: what I call an "accident," what the shrink-monster considers a kind of Freudian slip), they confront not me but the shrink-monster. The shrink-monster lies to them and tells me to do the same: Miss Maxfeld was in love with me but I didn't respond. I'm paralyzed, an animal caught in headlights, and do as told. I don't suppose my parents *quite* believe this, but it functions to get our lives back on track, and to impress on me the *hideous unspeakableness of what I have done.* (Decent people cannot talk about this—not even my parents.) My shrink impresses upon me the necessity of *never* seeing her again, but I do, in her car, as we drive around the waterfront highways of Manhattan and I tell her I can never see her again. She begs me to come up to her apartment, but I'm too frightened of what I may allow myself to do.

Well, almost. A couple times, over the next several years, in summer when the heat and humidity destroy rational thinking, when the urge to have sex with a woman—*any* woman—utterly overwhelms me, I call her up and go over. My timing is impeccable; the art teacher is out of town and we engage in a bit of the old tribadism. (Once I encounter another young student, who takes her time about leaving: Miss Maxfeld swears the relationship is innocent. I believe her.)

The affair was traumatic. I mean by this something very visceral— even after all these years my body responds to the thought of it with a surge of adrenaline more suited to a horror movie than to an at least *relatively* consensual sexual experience. Why I reacted this way is unclear—no doubt the disparity of age and her physical unattractiveness contributed to it, but mostly, I imagine, it was the repressed quality of her own sexual life and the agony about being homosexual that got transmitted to me. Certainly I would have been far better off sleeping with a friend my own age in high school or college. But as torturesome and guilt-ridden and frightening (in terms of my future life) the relationship was, my shrink's and my parents' reaction—and our conspiring together in a gigantic lie—was far worse. I do not think I have ever gotten over the shock of the discovery. It is why, I am sure, I have written so extensively about my sexual life ever since—an attempt to excise by repetition a shame I am still unable to shake.

COLLEGE

Having read, in books, about the "irresistible impulses" of homos— an urge that overwhelms them in public bathrooms so that they do horrific acts that get them arrested—I spend my time in college avoiding the gaze and companionship of attractive women, lest I myself be similarly overwhelmed and leap, for instance, across a counter at a coffee shop or bookstore and kiss some woman on the lips.

In summer, when the impulse is at its worst, I retreat to Central Park, in search of an older woman (the only kind I know) from the Upper East Side, an elegant type who lives in a building with a doorman (fuck hippie shit!), hoping she'll brush the hair out of my eyes and ask me to go home with her. I get my courage up and go to the Metropolitan Museum, a pleasantly deserted place in those days before Thomas Hoving's "Harlem on My Mind" show forever changed the notion of what a museum was, and hang out in the ladies room. Queers like art, don't they? and they get impulses in bathrooms. Women look at me strangely, but no one brushes the hair out of my eyes.

My main indulgence is confession. Not Catholic, of course (though conversion tempts me, for this sole reason), but to my friends. Over and over I tell them of the awful thing I did in high school. Despite those endless jokes about Miss Maxfeld being a "lezbo," and how I was a "lezbo" myself for sleeping with her, they are all dutifully and pleasingly astonished by my story, in what sounds like the same kind of astonishment I felt that first time when Miss Maxfeld actually kissed me on the lips. They "forgive" me (except one, who ends our friendship), and blame Miss Maxfeld, and I am soothed by their forgiveness, even though the telling itself *arouses* me. I realize I am waiting for one of them to reach out a hand, brush the hair out of my eyes, and succumb to some irresistible impulse. They don't, but their absolution functions somewhat as orgasm does, by quieting the intense anxiety I always bring to such confessions.

These confessions are certainly the most erotic moments I experience in college, for once intercourse enters the picture, finger-fucking departs, and I no longer enjoy long moments of relatively goal-less wetness. Because I am still a subversive, a counteragent, I fuck lots of guys to prove that—in spite of my moment of perversity—I'm not a queer. My years of childhood mimicry of "normalcy" serve me well here, for I'm usually told I'm a "good lover." You can't fool women like this, and this knowledge, of *how stupid men are*, is in the consciousness of virtually every queer woman who has ever slept with a man.

Long after college, when I am finally sleeping with women on a regular basis, I continue to get a charge out of these confessions to new friends, professional acquaintances, and guys who want to date me. It's the erotic impulse behind "coming out," and the thrill lasts for years—an unveiling of the real world to the dumb and smug.

SUMMER, 1969

I've spent a year at the Writer's Workshop at the University of
Iowa (biggest drug drop between Chicago and Denver), smoking
pot, dropping LSD: already I know I'll *never* have a regular job.
I've continued fucking lots of guys, partly to continue proving I'm
not a dyke, partly out of competition with the other Writer's
Workshop females (not all that many back then), and partly out of
a kind of peculiar logic that is expressed in the following bit of
dialogue. Wayne (married, drunk): "You fucked Bill, why won't
you fuck me?" Excellent point, irrefutable to one used to dealing
in self-annihilation, although in this particular case the premises
didn't support the conclusion (I *didn't* sleep with Bill, so I *don't*
have to fuck Wayne). Meanwhile, I'm "in love" with a heterosexual poet I'll call Hermione. By "love," of course, I mean what you
call a "crush," but from that day to this I am unable to distinguish
the intensity of the two. (If anything, a crush is stronger.)

As it turns out, I learn (alas, too late) Hermione would have slept
with me. Not because she loved me (she was straight, in love with
some guy), but out of curiosity and desire. But at that time my brain
just can't encompass a woman sleeping with a woman out of any but
the direst, most compulsive and sickest need—which includes *both*
being a dyke *and* being in love.

So, it's Woodstock Summer, and I *still* haven't had sex with any
woman other than Miss Maxfeld. I'm in NYC, and though I won't
know it for another few years, Stonewall is about to happen, perhaps
is happening this very night, as I head for the Village with the guy
I'm "supposed to marry" (in medical school in a city conveniently far
from both New York and Iowa, allowing us plenty of time to fuck
others before starting our "real" lives). I am telling him, not for the
first time, about this incredible urge I have to sleep with a woman.
He's not jealous—these are ecumenical times, we have dropped mesca-
line together, and everyone is free to do anything—and he urges me
to "try it."

Okay, but how? We walk into the old Sheridan Square Book-
shop and ask where there's a "homosexual" bar. (No "gay" in
those days, and "queer" had the status of "nigger" before blacks
began to use it.) Because it's the Village there's one a few doors
down. We walk over and I peer in, but there's a curtain over the
windows, so I can see nothing. No, I'll have to go in. My boyfriend
offers to accompany me, but I don't want this: how will someone
know I'm alone and on the prowl? But I lack courage, and circle

around the block, quietly checking, as I walk past the door, to see who's entering and leaving.

Twenty minutes or so later, I descend the few steps and open the door.

I see tables, a bar, some people standing. Everyone looks at me. Someone even says something—friendly, I think. But I can't take it. I run out.

My boyfriend's still there. We wander over to Sixth Avenue and Eighth, and go in the old McKay's drugstore. A black guy approaches. He asks what we want (probably he thinks we're looking for drugs), and, because it's this hot crazy night, and he's black and it doesn't matter, we tell him.

"I can find you what you're looking for," he tells me. And because it is 1969, and everyone is dropping acid and sleeping with everybody, my boyfriend says good-bye and leaves me with this man.

We visit friends of his on 9th Street. They are smoking dope on their fake polar bear rug as he tells them what I want. They're laughing at me and though it is embarrassing, I am a subversive, a spy, I'll put up with anything for the sake of my country. Excluding several brief moments of tribadism with Miss Maxfeld, it's been five years, I'm a desperate girl. So in front of me they talk about me, and who might like me, and the guy I'm with makes some phone calls, and eventually he announces he's found a woman who's willing to sleep with me. Smiles all around; I smoke some more dope.

Only catch is, because I'm inexperienced and may not be any good, he has to "try me out" first.

Now what do you think this Phi Beta Kappa girl did—run out of there into the night and hop on the subway? Call up my boyfriend? Go back to Sheridan Square? No. Although my dreams were running out and there was much implausibility to this equation (would I, after all, need someone to "pre-test" a woman I was going to sleep with?), there was logic there too: after all, it's been five years, probably I'm *not* any good. And, of course, all this time, I have not lost my sense of the world being incomprehensible, of my having to imitate what "normal" people do in order to survive. And although this testing doesn't seem "normal," for all I know it's "normal" among blacks, among "hip" people, among people who live in Greenwich Village, among homosexuals.

So I say yes, and follow him to his apartment, and he does what he wants to to me, and I know, as he is blowing air bubbles up my ass so I will fart in his face, that this is yet another night I will not get to sleep with a woman.

FINALLY

As I'm tooling up to the Mill, the Writer's bar in Iowa City, Iowa, the home of the Writer's Workshop, on my Sears Moped, I see a woman—tall, blond, beautiful, everything I looked for those days in Central Park (except younger)—opening the door of a car. I don't yet know that it's a Mercedes 190 SL, but I do see it's a two-seater sports car, with the top down.

I used to go to double bills every Saturday as a kid. I took the stories and the images in them seriously, and if you take movies seriously, this is the kind of woman you're supposed to be fucking. So I ask god, "Why can't I have her?" and I shut my eyes real tight and make a kind of prayer that god sends her over to me.

I suppose, if god never again answers a prayer of mine, that one should suffice, for even as I was opening my eyes she began closing the door of her car. She walked over to me (not, she says, on account of god but the Moped. She spent a year at Oxford and everyone there had Mopeds. I say god will use Mopeds if She has to), and we began to chat about Mopeds, England, art. We exchanged phone numbers. My roommate, who knows her, tells me she's straight, but I sense something; a few nights later the hair is brushed out of my eyes, within a week we are living together. She's had more experience than me, in pretty brick dorm rooms up in Massachusetts, but desire is the great equalizer, and it is I who initiate the great experiment of why someone would want to lick someone's genitals.

She's a wonderful person, but even then I know I've met her too soon. Years of deprivation have overlain (what I at least pretend is) my essentially monogamous nature with such humungous oceans of desire that one person cannot satisfy me for long, no matter how perfect an embodiment of my fantasies she may be. I've got too much to make up for—not just the women I *didn't* sleep with, but the men I *did,* out of all that reflexive self-denial.

I'm still working this one out.

But the pattern is set: to find the straightest-looking (or, preferably, *straight*) women I can, to prove—to my father, to myself, and to every other human being in the entire world—that I am no breast-binding bulldagger forced to sleep with women because men won't have me, and that I can get a woman as "good" as any man (i.e., my dad) can. That this is a self-destructive pattern, that women who sleep with men *before* me may perhaps choose to do so *after* me (or even *during* me) is something it takes me almost twenty years to acknowledge.

It takes even longer before I even begin to admit that, yeah, there are times, maybe, that I *want* a tough, swaggering, truck driver.

EVEN LATER

After graduate school, I return to New York. (I think of moving to San Francisco, but decide, in the startlingly obtuse fashion that is the flip side of my standard intuition, that it's not gay enough.) My lover follows me, but that's not enough either. So, sometime in 1970 or 1971, having read an ad in the *Village Voice,* I find myself entering a room in the second floor of an apartment on Prince or Spring Street in Soho. It's a meeting of the Daughters of Bilitis, the organization begun in the 1950s to help dykes deal with themselves and the world. The room is filled with women and, if everything I have read about the Daughters of Bilitis is correct, the women are lesbians.

All I can do is enter the room. I cannot move across it, let alone do anything so sophisticated as sit down and talk to somebody. Not counting high school assemblies (where I knew, courtesy Miss Maxfeld, of the sexual proclivities and apartment arrangements of the spinster teachers), it's the first time in my life I have knowingly been in a room with more than one other lesbian in it. It is, in fact, the first time in my life I actually *believed* there were other lesbians in the universe (as opposed to merely accepting assertions concerning their existence), and I could not have been more aston-ished by the sight than if I had found little tyrannosauruses parading around that room.

Even so, I did not *quite* believe it. It was clear these women *wanted* to be lesbians, or wanted other people to *think* they were lesbians, or perhaps—out of some feminist impulse—were *pre-tending* to be lesbians (like the women in my C-R group for whom I was soon to become their token dyke experience). Yes, they were *ideological* lesbians, but they didn't really want to fuck women. If they really wanted to fuck women, what were they doing standing around talking in this room, instead of pouncing on top of each other like bunnies?

I'd be standing there still, perhaps, if some kind officer of the organization had not come over to me and, grabbing me forcefully by the hand, dragged me over to the drink table. Although I gulped wine, I was unable to speak, even to utter my name. She offered to dance with me, but this was impossible, as my legs refused to move.

After this, I forced myself to attend coed dances at the GAA Firehouse in Soho (soon to be torched), then Bonnie and Clyde's and the Duchess. Beer in hand, I'd lounge at the bar with contradictory thoughts: part of me convinced that nobody in the world was good enough for me, and part of me convinced that there was no woman in the world whom I would not go home with, out of my terrible embarrassing need. This was partly due to my years of deprivation (in college, I'm sure, I would have gone home with any woman in the world), partly because, out of my experience with Miss Maxfeld, I had come to associate disgust with desire, and partly because, on some level, I believed—and still believe—any human can be attractive, if you can only find the way to see it.

Liquor helped in these endeavors. Eventually I was able to talk to women, even dance with them. It took time, and practice, but like any discipline, the more you do it the easier it gets. I'd stand around waiting for someone to brush the hair out of my eyes, and when after three or four hours of solitary drinking and staring that didn't happen, I might force myself to go up and talk to somebody, even if only at last call. By last call, even a rocket scientist such as myself gets around to realizing that a woman still at the bar at that hour is probably not *utterly* averse to getting laid. So I began working off my lonely years of desire.

Bars have a bad rep. But I say: bars saved me. In them I met women I would never have met otherwise, women who on account of education or class or background may not have been "suitable" for me to share a life with (though I met two of the people I lived with in bars—three, if you count the woman in Iowa), but women who were certainly worth spending a night or two with, for what they taught me about themselves and a world I would not otherwise have known.

And bars were a space of wonder. For many, many years (perhaps, at times, even to this day), I felt it, each and every time I walked into a woman's bar: wonder that such a bar existed, wonder that in it there were women like me—women who sleep with women, women who *want* to sleep with women, women who'd actually rather sleep with women than with men, women who'd *rather* sleep with women than sleep *alone,* women who might—if I was terribly lucky and had the perfect timing and the stars were all in the right place—have sex with me that *very* night! This wonder was clearly an artificial construct, a fallout of shame, guilt, and trauma, but whatever its genesis, a glow of desire was created that burned so bright, that lasted so long, that at least one spy feels that perhaps, after all, it was not a totally unambiguous blessing to come in from the cold.

Bridesmaid, 1964

Wilson DeLynn

MY DEBUT

Blanche   McCrary   Boyd

I grew up in Charleston, South Carolina, where coming out meant
wearing a long white gown and a wrist corsage, so I've never been
able to think about coming out as a lesbian without snickering. My
debut occurred in 1970, at the end of a radical feminist occupation
of a building at Harvard. After an eight-day stand-off with police, my
comrades and I marched outside declaring victory, and a photograph
with my face decorated by warpaint made the *Boston Globe.* Of course
I sent this photo to my mother, who phoned with a comment about
appropriate makeup, then asked if this was where a Northern education must inevitably lead. "And listen, honey, if you keep associating
with these women, you're going to get tagged as a lesbian!"
"Momma," I said, "I have something to tell you."

   The letter I wrote my mother detailing my newly discovered revolutionary status sent her to bed for a day, but when she recovered,
she was no more impressed by my claim to be a radical lesbian than
she'd been by the pictures of debutante cotillions in the newspaper

when I'd been a teenager living at home. Together my mother and I had mocked the debutantes lined up for display with their tuxedoed escorts discreetly behind them, and now she ridiculed me: I looked normal, I was her daughter, I'd been happily married for seven years, I was going through a phase. How on earth, she said in a raw moment, could her own daughter turn out to be one of the women in this photograph?

Thirty years later, I still don't know the answer. I have an alcoholism version, a political version, a genetics-as-destiny version, and a father-died-in-my-adolescence version, but at the heart of my mother's question lies the mystery of choice.

When a psychologist first suggested to me that I had chosen to be gay, I scoffed. Choice might entail whether to go to Charleston for Christmas, whether to go to bed with a specific woman, but it certainly did not include the hard wiring of love. An acorn, I said huffily, does not choose to be an oak instead of a pine. Yes it does, he said, in the deepest sense. And notice, he said, how a tree will twist and bend toward light.

At first, bending toward this peculiar light, I was as stunned as my mother. The women's liberation movement had hit my core as if it were a tuning fork, and what little I understood about myself at the age of twenty-five was entirely sheared off; the path of rage I cut through my marriage remained a source of regret for many years.

My sister says Southerners are like other people only more so, and that is the way I made my debut—hard and fast, with no aforethought. Unpremeditated lesbianism. If it was a fate worse than death, I alternated between horror and delight, and smoothed the edges with drugs and booze.

For several months I lived in a lesbian commune in Boston, where we did "actions," such as running a flag up a corporate flagpole with the slogan "Lesbian Mother's Day" proclaimed in red. I'm not sure now why we thought behaving like this was important, but spray-painting buses in the middle of the night was exciting, as was chanting in demonstrations, "Out of the bedrooms and into the streets."

There were seven members of our group, and, in a bad moment, I realized I had been to bed with five of them. (The sixth was my roommate and she was now hitting on me too.) None of them knew about the others, and, in the next house meeting, I might not be classed as revolutionary any longer; I might be accused of acting like a man.

The truth was simple: I didn't want to hurt anyone's feelings, and I didn't know how to say no. My teenage years had coincided with

Bill Clinton's, and, though the rules for nice girls strictly forbade sex, that only meant penetration by a penis. Everyone I knew was into heavy petting, what Monica Lewinksy insisted to Linda Tripp was "fooling around." I'd had orgasms with boys, but the reverse was not true, and here, perhaps, is where I revealed my incipient lesbianism. I was unconcerned with boys' sexual distress, but women made me feel like Warren Beatty in *Shampoo*. I cared about women's desires and felt a great deal of tenderness for them, whether I found them sexually attractive or not. With the lynchpin of intercourse removed, when I was alone with a woman, one of us just seemed to start taking off her clothes.

Before the next house meeting, I moved to Vermont and joined a commune of dropped-out intellectuals among whom I would be the token, newly-minted lesbian. This was an arrangement in which we could all feel revolutionary, and I could get some rest.

In Vermont, temporarily celibate, I discovered that under my bravado lay sexual shame, and grief about my marriage. If one version of me believed that sexism and racism might make political revolution necessary, a deeper version of me was just a nice girl from South Carolina who believed in getting married while still a virgin (I had) and maintaining the sanctity of those vows I'd made before God. It was a rough spot, and I soothed it with alcohol and drugs for ten years.

For most of the seventies my life appeared to stabilize: I lived with a woman in New York and wrote two novels I don't much like. But throughout those years alcohol and drug addiction were an escalator that slowly descended. Sometimes I'd reach a plateau, and then another lurch would take me farther down. I moved home to South Carolina, where I became adept at dissembling, so that neither my family or my friends realized the extent of my problem. Then, in 1981, an off-and-on lover shot herself while on drugs that we had just bought together. I got help and managed to quit.

Sober sexual interaction was an unknown; it was necessary to "come out" all over again. Surprisingly, without chemical crutches, I discovered that I didn't want to be gay. I no longer wanted the confusion, the lust, the broken relationships, the trouble with family, or the risks with jobs. Yet this door, once opened, proved impossible to close, and, in accepting that impossibility I found peace. At the Beijing conference for women's rights, a Chinese lesbian said something to an interviewer that struck me: "Making love with a man is like swimming in a river. Making love with a woman is like swimming in the ocean. If I have been in the ocean, why would I go back to the river?"

My second debut occurred slowly, over the course of years, and the only attendant was my deepest self. The complexities of this process are too delicate to tease out, but I like to say that one of God's jokes has been, for the last decade, my increasing happiness. It's Thanksgiving weekend as I'm writing this. Leslie's mother and my mother are both visiting. We forgot to take the magnets off the refrigerator that say "Satan was a Lesbian," and "Queer for Kicks," but neither of our moms has noticed. Last week, Leslie was inseminated, and soon we'll find out whether she's pregnant. Her mother is excited, and mine is bewildered. I'm going to be a mommy, too. Or a daddy. Or something.

When Leslie and I first started talking babies, I began collecting orchids. I have more than forty now, and our living room looks like a hothouse. Orchids are distinguished from other flowers by a central column containing both female and male organs, and by exotic, erotic lips. The most beautiful orchids are hybrids created artificially by breeders. It's all a matter of taste, inclination, and genetics. So, although I'd never wear a corsage on my wrist, on my forearm is an orchid tattoo.

Charleston, 1980

RED LIGHT, GREEN LIGHT

Beatrix Gates

ON the first day of day camp, I showed up poolside in my brother's swimming trunks, pale board of a chest thrust forward, pebble-sized nipples barely visible. My thighs were small inside the baggy gray folds, but the navy stripes were crisp down the sides and the wide elastic waist hugged my middle, so I had been able to pronounce, "They fit," as my mother looked hard that morning at my proposed swimming outfit, her index finger crossing her freshly lipsticked mouth without touching it.

"I suppose it doesn't matter," she said, then relaxed her brow, "and it's one less shopping trip." I slapped proudly across the hot pavement to the edge of the pool, ribboned light flowing across the lanes marked off for the relay race.

Another camper in an elasticized torso-hugging floral print edged with a ruffle at her nonexistent hips padded up and asked, "Where's your suit?" delivered more like "Why don't you have any clothes on?"

I turned and beamed, "This is it," and as she continued to look at me as if I hadn't really spoken, I realized I would have to fill the space between us with a happiness so great it would outweigh any and all doubt she had ever had. I was thrilled with my suit, but learning to play like this was new, and I was entering a kind of theater, no applause, and feeling increasingly uncomfortable in the spotlight. "Did you see the navy stripes?" I offered. "They're official, from Camp Chewonki, a camp where you go away and only boys are allowed."

"How'd you get those trunks then?" My sister camper really wanted to know now. I explained, as I had often heard my mother say, "You have to have connections." I saw the camper's face begin to change, and I knew she was beginning to see me again. It was as if I had disappeared for her and now I was filling in again. I saw her see me, and I smiled. I was not dangerous in my gray trunks, and I was *not* taking them off—the suit I had admired for two years, the suit I had seen fall around my knees all the times I borrowed it to try on in my room. No, not this suit. I leapt into the pool headfirst, and the water ran in a delicious stream down the full width of my chest.

Dream at ten: I swim underwater and three full strokes down into the green-lit world, I realize I can breathe. I arch and dive, eyes wide as I glide in the revelation of another world. I share my new powers with no one and believe in the impossible. There will always be a moment of questioning, of quick blood-cold dread, when I ask the water itself if it is still possible, then, contacting a stream of breath big enough to power me forward, I swim. Other times, I dream I rise away from the ground, and if I pump my arms too hard, I fall, and if I let myself rise, I do. I fly, I fly.

In daylight and in the eyes of others, I began to understand there would be no easy way out. Following the rules of the child's game Red Light, Green Light, I ran and froze, a chameleon seeking cover and seeking meaning for myself, not yet understanding there would be no security or winning way to deal with the world's opinion of who and what I was. As a child, one of my favorite things to do was spy. I watched house traffic quietly from under the kitchen table and ran experiments to see how long I could go undetected, protected by silence.

Green Light: Run. The figure begins to turn and I begin to freeze. Gather strength, see another fight ahead. Our shadows are tied together and I breathe hard, sweating and trying not to fall forward as my body yearns to, as I am watched for one false move and as in turn I learn to watch for the red light marking constant betrayal and danger.

I dreamt many lovers, took excursions in my dreams where I flew alongside the wind and descended from the sky to press full-length against the body of my music teacher, her full chest held tight under a white button-down shirt, khakis smoothing her hips. I would wake surprised, aroused and wanting to rediscover the heated sensation leaving my pelvis. I was very happy, and of course wondered if she knew that we met at night, hips clasped hard against each other, while in the daylight hours I sang as loud as I could in the chorus she gustily conducted, her arms rising rapidly as the sweat grew and dampened her shirt and her chest heaved and sighed to our communal song. I was eight or nine years old when I discovered she could move me beyond song and into the forbidden and delicious realm of sexual obsession. I learned to pay close attention to my dreams and to her every excited movement as she conducted the energy behind the music into the collective achievement of our all-girl chorus.

My clarity and sense of self never lived long inside me, a stuttering flame, and I often wondered why, even as I strove to find a way for inside and outside to fit together in fluid relation. My heart reached one way only to be dead-ended by isolation. *Red Light, Green Light.* As I searched for others, I kept up a double vision, always watching the outside and monitoring the effects of my behavior. I wanted to fit together, and I felt shapeless and sharp, torn and flickering, hidden under a surface of fluctuating needs, a sense of duty and finely tuned sociability. Red Light, Green Light became a metaphor for my progress as a young person seeking my lesbian sexuality. Control of my own path would not often be in my hands. The stop-start dance mimicked the frustration I felt in the world, the constant interrupting of my explorations of lesbian life.

Sixteen going on seventeen in 1966: the headmaster called on the phone and dropped the bomb. I wasn't being asked back to the private girls' school in Brookline where my mother had let herself boast about how well I was adjusting. Her fury took over the house: "No warning, they gave us no warning. We're paying through the nose and they can't even call us in." I had stopped doing any work and tried to warn her, even though I couldn't have said that's what I was doing. I fought with her every day about going to school.

Every ten days or so, I'd do a marathon—take No-Doz and try and write one of my overdue papers. I wrote one riffing off of *The*

Canterbury Tales that was more than twenty pages of my illegible script, but I couldn't reorganize it the next day in study hall. I had a hard time reading my own handwriting, and I couldn't get my mounds of paper together after a night without sleep. I despaired in that hideous hour before it was time to turn in the paper. I bragged I had written a twenty-page paper, just had to copy it over. Meanwhile, I was watching the light change across the yellow pad I'd filled, frozen in dread, too proud to let go of my hope. The top of the desk seemed impossibly cold, the beige swirls of plastic and the mocha metal legs I sat caged between. I looked out the window and couldn't imagine how anyone did this—went to school, understood what was going on, listened, participated, went home, did homework, had friends, went out with them, had dinner, talked with parents, watched TV or listened to the radio, slept and got up to do the same thing over again.

I hated everything I was supposed to be—on time, pretty, not-so-smart—and liked blowing their images, doing well in math, falling behind in French and Latin and rocketing forward in English. Nothing if not unpredictable. I succeeded in getting thrown out when my long line of absences had finally overtaken the actual number of days I had been in school. I hated telling anyone anything, and I still had to go talk with the headmaster.

I sat on a modern brown nubbly couch in his office with thin purple pillows behind a teak coffee table where I studied his gray complexion, the purple ringing his eyes and the shock of mouse-brown hair above his large dull watery eyes. He seemed to me the oldest young man I'd ever seen and I wondered how he got that way—something stronger than No-Doz. Soon he bore down on me saying how important it was for me to admit that my absences were unnecessary, to say that I lied, that I wasn't really sick.

But I never knew when something was wrong with me. My doctor told me I masked my symptoms, so my bladder infections raged without detection. I had been on medication for my kidneys since I was a kid, but my doctor didn't acknowledge the side effects, my daily dizziness and nausea, until much later.

Mr. Grayson finished by telling me that his seemingly overbearing attitude was for my own good. I agreed, sort of, to get him to shut up. Declaring me "a health risk," he stood up and took three of his famous long-loping strides to the door. He smiled and offered me his hand. "Your place needs to be filled by someone who will make the most of it." This never was my place, I thought, as I bumped into the coffee table and left.

I felt relieved to be catapulted out of the nightmare I had inhabited that last year, half-knowing what was going on in my classes and hating the concerned smiles and strained how-are-you's that washed over every dreaded trip down the long hallways. The hard part was where was I going to find any friends now? The girls at my old school all stuck together, and these people from the suburbs south and west of Boston weren't about to reach out to a misfit from Cambridge. After all, where would it get them? I had entered another netherworld. I stopped sleeping and made the radio my solace, my all-hours friend with the songs of Brook Benton and the Platters making everything all right.

I would have to stay back. I spent the next year at Manter Hall, a school for kids who had been thrown out of public school and private school, missed a lot due to illness or disability, gotten pregnant, or been in the service before completing high school. We were a band of misfits (who knows how many of us were gay and lesbian?), and there was no GED, no program for pregnant teenagers, Disabilities Act, no counseling. Manter Hall was located in Harvard Square over Elsie's Restaurant, and had an all-male faculty who could "handle the kids." A year there leveled me out—and took care of any of my mother's hopes about creating a socially acceptable young woman. I got my first leather jacket from Harry the Greek's, a giant cooler of "second-hand" leather in Boston, and settled into steadily smoking Marlboros or whatever I could bum in the smoky yellow air of the girls' lounge.

When I heard about a new school spanning the last two years of high school and the first two years of college for talented, underachieving kids, I begged my parents to drive out to the Berkshires to see it. The founder of Martin's Falls was Frederica Ball, well-known for many years as headmistress a prestigious private girls' school in the Boston area. This helped sell it to my mother. Freddie Ball drove a white Jeep, a new International Scout, and gave us the tour of the proposed school, a construction site mired in mud and melting ice, locked in 4-wheel drive. She drove fast over the frozen dirt piles, strode into the concrete shells and gestured wide, grinning and laughing from a leathery face, talking about taking risks since it was clear that higher education wasn't moving fast enough to keep up with kids these days. My parents knew I was such a kid. I knew I liked the way she drove.

Maureen Larson, the Dean of Students, shared a cottage with Freddie Ball on the country estate her grandparents had built outside Great Barrington, the site of the Martin's Falls campus. The two of them kept two Lhasa apsos in a house that was nestled beside a small lake and looked southwest to where the geese migrated and courted over the seasons. Freddie Ball's husband lived in the Boston area and commuted to the Berkshires when he could get away from his law practice, as the story went. When I think of Maureen Larson, she comes immediately to mind as a friendly woman with a whimsical streak and a delighted spirit who took in the world in gasps and laughed in a high register punctuated by more gasps. She had a generosity that played across her wide Nordic face and brightly-lit, pale blue eyes, and she also possessed a thoughtful attention accompanied by its opposite, the sudden rush of flight, like a shorebird skittering away from a perceived predator. Like many others, I fell for her warmth immediately, never seeing the warp of fitful nerves underneath.

By the time I got to Martin's Falls, I was starved for a relationship where I was seen, recognized, or mirrored back in any form at all. It was for this reason that I fell in love with my English teacher, a cynical, sensitive, and fast-witted young Brit named Rosamund Fay. I wasn't sexually attracted to her, but I had looked to my English teachers ever since I decided writing was my only truly free zone. I worshipped the blank page and all it had to offer. I turned every muscle of my attention toward any person who could offer hope. The live example became my teacher—two teachers, really, since Rosamund lived openly with Jess Stewart, a faculty member in History. I was fascinated by the fact that they lived together. I sought them out wherever I could. They wore identical pinkie rings, and at home they kept up a running commentary of devotion directed toward the two barkless basenjis they spoiled. They seemed to have perfected the art of mystery, their postures somehow changing at fish-fin-flicking speeds, as they juggled identities and became invisible and glaring, both at once.

As I came to know Rosamund Fay, I was shy, despite my dependence on her opinion of my work and my huge and extended need for being understood. I had found poetry two years before—a place where every word counted and I owned the page. I cruised every inch of the poetry sections in bookstores in the Harvard Square bookstores—the Paperback Booksmith, downstairs at the Book Cellar, the second-hand store on Church Street run by father and son, all the periodicals at Reading International, the Mandrake, and, if I felt brave enough, the stacks and piles at the Grolier. Only one room, the Grolier was a hard place to hide out unobserved, and I was too shy to say I wanted to look at everything, so I stumbled out, intimidated by the legendary Gordon Cairnie's gruff questions. I liked to be a quiet detective on my own private search when I went scouting poetry. I scoured the books to see where the poetry came from—how poets changed the length of lines and where, how the books were made, who published them—and began to notice how the poets might connect to one another through their publishers: New Directions, Black Sparrow, and Broadside Press.

Rosamund introduced me to the Romantic poets, and I loved studying Keats and Wordsworth, going over the work line by line. I had begun to occupy my first, firm avenue of expression with a passionate recognition and appetite. The realm of poetry became everything for me, and I was nurtured and fascinated by my teacher—sometimes struck dumb in conferences with all that I had begun to utter. The naming of my feelings had just begun to have a space, if only on the page, but to me this was huge—the great blank expanse, the equivalent of permission to occupy my true self in a real way. I began to write poems and show them to her. To trust a reader was to begin to tell the truth, and I trusted Rosamund to know the difference between who I was and who I was pretending to be.

My concentration on Rosamund went from tracing her every physical aspect—lean figure, wide mouth and gap-tooth front teeth—to her penetrating intelligence and facile wit. Although she always dressed in skirts, she wore all her clothes as if saying, "Oh, so you want me to dress up?" She always wore something different, so she had an unexpected look, and yet the clothes were prescription conservative. Technically, all the parts matched—always loose, rarely repeated—and yet she seemed theatrically invented. What *was* it that didn't seem quite right? If there were a pillar nearby, Rosamund would be leaning on it, smoke rising in two streams to her nostrils, French-inhaling and asking that very question, her mocking, deep-blue eyes coaxing awareness. Full lips painted red, tongue poised behind her teeth, she loved to smoke, and she was, for 1966, very gay—her dress, her pose, her clear companionship all flaunted her lesbianism right next to the purposely sloppy camouflage that teased at the edges of recognition.

I sensed that Rosamund felt a real duty to educate women, and I watched how she guided the more problematic among us, especially the other writers, toward what they might need. I saw her direct a fragile/tough student to Woolf, leaving space for the unsureness and arrogance that masked the student's adolescent rage, so that she could emerge whole from her teenage pose and grow as a writer.

When I tried to make Rosamund into everything I needed, I discovered she had the insecurity I found among most teachers I had known—a fear of not understanding enough about poetry. Although she read my poems and made good suggestions, never telling me to give it up, her encouragement was often prefaced by a disclaimer about perhaps not being the best person to comment. I had already learned that I had to search out the people who weren't afraid of poetry, and, too, that they weren't always English teachers. I had grown accustomed to having to tease my teachers along into reading poetry and admitting the ways it moved them. I took up the challenge like seduction. Many of my teachers were fine readers, they just didn't think they were, and the fact that they felt somewhat exposed only excited me further. I wanted to be seen, and they felt exposed by the nature of the work, so I was not only visible to myself but also had created a spark of recognition, touched someone else. How delicious.

Despite Rosamund's disclaimers, she carefully read a developing series of poems for a special mid-winter term project. I was half-crazed with the need for meaningful contact, and yet in conference, I was plagued by speechlessness and an embarrassment that seemed to travel from my bones to the surface with no mediating intelligence. Her expressed interest, concern, and affection was almost more than I could bear, and yet my hunger for recognition continued unabated.

In one conference, Rosamund had just commented about the power of my work, when Jess stopped by. She excused herself for barging in, friendly and large in the doorframe. Rosamund said, "Here, read this," and handed her my poem, "Our Hands, Our Needs Outreach." The poem was about a sexual encounter not serving or reaching deeper needs, a poem I had written after a night with a friend from Cambridge left me feeling largely empty. At sixteen, this new emptiness was an unwelcome surprise that settled as a disappointment.

The poem was, as usual, way ahead of me. But as Jess read it, she began to color—hurt, anger, and recognition flowing over her face in a wave. I saw the power of my words and her inability to avoid the impact. This was the beauty of Jess, I see now—her direct response. She handed the poem back, barely able to sputter, "These damn poets, they don't know what effect they have," then turned and left. I wondered what I had mirrored for Jess. My young instincts told me that Jess asked a lot of those close to her, and that her commanding presence and emotionally vulnerable nature got her into trouble, trouble she herself didn't always understand. Rosamund knew the exact combination of hard and soft edges in Jess's personality. That much was clear, and without exposing the repeating steps of their own dance, Rosamund showed me the emotional effect my poems could have.

Rosamund and I were on the same side—or were we? I felt

horrified, powerful and pleased. When Jess left, Rosamund seemed satisfied, as if she'd won an argument I had never heard. Having just topped Jess in public, in front of me, the young woman who had an emotional stake in every word, she was letting me see that not only was there an emotional bond, a deep one, between them, but also that I had a place inside that world. My poem related directly to their experience, and she let me inside the circle. Now what? I didn't read their inclusion of me as a signal of rivalry but as a way of showing me that my feelings were real—as expressed in my poem and in my need to be seen by others and by myself. Rosamund had helped me see myself.

I went to visit Rosamund and Jess during the summer on a very hot day. I had been looking forward to the visit, borrowing a car and sticking to the seat all the way over from Stockbridge. They'd been given the tenant farmer's house by the road to live in during their tenure. When I got there, Rosamund answered the door, trademark cigarette holder and Old Gold between her teeth. Rosamund had great attitude. Her usual rolling sarcasm and dry wit, which I cherished, had an extra edge that morning. *"You* have arrived on a day of hell," she announced in her British accent. "No point dressing it up." She eyed me keenly, read my look of shocked, complete attention, and seemed to be saying, "Get ready," as she pushed off the doorway and hit her languorous stride. Her bones traveled ahead of any musculature, giving her a slightly rag doll affect, head bobbing on her neck and expressing unequivocal disgust at the idea of having to flex muscles to get any-where. Normally an expert in hard and hilarious truth, today she moved with an unbearable slowness followed by a series of compensa-tory jerks to get her body through the world. Every joint had become a hyphen, and what followed came as a surprise. The parsing of senten-ces, the stream of narrative, had come into question. And how was her life changing in the air before her?

Rosamund sensed my observing eyes at her back and recovered, exclaiming "Oh hell," as I trailed behind, and we crossed the threshold to the living room. She pulled together as Jess came into view. Jess was sitting in her favorite chair, a stolid wood frame with leather seat and half-back. Her square shoulders and open face had always ema-nated direct enthusiasm, laughter, and a penchant for blushing with emotion. She was blond and blue-eyed, a WASP butch, and possessed a transparency as striking as Rosamund's satiric and languid presence. A product of Main Line Philadelphia and Bryn Mawr, she had had a hard time, it was rumored, breaking from the strict, social expectations of her family. Teaching had become her life.

Today, an eighteen-inch pile of Kleenex grew beside the chair. Jess was blowing her nose as she said a muffled, "Hello, nice to see you." Her usually combed and parted blond hair was now tousled locks falling across her forehead, red eyes swollen beneath her brow.

"We've been canned," Rosamund piped up. I didn't know whether to sit, go to Jess, or stand some more.

"I feel so betrayed," Jess offered between nose blows.

"Frederica Ball fired her yesterday and assumed I'd quit. I didn't. I made Frederica Ball fire me too." Rosamund says this with small satisfaction, Freddie Ball's last name delivered like a thrown-up flare of disgust that ensured the bearer bad tidings for life.

I start with *Why*, and Rosamund says that Frederica Ball wouldn't say *why,* claiming it would hurt Jess too much, and that Freddie Ball then had the nerve to claim she was protecting Jess. Jess shook her head, wondering out loud what in the world she could have done.

As the details unfold, my stomach falls and clenches, and I have the twin sensation of Rosamund and Jess moving closer and further away. At first, I want to separate them, desperate to keep Rosamund in my life, as if I could "save" one of them, at least, for me. All the signs of their shared life seem to speak in amplification. I weave between the shock of dual perspectives—the wide, bright path of kinship that I am standing on and the knowledge that I will be cut off by the end of the day. The three of us tangle inside a moment of rupture and intimacy, even as they are being excised from my life. I will be returned to solo flight, fully aware of what I have lost but unable to say it, even as my defiance is rising. I can't believe my life is running away from me again, when I have just arrived. I look at Rosamund, see her anger and defiance next to Jess' temporary undoing.

The day before my visit, Jess had returned to see Frederica Ball with another colleague, a witness who demanded to know the reasons for the firing, a faculty member demanding the right to know what grounds were being used. Frederica Ball still wouldn't budge. The only time she gave in to pressure from the outside was when she fired the two lesbians who had loyally defended her every act up until that point. The board had been challenged by homophobic parents, and Freddie Ball responded quickly, firing Rosamund and Jess in an afternoon with no explanation, apology, or severance pay. Why were these two teachers fired in this way? Why was it so sudden, with no means of redress? She did it to save her own neck. Her willingness to purge would remove any doubts, real or imagined, harbored by these same parents about her and her woman partner of so many years, the Dean of Students, Maureen Larson. So Frederica Ball stood lean and shadowless, her dean absent from her side. French doors behind her, she said dryly that it would be far better for Jess to just *go*.

"I've never done anything but teach," moaned Jess, tears spilling from her face. "We left a traditional school, we were fine there, we joined this crazy place, because it sounded good. What gets me is we backed her up through everything this first year, we didn't listen when the others called her judgment into question claiming she was arbitrary and dictatorial, we sided with her every time, all the time. Period. The End."

We all sat quietly for a moment, then Jess sobbed again into her handkerchief, and the usually restless tan dogs stayed quiet. Rosamund gave them a look, commanding and praising without uttering a word. She ran her free hand through her short brown hair, and got up to make some fresh coffee, "Not that we've slept to need waking up," she muttered. By the time I left them, I was not only heartbroken, but I also harbored a deep feeling of betrayal by Frederica Ball. Rosamund pretty much ordered me not to waste my time getting involved, holding me with a penetrating look, and I promised her not to take it on. Inside, I vowed justice, in some form as yet unimagined, and knew they'd hear about it. She had reason to worry about me. I was stunned to think I had no idea when or if I would see them again, and revenge was on my mind.

My showing up the day after Rosamund and Jess were fired was an accident. Or was it? My summer plans had been partly created by the fear of separation, even geographically, from my favorite teachers. They'd told me by their actions that I could be real and live. I wanted to know how they did it and didn't know how to ask, still feeling I had to be a voyeur to see a way into the life.

The next fall, my friend Ellen Fishbein and I, having absorbed the shock over the summer, set to organizing. Our goal was to break Frederica Ball's dictatorial rule, having seen one too many faculty members as well as students disappear for bad reasons. We demanded the creation of a democratic process for faculty hiring and firing. We met in the bottom of the new dorm, presented the points of a petition to our sister students, and talked together in small and large groups over the period of a week before setting a date for signatures. Some said it was asking too much for the faculty to sign and risk losing their jobs, so we decided to circulate the petition at the next faculty meeting on the same day we turned it in to the board of trustees. We hoped student dissatisfaction could translate into a real threat of transferring out and that the faculty could be moved by student support to further challenge the administration policies.

Ellen and I were passionate political strategists. At the beginning and end of each day we pored over every action, nuanced comment, or student rumor to read how the student movement was playing, discuss how to cultivate more support and put more pressure on the administration. We demanded that the community stop being afraid and that the administration stop violating the democratic principles put forward as sacred at this new, progressive institution. Determined to shake the school to its roots, we delivered the first petition to the board and the administration, signed by all but one student, the granddaughter of the U.S. ambassador to Vietnam in 1967.

Through this experience, I began to walk in my own shoes. It was the first time I felt a true alignment with myself. I was in the right place at the right time. Regardless of the consequences, my actions grew out of my words and the words came from my heart. I came out to myself, and I began organizing out of love for these two women.

A year after the firing, Ellen told me that her father said that everything had come down the way it had because there was "a really big lesbian thing going on" at Martin's Falls. She let me know that the school had called on him, a psychologist known for his broad perspective, for advice in the aftermath of the firings. David Fishbein was someone I admired and loved, a proud and interested father to his daughter, and a friend to me. The summer of the firing, I had stayed with Ellen, her mother Rosie, and David, in a household devoted to art, politics, and the life of the mind. They had always been ready to talk about anything and ask questions, any questions. So to hear this a year later, not even from David directly, made a deep impact. I wondered if I would ever find true allies again, and was even afraid to tell my dear friend Ellen how dispiriting her father's words were to me.

Rosamund and Jess had let me see their devastation and their courage. They stood firm in their life, lost their jobs, and still traveled together inside their love. Now that was the truest test of commitment among two people I had seen to date. I began organizing out of love, knowing how privileged I had been to have these teachers—and I learned definitively that there was no protection for lesbians. The prejudice fueled by hatred, irrational and all-encompassing, took over every territory I had known as welcoming, progressive ground.

I return to the four killing words—a "really big lesbian thing."

These words implied that there were many more lesbians at Martin's Falls than had first been thought. Countable numbers—as opposed to the hidden, closeted, and passing, who could not be counted—spelled out immediate, serious, and irreversible harm. "Really big" also suggested a conspiracy: any number larger than one always led to conspiring. The agenda of this unknown, conspiratorial group was left vague and unanswered, as if even to imagine concretely was far too risky a venture, especially for people with important business, like the board or the parents of the richest kids at the school. It was those kids, it turned out, who had lodged the complaint about the two teachers. "Really big" also implied the threat of a large following and high rate of conversion, neither of which I had experienced directly or even heard about—though I should have been assumed to be first in line. I had never been asked into Rosamund and Jess's social realm, I had never been approached sexually, never invited over to their home by myself during the school year. I was simply listened to and encouraged. Rosamund had asked me to think over the many aspects of my writing—my relationship to who and what I was writing about—and asked if I had ever thought about writing plays, to get the different voices out. She talked to me about my talent, careful not to praise too much, but sought to inspire me to reach further outside myself. As a teacher now, I can see how she thought about what would help me, then tried to pass it on in a way that would take hold.

My friend's father had offered these blunt facts to his daughter to pass on to me, not speaking directly—as if even the word "lesbian," uttered openly, might send the hearer running, cringing, or folding. He spoke as if his words required no further explanation, hard with an edge I had not encountered before. His last word on the subject: "They had to get rid of them." "They" in this case was Freddie Ball, who, to be absolutely sure that she and Maureen Larson were not recognized as another dyke couple, had to cut Rosamund and Jess loose. Witnessing this particular cruelty delayed my own journey to a woman lover by five years. The experience also showed me that being a lesbian at Martin's Falls in 1967 meant expulsion from the teaching community and the murdering of at least two careers. Frederica Ball steeled her continuing reign and garnered respect for her toughness (now an asset) from the board, while Maureen Larson proved over time that she held nothing in higher esteem than Frederica C. Ball. She remained loyal, territorial, and devoted to her and the righteousness of her rule.

Early one morning at assembly, when I sat with ice melting around my boots, I heard my name read for having overdue books and cast my mind immediately to the piles of untended term papers and books hastily shelved in favor of organizing. Maureen Larson raised her hand, leaning forward over her heavy breasts, and rose, scanning the assembled crowd, then began, voice shaky with urgency, "I think what we've just heard about library books overdue by two weeks is despicable, a despicable act. It's an act made to undermine the most basic rules of respect and sharing in a community. It's a gross violation of the community's trust. That's all I have to say." As she sat back down, I realized that my teachers had been quietly protecting the fact that I was barely making it to classes and turning in papers. If this news had reached the dean, she wouldn't have bothered with simply shaming me with my overdue library books. She surprised me on the way out that morning, and said she needed to speak with me right away.

When I came into Maureen Larson's office, she was blinking behind her glasses, shaking her head as if she couldn't get the words out. Had she been crying? I sat down and knocked the ice from my boots, not at all sure what she wanted from me. Would this be a preliminary talk about the demands in the petition, a hysterical reprimand, or would she be asking me to leave the school?

Gathering her thick Norwegian cardigan around her, she looks as if she can't reason with what's in her head any longer and blurts out, "You're destroying the school. You've got to stop."

"I can't," I throw back.

"Why not? Don't you have any sense of responsibility?" She looks at me, incredulous.

"It's not just up to me."

"And these ridiculous demands, they threaten everything."

"The petition was signed by everyone because that's how we all feel. We want a say in decision-making, especially about faculty."

"Well," she snorts, "I understand you practically forced people in that meeting to sign, bullied students."

This tears it, as I say, "You're the ones who took people's jobs and had them disappeared without any process." I get up to go.

She gets up too, her face flushing. "You have no idea what you're doing. Don't you know how hard we've worked to create this school? You've got to stop, everything's falling apart." She looks at me directly for a moment, gauging my reaction with a puzzled and desperate look. I take it as a softening.

"I'm not trying to hurt the school. I'm part of the students who want, we just want a way to—"

And she hardens, interrupts, "I don't know what's happened. You used to have more respect."

"That's right, I did," I answer, and feel my words echo into a larger sense of my life and those around me. She begins to sob and now she's sliding down the wall, head back, face skyward, her eyes shut, tears along her cheekbones. It's a slow letting go, and I'm wrenched by seeing her breaking apart.

"I can't do anything else," I say, "I'm sorry," and begin to back away. I can't make the natural gesture, reach out and comfort her, and I feel as if we are caught under a giant net together as I turn for the door and air.

"Please," is the last I hear as I go. I'm shaking when I get outside. I look across the hall at what used to be Rosamund's door. Jess and Rosamund paid, and now Maureen is paying, but it's still not the same price. I hated seeing her like that. She almost broke me, I think as I hit the frigid air.

The deeply etched words—"a really big lesbian thing going on"— haunted me. By the time I left Martin's Falls, I knew it was no explanation, and I wanted to know more—who? where? how? My interest was acute, and yet now I feared the very subject, knowing that bringing it up would deep-six it forever. I now knew exactly what I was facing in my life: persecution, joblessness, and an assumption of criminal behavior, or behavior so morally questionable it could ban me from the community I had set so much store in, my first real community of women and the first place where I had power and exercised it—for myself and for others.

Red Light Green Light was no longer a game. All action must freeze—even the hot breath and sweat must evaporate into sudden pure stasis. *Red Light:* Unmoving. Unmoved. Unexpressed. Inexpressible. Unrevealed. Stopped. Never be caught in motion, yet always be closer to my goal.

Green Light: Run until the shadow begins to turn. I hear the numbers counted slowly out loud, know I only have a few seconds to reach the figure whose back is turned. This is the one who freezes me and all of us with judging eyes, who laughs, who says nothing and walks away to start the game again as we are made to return to our original positions. I push forward from the earth and strain to the tips of my outstretched hands to touch the shoulder now turning toward me. I am right there in the face of it—fear and all its followers dropping away as I run past and remember the feeling in the dreams, the flood of energy as I flew. But this time, I have caught up with myself and slow to stand my ground.

D. Gates, 1972

A VISION

Rebecca Brown

WHEN I was six my family moved to Spain. My father was in the military, and though my mother had not been happy with the peripatetic life our family led, she was excited about this posting. This posting would let her go to Europe and take her daughters, my older sister and me, to museums and historic homes and castles. My brother wasn't interested in any of that. Like my father, he preferred duck hunting. But "the girls," as my father and brother called Mom and us, loved going to museums. My sister, who wanted to be an artist, liked looking at the paintings. I liked looking at the armor. I loved those huge tall statues of silver and bronze, with their shiny shins and pointy, sectioned feet that looked like armadillos. I liked the plush royal blue-and-purple brocade and quilted cloth and chain mail. I liked looking at the face-guards with slits and wondering what it looked like inside. I loved the plumes on the helmets, the gold carved handles of the swords. I loved the red-and-white-striped and blue-and-gold-checked skirts the statues of the horses wore. I loved the stories I was learning to read about the olden days. I decided that I wanted to be a knight.

My best friend was our neighbor, Chuckie Thom. Chuckie and I would get ratty old bath towels from our moms and draw insignias on them with magic markers, dragons or castles or lions or gargoyles, and safety pin them around our necks so they'd hang down our backs like capes. Then we'd run around waving our rulers or our big brothers' baseball bats as if they were swords and yell, "But my Lord, I am not worthy! I am not worthy!" while we stabbed out the innards and chopped off the heads of our imaginary foes. We'd turn garbage can lids into shields and our fathers' pool cues into lances and joust, or go on a mission to find my brother's baseball trophy, the Grail.

Most often Chuck was King Arthur, but he also got to be Edward the Black Prince, Henry the Fifth or Richard the Lion Hearted. He had a choice. I, because I was a girl, was always Joan of Arc. Except for how she was burnt at the stake and her religion, which I didn't get, I liked Joan of Arc, so mostly I liked being her.

Sometimes, when Chuck had been called home for dinner and I played late alone, I would imagine things. I would get very, very quiet, then I would lift my arms straight up toward the sky, close my eyes and tip my head back so far I would get dizzy. Then I would wait. I waited until I could almost feel against my skin, or at least in the air above my skin, a touch. Or if not exactly a touch, at least the passing of something through the air beside me, a spirit or someone right next, or at least near to me. I waited until, although, because my eyes were closed I couldn't see I could, almost, or so it seemed, see something like a figure, like a ghost, a shape, or colors, inside my tight shut eyes. I waited until I almost heard, not in my ears, but in my head, a sound, like someone was saying something, whispering, as if someone was telling me a secret. I stayed like that, my head tipped back and waited for, like Joan of Arc, a vision.

When we moved back to the States, it was to Texas, where we had never lived before. The next year I entered sixth grade. All of the sixth grade teachers at Stephen F. Austin Elementary School, except the football coach who was also the principal, were women. All of the women teachers, except one, dressed up for school. Mrs. Kreidler, my homeroom teacher, never wore the same dress twice and her shoes always matched her dress. Once she brought a record to class and sang to us in her high thin voice, a song about the mountains. The dress she wore that day had a pattern of mountains and stars. Miss Bryant, the art and music teacher, wore pink or other pastels, usually suits with big shoulders and you could smell her perfume all the way inside the room when she walked in the hall. Mrs. Grant, the science teacher, was old and wore lots of powder and had bright, red, perfectly round circles on her cheeks and lots of shiny rings on her knobby hands. Sometimes she tripped on her heels.

Miss Hopkins, however, was different. She had short, straight black hair that she never curled and you could see that it was shaved at the back of her neck. She always wore penny loafers or flats, never heels. Her clothes were plain, black or gray or navy A-line skirts with light blue or white or beige open-collared shirts. She never wore dresses and never patterns or pastels. Her glasses did not have cats' eye frames or pointy frames or frames held on with a gold-looking chain the way the other teachers did. Her frames were plain and black. She taught us math.

The first day of class Miss Hopkins told us that our grades would be based "strictly on class average," the average of all your homework and tests. Miss Hopkins did not give extra credit. There was no arguing, no mickey mousing with Miss Hopkins. Everyone was afraid of her. Nobody misbehaved with her. Not even the football players or the cheerleaders.

This was different from other classes. Football was a huge, huge deal in our small Texas town. Football boys were let out of class to practice. Some of the teachers flirted with them, or with their dads, or looked the other way when the football boys copied from the smart kids during tests. Some teachers had been known to hold some big boys back a grade so they would be even bigger and play even harder the next year. Miss Hopkins, however, did none of that. She treated the football boys and cheerleader girls like anybody else. She treated everyone the same. She had no pets.

Every fall there were cheerleader tryouts, and for the weeks before the tryouts our gym periods were devoted to learning cheers. We'd have class on the playfield outside learning cheers, where, instead of doing softball or track or even exercises, we did cheers.

I hated cheers. I was bad at them and couldn't get my hand claps and my jumps and arm flaps to coordinate. I couldn't do the splits and I hated the leg kicks that you were supposed to do in a line like the can-can. I hated the way you were supposed to wiggle your butt and smile and squeal and yell that high stupid way. But it was class so I had to do it.

Most of the girls, the Brendas and RaeAnns and Darlenes, the cute ones, liked working on cheers and were looking forward to the tryouts. These were the girls who had a chance. But there were also other girls. Girls with names like Carmen or Maria or Rosa, girls with the wrong religion because they were Catholic. Or girls who were fat or smelly, or wore dirty, old-fashioned clothes. Girls who only lived there for a while before they had to move again. There was one girl with a limp and one girl who had peed at the Girl Scout meeting once and one retarded girl. These were the girls who did not have a chance.

I didn't have a chance either, but not because I was Mexican-American or poor or fat. I didn't have a chance because I didn't want to. I didn't want to be a cheerleader. I didn't want to wear the little skirts they did and worry—or hope—that the boys would see my underpants when I jumped up. I didn't want to go out with the boys and I didn't want to act the way girls did when they were around them. I was the only girl in the sixth grade class who didn't try out for cheerleader.

By the time I went to college in 1975, very far away from Texas, I wrote poetry, listened to cool music, ate vegetarian, had sex with boys and girls my own age and told stories. It was fun to tell my artsy, liberal, drunken, feminist young friends stories about Texas. I shaped the story of my not trying out for cheerleader as a mock heroic tale of escape from an oppressive, Southern-style femininity. Though I was a white girl who got to go to college, I allied myself, in my retelling, with the Mexican girls and the fat, poor girls who couldn't get away the way I did. I attributed to myself a sassy rebelliousness that I had never actually had as a kid. In fact I was self-conscious and any rebelling I ever did I only did in private.

A lot of my life occurred in private, more and more of it as I slipped away from childhood and toward whatever difficult thing was coming next. More and more I imagined things. I often did not understand them or admit them to myself and I certainly never told them to anyone else. But I imagined some things so earnestly, so hopefully and longingly, that in my mind, I think, I almost saw them.

It's right after the tryouts and it's a huge, huge deal that I have not tried out. It is the talk of the school. It is notorious. I go to Miss Hopkins.

No. No—she comes to me.

She comes to me. She puts one of her handsome hands—for I have looked at her hands and they are handsome, square and firm, with short, round nails, clean. Her watch is face down on her wrist, not face up like the other women's watches, and the band is dark brown leather, not thin and gold-looking like a bracelet. She puts her handsome, competent hand on my shoulder. I feel it on me. It feels firm as if it steadies me but also light, like pulling me, like lifting me toward—toward—. I can smell her skin, like Irish Spring soap, right next to me. I feel so much, like everything. And I can hear, I think, the sound of the air, its breath, as if the air is alive, around her marvelous hand.

She leans her face down close to me and says, her breath like mint, "I heard you didn't try out for cheerleader."

I can't—I don't—but I don't need to say anything.

Because she knows.

I look at her and, for the first time ever, see behind her glasses. Her eyes are blue, lighter than blue eyes usually are, like ice, but also with a warmth to them, like water, like you could fall into and be swept away. I see her start to smile, her thin lips somehow fuller, softening, and the skin creasing around her mouth and I see the shine on her white, white teeth, one canine slightly sharper than the rest. Her tongue is wet. I hear her do this little laugh, then something else from inside her throat as she removes, first, her plain black-framed glasses, then mine.

She tips my head back a bit and I close my eyes and tip my head further back and I am very still then feel something near my skin and hear a whisper, telling me.

I can't hear what she says.

Of course that didn't happen.

Not that, exactly. Not exactly then.

Her name was not Miss Hopkins. I was not thirteen.

But someone, sometime somethinged me. There was some thing I almost felt, if not beside my body then above me, in the air. Something or someone passed nearby. Or someone came toward me and I heard, almost, if not a voice, then something, then I saw and someone kissed me.

Though neither that, exactly.

I kissed *her*.

It happened later.

She turned a corner in the hall I couldn't see (though I have seen it since, yes, many times in memory and still I do). She stepped down the steps by the window in the hall I was standing in. I was talking to someone else who I forgot immediately because already it had happened.

I saw, in the light of the late afternoon, the perfect light go over her. I saw illuminated her perfect face, her slightly open mouth. A brilliant light surrounded her. It pulsed around her everywhere and I was almost blinded. Her hair was black, her eyes were blue, her mouth was slightly open. There was the way she breathed, the way her chest and shoulders rose and fell. There was the way her throat moved when she swallowed. There was the line of the throat. There was the cup in the flesh at the base of her throat. There was the light in the air around her. She was beautiful.

I wanted to put my mouth on her. I wanted to eat her alive. I wanted to possess her, to devour, to consume her. I wanted to . . . something . . . her into next year and back and back again. I wanted to, with her, annihilate myself.

I was, however, half her age.

For this and other reasons this did not occur.

Not then.

Later.

Later I went back to her and took us to the bed. Therein did we do what we were meant.

I still believe, despite the rest, that this was good.

I loved her.

I saw in her the possible. I saw the real embodiment of what, in some way, I had longed for years. I saw she who, though I could not possess, I might hold for a time.

I believe what I remember.

I believe that what I saw and did continues in a place outside of time, that it remains.

I believe that what remains occurs and will again.

I believe the vision I was shown, the body I was given.

I believe what I desired was made manifest as love.

This is what I tell of my religion.

Class photo, circa sixth grade, 1968-ish

RICHARD NIXON AND ME

Heather Lewis

I never thought I'd write my coming-out story because I never thought of myself as "in"—as in: in the closet, in hiding, incognito. If I was any of the "ins," the only one that fit was indiscreet. Though, in truth, I didn't realize this at the time, either. There was no need to. I grew up in a family where the kids could pretty much do as they pleased. Out of sight, out of mind—this worked pretty well for all concerned.

My early "cross-dressing," far from frowned upon, was convenient. I could wear my brother's hand-me-downs. This saved money. Something important, because my father spent wildly on luxuries, which in turn made necessities hard to come by. While Dad leased two vintage Bentleys and a Rolls Royce, Mom drove a VW bug. I paid the household oil bill, which ran at least $1,000 a month—more, once the five-car garage had to be heated along with that leviathan house and its out buildings. How did a kid that age come up with that kind of money? Don't ask, don't tell.

My brother and I lived a childhood full of the freedom that comes with neglect. That I got away with tomboy clothes was one thing, but he got away with skirts. No small feat for any young boy, though he knew enough to wear them only at home. I always figured we were lucky. From an insanely early age, we could do whatever we wanted—drink, do drugs, have sex. My parents traveled a lot, were hardly ever home, and were not the best at arranging childcare. They had larger concerns.

I remember the time one of our babysitters discovered our pot plants. Not that they were hidden. We'd never seen the need. She came to confront me, I suppose. Had my brother in tow, carried one of the baby plants. I was watching Mike Douglas, and—as was my habit after a hard day of fifth grade—sipping at a large glass of vodka I assumed passed for water. She backed away from this sight without uttering a word. My older and wiser eleven-year-old brother stuck around long enough to tell me I wasn't fooling anyone. He knew it was vodka. The message was hide it better, keep it under wraps. Something he was always much better at than I was—no doubt from necessity, given the skirts.

So looking back, it's probably not altogether surprising that what stands out are those times I suddenly and unpredictably took center stage. And while these times did revolve around "curing" me, straightening out my kinks, even then I understood I was a sideshow, a diversion. Something to take my parents away from their own considerable and mounting troubles.

This is where Richard Nixon comes in. If he hadn't been caught, I wouldn't have either. Though "caught," while it might be the right word for him, wasn't really the right word for what happened to me. *Noticed* was more like it. The whole story here, the long one, would take years to write, so this is the short one, the highlight show. Suffice it to say my father'd gotten in tight with Nixon. Wound up in the deep end.

At first, Nixon meant trips to the White House, not just for my parents, but sometimes my brother and I went along, too. For these excursions he wore one of those little boy suits—gray flannel, short pants. I wore little girl suits, handpicked by a saleslady at Saks. But when Nixon came to us, when his helicopter dropped him off for a power dinner party, followed by a sleepover, it was me, not my brother, my father decided should dress up in uniform. An FAO Schwarz admiral suit to be exact. Another instance where my cross-dressing was convenient.

These were strange times, surreal even. That visit especially, what with Secret Service there days in advance. When they scoured the property, the toy rifle that gave them a scare was mine, not my brother's. I didn't know until after Nixon left that there'd been protestors at the foot of the front driveway. That they'd camped there for weeks. That this was why we kept taking the back driveway. Maybe my parents were afraid that if I knew I'd run down and join them.

My politics were already a complex mush of Joan Baez liner notes and nightly news horror. I went to a small Quaker school because they had nursery school, while the tony private school started with kindergarten. My mother wanted us out of the house that extra year early. At school, the teachers wore moratorium armbands—the men had long hair and beards, the women wore miniskirts. The kids wore uniforms, but nearly everyone, it seemed, had a guitar, or beads, or a POW bracelet. I wanted to be older. By fourth grade, I could argue either side politically.

And I did argue—at home and at school—though my position and intensity depended entirely on location. At home, dinner was warfare. My father and I became enemies in battle. I wouldn't know for over two decades that I'd intuitively picked hobbyhorse causes to match operations in which he was directly involved. The bombing of Cambodia, various coups in South America—I didn't know I was hitting nerves, but somehow I did know. The personal wasn't political, the political was personal.

What somehow slipped by me was Watergate. Perhaps the same instincts that knew where to hit knew what not to touch. And, too, I had my own distractions—women, chief among them. By twelve or thirteen, I couldn't get girls, but I could get women. The girls I knew at that age, at that time, were scared of other girls when it came to sexual encounters. And, truthfully, I wasn't much interested in girls anyway. I was already more used to grownups, more comfortable with them.

Of course, it's not unusual for girls to harbor crushes on older women. It's practically expected, possibly even accepted. I do admit that actually getting involved at that age, with a woman of a considerably different age, might be somewhat unusual. But it seemed I had a knack for turning these girlhood fantasies into realities. And there seemed no end to the elaborate entanglements I'd wind up in.

In part, this kept happening because I was always looking for a place to stay—to get away from my parents if they were home, or to get fed and have some company if they weren't. If I couldn't get something together it meant either endless fighting or too much time alone in that big empty house, scrounging for food. So getting involved with older women—ones with cars and houses and who knew how to cook—solved multiple problems.

This system actually began very early and innocently. I'd worked versions of it since I was eight. My parents liked to tell their friends I rode horses, so I'd been hanging around stables since I was four. By eight, I'd started staying with my riding instructor and her husband— they'd let me drink, but there wasn't any sex. Or I'd stay with the families of friends from school, but let's face it, no one can stand a houseguest for months, especially not one with chronic bronchitis. I needed to keep moving around. I needed to keep looking.

By about twelve I'd found what I was really looking for: women. Women who provided a much more interesting solution to my housing problem. These women ranged from mid-thirties to forties. Some were newer, hipper riding instructors, or other women who hung around horses or horse shows. They were usually married, or had boyfriends who were.

I usually managed to play multiple roles: surrogate daughter, lover, confidante, whatever. And it helped that I'd fuck the men, too. When I was older I learned to make money off this particular flexibility; moved up from what you might call "trading" or "being kept," though I didn't think of it that way at the time. So this system, for the most part, was quite pleasant and lucrative, though not exactly risk-free. I would eventually find myself subpoenaed in a particularly nasty divorce, labeled as the wife's other woman. The wife's solution to this problem was that I protect her through perjury. Let's just say that, by then, I'd wised up.

But what I did away from home, to get away from home, isn't really the point. What was happening at home—what I knew and didn't know, couldn't know or couldn't let myself know—led to my own peculiar outing. However improbably, Watergate led to it. As I went from preteen to teen, Nixon crossed a line, too. Now there was a ceasefire, an end to dinnertime warfare. And while I'd always been the smartass, I was suddenly dumbstruck and dumbfounded.

The outside tensions mounting on that big showy house put all internal disputes on hold. Watergate brought our family together in a heretofore unheard-of way before tearing us irrevocably apart. I remember that time in confused moments. I remember that time fondly. Only much later would I learn the extent of my father's involvement, and I would learn it from books. At the time I assumed I exaggerated his role. Later, I discovered I'd minimized it.

There was a lot of traffic in and out of the house. Bebe Rebozo would come in the middle of the night. So would others, but they're still alive, so I'm not going to name them. If I learned nothing else from this time, I learned paranoia. After these visits or a phone call, my father would disappear. When I asked where he was, my mother invariably gave one of three answers: Washington, Zurich, or London. Unlike my father, she wasn't much of a liar.

When put on the spot about whether he was having an affair, she was similarly blunt, saying, "It's a woman in London." Actually, I hadn't asked if he were having an affair. I'd asked if the affair he was having was with his secretary. An unintentional trick question. I think I was eleven.

It turned out that the "woman in London" was just one in a long line. Again, much later from books, I'd learn he'd siphoned company money for her. As CEO of *Reader's Digest*, he'd used his position to advance hers, just as he'd done with Nixon. He set her up with work, an apartment.

I'd learn later, too, from books, that he'd run money out of the country. That a call from Nixon's secretary, Rose Mary Woods, arranged the most damning of these trips. He'd flown down, picked up $100,000 in cash from the White House safe. Next he took it to true safety in Switzerland, depositing it in a numbered account. By now, Carl Bernstein, under Deep Throat's instructions, was following the money. This in turn meant trailing my father, who managed to dodge Bernstein's repeated calls. Bernstein was endlessly told my father was out of the office, out of town, out of the country. At least this was true. He was busy in Zurich again.

Another call from Woods, late in the game—by now everyone knew what we'd known for some time—was answered by my brother. He asked if her foot could reach the pedal for the tape recorder. The tapes, and the famous erasure, were common knowledge by now, as was the contortionist's stretch Woods had performed to explain it. My mother, who quickly took the phone, couldn't help laughing. Though afterwards she reminded him and me both that Rose Mary Woods had always been so nice to us kids at the White House. That it was mean to tease her.

As I remember it, the three of us—my mother, brother and me—were on some sick, giddy high. She'd whisper that the phones were being tapped or loudly announce that Martha Mitchell was the only one telling the truth. My mother got quieter after Martha Mitchell had her phone yanked from the wall while talking to Helen Thomas. So did Mrs. Mitchell, who was drugged and locked up. She briefly resurfaced, calling herself a political prisoner, saying she knew all about Watergate and would leave her husband, former Attorney General

John Mitchell, if he didn't get out of politics. Mitchell by now was running CRP, a.k.a. CREEP—the Committee to Re-Elect the President.

John Mitchell would, of course, later be a prisoner himself, go to jail. Not so my father who, like Rebozo, eluded indictment despite the efforts of prosecutors to trace the mysterious movements of that same hundred grand Dad had spirited out of the country. A grand jury was impaneled. It would be years before my father would attempt to explain away that hundred grand. In an interview with Bob Wood-ward, my father steadfastly proclaimed his innocence, employing a logic even more circuitous than the path he'd taken to hide the money in question.

By the time he gave that interview, it was 1976 and I was fifteen. The giddy highs of the early seventies had long since passed. Watergate had wound down, and we were all wrung out. Nixon had been forced into resignation two years earlier. Now my father was about to be forced into mandatory retirement, and I was about to be forcibly removed from boarding school. He and I had embarked on a collision course. But before we collided, our simultaneous disgrace provided one of the handful of tender moments of our embattled relationship.

Right before Christmas vacation, I'd gotten caught at school not with a girl, but with drugs and boys. Probably an inevitable turn of events—the drugs, at least. I'd come back to school after a summer on the horse show circuit, strung out on smack and hung up on a woman twice my age. I was neither the star athlete nor star student I'd been the year before. Now, I spent most of my time trying to feed both my habit for the drug and my hunger for the woman.

The first day home after this debacle the family went out to din-ner. Not just the immediate, but the extended family. The dinner was painful. I was waiting to hear my fate, slated to be delivered that same night by phone. My father looked at me somewhere between entrees and coffee, and said something like, "You want to get out of here, don't you?" We drove home together. The way I remember it, the phone was ringing when we came into the house. I answered it, hearing the voice of my field hockey coach. She was yet another woman I had a painful hunger for, which in part led to her catching me with drugs I quickly hid.

If anyone else had caught me I might not have confessed. She lived in our dorm, was responsible for what went on there. She heard noises, came to investigate. The boys partying with us literally jumped from the third-story windows. I got caught on the stairs with the stash in my hand. I knew she knew. I had to come clean. So I went down to her apartment, where I stood in the entryway and gave up the goods, oblivious of her attempts to shut me up.

It turned out another faculty member was there. She tried to persuade him to let it go, cover it up, it was just a little bit of pot. But he wouldn't budge. Now she was the one who got to deliver the news. I knew it was bad when she asked to speak to my parents. I made her tell me. They'd booted me and the boys; the other girls were off the hook.

Now both my father and I had been booted. Again I'd learn later from books that he'd kept his CEO job this long only because his boss, DeWitt Wallace, had decided it was safer to keep Dad on salary, under his control, until the outcome of the grand jury investigation. Nixon's resignation marked the end of Watergate for most, but not us. Things had changed, though. My father now dodged Nixon's calls, not Carl Bernstein's, and he'd actually talked to Bob Woodward, however evasively. While certainly no fan of Nixon's, I remember feeling Dad should've stuck by his friend. Good thing it'd be twenty years before I found out his exploits had landed Lila Wallace—DeWitt's wife and *Reader's Digest*'s cofounder—in a hospital with a perforated ulcer.

She was my godmother, I was very fond of her. I sat enthralled, watching her drink martinis from a solid gold goblet that came from King Tut's tomb. She gave me my name. And during that infamous Nixon visit, she sat me on her already frail lap in my full dress admiral's uniform and told me she owned me, could take me home whenever she pleased. Admittedly the wording was a bit odd, but I wished she'd done it—taken possession.

But again, I digress, it's hard not to. Back to the end of 1976. Conventional wisdom still said my father was headed for jail. The aforementioned grand jury was still impaneled, but would soon be dismissed. Now off that hook, he was out of a job. Not that he'd actually been doing his job during these years. As one account puts it: "His only memorable achievement, in the twilight of his career, was to drink champagne from the shoe of retiring editor Audrey Dade." And it turned out that the girlfriend in London would do him in, provide the proverbial last straw. The second question DeWitt Wallace put to my father's successor before handing him the job was: "You can get rid of Hobe's girlfriend, can't you?"

An editor would be assigned to deal with this woman, who was by now reading manuscripts and insisting they be delivered to her by limousine. Perhaps this woman's extravagant tastes had something to do with why I paid the utility bills, while my father wore custom-made shirts from Turnbull and Asser.

Now retired, Dad busied himself for a time, as did I. I plunged back into horses, drugs and the woman. But he soon grew bored with his activities and began meddling in mine. He tried, I guess, to play country gentleman, exhibiting a newfound interest in horses. But while his pension was generous this front was impossible to maintain, way beyond his considerably scaled-back means. That monstrous house and anything else with any conceivable value was being sold, all at bargain basement prices. We were liquidating, liquefying.

Meanwhile, I was having similar trouble keeping up appearances. Keeping up at all. Now at public high school—at least my disgrace saved my parents the expense of boarding-school tuition—I played mild-mannered A student in the morning and championship rider in the afternoon. But nights I devoted entirely to scoring drugs and the woman. By now it'd become impossible to determine which had the greater hold, the two were inseparable. Things were getting harder to juggle, but I managed.

I managed until my father's still-wandering eye landed on this same woman. Goes without saying his London girlfriend would have little interest in an ex-CEO. Turns out my girlfriend was similarly disinclined, which meant disaster was imminent. Dad was jealous, though whether of me, or this woman, that's still hard to gauge. The simple answer is both. It's probably the right one, too. All of a sudden, after years of who cares, my penchant for women, or at least for this particular woman, had become not only a problem, but my father's pet problem. And what with his so-called retirement, he had considerable time on his hands. Given the circumstances of that retirement, he also had plenty of fury, frustration, humiliation, you name it.

You could say "curing" me became an eccentric man's hobby. One he worked at with vindictive precision. And one he could afford because his pension plan included extremely good health insurance. It began with sending me to a shrink. This guy told me my father had said I was in love with a woman. Before I could say anything to this, he said not to worry, I wasn't gay, just rebelling. He then said he'd been told I'd got kicked out of school for pot. He pulled out his prescription pad. As he scribbled, he told me I was addicted to pot. That the pills he'd prescribed would take care of that.

Admittedly, I was confused. I'd been diagnosed as addicted to one of the few drugs I'd never much bothered with and told I wasn't gay. Maybe the shrink was confused, too. In any case, I left his office with that little piece of white paper. I liked drugs. How bad could it be?

I had no idea what I was in for. My father, however, had accomplished several things at once. I just didn't know it yet. I still don't know whether he knew it, whether this was design or luck, or again some combination of the two.

The pills turned out to be old-school anti-depressants, meaning the kind that depress you, flatten you, literally cloud your vision. I was advised not to drive on them. Driving was another thing my brother and I had been doing since we were kids. And now, when I actually had a driver's license, I suddenly couldn't drive. Any suburban teenager's nightmare, but in this case catastrophic. My life up until now had been almost entirely unsupervised. I hadn't even lived at home in years, what with boarding school and life on the road with the horses and the woman. Now one visit to a shrink and I was under a microscope and marooned in my parents' new and much-smaller house.

Worse still, I was cut off from the woman. I guess if he couldn't have her, I couldn't either. This in itself was agony, but add to it being cut off from Quaaludes, our then drug of choice. I learned later, again from books, that what ensued was classic barbiturate withdrawal. Maybe begging my terrified drug-phobic mother for a Quaalude should've tipped me off sooner, but it didn't. I thought I was truly mad, truly insane, I thought I was going out of my mind.

My mother was assigned to dole out the pills—a blessing in disguise. She didn't quite believe in them. And she was the one who figured out they were the reason I could no longer read. She had cause for suspicion—another thing I would learn years too late. This same shrink blamed her for whatever he couldn't pin on me. He'd tried to get her hooked on Valium.

My father went blameless. These two men became a formidable tag team. I'd listen to the shrink tell me to go on dates with my father, that he wanted a "relationship" with me, meant well, and on and on. Meanwhile my father'd slip in and tell the guy whatever he felt like—all, of course, with my best interests at heart.

Some things eased up. I got through withdrawal, regained my senses. Having me around was a bit of a bother, let alone driving me around. My mother stopped doling the pills. I started going to CBGB's, Danceteria, and that afterhours club Berlin. Things went back to semiabnormal, but they weren't over. The worst was yet to come, only I didn't know it—no doubt a good thing.

A few years prior, my ever-contradictory father had put me on to Patti Smith. Because he'd suggested I'd like her, I was determined I wouldn't. But being all of thirteen when her first album came out, and having come out myself way before then—androgyny, drugs, bisexuality—she naturally presented an irresistible package. I'd gone to CBGB's back then, too. I'd gone wherever she played. Another thing nobody'd much noticed.

This time around, though, my father cast her as not just a threat, but *the* threat. He'd convinced himself I was fucking her. He also convinced the shrink. I wish, but my groupie skills were not yet that well developed. I didn't talk to the shrink, but based on my father's delusions, I wound up on Thorazine. From here things got more aggressive, and given this drug, which I knew nothing about, I was fast losing any means of self-defense.

I graduated from high school, much against the advice of this same shrink. I'd carried a large course load after getting kicked out of boarding school, so by senior year I could make it through on very few classes. But the shrink did make sure I didn't make it to college. By now it was hard to determine how much this guy acted on his own and how much in collusion with my father. It still is. Add to this a terribly tangled relationship with this shrink's young, pretty, and inexperienced protégé, who I'll call Beth. While I talked, and flirted, and soon wound up having sex with her, my father made strategic strikes.

I'd been assured by Beth that what was said between us stayed between us, unless it presented a danger to me. Somehow, though, drinking, taking nonprescription drugs, or even the occasional single-person car wreck didn't seem to qualify as dangerous. But my reunion with the aforementioned woman—or sex with any woman other than Beth—got immediately reported back to the shrink and then to my father.

I'd find this out only when the shrink would call me in. First came the threats to lock me up. Next, scared-straight style visits to loony bins. Next the first lockup. Against both the judgment and wishes of Beth, our hapless young therapist, I was sent to a "therapeutic community/school." One of those "your bags are packed" ambushes where you either comply or get stuck with a syringe. My new roommate cheerfully informed me she'd been raped by an older woman, too. Presumably this meant we had much in common, would get on just great.

It didn't take long to learn that the so-called teachers who'd been advertised as therapists were actually all in therapy. A not-so-subtle distinction. My chemistry professor often came to class catatonic, clutching a teddy bear. Meanwhile, Beth's attempts to visit were blocked, our phone calls first cut short, then cut off entirely. It was not out of the question that the object of this little foray might be to separate us.

I managed to get out in three months. While out on parole for Christmas, I begged my father not to send me back. In another of our few tender moments, he caved. And he was the one who went to collect my stuff from this place. He returned so shaken he couldn't talk about it beyond mumbled regrets. He'd never actually seen the place. These mumblings marked a third tender moment.

I had a reprieve, but not for long. I still hadn't learned my lesson. The cure hadn't worked. And I was still under the care of this same shrink, which meant still seeing Beth. I made the same gaff, telling Beth about yet another woman, and again she reported back. My father, having been informed, made his last strategic strike. This time he told the shrink that his sister was manic-depressive, and perhaps I was, too. Eureka, they'd solved it, solved me.

Once more I was called into the shrink's office. I listened to a masterful pitch for Lithium. He made it sound like a drug addict's dream. That it would allow me to manipulate my mood at will. Next he described me as a Virginia Woolf–type time bomb. I'd certainly kill myself by forty. Now I was some kind of suicidal genius. But through the miracle of Lithium I could be saved. The flattery worked, the pitch worked. I fell for it hook, line, and sinker. Took another script to the drug store, this time believing in magic.

I didn't know you needed a blood test for dosage, but presumably the shrink did. For the next ten days I didn't eat or sleep. No need to, this stuff made me high as a kite. Unlike most actual manic-depressives, I had no experience with mania. And while I'd done speed, of course, and coke, downers were always more my thing. I'd never gone so hyped for so long. You could say my judgment was a bit impaired. This set the stage for the last act.

The shrink suggested I sign myself into a hospital, just for a couple of weeks to stabilize the dosage. Even impaired, I didn't immediately bite. So Beth was brought in for bait. Unlike me, she'd learned her lesson, was on board this time, though I didn't know it yet. She coaxed me and I began to waver. I don't remember why, but I was at my brother's house when I called her. I do remember I was alone, staring into his kitchen, which had this amazing pile-up of empty Dewars bottles. The same scotch my parents drank by the gallon. The sight of all those bottles seemed to be what made me call.

It was night, a Friday, I think. I know Reagan had just been elected to his first term. Time had passed. I'd later joke it was his election that tipped me over. Beth came and picked me up. Took me to this place. I signed myself in. My parents didn't even know. The weekend meant two more days of no sleep or food, even so I realized I'd made a mistake, a big one—been duped.

My father bailed me out, took me home. That might have been that, but it wasn't. I was still on the stuff—the lithium. By now it'd turned me into some punk girl version of Travis Bickle. For reasons I don't recollect, I was wearing army fatigues, combat boots, and a lot of those heavy silver biker rings. My mother was in the kitchen cooking dinner. My father and I were watching the news. As my kind of luck would have it, Cambodia, perhaps then still Democratic Kampuchea, was news that night—the Khmer Rouge, Pol Pot, the killing fields—they were dredging it all up again, showing old footage.

That's all it took. The fuse was lit. The only question now was who'd explode first—me or Dad. I think it might've been simultaneous combustion. But he was the one on his feet first. When I hit him, I believed it was self-defense. If I hadn't been wearing the damn rings, I might not have done damage. My mother tried to break it up—a first. Somehow she and I wound up on the stairs. But how she fell, honestly I don't know. I only know I didn't intend to hurt her. I think I was just trying to get her attention.

She wasn't badly hurt, not physically. But she sat at the foot of those stairs yelling she never wanted me inside their house again. Meanwhile my father was on the phone to the cops—or rather a cop. A friend/employee of his. This guy drove me back to the snake pit. This time they took my jewelry, hell, they took everything. This time they doped me to the gills. This time it was progress when I finally got out of a tiny cell to roam a locked ward with women who'd had lobotomies, and I assure you I'm not exaggerating.

I'll spare you the gorier details. Things you'd expect but might not believe. After all, nobody believed Martha Mitchell either, at least not until it was way too late to do her any good. So let's just say that given the condition of the other inhabitants, I was a real find for the night nurse. She made a bundle pimping me to the orderlies. I did eventually engineer my release, aided and abetted by a young woman working in occupational therapy. She was the only person who knew or rather cared that I didn't belong there. She coached me.

For added insurance I managed to get a guy I knew to come pose as my boyfriend. We went so far as to announce our engagement, and I was released shortly after. At the time I believed the engagement stunt was what cinched it. Now I assume it had less to do with the insurance I'd arranged than with my parents' Blue Cross, which no doubt had been bilked to the max.

The doctor who released me was the same one who'd been there the night I'd signed myself in. I hadn't seen him or any doctor since, save the one time he'd called on me to act as playmate for a wealthy woman friend of his who was there taking a much-needed rest from the jet-set. If my whole time there had been like that one week with her—good booze, good drugs, good food, and good sex—I might never have left. But it wasn't. It was a beautiful fluke amidst grueling ugliness.

As this guy released me, he laughed, even gloated about the amount of Thorazine he'd managed to pump into me. I'd remember the number. Again, I learned from a book that this dose was more than double what was considered safe for an actual psychotic. I got the point. I resolved never again to display an emotion, never again to state an opinion, and never again to fall in love with a woman.

Needless to say, I got away from my family. But I still kept those resolutions for nearly two years. The first two fell away first. The last one was lost to a woman I'll call Ingrid. And while falling for Ingrid would begin yet another sordid story, it's the end of this one.

The author (right) during the '70s with a woman whose name she can't remember

CHERRY PICKER

Chrystos

COMING out from compulsory heterosexual strait jackets is a star quilt of many colors, slowly sewn. A pale blue inner circle of diamonds is her small convertible driving away with my heart in the backseat when I was four. I don't remember her name. I can't ask my mother, as we carry angry silence between us. From hidden photos I found sorting through boxes in the basement as a young girl, I know my first love was a pilot during World War II—a crop duster like my mother, flying over the fields of California with loads of poison. I didn't think to steal & keep the picture of them leaning against a tiny plane in khaki slacks, their arms slung casually over each other, squinting into the light with sunny grins. My father took off after I was born during a fight about money, leaving my mother with none. The sleek pilot courted my mother until the devastating day when she drove away. I knew even then I wasn't allowed to ask why. I'm still coming apart with love of her memory.

A river-green flourish of diamonds, the color of JonnieLee's eyes, surrounds the blue. She took me down to her basement, where we climbed in under the floor by way of an access door to the crawl space. In the delicious darkness she whispered that I needed to rub cream on her breasts so they wouldn't be dry. Oh, did I need to. I was gawky, just ten. She was my goddess, empress and fire. I wasn't good enough to be her friend. She mocked my adoration as we roamed the streets kicking the can or calling out, "Mother may I?" Her Navajo mother was my mother's best friend. I wanted to be JonnieLee, to crawl into her confident, mocking skin & taste her arrogance from the inside.

Spangled with glints of gold are the pieces of Lynne, whose red Irish hair was thick & curly. We played boyfriend (Lynne) & girlfriend (me) on our porches, with old nylon stockings knitted together as my mink stole. Her imaginary red convertible had a real steering wheel we'd found in one of many vacant lots of debris. She loved to drive, cruising very fast, her arm shielding me from the wind. We practiced kissing for hours, supposedly so we'd be ready for the boys, none of whom ever kissed that well. When she slept over, my mother gave us her bed, because mine was a small & narrow iron cot. Lynne let me touch the beautiful wild thatch of hair beginning below her belly, hair as glorious as that on her head, especially fascinating to me because I didn't have any yet. She guided my fingers to please her, but I was too frightened of the catholic curse of sin to let her touch me. Years later I heard she wasn't married & had a red sports car, but I didn't pursue her. The simplicity of our explorations couldn't hold the complications of my activism and her comfort. I continue to smile when I see women with that red gold hair, imagine kissing them on a porch, pretending to go very fast.

I was taken to psychiatrists by the school because my grades didn't match my IQ scores. I was obsessed with a succession of best friends. One of the cheerleaders shouted at me that I was a lezzie, so I beat her up & got suspended. My French uncle continued to rape me regularly. My mother's drinking & rage worsened. I tried to strangle her. I was sent to juvie where the other girls beat me up because I was the only Indian & hadn't figured out how to beat up gangs yet. During PE one day, Charlene, whom I didn't like, jumped on top of me & started kissing me. I threw her off & so the dyke PE teacher suspended me again. I discovered the bliss of beer, the delights of drugs. I fucked high school boys and older ones without enjoying it, in a frenzy to disappear, to obliterate my uncle. I worked as a hooker when I left home at seventeen. I couldn't turn tricks without heroin, like most women. I spent my eighteenth birthday in Napa State Hospital (the loony bin), buried under their drugs, which were considerably less interesting. None of these years held any stars.

The shrinks moved me off the violent ward to the pink cottage where they kept the women they thought they might let go someday, after they tested my IQ. Terry & I fell into each other's haze. She showed me how to cut my arms with razors to let out the pain. She collected her blood in a coffee cup to take to her psychiatrist. I carefully let mine gush into the toilet where I could flush it away & not be caught. I pulled my black cardigan state sweater down over my relief. I was still alive despite their drugs. Terry's hair was long & thick, bleached blond, perhaps because she wanted to be a princess in a fairy tale instead of real. We wrote letters to one another, passionately declaring our eternal love, which the technicians stole. One night when she was sitting on my bed in the dorm after lights out, as I brushed her hair, they threw on the lights in a frenzy of disgust & separated us for being lesbians. We were too drugged and too frightened to do more than hold hands. The head nurse was a lesbian, who called Terry's mother, who came the next day to take her home to her psychiatrist father, to whom she had not spoken in over four years. I was sent to the old women's ward for punishment, where my job was to feed the bed-bound ladies, some of them in restraints all the time. The stench of urine & untreated cancer was overwhelming. I wrote long, intense letters to Terry, which I could not send, hiding them under my green plastic mattress. Terry's stars are deep burgundy, & I bleed into the other colors when I mourn that we never made love.

Then Maggie was dragged onto our ward, in hot pink tights & purple smock, her teeth glittering with mischief. Far from being depressed by the surroundings, she sang bawdy songs to the old ladies she fed, opening our misery with laughter. She was from a wealthy Marin family who sent her there to straighten her up & scare her into agreeing to marry the man they wanted to sell her off to, although they wouldn't say it like that (she did). Somehow her wedding veil was among her belongings. She liked to wear it to the vast dining barrack because it annoyed the nurses so much. It was very beautiful, expensive lace which she trailed behind her like indifference. One day Maggie & I decided to get married. The guy who thought he was jesus was happy to perform our ceremony, held in the courtyard of our adjoining wards, surrounded by hundreds of old glass windows barred with iron grates. I wore Maggie's veil & my Napa State Hospital white cardigan tied to make a train. We both carried huge bouquets of lilacs, which were blooming wildly in that hot, dry country. All our patient guests cheered & clapped so loudly that we couldn't hear what jesus was saying. We only got to stroll down the sidewalk, showered with rice that Edith had filched from the kitchen where she was one of the cooks, before our union was rudely interrupted by burly male guards straining with anger in their white uniforms.

Everyone was locked down, some of us in solitary, & the bells went off for riot alert. Maggie's poor veil was ripped apart by their feet & rage & arms. The head nurse (another lesbian) called Maggie's mother that night, & before I had a chance to kiss her hello & goodbye, Maggie was driven away the next morning in her father's limp-dick limo (her words again), as we ate our powdered eggs, silently depressed.

However, Maggie was a very sneaky & smart girl. She calmly arrived the following day in her VW bug (custom-painted purple, as are her stars) & said she had come back to collect her belongings, which no one had thought to pack up. Her mother, a master materialist (probably hoping for the veil), was very understanding. The hospital wanted to be accommodating in hope of future funds. So Maggie surprised me by returning to busily pack up not very much. We weren't allowed to talk, & the nurses were watching us sharply until Ursula, understanding our need, threw her tennis shoe at the TV, screaming. Maggie palmed me a note to meet her by the lilac hedge behind the building, where she had conveniently parked. I left as though going to my new job at the dairy (cow shit apparently being a step up from human shit). The other women realized Ursula's intentions & took off their keds, too. My last sight of that day room (where I had been declared incurably schizophrenic) was of flying sneakers, screaming technicians, breaking glass, & laughing patients—a really lovely melee. Because, of course, Maggie had returned to rescue me. We pulled out the backseat of her bug & I lay down across the battery. She laid a Mexican blanket over me, while I tried to project looking like a backseat. She piled her boxes, mostly empty, on top of me. The guards at the main gate were distracted by another call from the ward where the women who weren't strapped down could not be contained. Maggie smiled, they gave her back her driver's license, & off we went. On the other side of town, Maggie freed me from my seat charade & I tasted the wind in my hair for the first time in more than a year. She drove me to Big Sur, where I'd never been & they wouldn't look for me (I had seven previous escapes, which is why I was on the violent ward so often, a curious juxtaposition—is freedom indeed violence, for lesbians?). In her trunk she had a sleeping bag, some food, money, & clothes that didn't say Napa State on them for me. She dropped me near an overpass under which fellow fugitives of all kinds were camped, driving back to Marin, where perhaps she did escape marrying him. My belongings & three cartons of writing may still be in a dusty storage room at Napa. I guess I'm AWOL. Freedom's worth the loss. If not for Maggie, I'd still be in the loony bin, incurable & terrified, not allowed to be a lesbian except with technicians. But I ripped that nurse out of the quilt.

Big Sur was rich with empty summer houses we raided for canned goods as a gang of teenage runaways, Vietnam War deserters, Rez escapees & drug dealers. We caught and roasted a wild pig. We hid out from the park rangers. We flirted with soldiers from the base for bags of potato chips, Hostess lemon pies, & chocolate bars. It was my theory we wouldn't get scurvy if we ate the pies. We dropped acid & had orgies & stole into the mud baths at night. I was in a fog & detoxing from the nuthouse drugs, until one dusk when my eyes became diamond sharp at the sight of a thin young guy getting out of a hitchhiking ride at the convenience store near the campgrounds. He had black wavy hair cut in a DA falling forward over his face, wearing a leather motorcycle jacket that oozed sex. Our eyes caught across the parking lot & I fell in love like slamming into earth. I walked over, offering my open bag of BBQ pork rinds. Her reaching hand made me laugh & I blurted out, "I thought you were a guy." She looked me up & down intensely, startled me by stroking my crotch with a quick secret movement, & growled, "Good."

Sherri was an excellent con artist, but I thought she was my dreams finally coming to my bed. She convinced some soldiers to take us out to dinner at the fancy hippie restaurant called Nepenthe, where with awe I watched her manipulate them for drinks & drugs & money. I'd never seen a woman who could get things out of men without having to give too much up. Then they wanted to go down to the beach & have a fire, which I knew was illegal, but I remained silent. The four of us built a roaring one while Sherri continued to beguile them with tall tales. The boys drank from six-packs, while she matched them beer for beer without seeming to get drunk. I became bored and decided to wander off down the beach. I was watching the lace come & go until I heard the small brass bell from India she wore on her ankle coming toward me. I went still because I knew I was about to fall right off the flat, known universe into a sea of colors. She turned my face with her hands & kissed me with her tongue, opening every pore in my body. I gasped, "I've never kissed a woman before." She chuckled, slapped my nipple lightly & said, "Now you'll never stop." All those strait jackets had wiped Lynne from my mind.

Sherri & I staggered over the sand dunes, kissing, her hands on my breasts, looking for a depression to hide in. My shirt was off & she was sucking my nipple when the soldiers came over the rise with a blaring flashlight & started shouting that we were gross. Perhaps they would have killed us then, except the Spirits were with us. From the opposite way came an angry park ranger who had seen our fire & was only interested in chasing all of us out. Sherri managed to convince our "dates" to drive us back to the cabin where she was staying, arguing all the way. Frightened, I huddled in her arms & longed for our own convertible & the wind to blow the soldiers away.

The cabin was dark, without electricity. She lit candles on our way to her bed, which was hard & strewn with clothes. Her kisses became abrupt & jagged, as I embraced her weight on me with an entirely new joy. She rocked her hips into me, coming with a gasp & then silence, as she fell asleep. I was accustomed to not having an orgasm with men, but I expected differently once I finally figured out how to be with a woman. All night I was restless as she slept, afire with pain, uncertainty, arousal dropped off a cliff. Around dawn I finally slept. I was awakened when another woman came into the room with a tray of grapefruits cut open & a shivering white bowl of yogurt. Her name was Sandy. I gradually understood that she was Sherri's lover, who had put aside her feelings of betrayal to be gracious to me, an act that continues to catch me by surprise. Not long after, Sherri hissed at me that I was nothing but a straight girl as she dressed & took off abruptly. Perhaps I was supposed to become the source of a raging fight. I still admire Sandy's deftness in out-maneuvering the manipulator. Sherri didn't return that evening. I wept. Sandy comforted me, explaining that Sherri always did whatever she wanted, would not make any kind of plans or commitment with anyone. I understand now that she was running hard, maybe from admitting that she was a lesbian. As far as I know, in those days, not one of us was proud. Our strutting arrogance was a cover for fear of being killed.

For two days, Sandy & I talked about Sherri, waiting in the cabin for her return. Sandy wanted for us to make love, but I was fruitlessly focused on Sherri & thought that would be a betrayal of her. Then we hitchhiked to San Francisco, where my life continued to be a hustle for drugs, for food, for a safe place to crash. I was beaten up in the Doggie Diner for being a queer by young thugs before I even had my first orgasm with a woman. I turned tricks, dressed up as a dominatrix because it was better money, I drank, I roamed the streets looking for Sherri, the torch burning me inside out. My first orgasm was with my stone butch pimp, named Two Bits, in front of about ten men who had all paid $50 to watch us. I wasn't in love with her, although she claimed to be in love with me. Maybe. More likely, I was good money for dope. The stars were crooked & Sherri left a bloody wake. Almost ten years later, dancing at Amelia's, I was sweaty & high when I carried my empty glass to the steel shelf near the bar where the dirties went to the dishwasher. A hand reached for my glass. I became absolutely still. Sherri's hand. I ducked down & shouted, "Sherri!" Her eyes were dull & angry as she snarled, "What?!" She had no idea who I was, this woman I had loved passionately, foolishly, in the underground tunnels of my heart, right through all my affairs with many other women. I cried, "You brought me out. You were my first lover!" Tears ran down my face as I folded my humiliation into a hole of oblivion. She looked me over in an abbreviated parody of our first night & said, "So?" turning away.

Late that night on the way home, I took off the bell I'd worn on my ankle & left it on someone's porch step. The leather thong was so old & hard that I had to cut it with the butch's pocket knife I had with me. Sherri was the only one who didn't actually get any cherries. Her use of me didn't matter, because I found out how to get in bed with women. I sewed her dark diamonds down with tiny black stitches, in a quilting pattern that says, I am too a lesbian, I am too a lesbian. I'm still coming out.

With her niece, circa 1978

BORN QUEER

Judith Katz

IT is 1972. I have been an official lesbian for about fifteen minutes. That is to say, I have just had sex with a woman for the first time. Up until this minute, I have enjoyed a number of close calls and have lost my job as a dorm counselor for declaring my (unrequited) love for another (woman) counselor. I have danced around a married-to-a-man-but-actually-queer head of residents' apartment to Laura Nyro's *Gonna Take a Miracle* album with a lot of other almost-dykes or already-are-but-never-talked-about-it-until-recently-dykes and one really big dyke who has been in the army. All of us are students at UMass, Amherst, or girlfriends of students. In about a year I will sit in a room with the dyke from the army and a dozen other women and realize that we have all slept with her at least once. In about two years I will look around my own life and realize that I have slept at least once with about half the women I know. But until those fifteen minutes ago, when I went to bed with a crazy woman named Helen Anderson who is also a student, I was just on the edge of remembering who it was I'd been afraid of being for the past fifteen years. Now, I know exactly who I was chasing away, and I am so glad to be welcoming her back.

To get myself in bed with Helen I take a carelessly designed cocktail of pot, beer, and Quaaludes. Someone down the hall is playing Jefferson Starship. I have been after Helen's friend Laura for months, that's who I lost my job over, but now it doesn't matter. It doesn't even matter that Helen kind of spooks me because she doesn't talk so much as whinny. The fact is, she expressed an interest in me, and I had been wanting to go to bed with a woman for months, and so Helen and I tumble into my little bed together and make love. There is a lot of biting and some howling. It is delicious and liberating and easier than anything I have ever done in my life. In that narrow little bed in the basement of a university dorm, I come free.

The next day, I am out everywhere—affable, twenty-one, and big-mouthed, I extend my hand to everyone—professors, dormmates, classmates, counselors. Hi I'm a lesbian, ask me a question, I tell them. I volunteer to talk in front of classes about being a dyke. I confront all my literature professors because every book, play, and poem we are reading is about women and men or men only. I start writing scenes in playwriting class that are about women together. At last I am out of some closet, some big box, although many people who met me at college assumed I was queer the minute they saw me.

This is 1972 in Amherst, Massachusetts, home of Emily Dickinson. Women's Studies is just evolving into an academic field. Some women are excavating an invisible history and culture, while others are inventing it. Feminism provides a key and a permission: to wear overalls and work boots; to talk publicly about rape and report it; to consider sex as pleasure in a public way. Betty Friedan's *Feminine Mystique* sits on the same shelf as Judy Grahn's *Psychoanalysis of Edward the Dyke* (although soon Friedan will beg the lesbians to keep a low profile in the National Organization for Women. They will respond by wearing Lavender Menace tee-shirts at a NOW rally in New York City as they rush the stage). Somewhere in New York City, Audre Lorde and Adrienne Rich are making theory into poetry. Jill Johnston is right up the hill in Goshen, Massachusetts, writing *Lesbian Nation*. Books with titles like *Sisterhood Is Powerful, Sexual Politics, Woman Hating, Housework*, and *Black Women in White America* are sticking out of women's backpacks. I have walked into my lesbianism at this peak moment in women's cultural history. Of course I am announcing my lesbianism to everyone. I am one of the luckiest women on earth.

★   ★   ★

Six months and several girlfriends later I have a job at the University of Massachusetts. I am the student coordinator of the Southwest Residential College Women's Center. It's an organization started by a few straight and a couple of soon-to-be-lesbo staff people working in my residential area, which is the same area that houses two alternative living/learning dorms called Project 10. This residential area has the newest buildings, and was the first on campus to organize co-ed dorms, one of which I lived in back in the good old days when I was still thinking I was straight. In other words, the women's center is only one part of a little city with a relatively forward-thinking student community. There are still some jocks living in this area (when Billie Jean King beat Bobby Riggs at tennis, some of them shouted out of the high rises, "Billie Jean King is a whore!"), and some students who live here are still studying conventional topics like science and history. But there are also many people like me who can think of no better way to spend their days than organizing political events, smoking pot, and substituting required courses for newer, more socially relevant ones.

At the Women's Center, where I am the student boss, I spend *my* days answering the phone, getting high, organizing the ever growing library of books by and about women, masturbating, and thinking about girls. The staff in charge of me, my bosses, plan parties, host parties, and help me to organize guest speakers. The parties are actually consciousness-raising groups, poetry readings, and classes. The guest speakers are sometimes nationally known feminists from out of town. Everything feels like a party because the Women's Center is in a huge, barely furnished faculty apartment consisting of a bedroom cum library/counseling room, a kitchen, and a living room/classroom; we have a stereo, and all events except classes are accompanied by music; huge bottles of Almaden, white and red; fancy crackers; and various groovy cheeses which the (white) faculty members purchase especially for these occasions. Also, everything seems like a party because even though the meetings and consciousness-raising sessions, the readings and classes are often grueling, there are real topics—fiscal inequity, violence against women, racism, homophobia, classism, rape—being revealed, discussed, denied, sung about, dramatized, painted, and argued about—and when we get together there is real work happening as we try to puzzle through all of this new information. There is also often amazing sexual energy and tension between women—even straight ones—flying in all directions. It is a general excitement that comes from dozens of women discovering, disagreeing with, and coming to terms with things that matter to us intellectually, politically, and personally all at once. We have touched some hard issues, but we haven't really struggled with the things that truly frighten us. There is little discussion of sadomasochism, for example; dildos and vibrators are still unspoken private sexual pleasures; and when we talk about race and class, many of us acknowledge the problems in a purely perfunctory way. We agree that problems exist, but most of us (white, middle-class) women really don't get it yet.

In a few years, it will be very clear to many of us that this lack of understanding has caused huge damage to our movement. In a few months, we will start to fight amongst ourselves. Some lesbians will want to have nothing to do with straight women; some straight women will want to have nothing to do with men. Sexually curious heterosexuals will experiment their ways into lifer lesbian status. Some lesbians will find themselves twenty years later married to men. But for right now, feminism, at least in the Southwest Residential College of the University of Massachusetts, is very sexy and lots of fun.

One day, while I am sitting in the Women's Center, doing my job—that is, sitting at my desk, listening to a Tracy Nelson album and thinking about getting loaded—the phone rings. It is the girlfriend of one of my dancing pals. She is a medical student. She is calling to tell me that Bill (not his real name) Bosco, who in the late sixties and early seventies runs abortion clinics in Boston, is coming to speak on campus about women's reproductive rights. Mr. Bosco at this time is notorious because he is constantly in a tangle with Massachusetts legal and health authorities. Massachusetts is a Catholic state, home of the Kennedys, and Mr. Bosco is also in constant conflict with the Catholic Church. Because of all this, Mr. Bosco's abortion establishments are in perpetual danger of being shut down. *N.B.,* Bill Bosco is no feminist, but he does have a big mouth and has enabled many young women to end their unwanted pregnancies safely, that is to say without knitting-needles or back-alley abortionists, and therefore has saved many women's lives.

The medical-student lover of my friend wants to know why this guy—and not a woman doctor or doctors—is coming to campus to talk about women's reproductive freedom. Being a medical student, she actually knows a couple. Here is a list. I agree that I will ask my bosses, the ladies with the Almaden, what the best way might be to proceed. I have ideas but no power in this setup. I also have a big mouth.

Somehow, we register an objection to Mr. Bosco's appearance on campus. We would like there to be a woman speaking instead of him or with him. As I have stated, Mr. Bosco helps women out, but really, he isn't our friend. He organizes abortions for women, but he doesn't really like us or think we know much. Also, he loves attention.

Two days later, I am sitting at my desk, listening to Roberta Flack and actually stoned. The door swings open and into the Women's Center walk two male students and a man older than us whom I have never seen before. One of the students is holding a camera. Before he even tells me his name, he's taken my picture. "What do you guys want?" I growl.

The photographer takes another picture. The other student with him smiles. The man between them also smiles. "I'm Bill Bosco." His grin grows bigger but not warmer.

"What do you want?" I am leaning forward a bit like a dog with my eye on Bill's jugular.

The camera snaps. The photographer snickers.

"What do you feminists have against me coming to talk about abortion? I thought you were in favor of abortion."

The boy with the pad has his pencil poised. I recognize him immediately as one of the reporters from the campus paper, *The Collegian*. I lean back. I put my hands on my hips. My upper lip curls. "We are in favor of abortion," I tell him. "We just think it would be nice to have a woman talk about it for a change."

"Because you hate men," the student reporter chimes in. His friend snaps another photo.

"No, because we think it's time for women to give voice to our own ideas."

"Because you hate men and you don't trust us," Mr. Bosco tells me.

"I don't hate men," I say. I wonder in that moment why I am lying.

"But you're a lesbian," the boy reporter says with smug satisfaction.

"So?" I can feel my hands form into tight fists.

"That's why you don't want Bill to talk. You lesbians hate men."

Somehow they collectively decide it's time to leave. The next day, there is a small picture in *The Collegian* of me looking surly and a medium-sized article about the man-hating feminists who want to stop Mr. Bosco from coming to campus. Censorship! Denial of free speech! Man hating dykes! Coordinator of Women's Center! Judith Katz!

I am a tornado of indignation. I have been an out lesbian for six months and already all hell is breaking loose. My overalls have hardly begun to wear out at the knees. My work boots are barely scuffed.

My hair is still long. And this butt head who is simultaneously anti-feminist and pro-abortion is telling me I hate men.

I blurt this all out to anyone who will listen. One of the people who is listening is a young gay man named Ron, whom I have known for most of my college career, even when we were both straight. I can't remember now if I slept with him or not. He is the fine arts editor of *The Collegian*, which on Fridays publishes a supplement called *Poor Richard's*. He knows those boy reporters who came in with Bill Bosco to entrap me and he hates them. He tells me that if I write an article telling my side of the story, he will put it on the front page of *Poor Richard's*. The article has to be written by Thursday. Today is Wednesday. I look at all the other people sitting in Ron's dorm room. Someone hands me a joint. I say, Sure.

Several hours later I am in my friend Bonnie's room with her stereo up loud typing out my side of the story. People keep bringing me cigarettes and joints and cans of Coke. Someone might have even provided me with lines of coke. Bonnie has left me in her room with her stereo blaring. From time to time she comes in to see how I am doing. I am in mad scientist mode, one that over the years, with and without marijuana, will signal that I am in the act of real writing.

The idea of this *Poor Richard's* piece is to debunk the annoying assumption that women become lesbians or even feminists because they hate men. I am a lesbian, I state, because I *love* women. Men are irrelevant to the conversation. We don't want Mr. Bosco to talk about abortion not because we don't want to hear about abortion. We want a woman to talk about abortion because we want a woman to talk. I make these points over and over again for about 5,000 words and it is very satisfying. When I am done, I have Bonnie call in the troops and cheerleaders, we all get loaded, and I read the article out loud. Everyone loves it. I call the article "Hard Ass Dyke Tells All." Ron snaps the pages up and with them a black-and-white photograph taken by a friend of me in mirror sunglasses and a flannel shirt. My hair is a mass of wild curls. I have a shit-eating grin on my face.

The week moves on, full of smoking, drinking, and maybe some studying. Friday is going to be a big day. Not only is "Hard Ass Dyke Tells All" coming out, but the Women's Center is sponsoring a reception for a visiting nationally known feminist. Wahoo. What a triumph. Bill Bosco becomes irrelevant. Friday arrives. The paper comes out. Ron has blown up my picture so that it takes up seventy-five percent of the front page of *Poor Richard's*. The headline, "Hard Ass Dyke Tells All," is in twenty-five point bold type over my mirrored, curly head. And there, right under my picture is my byline, and under that, my article begins.

The elation is brief, for within minutes of *kvelling* over my own handiwork, light, as we say in Massachusetts, dawns on Marblehead. For the first time since I slept with Helen Anderson or told anyone whether they asked me or not that I was a lesbian, I remember that at least a third of the population of this campus comes from my home town. This is a state school and I am from the second largest city in that state. With a sickening thud it hits me that if Martin Donatello who grew up down the street from me knows I'm queer it's only a matter of time before his mother knows I'm queer and that my mother will know about fifteen seconds after that.

Trepidatiously, I pick up the telephone. My mother answers on the first ring. "What's wrong?" she asks me before I even say hello.

"I've got something to tell you," I tell her. "I'm coming home."

It takes ninety minutes to drive from UMass to Worcester, where my parents live. They have lived there all their lives and all of mine. They are first-generation Americans descended from Russian and Polish Jews. Somehow I got the impression that they met at a Communist picnic before my father went off to war, but that may not be true. When they were married they lived with my grandmother and then with me too over my grandmother's grocery store. When I was three my mother and father and I moved across town to a newly-built house and my brother was born.

All the other people who live on my street have escaped the old neighborhood too. All of them, except the two Italian couples and the Armenian one, grew up together in the Jewish neighborhood on the other side of town. Every household has children the same age. We have parallel families and parallel pasts. Two of the families on my parents' street are actually related by blood. The fathers of those families are my father's business partners, so in a way it feels like we are related by blood as well.

Our street is a hill so steep that coming home after school on an icy winter day was a Sisyphean task. I was raised on that hill as if on a kibbutz: when I was little we children spent summers running and winters sledding through each other's backyards. We played in each other's houses, walked each other to school, sometimes ate meals together. Anybody's mother might discipline us and we either obeyed that mother, ignored her, or sassed her back. If we sassed we were punished by our real mother later that day.

When I was a girl, my entire body was compact. I was slim and sturdy, my hair was short, my chest was flat. I was always allowed to wear pants like a boy, except to school or synagogue, where I was required to wear a skirt or dress like a girl. But when school was out, when services were over, I changed right away from my pleated blue skirt or my gray skirt with pink kittens into trousers and one of my favorite long-sleeved button-down shirts. These were my sword-fighting shirts. They made me feel suave and debonair as I swashbuck-led around the basement and backyard with a yardstick cutlass. That felt like sex to me, and so, when I finally mastered it, did riding my bicycle, which I did around the paved backyards on our street. When I was alone I pretended I was Robert Goulet as Sir Lancelot in *Camelot* and my blue Schwinn was a blond palomino.

Other girls on my street excelled in physical activities as children. One played tennis and won trophies. Another could spin and flip through any hopscotch configuration or jump-rope tangle imaginable. Some were expert at dodgeball, softball, and tetherball. I, on the other hand, couldn't hit or pitch to save my life. I was totally passive when I was "it" in dodgeball and was known by all the children on my street as an easy out. Hopscotch and jump-rope confounded me. I was much happier when I swashbuckled by myself or played with two of the boys on my street. Dennis Tenneti and Henry Gold were my age, and maybe we liked each other because they were born queer like me. Henry passed the time drawing figures and landscapes. Dennis drew cartoons. I wasn't as good a visual artist as either of them, but I shared their good imaginations and could imitate Ed Sullivan. All three of us shared a bond of sports hatred.

Dennis and Henry and I built shacks in the woods which we called camps. We play-acted elaborate games based on kids' movies we had seen or TV shows we liked, like *Old Yeller* and *Robin Hood*. Henry particularly liked games that involved royalty so that he could wear costume jewelry. I liked games that involved fancy duels. Dennis was particularly fond of a game he and Henry had invented called Tom and Tom, which they had been playing for some time before I joined in.

Henry and Dennis probably used their actual anatomy when they played Tom and Tom without me, but when I played, we were always fully dressed and the body parts were imaginary. Tom and Tom, and when I was there, Tom^3, were human cartoon characters who ran around together and got their genitalia caught up in all kinds of elastic knots and snags, just like Coyote's tongue did in Road Runner cartoons. The sex of Tom and Tom was all about those thrilling imaginary knots between our stretched-out giant penises.

It thrilled me to act like a boy with Dennis and Henry, like a gay boy, a little fag like both of them. Really, what I wanted was to be a gay boy like Dennis and Henry. I wanted to play Tom and Tom in a million settings like the Gidget movies: *Tom and Tom Go to Paris; Tom and Tom Go to Hebrew School; Tom and Tom Go to Hawaii*. In Hawaii the Toms meet Annette Funicello, who falls in love with me, Tom³, breaks up with Frankie Avalon, and comes home to Worcester where she marries me and officially replaces my mother.

I had to use my imagination more than Henry and Dennis did during Tom and Tom because I didn't have a penis, but I didn't want a penis, either. I didn't feel like a girl or a boy, but I liked my vagina, for which no euphemism was ever used in my house.

When I played Robert Goulet and swashbuckler, or even Tom and Tom, I didn't mind if anyone else saw me. But there was one pleasure I only engaged in when my parents' house was entirely empty. When my father was at work, my mother down the hill or across the street drinking coffee or playing cards, my sister and brother outside running around, I crept into my brother's room and opened his closet. There, with the house completely quiet, I slipped into my brother's sport coat, clipped on a bow tie, and slicked back my hair. I stood in front of my brother's full length mirror and pretended I was one of the Toms, or sometimes I became Perry Mason and engaged in lively legalistic oratory.

Sex for me had nothing to do with kissing or naked bodies. It was my brother's sport coat, my flat chest, my short, slick hair. Penises just seemed like annoying bundles of skin. I liked my compact vagina, even if it meant I had to pee sitting down. I liked my flat chest, but I spent very little time touching any part of myself, except my lesbian-to-be hands and arms, which I spent hours studying alone in my room, or while spacing out at school, or sitting in *shul*.

Though, to tell the truth, I did engage in another kind of sex. Sometimes . . . often . . . I went down to the basement on my own or with Henry Gold, and studied my father's *Playboy* collection, which sat in stacks near my mother's surplus canned goods. Henry liked to examine the centerfolds and admire the big breasts the women displayed to the camera. I was more interested in the mechanics and psychology of fucking as shown in cartoons. I was particularly interested in the Annie Fanny cartoons, because while the heroine of these was often tricked into sexual encounters, she always seemed to enjoy herself. I graduated from *Playboy* to my father's softcore porn collection, which included paperbacks in the *Man from O.R.G.Y.* series which he kept in the bottom drawer of his nightstand along with a big box of condoms.

It was somewhere in the early sixties, reading these books and others, which I would take into my brother's room when no one was home, that I began to sense that something might be wrong with me. When I read the hot parts, what turned me on was imagining myself the teller, the fucker, never the woman being fucked. I was convinced I was a sexual misfit, monstrous, dangerous to myself and others. Not because I enjoyed porn, which was, after all, a kind of groovy thing in my house in 1962—my father read his *Playboys* out in the open, and my mother, on more than one occasion, was busy looking at the centerfold herself. I thought I was monstrous for how I enjoyed my consumption of naked women. I tried time and again to put myself on the bottom, on my back, under the Man from O.R.G.Y., to writhe and wriggle, only to find my reader's mind placing me back on top pumping and thrusting. In real life today, as a middle-aged lesbian feminist who does not identify as butch or femme (and not for political reasons, either—facing facts, I'm just a kai kai girl who gets off on flipping girls sometimes, but who also gets off on being flipped) my identification with male partners in heterosexual porn interests me, but it doesn't surprise me. The storyteller in these tales is the active partner, and in most cases, to my mind (and taste) he is having all the fun. The women are not simply passive in these tales, they have no voice. The entire sexual experience is related from the fucker's point of view and the pleasure is always his. But back then, Laura Mulvay and Julia Kristeva were just a twinkle in their mothers' eyes, and my identification with the fucker in the stories was pervert proof to me. Topping this off was the mysterious information about masturbation I found in the sex mis-education book my mother gave me, *The Stork Didn't Bring You.* The main message here was that if a person masturbated she would grow up to become a lonely (read perverted) individual having solitary sex *in an attic* (!) for the rest of her life.

While I looked at *Playboy* and creamed at the hot parts in those *Man from O.R.G.Y.* volumes, I hardly touched myself while I was awake. But I did wake up from time to time with my hands up inside myself in a cold sweat. Tom, Tom, and Tom didn't scare me, my brother's sport coat didn't scare me, but all of a sudden I began to realize that what turned me on was somehow dangerous, no matter how slick and trim I was, no matter how adroitly I could slash that yardstick sword through the air. Maybe it wasn't good that I loved it when my aunt Raisel took me up in her arms and hugged and kissed me and that I hated it when my uncle Melvin did the same. Maybe my imaginary penis as Tom[3] was catching up with me and the attic wouldn't be a bad place to hide. All of this shook through me like a psychosexual earthquake the summer of 1963, when not only my imagination but my body began to betray me. Almost overnight I went from Judith Katz, world's cutest boy/girl to Bizarro Judith, monster twelve-year-old: where once I had an adorable smooth and boyish face, I now had a full crop of acne; where once I had straight, sleek hair, I now sprouted frizzy strands of steel wool. My once smooth legs now became thick with hair; and on my once flat boy's chest, breasts began to grow—and not pretty ones either like those pink shiny women in *Playboy* sported. Mine were unwieldy masses of pudgy flesh that made my dueling shirts puff out at the chest. Even my trusty vagina began to turn on me, not yet spouting blood, but offering up strange smells, odd drips, surrounded now with wisps of hair.

I wasn't the only one freaked out by this transformation into a child monster. My mother seemed particularly offended by my appearance and my scent and did everything she could to fix it: braces, deodorants, astringents. She constantly manhandled me in an effort to make my clothes—now almost always dresses and skirts—look right. Also, she was obsessed with my hair, which never looked right to her and was a constant battleground between us—one she took up physically as she pulled at it and raked a comb through it in an effort to calm it down. Twenty years later I would begin to translate this experience into art. My mother's invasive behavior would become the basis for the first chapter of *Running Fiercely Toward a High Thin Sound*. Right at the moment, I just wanted to be dead.

Once, each night before I went to bed I imagined myself as Perry Mason getting some poor wrongly accused girl off the hook for murder (of her mother?). Now every night I fantasized a funeral and mine was the body. Gay or straight, a TV lawyer no more, I was a queer little girl, a little queer girl, once an adorable smarty pants boy of a girl with a sweet smile and a Pixie cut, now and for the next five years, stammering, chubby, wild-haired and stupid.

In this condition, in the fall of 1963, two months before John F. Kennedy got his head blown off, I was on my way to junior high school. Tom[3] no longer, I was the queerest girl in the world, though I was not a lesbian yet.

When I get to my parents' house, my mother is hovering in the doorway. I park the red Toyota on the steep incline of my childhood street and haul myself out of the car. My mother doesn't come out of the house to greet me, only stands there, filling the front door. I wonder how I look to her, how big and unruly she finds my hair, whether she will object to the fact that I am not wearing a bra, how she sees me in these big orange work shoes. But she doesn't say a thing about how I look today. She leans into me and puts her arms around me, squeezes me and lets me go. She moves aside just enough to let me pass into the house. She is grave and distracted and there is nothing that tells me she loves me. As much as this woman has tormented me, she has also set a standard of distant affection for everyone I fall in love with from now until the middle of my forties.

Not that my childhood and teenage relationship with my mother was all verbal abuse and body searches. As a little girl I spent a lot of time sitting on her bed in my pajamas watching her scurry around the bedroom in her underwear getting ready to go out for a night on the town with my father. It smelled wonderful around her and she looked so pretty in her bra and slip. I loved watching as she screwed on a pair of mother-of-pearl earrings or ran a tube of lipstick deftly across her mouth. I think I even saved some of her tissue blotters for their perfect impressions of her lovely red lips.

It was sometimes my job to stand on the bed and zip her up. Then there she stood before us all, an art project, a masterpiece, perfectly coifed and ready for some big synagogue social event—a wedding reception, a Bar Mitzvah party. My father always looked handsome at these events, but my mother shone. She was peaceful then, and her attention was on herself, not me at all. By the time the baby-sitter arrived (or later, when I was the baby-sitter), there was a perfumed order in the house, a kind of tranquillity that would last at least until they came bursting back from their party, my mother talking at ninety miles an hour.

But right now, today, she is neither beautiful and loquacious, nor is she invasive and scrutinizing. Right now, this minute, six months into my lesbian life, my mother is cold and far away. In the future, this quality will also continue to sexually interest me. But I don't feel aroused now. I feel tongue-tied and terrified. My entire physical essence is in my front brain and my rapidly pounding heart.

I go right into the bathroom, unhook my overalls, and empty my bladder. When I come out, my father is standing at the end of the hall. He looks lost, although, like my mother, he seems to completely fill the space he occupies. Like my mother he is emotionally distant. He touches my shoulders briefly, then ushers me to the kitchen table, which is set with placemats, glass cake plates, and teacups. A platter full of homemade pastries sits in the center, including my favorite, my mother's maraschino-and-walnut-filled ice cream strudel. It's more like *Shabbes* evening than bold confession time. I keep expecting my Aunt

Raisel and Uncle Melvin to pop in at any minute. But they do not. Though the table is festive, the mood is grim. Both parents are battened down tight around me. My father, without an open newspaper protecting his face, looks old and terrified. My mother is folded into herself, her hazel eyes glisten with what looks to me like rage. We sit in awkward silence until the tea kettle boils. Then my mother jumps up and pours the scalding water over three tea bags in three shallow cups. When she has settled back, my father looks up at me. "So?"

Ah. Well . . . "There is an article," I begin, "in this morning's school paper, and I wrote it."

My mother glares. My father looks at me blankly. No one says anything.

"The article is about Bill Bosco, but it's also about me."

My mother sits up stiffly. "The abortionist? You didn't have an abortion?" She sounds almost hopeful.

I gasp. "An abortion? Me? Absolutely not!"

"Are you pregnant?" Again there is a glimmer of hope in her voice.

"Am I?" This bursts out of me in a kind of shriek, more like my paramour Helen Anderson than myself. I look down at my completely lesbian self in all its significators: overalls, work boots, flannel shirt. "No, in fact I've come to tell you just the opposite." We all are holding our breath. "The article in *The Collegian* is a response to Bill Bosco, but really it's about me."

"About you?"

"Yeh. It's about me. I tell why . . . uh . . . why . . . uh . . . I'm a lesbian."

At first there is terrible silence. Then suddenly my mother's hand comes down on the table and all the dishes shake. "What does that have to do with Bill Bosco?" Her voice is broken and ferocious simultaneously.

"Nothing, really," I say. "It's a weird coincidence."

It is very quiet at the table. All of my easy, Hi, I'm a lesbian ask me a question jocularity has evaporated. I'd be happy to slink back into my car—the car they bought me—and disappear forever. Instead, I take a sip of tea.

"Well," says my mother after what seems like an hour, "it's not as if this is a total surprise. It's not as if we never suspected." She is remembering all the unnatural attachments of my youth. Not Toms one and two, or the Man from O.R.G.Y. My mother is remembering, as I did that night I slept with Helen Anderson the first time, my obsessive attraction to Janet Kaplan.

★   ★   ★

Janet Kaplan was Jewish, sarcastic, hilariously funny, beautiful, and cruel. She sat in front of me in home room my first day of junior high and I fell in love with her the second I saw her. I laughed at all of Janet Kaplan's jokes, but in her actual presence I could never think of any of my own, even though Henry and Dennis thought I was the funniest thing since *Laugh In*. I was helpless, breathless, and stupid whenever I was near Janet Kaplan. What other person made me feel that way? Of course, my mother.

Being in love with Janet Kaplan did not make me feel powerful and safe like my level one queer activities, cross-dressing and sword-fighting. It made me feel nervous and endangered in much the same way reading those *Man from O.R.G.Y.* books made me feel. I wanted to be with Janet every minute. I wanted her to see me as cool, the way I saw her. I wanted shaved legs, bras, and mysterious eyes via shadow like Janet had. All of this was forbidden to me by my mother. Ironically, years later, my mother and I would constantly jostle over why I would not wear a bra. She would belligerently wonder why I hadn't shaved my legs and where my eye makeup was. But then, my mother forbade all those signs of girls growing up fast, and I complied. Except in my adoration of Janet Kaplan, who was bad and fast and dated gentile boys. I took up smoking to impress Janet, I shaved my legs to be as good as her. I lived for Janet, and to Janet I was a mere speck.

Which I kind of liked. Where my mother was all over me like a cheap suit about everything from the way I smelled to how much hair there was under my arms, Janet Kaplan was cool and impossible even when she was sitting three inches away from me in homeroom. On the rare occasions when she turned around and actually touched me, though—oh, I could live through any of my mother's humiliating opinions about me for another week.

Now every night before I fell asleep, my fantasy funeral was off. Instead, I was in the hospital because Janet's older brother Dukey had run me over with his car. There in my imagined hospital bed, all limbs in traction or in a Hollywood coma, Janet would come to me, her arms full of flowers. How she begged forgiveness for Dukey's bad driving! How she apologized for being rude to me all those days in homeroom! Sometimes in these fantasies, Janet even held my hand.

Eventually, by our junior year of high school, Janet Kaplan seemed to like me well enough to hang around with me and let me in on some of her secrets, even though Dukey never hit me with his car. My mother hated her, which made me love her all the more. Janet Kaplan's favorite song then was Janis Ian's "Society's Child," which was also my favorite song. When she sang along she thought about all those goy boys she dated. When I sang along I was singing to her.

Of course back then I worried that I might be queer. I looked up homosexuality in the card catalogue like every one else, and made a special effort to skip the masturbation parts in *The Stork Didn't Bring You* in favor of its meager offering on homosexuality. Years later I would learn that there were girls in my high school who did date each other. For three years Patty Feldman and Melissa Levine had a public war over the same boy when in fact they were privately kissing.

I wasn't that brave. I just hung around and drooled while Janet Kaplan told stories about dry-humping some Protestant boy in the back of his car. Even though I was often alone with Janet Kaplan and stories of her salacious escapades, even though I am sure there were ample opportunities to make an ass of myself and try to kiss her, I never did. Instead I carried a razor blade around in my wallet, and not to cut cocaine with either. I was a queer, terrified teenager with a crazy mother and a sex life that wasn't my own. The razor blade was my private insurance policy. I was queer all right. But really, I didn't even know how to spell lesbian yet.

My father's next remark, coming as it does through surprising tears (his), confounds me. "We always thought you would get married." He is really crying now, and this is shocking to me. "I wanted to give you a wedding." This is particularly intriguing since the entire time I lived under his roof I had about half a dozen dates with men, which averages out to one a year from junior high school to high school graduation—not exactly prime material for the marriage mill.

"But I never even had a boyfriend!" I'm shrieking.

"You never tried very hard either," my mother says.

"What do you mean I never tried?" I am right now remembering embarrassing dates with boys more queer than I was in high school, and not gay boys, either.

"Look," she says, and I am not at all prepared for the curve she suddenly throws into our conversation. "I want you to know," she is stern now, as if suddenly she is Hamilton Berger to my Perry Mason, "this is not my fault."

I am blown away. There we are, sitting around cookies and tea like it's a party, my dad home from work especially for this, he is in tears because I'm not getting married and she is absolving herself of a responsibility that never even occurred to me. If anything, given my relationship with her, I wonder in that moment why I didn't become a raving heterosexual.

Actually, I was a heterosexual for about a year and a half in college. Maybe my dad remembers this and that's why he's crying. Maybe he remembers coming to visit me one day a few years back when I was at summer school and I was stoned on my ass. I was miserable when I opened the door and found him there, and not Eddy Finn, the boy who taught me how to fuck. Maybe on some unconscious level my father thinks he scared Eddy Finn away. He doesn't know I'm much happier now without Eddy Finn.

Eddy Finn was a working-class Irish Catholic guy from a town outside Boston. He was just a year older than me, but he was much more sexually experienced. For one thing, he had been fucking his high school French teacher when we first met. After college he was gay for a while, but eventually he married the French teacher. Eddy not only taught me how to fuck, he also taught me how to blow him and how to do drugs. I fell in love with him and marijuana simultaneously. I was obsessive and passionate about both, although my time with him was over in under nine months and my love affair with dope lasted for fifteen years.

The most important thing Eddy Finn did for me was divert my attention from my queerness. Fucking him felt great, and it felt great the first time we did it. When Eddy *told* me that I had had an orgasm that first time, a wave of gratitude washed over me and swept away all of my shame and fear around being the guy in *The Man from O.R.G.Y.*, around loving Janet Kaplan and all the girls besides Janet I had crushes on and never kissed. I was relieved of the burden of my desire for other girls, for women, for sexy aunts and friends of the family, for my own mother even and even my grandmother. I felt normal for the first time in my young adult life, but also cool, nonconforming, wild.

Fucking Eddy Finn made me a normal woman, but loving him made me crazy. Like Janet Kaplan, Eddy Finn was adorable: he was big, sexy, and very funny. He was also distant, cool, and completely into his own pleasures. Marijuana and sex with me were only two of these. He was sleeping with his male roommate, maintaining his relationship with his French teacher, and *shtupping* one of my friends from high school, Lizzie Goodman. I was devastated because he dumped me, but I was also torn apart because I wanted to have sex with Lizzie Goodman too.

To his credit, Eddy did try to take care of me. He pointed out other boys who he thought would be much better boyfriends than he was. I wasn't interested. I was rejected because I wanted too much, and I never understood then too much of what. My adolescent hospital fantasies came rolling back over me. This time Lizzie Goodman had hit me with her car and Eddy was coming to visit and apologize.

And then my life became another life. I moved into another dorm. I became a resident counselor. I took a women's studies course called Woman as Hero and playwriting classes across the river at Smith College. I began to forget about Eddy Finn and slowly, like coming up from some underwater adventure, I began to find out who I actually was: a girl who liked to write and was pretty good at it, someone who understood feminism the minute it was presented to me, a young woman who had once been in love with Janet Kaplan not so long ago.

This wasn't some easy breezy transformation. I suffered a lot. I was in love a lot with women who, like Janet Kaplan, treated me like a speck or who were straight and terrified of me. I lost my job as a dorm counselor because I was in love with another dorm counselor who had a textbook case of early 1970s homophobia. Slowly I located all the actual dykes on campus and began to find a community. Then I slept with Helen and I became uncorked. I saw my entire universe through a lesbian lens. This has made it possible to write my "Hard Ass Dyke Tells All" article and have the horrible conversation I am having with my parents right this minute, right now. I can't remember if I kiss my parents good-bye before I climb into the car this October afternoon to head back to UMass. I think my father hugs me and my mother turns away. For months after this, I will call and she will hand the phone over to my father. They will send my favorite aunt, Raisel, out to visit me. Raisel will tell me I am going through a phase. I will tell her again that this is no phase, that I am really a lesbian, a lifer, that this is what my heart and every fiber of my body is telling me to do. For years after Raisel's visit, I will barely be able to engage in civilized conversation with my mother, and this will depress me. I will have years of therapy where I will try to untangle not the knot of my queerness but the knot of my family.

But right now, after this strange, sad parting, I climb into my red car, light a joint, and sail over the hills of Route 122 to Route 202, then on to Route 9 and become suddenly elated. I drive right to the Women's Center and burst in on a lively Friday party, where wine-drinking feminists, lesbians and straight, are feting a celebrated author from New York. Everyone stops to cheer and toast me because not only have I warded off Bill Bosco in public, I have come out to my parents and made it back alive. I am a brave baby dyke. If this were the kind of crowd who carried people around on their shoulders to show their appreciation, I'd be held aloft right this minute. I am happy and not happy. The fact that I have finally become that lesbian I was all along pleases me. The fact that I feel like an orphan does not.

Years will pass. I will wrestle with drugs. I will find love, lose love, drive love away. I will become a writer of plays and novels. I will reconcile with my parents after years of therapy (mine) and chemical dependency treatment (also mine). I will live in the middle of the country and be homesick for the East Coast often. My lesbianism will continue to be an integrated fact of my life; my life will become the center of my work. At age forty-seven, I will look at myself: a middle-aged, single, Jewish dyke who owns a dog and a truck and plays guitar in an all-woman Klezmer band. Born queer, I have grown up to be one of the luckiest women alive.

Kathryn Kirk

WHAT COMES FIRST

Holly Hughes

I left the Midwest for New York City just as the sun was setting on the Carter Administration. I had signed up for the first semester of classes at the New York Feminist Art Institute. Perhaps it is presumptuous of me to assume that readers are familiar with feminism; for the purposes of this story I'll describe it as a seventies kind of phenomenon, not unlike polyester, disco, quiche (as a health food), and John Travolta. I wish I could report that either quiche or feminism had been able to make as successful a comeback as has Mr. Travolta, but alas. Let's not open that door or we'll never get it shut.

"Feminism, my foot!" exclaimed my mother as she cremated the meatloaf. "This feminism thing is just a cover for being a lesbian." Perhaps that is not an exact quote; you see, my parents' first language was silence and I've had to translate here. But I was able to decipher the vast stillness that followed the announcement of my move and realize they were on to me. We all knew that being a feminist was something I could have done in the privacy of my own home in

135

Kalamazoo, whereas having sex with women, well, clearly one would have to go out of state for that.

I arrive in New York with visions of all the sisterly nonhierarchical art we're gonna make; how we're gonna topple the military industrial complex by festooning public spaces with giant soft-sculpture vaginas. How we're gonna reverse centuries of racism and imperialism by re-naming ourselves after our mother's favorite condiments.

Alas, the school is of course a collective. By the time it opens for its first semester, none of the members of the collective are speaking to each other.

My lesbian career is also stalled, despite the fact that I thought I had impeccable credentials. I had already constructed somewhat of a public identity as a lesbian, had already survived a bit of bashing in the college cafeteria, when someone threw fruit cocktail at me. I had done all the assigned reading, from Adrienne Rich to Mickey Spillane. Actually I think Spillane was more helpful in forming my identity. His books, and those of other pulp fiction writers, were riddled with queers of every stripe. Okay, so a lot of them were dead; they had a lot of fun getting there.

There was one small problem; I had yet to have had sex with another woman. I had gone in on a subscription to *Playboy* with a man, but I guess that doesn't really count.

Turns out that being a lesbian outside of the privacy of your own home was quite hard. I'm not talking about the various manifestations of homophobia—oh, that old thing. I'm talking about scoring. Picking up chicks. (As it turns out, I would come to prefer the type of woman few would recognize as female, the type who would cheerfully deck you if you called her a chick, but might, if I were lucky, see me as such: a chick, a babe, a femme fox.)

In the *oeuvre* of Mr. Spillane, being a lesbian seemed so easy, like shooting fish in a barrel. In my favorite lesbian novels, *No Blonde is an Island* and *My Gun is Quick,* all a gal had to do was brush up against another woman by the water cooler and, watch out, the sapphic sparks would surely fly. Lesbianism was something any woman could do, no special equipment, messy creams or liquids were required.

But when I walked into my first dyke bar in New York City, I had a rude awakening. It was like transferring to a new high school. No, it was worse than that. A new junior high school. You walk into the class on the first day and everyone turns to stare. Your clothes, your hair, the way you move, it's all wrong. You have to change everything or die a horrible and lingering death.

I guess the moral of this story is that there are some pursuits, such as lesbianism, that one can't learn from a book, no matter the author. A more crass sort might make some tasteless jokes at this juncture about "boning up" on lesbianism, or about "hands-on experience," but the reader can be assured this dyke will not sink to that level.

I watched the other women dancing, talking, flirting. All transactions were conducted in a lingo as incomprehensible to me as straight guy sports speak. My late-seventies disco fever look was out of place here. Everyone looked like they'd raided the closet of their bigger, older brother while he was out repairing refrigerators.

I was the only one wearing makeup.

Someone approached me: "This is a *gay* bar." I shriveled up and a gust of wind blew me out into the street.

I had no skills. No lesbian skills. I was stared at, rather than cruised, at the bars. I couldn't find a way of signaling to another dyke that I was open for business, a friend of Dorothy, in the life, on the bus. Let alone desperately horny.

Somehow I managed a few invites to lesbian parties. I'd figured out that wearing lipstick was wrong, but I was still doing it. I'm such a congenital WASP that my lips disappear without makeup; I couldn't imagine having sex without lipstick. I had tried to pull a lesbian look together: oversized second-hand men's clothes, an unbuttoned black vest, but Annie Hall does not work on someone five feet tall.

Nor could I play softball. When something is thrown at me, even if it is specifically designed for that purpose, I automatically duck. All I had going for me in the lesbian skill department was ownership of a cat. Enough to break the ice, but not cinch the deal.

Certainly I couldn't just come out and ask some other dyke to show me the ropes, so to speak. The seventies were still going on even though it was now the eighties. Feminism and lesbianism had kind of merged, become one big multinational entity with Andrea Dworkin as CEO. You had to be sneaky to get laid.

Yikes. It had been so easy with men. All you had to do was bend over at the bowling alley and something would happen.

After two years, the drought ended. I saw a sign that advertised: "Double-X-Rated Christmas Party for Women." The party was held in the basement of a Catholic church. Perhaps the priests had passed out upstairs and had no idea what was going on. Or perhaps the priests were the drag queens working the bar. Nevertheless, I was there as soon as the doors opened. And the doors were not the only thing that opened.

I walked into the basement where the party was taking place and saw rows of thrift store tuxedoes, second-hand prom dresses. The doorperson made it clear that these outfits could be borrowed for the evening. After they checked their coats, many party-goers were borrowing outfits from the racks and disappearing into the bathroom to amend their attire. As the evening went on, I noticed more and more women trading in their flannel and denim for sharkskin and taffeta.

At this, my first encounter with the women who produced the WOW Festival and would later open the WOW Café in a tiny linguini-shaped storefront on East Eleventh Street, I fell in love. In love with all of the women, with their outrageousness, their unruly desire. I wanted desperately to be a part of whatever it was they were doing . . . if the WOW Café had been a support group for lesbian skeet shooters, that's what I'd be doing now.

Instead, I found theater, or it found me. And the theater, it seemed, offered a wonderful solution to my involuntary celibacy: the casting couch. In theater you are encouraged to have sex with as many people as possible; it's an integral part of the process. At least at WOW it seemed like the shows were almost an afterthought to the flirting, a byproduct of the endless parties where women of every imaginable gender rubbed up against each other.

This last paragraph reads like a natural cue to cross-fade to the Story of the First Girlfriend, doesn't it? At this point, I should see a stranger across a crowded room, our eyes should lock, and the violins should swell like wieners on the grill. But this scene isn't part of my coming-out story. Who even remembers my first girlfriend? Not me. I remember lots of bodies, I remember rooms lit by lots of small lights, and above all else, I remember lots and lots of Rolling Rock. This movie doesn't end with a soft-focus closeup on two women kissing; this is a coming-out story that crescendos into a crowd scene. It's a wide-angle shot. The climax of my coming-out scenario isn't a closeup on a lesbian couple but a panorama of a lesbian world.

Jump cut. Setting: the present. I'm an out artist who's always being asked which comes first—the lesbian part or the artist part. Or I'm asked when I'll start writing about something else, something that could, I'm told, appeal to a broader audience. Often the question is about sex, why do I insist on writing about it?

And I want to say something about how I can't separate my love for theater from my desire for women. I want to say something about how I imagine my work to be like the small glass tumbler I'm holding in my sweaty hand, unremarkable but important because it holds something we need. I try to say something about making work that is filled with something as clear and necessary as cold water, then giving that water away. But it'll always be water from my well, warmed by the heat of my body.

When I am asked these questions I remember that first night at WOW when my dreams of being a lesbian and of being an artist took shape. If I hadn't walked into that room that night, I imagine I would still be fluent in the dialects of silence, I would be a woman who wears her body like someone else's clothes, I would be my mother by now. Underneath my heart there is a big dark underground room full of women wearing tuxes, blue eye shadow. It's too dark and crowded to tell where desire starts and art ends, but this is a place to which I always return. This is where I go to get the water I promised you.

Dona Ann McAdams

HOUSE OF CORALS

Cheryl Boyce Taylor

I wish I could put my finger on the exact moment when I knew that I was attracted to other girls. Perhaps I would make a big deal of the day, make it special, like New Year's or Christmas, celebrate with Veuve Clicquot, roasted garlic, long-stemmed strawberries, and a sage bath.

"Lesbian" became a part of my vocabulary only in the late eighties. What did I call myself before that? I am not sure. It was twenty years before I gave myself a name and twenty-five years before I came out to my family.

When I was growing up in Trinidad in the early sixties, there were many names for girls like me. Negative names like "zami," "zami queen," "man-oman," "he-she," "nasty," and "sodomite." As a child, I was unfamiliar with the true meaning and impact of these words—that was "grownup people stuff." I never attached anything negative to the innocent pleasure I was having. I enjoyed the tickly and giddy sensations I experienced with my little girlfriends. Years later, I understood the hatred and threats in those words. Even so, nothing has interfered with the joy and satisfaction I've felt being with a woman. The sacredness and passion I've felt for my lovers has outweighed any names I've ever been called.

I remember that the first time I kissed a real, adult woman, she returned my passion. It was like my birthday, the birth of my child, and Kwanzaa all rolled into one. I thought, "This is not like the way any man has ever kissed me." I was fascinated . . . elated. I was *high*. I floated . . . I drifted . . . I was in love. It was days before I landed again. As the months hurried by, I knew I had made the right life choice. I have never doubted that choice. There have been many times when this decision has tried me, tested my faith. Still, somehow I knew it was right for me.

My earliest memory of petting with one of my little girlfriends was at age seven. After a long day at school, we arrived home weary, but eager to get changed and play. My grandmother gave us a snack of toast and orange marmalade. We ate quickly, announced loudly that we had homework, and headed for the bedroom. My mom was not home yet, but Gramma was puttering around, cooking dinner, washing dishes, dusting, doing her regular household chores. I got down my geography atlas.

I remember this book as if it were yesterday. Stupidly, we used this book as cover, thinking it would hide us if someone unexpectedly came into the room. The book was dark green, oversized, slender, about 16" x 20". There were many maps with lines and colors indicating areas of terrain. There were equator lines, mountain ranges, swirly lines that indicated bodies of water. Most important were the bright colors designating far-off countries. In many ways, this book was my ticket to fantasy land. I remember it well. I also remember the distinct smell in the room that day. It grew stronger as we played; it hovered in the room all afternoon. To this day, that slightly funky smell makes me giddy and excited.

My friend Mauve and I looked at the book, chatting about the colors and countries. After a while, we pretended to go on an enchanted journey to one of the countries. We took turns lying down and traveling there. Pretty soon we began touching and examining each other's bodies. The vagina seemed most mysterious of all, so we lingered there, probing until one of us got tired or impatient for her turn. There were times when I did not want to examine Mauve's pussy for long because it smelled a little stinky, and anyway I was anxious for her to do me. I always wanted it to be my turn. It was my house, and I felt I should have my way. She would get cross and tell me I wasn't playing fair, but next day she would be back at my house ready to play "school" again. After Mauve got mad, we snuggled together and pushed our bodies very close. This was great fun. Pretty soon, it was time for Mom to arrive, so Mauve went home.

One of the greatest and most challenging gifts in my life was being born into a Caribbean family. I grew up in Trinidad in the fifties and sixties, in an extended family. My maternal grandmother was head of the household in which my aunt and uncle, their three sons, my mother, my brother, and I also lived. My two male cousins, though they were shuttled back and forth to their parents' home in a nearby town, were there often enough to be counted.

Members of the Boyce clan were known for working hard and keeping to themselves. Yes. We were such a huge family we thought we didn't need other folks. Gramma was the boss. She believed in being proud no matter what. She said, *"If yu only hav one dress le it be wash an press so yu always lookin good and clean so people doh ha tu kno yu business."* She believed that silence was golden, religion was necessary for salvation, and education was the ticket to freedom. The adults in my family were determined that their children would have the educational opportunities they themselves had desired but not gotten. My mother, especially, wanted me to be a college-educated woman, *"so yu wouldn't ha to depend on no man,"* as she put it. To reach the goals she set for her children's future, she worked as a nursery school teacher by day, a tutor evenings and weekends, and a milliner on the side.

The Boyce clan also had many secrets. Sex and sexual relationships were never, never discussed. There were so many things I wanted to know. Whether my grandfather hit my grandmother, who my cousin Ton's father was, and how his mother had died. Did my uncle really have a mistress and two daughters living only two blocks away from our family home? And what had happened between my parents right before I was born? Why didn't they live together? I spent a lot of time at my father's house a few blocks away. His cousins loved and cherished me. I called them Aunt and Uncle, but I called my father by his first name, Roy—never Dad. None of the adults ever told me to call him Dad, not even my mother. I did not know at the time how strange this was.

You might say that my parents coparented me, my mother making ninety percent of the decisions. When I asked my father what had happened between them, he never gave me a straight answer. My mother never answered me at all. I continued to ask, but the only reply I got was "Go outside and play, and don't stick your nose in big people business" or "Children should be seen and not heard." In this climate of secrets and silence, I grew up and learned to thrive.

In her own strange way, my mother taught me freedom of expression. As early as I can remember, she said, "Always tell me the truth, and you will never get a beating. Never be afraid to tell me anything." On the other hand, she upheld the family tradition of keeping secrets and keeping to ourselves. This mixed message was confusing for me as a child and continued to confuse me even into my adult years.

The only girl in this family of six boys, I got my way quite a bit. I was the only one who traveled out of the district to go to school. I took two buses while the boys walked. I always had stories to tell, and even though my family got sick of my incessant talking, my mother had encouraged me to talk and would not go back on her word. I loved my mother and trusted implicitly her plans for my educational future. I took piano lessons, had a tutor for math, and recited poetry at church and community functions. Her plans fit easily into my life, since I loved reading, writing, and performing. I dreamt of becoming a nurse or dentist someday. My favorite teacher told me you had to study hard and be very disciplined for such a career.

By the time I was eight I had learned to do the things that thrilled Mother, but I also knew how to get the things that thrilled me. I was growing into the sneaky, rebellious type. In front of my mother's face I yessed her to death, and the minute she was out of my sight I did as I pleased. I still brought home good grades and was enthusiastic about her plans for me, but I knew I had to find ways for my free-spirited personality to thrive. I knew that I was special and that I had to carve out my own set of rules, apart from my family. In retrospect, it was not so clear then, but I knew something *big* was going to happen.

The year I turned nine, my life changed dramatically. I was never the same again. I awoke on a bright sunny Sunday to find red stains in my "good" church panties. We had gone to a festive school affair the previous night. As always after church and after any special occasion, my mother had instructed me to take off my "good" clothes. These items included my frilly ankle socks, white lacy camisole, and matching panties. I was lazy that night and decided to take a short cut to bed and not remove any of the good stuff.

So here I was on this beautiful Sunday morning facing these horrible red stains and not knowing what to do. I knew I had better not tell my mother; we did not talk about such things. Mom never mentioned intimate parts of the body, especially the genitals—somehow, I knew it had to be bad. I had disobeyed her and slept in my undies. She had also warned me not to play with boys, and I had. The picture was bleak.

My mother went to her Red Cross Volunteer Corps meeting, and I was left in the care of my grandmother and aunt. I did not tell them anything; instead, I changed my panties every few hours and hid the soiled panties far under my bed (the bed I shared with my mother). Later that day, my six-year-old cousin arrived. Relieved and frightened, I told her my story—that I had cut myself "down there" but wasn't sure where. She had me lie on the bed and she looked for the cut. So there I was, lying on the bed, legs spread as wide as they could go, while she looked for the cut with a little bandaid in her hand, waiting to put it on when she found it. After a while we gave up and I resumed changing my undies for the rest of that day.

My mother arrived home and I still did not tell her. Next morning when I awoke, there was a big ugly stain on my mother's sheets. Through tears and terror I sobbed to my mother that I had not done that. My mother shushed me and went to her closet and got out a large piece of white cotton, folded it in a triangle, and handed me a piece of elastic and two huge safety pins. She then helped me tie the elastic band around my waist, put the cloth on, and fasten it securely with the safety pins. I was humiliated. At recess on that first day, I stood against the wall and refused to play. I was afraid that if anyone, especially a boy, bumped into my back, he would know, would tell the entire school. A fate worse than death. *Humiliated for life.*

Thus began my introduction into womanhood. My mother had not comforted me or talked me through this major rite of passage. Unable to discuss it with me, she wrote to her older sister in New York, who sent me a book on "the curse" some six months later. Not even my brother knew about my curse. When the dust settled, two things were clear. I should never talk about sex and I should not play with boys. This cemented my belief that playing with girls, especially sex play, was the right thing to do. Boys were out. Girls were in. For me this was good and right.

Nine must have been the magic number. That was the year I met Coral. She was thirteen and had something that looked like a small Adam's apple, hair on her chest, and hair coming out of her nipples. She usually smelled of oranges, but also had a strange, almost male, musky smell under her arms like my brother's after he had been out playing all day—Gramma would yell at him to wash up before dinner, saying we smelled as rank as horses. Coral's family attended the same church mine did, and though I usually hung around with girls my own age, Coral was friendly, and we became fast friends.

On Sundays, the children had club meeting from three to five, then we had evening church service at seven. Between the hours of five and seven our parents sat around on the church porch talking while we played or went for a walk to the parlor (candy store) or to somebody's house nearby.

Coral lived very near the church. Looking back, I think she must have been a lonely child. Her parents, an older couple who had married late, were often away or busy with their furniture business. Coral once described herself as an afterthought, an accident. One Sunday, we walked to Coral's house for snacks. We sat around eating oranges and talking. Then she asked me to lie down on her bed with her. It was a small, rickety, black-frame metal bed. The springs sagged and squeaked as we lay on it together. Coral began to push her body very close to mine. She touched my face, my hair, and rubbed her fingertips very lightly over my new breasts. She pushed her breasts softly against mine, then a little harder, letting our firm button-tips touch. Not too hard, but just enough to ache a little. This was a new sensation for me. My legs felt hot, my face flushed and damp. I loved the way she made me feel. We pushed close together, rubbing our bodies frantically, our clothes still on. Coral put her hands in my panties and touched me "down there." I did the same. My head felt giddy and light. I started to giggle. She put her hand over my mouth, but I could not stop laughing. She didn't like that very much, so she stopped touching me there.

A week went by. I thought about her a lot. Next Sunday, I was back at Coral's house. This time we didn't eat any oranges. We headed right to her room. She removed her shirt. I was amazed she had hair on her chest and hair coming out of her nipples. I watched in wonder. I had never seen that before. She came over and put her nipple in my mouth. I nibbled at it the way Coral had done to me. I felt unsure: I didn't really like her nipple hairs—they felt funny in my mouth. Plus, she had that musky boy smell. It repelled me as much as it excited me. I did not quite understand, but it all felt good, and I could not wait for it to be my turn. Coral got on top of me and angled her body so her mouth was at my little breast. She kissed and rolled it around in her mouth. After that we rubbed and played until we were both laughing loudly. We thought we heard someone at the door, so we jumped up, got dressed really fast, and headed back to church.

We began to meet regularly. Since I traveled to school, little attention was paid to the time I arrived home. My mother was usually tutoring, and Gramma was always busy with household chores. I began leaving school promptly after classes and headed to Coral's house. One day, I told Coral that I wanted us to rub our pussies together. I thought if we did this something magical would happen. We had already been experimenting for some time, and when we rubbed our bodies together, any slight vaginal contact would cause an overpowering sensation. But we were little girls, inexperienced, and hadn't explored those feelings long enough to see what would happen. I asked Coral to try, but she said no. I was disappointed but did not push. After a few weeks, I asked her again, this time insisting. Finally, she said in frustration, "I don't want to try it because it doesn't work."

"How do you know?" I asked.

"Because I tried it with Betty already, and it doesn't work."

That satisfied me, and I left it alone.

I never got jealous or mad when Coral said she had done it with Betty. Somewhere in my head I knew I would try it with someone else and make it work. A few days later I tried it with another girl, Hayden. We tried it a few more times. It never worked, so eventually I gave up on the idea. I often wonder if this was the beginning of the nonmonogamous life I would successfully lead later as an adult. Coral and I continued to be lovers until I turned eleven and was sent to school in another district. A few months later, Coral and her family moved away.

As much as I blabbered on at home about everything, I never told anyone about Coral and me. I had learned my family legacy and was carrying it on well.

1964: The year I turned thirteen began another new era in my life. Still in pursuit of my educational dream, Mom sent me to New York to live with her older sister, Olive, so I could attend high school. She and my brother planned to follow within a few months, but that year the Immigration Service tightened their rules, making it difficult for two family members to get visas in one year. My brother was almost eighteen and being considered for military service in Trinidad. Our family plans took a strange turn. It was a year before my mother was issued a visa and five years before my brother joined us.

It was agony. I went from an outspoken, outgoing, daring child to a moody, insecure teenager. I missed my mother so much that sometimes I prayed to die. This intense loneliness caused me to seek solace in books and in writing. I wrote long, pleading letters to my mother to let me come back home. Finally, she joined me, and my world was complete.

I continued my relationships with girls and began dating boys as well. I finished high school and married shortly thereafter, as my religion and culture dictated. After all, that was what all my friends were doing in 1970. I married a loving, supportive Caribbean man. I was nineteen, he twenty-one. We had first met in Trinidad when I was twelve and he fourteen. It was a great marriage. We grew up together. We shared our language, our culture, and our family traditions. The birth of our son followed the next year. He was and still is the most magnificent gift his father and the universe have ever given me. I adored him.

The marriage lasted nearly two decades. During that period, we became involved in an open marriage. With my husband's support, I explored relationships with women. Since our son was so young, we agreed to keep this secret. We loved each other and our child.

The years were generous. There were parties, trips, and, yes, women. I believed my life could continue this way, telling friends I had the best of both worlds. When I met Alisha, everything changed. I fell deeply in love with her and she with me. I tried to keep my marriage strong. It was hopeless. We divorced. My family suffered intense pain, especially my son. I felt worthless and guilty, as if I had not been a good mother. Over the next few years, my relationship with my son took a severe beating. I felt controlled by guilt. Even now, writing this makes me very sad. I worked hard to make it up to him. Only one thing stood between us. The big "L" word: "Lesbian."

Summer 1992: We danced with zest, passion and a wild fever to the sounds of Buju Banton's hot new reggae jam "Boom Bye Bye." In Jamaica, Buju's island, and in Trinidad, my birthplace, it was #1 on the charts for a record-breaking number of weeks. In New York City it was also #1, making the rounds at every gay and lesbian party I attended that summer.

We held our lovers close, grinding and gyrating to the sounds of this seductive reggae artist. We did not yet understand the hatred and death threats of the words he sang. In the song, he bragged about how he hated gays and wanted to put bullets in their heads while they made love in bed. Buju had recorded the song in traditional Jamaican yard dialect. Unless you understood the dialect, you would not know what he was saying.

By the time we understood the full impact of his lyrics, a grave fear had spread among us. We learned that a group of young Jamaican men were beating up Caribbean lesbians and gays in the Flatbush area of Brooklyn as part of an initiation into a gang. This news sent a wave of terror and anger throughout our community.

Gang members would walk up to a queer person and shout "BOOYAKAH, BOOYAKAH," simulating the sound of a gunshot, then be verbally or physically abusive. A similar terror was hitting the island of Trinidad. Gays and lesbians there were being forced to come out of the closet. They organized, started an underground newspaper, and set up discussion and support groups. Back in Brooklyn, poets took to the stage with their rough words. Caribbean gays and lesbians took to the streets, many of us outing ourselves to our Caribbean community in the process. Funny, we'd been out to the rest of America, but not to our own people. Our Caribbean brothers and sisters, mothers and fathers, thought us sick. They believed we had caught the white man's *nasty* disease. In Trinidad, years ago, they stoned queer people and threw them out of their community. Still today, in Jamaica a person can be killed for being gay, and the police will look the other way. I was afraid to tell my mother I was a lesbian. I feared losing her. I had lost her once before and was afraid to take that chance again. I was already an outcast: as a black woman in America; an immigrant; a large, dark-skinned woman; a dread-locked woman; a woman with a white lover. How could I come out to my family? Could I handle much more? Most importantly, I feared losing my son legally as well as emotionally. But what about my life? This gang could take my life or the life of someone I loved at any time. Ours were some of the heads they sought. Nothing could protect me. Nothing could protect us.

We organized and for the first time became visible. After reading an article in the *Village Voice* disclosing Buju Banton's hatred of gays and love of guns, I responded by writing a message to him. A few people we knew had been accosted on the street. We were scared, but not backing down. My lover, a white woman, held my hand, comforted me, organized with us. She took photographs to help us document our struggle.

On the home front, I came out to my son in the middle of a shouting match. He hated my lesbian life. He said that he believed I hated him and his father. He said that he was angry at me for spoiling his life and that he could not bear the thought of me with a woman, especially a white woman. I asked if he believed I was a good mother. He said yes. I asked if he thought I loved him. He said yes. "Then what is the problem?" I asked. He had no answer.

Everything I had feared for so long was coming true. I was scared and didn't know what to do or say to comfort him. So I yelled back at him, telling him he had no control over that area of my life and that he should accept what he could not change. I felt like a coward. I felt like I had let him down. We did not speak for months. I cried like crazy.

At the same time, my sisters of color expressed increasing disapproval of my white mate. It was not easy to be a lesbian that year. We worked hard as a community and as a couple. We won that round. But my relationship with my son remained shaky. I was scared for a long time. I am still scared, afraid I'll hurt him or worse, lose him.

Buju finally apologized. It took awhile, but he did. The gangs seemed to go underground; a silent hostility remained on both sides. That year we marched in the New York Pride parade as a Caribbean gay and lesbian contingent for the first time. Some of us marched in the Caribbean Labor Day parade. We were heckled some, and it got a little scary, but we did it. My writing took on a new rage and a new pride. I loved my life. I loved my woman. We stayed together.

Syl, my closest cousin on my mother's side, has just returned from the Far East, where she now lives. She is weary and in need of rest. She is lying on her mother's (my mother's older sister's) bed. We have not seen her in three years. Despite her exhaustion, we gather around to hear her many tales.

We are the five women in my family: my mother is seventy-two; her sister, Olive, eighty-one; Olive's daughter, Syl, sixty-two; Syl's daughter, Kay, thirty; and myself, forty-one. The three older women begin talking about their youth, their parents, and their early family life. Their family consisted of eight girls, two boys, their mother, and their alcoholic, but gainfully employed, father. The discussion turns briefly to their father's abusive treatment of their mother. My mother and Olive say they can't really remember some of those old stories. Each seems sad and pensive. Then suddenly the mood changes. Syl goes into high gear, talking with great pride about how they were a family of secrets. Mom brags about how they were referred to as "the secret order" by the other families in their community. They congratulate each other on their ability to keep silent. Olive says she could keep a secret best. The others agree. Kay and I listen as outsiders. I feel myself getting angry, realizing that the secrets they are so proud of have been my greatest source of pain. Such silence makes me invisible, vulnerable, a target for anyone's vengeance and rage.

I leave my family's home. Hurt and angry, I take these secrets to my father. I am angry at him, my father, the co-conspirator; I want to hurt him for all the ways he has not taken care of me, for all the ways he has supported my mother in her silence. I tell my father I am gay because he has not taken care of me, because he has neglected and lied to me. He pretends not to understand. He wants to know why I like my mother best.

New Year's Eve, 1996: I am single again. I meet Cee at a party. She has a great sense of humor. She's bold and assertive in a way that I like. She has gorgeous locks down to her ass—I love that. We joke, laugh, share a dance. We exchange numbers, become friends. Months pass; she wants to spend the night with me. I want that too, but tell her to give me a reason. I am cautious.

Next day she sends a huge, exotic bouquet of Caribbean flowers to my job. The card reads: "Here's a reason."

My officemate runs over and asks in her bubbly, excitable way who sent them. She does not know I am a lesbian. I tell her they are from a woman I'm falling for. She laughs approvingly. I come out to her.

It's so easy. It's not always that easy.

I call Cee. I write her a poem of thanks. It reads:

Spread those dreads
Spread those dreads baby
make a bed
make a bed baby
I wanna lie down.

1965, age fourteen or fifteen

BRIDE OF CHRIST

Mary Beth Caschetta

MY mother always said I couldn't keep a secret. She said I wasn't really her daughter.

SECRET #1

My best friend Gina lived on Wide Waters Lane, her backyard stagnant from the Erie Canal a few feet away. Her brothers and sisters started the rumors: dead cows and baby heads. In 1977, we were forbidden to swim in the water, chemical pollution and river death still very popular. We moped around, while Jimmy Carter announced that natural gas, petroleum, and coffee were scarce.

We were running low on nature.

Gina was distracted by the new girls, sisters, whose family had been relocated by Kodak, their father a chemical engineer. They were exotic girls with movie star names—Charlene (Charley) and Louise—

dark-haired and black-eyed like us Italian girls. But they seemed more subtle—no hairy arms or wide hips—and I remember hearing they were Jewish, thinking they were beautiful.

Older by two years, Louise was the organizer. Games were her domain; House was her favorite. Five minutes in their cool carpeted basement, she'd lie on the couch, flip on a soap opera, and sink into a loud nasal tone, most likely imitating her own mother.

"You be the boy," she ordered.

I was the one with the brothers, but still it seemed unlikely.

I crossed my arms and sulked around the television set.

"Not the kid, stupid, the husband." More direction soon followed: "Start over: walk in the room, lie down on top of me, and kiss. Act tall, like you mean it. Now, squint your eyes. That's good. Okay, do it again like it's your idea." Kissing her was a disappointment; at thirteen, she had miles to go before her edges softened. She lay on the sofa, all elbows and teeth, game over minutes after it started.

The rest of the day we played Ping-Pong, or wistfully walked to get a look at what we longed for: a stagnant canal, no longer ours, poignantly commenting on our childhood.

In the woods, we poked leaves with sticks until it got late.

"I gotta go; my mother will kill me," I said.

Charley rolled her eyes. "Just set your watch back and say you didn't know it was slow. You get a whole nother hour that way."

It didn't fool my mother for a minute. "I don't like those girls."

It didn't matter what she said, or what I felt. Gina was entranced.

The Alligator Club was formed one day, after Charley watched a documentary on endangered species. Louise liked the idea of naming ourselves after something dangerous: Whitey, Croc, Scales, Killer. Half in love with both of them and persuasive through her lavish attentions, Gina managed to get me in. Louise suggested we write our favorite TV stars.

"Let's organize a bake sale and raise money for reptiles in the Congo," I said.

"Don't be stupid," Louise said.

One afternoon, they conducted a mysterious study with their father's *Playboys*. Sensing danger, I came up with countless excuses to leave, but they insisted on hauling the magazines out of the bathroom vanity.

I'd seen naked women before: my father was a big fan, and my brothers had boxes of them in their closets and sock drawers, under their beds; naked women on slick paper grew in every crevice faster than weeds. My mother had recently given up trying to throw them away.

I stood frozen, as the Alligators sat plucking out centerfolds like magazine tongues; hands behind my back, the furious activity took place all around me. In minutes, dozens of shiny pages gleamed up at me from a fuzzy blue bath mat.

"What's the matter with you?" Gina whispered, yanking my shirt. "Get down here and help. It's important."

I couldn't answer.

"What is it?" Charley said loudly, startling me.

I shifted weight from one foot to another, trying to be casual.

"You're smiling," Charley accused, putting a hand on her older sister: "She's standing there smiling."

"I'm not," I said.

My best friend Gina dropped her head in her hands, as if all had been lost. "You are."

I shook my head.

Charley volleyed. "I saw it."

"We all saw it." Louise got to her feet. "What *are* you smiling about?"

I tried to think.

Charley took out a notebook and wrote down my name in neat blue ink. "Three Alligator Demerits." Since the club had no purpose, demerits were harmless; still, I felt humiliation rise up and pink my cheeks. Riveted by the glossy girls with their pages wide open, I managed to say, "I think I'd better go now." But it was too late: I had already burst into tears.

"What's your problem?"

"Home," I choked out.

Home was where my brother's imminent departure to college had everyone tense. His constant hand-washing, moping, and grumbling had even sharpened my parents' dull sense of impending doom. Home was where all three of my brothers were due to arrive, piling out of separate car pools from football practice. In August they had double sessions: twice a day they pushed into the doorway—sweaty, huge, and hungry—half-dressed because of the heat. My mother met them in the hallway, forcing them to strip, so she could wash their muddy jerseys.

"Out of the way, Tuner," they told me.

Home was where even nicknames were secret. Where I stood in the driveway counting cleats caked with dirt, like dead animals.

I kept sobbing. Louise stormed out of the bathroom, disgusted.

Gina gathered the magazines back in their stacks, handing them to Charley, who shoved them under the sink, closing the cabinet doors. They led me to a bedroom and let me lie down.

"They were only magazines."

"Don't be such a baby."

They sat on the bed, staring at walls, getting wiser every second. I'd noticed before how much smarter they were becoming: "Stop crying. We'll go to the canal and throw some stones. We'll fish for dead cows."

I seemed only to be getting dumber.

Already, simple tasks had become mind-boggling; days jumbled, my brain easing from normal lines of thought. I was a train in danger of derailing starting from the first night my brother began coming into my room.

"Don't bug me," I'd say, half-asleep, convinced it was a joke.

As I fell back into my pillow, he'd roll to a belly drop and slither out.

Sometimes he'd speak. "What time is it?"

"I'm sleeping," I'd complain.

In daylight, he seemed his normal, grunting self, though at times I'd catch him staring at me, a funny look across his face, as if the sun were in his eyes and he couldn't quite make me out. Ten to his seventeen, I grew whispery and cautious.

In the dark, he sat on the edge of the bed, making it shake in strange labored rhythms.

It got worse.

"What time is it?" "Did you hear something?" "Tuner, is Mom in here?"—His questions interrupted my dreams. Soon I woke up with bruises, my skin turning colors from pinching.

I asked for a lock on my door.

"Stay out of there," my mother told him distractedly.

The next night, I awoke to find him with his hands in my pajamas. Mute, I rolled to the other side of the bed, got up, and went to find my mother.

She was asleep in the living room, TV blaring. "What is it?"

I made a stab, a semiaccusation, trying to name body parts, but the words were hard to get out. Somehow my mother translated enough to take action. The next day she bought him a clock radio: he'd explained that he came to my bed to ask what time it was. As if to organize a misguided game of Cat and Mouse, she put a string of bells on my door.

Years later she said, "Your father thought he was adjusting to puberty," though he was nearly eighteen. After a cousin explained my nickname to his sister, she explained it to me. Tuner, originally *Tuna:* "Even five-year-old cunts smell like fish."

I'm not clear whether my brother stopped coming into my room that summer, but I have a distinct memory of a time when I woke to find him fully grown, a junior in college, standing over me, drunk, breathing hard, leaning in to touch me.

"Get out," I said. It didn't seem to matter that I was no longer mute; my life had become an echo chamber, indistinct, with no hope of concentration or connection.

I learned to adjust, a weird kid with a secret.

SECRET #2

Kids hate the sight of a mess in their own image, the fragile flesh of another child turning to jelly. It makes them nervous, breeds responsibility. Maybe Charley, Louise, and Gina were just doing their job, a few days later, when they took me out behind the woods.

"We know," Louise said.

I stared at her gleaming black eyes. How could she know? I hadn't breathed a word, except to my mother who urged forgetting. Louise hadn't been to the club in weeks, snubbing us for new friends down the block. I wondered if they could tell I'd also stopped sleeping.

"We've been having meetings about you," Charley said.

"Secret ones." My former ally Gina spoke more tentatively, as she studied the dark dirt floor under her bright white sneaks.

"You might as well just get it over with and confess," Louise said.

"I, I, I . . ."

"She's an idiot," Charley interrupted. "Let's kick her out. She's no endangered species. She's not even special."

Gina tugged at my arm. "It's about the photographs. They arrived today."

I looked at the packages in Charley's arms addressed to "The Alligator Club."

"What were you thinking?" Louise snorted.

Sweat gathered on my upper lip, as Charley pulled out the pictures: "We wrote to Shaun Cassidy, The Osmonds, Davey Jones, Parker Stevenson."

Louise stepped in with another set of photographs in her hand: "You wrote to Police Woman, Kate Jackson, and some old lady."

"Can you see their point?" Gina asked. "Women!"

Charley threw the offending photographs at my feet. Angie Dickinson smiled up at me, an autograph across her Police Woman uniform, as my life turned away from the brick wall of my brother's touch and headed for the steep cliff of treacherous girls.

Louise continued with the evidence: "You like playing the boy when we play House, and you like kissing me. You know what that's called?"

I didn't.

"Don't forget the magazines," Charley said. "She loved the magazines."

I looked at Gina. "You did smile," she said in a low voice.

"She's a weirdo," Charley shouted. Her sister agreed: "Abby Normal."

The wrong question formed on my lips: "But am I hopeless?"

Surprised, they thought it over carefully, eyeing each other for an answer.

"You get one more chance," Louise said at last.

"But don't ask for help," Charley added. "You either act like us or forget it."

After the sisters marched away, Gina looked up. "Got it?"

I nodded my head, eyes blurred with relief.

"Good."

SECRET #3

I didn't go back to Wide Waters Lane, waiting instead on my own front porch for August to end—outside where it was safe, but not quite yet in the world, where it wasn't. I read books, rode my bike to the library, watching out for football players. Then one day, in the middle of the afternoon, a few weeks before I would turn eleven, a car pulled up and ejected four squat dark forms, all of them resembling one another, and somehow, me.

"Cousins from Ottawa?" my mother said, appearing beside me. "What are *they* doing here?"

Before long, my entire family was standing on the front porch.

"*Compare*," said the man in the driveway. He held out his hand. "We've driven for help, Doctor Cousin. Something terrible!" My father, an obstetrician/gynecologist, who drove a fancy sedan, shook the man's hand, smiling briefly at the fat woman and the two girls who cowered in the background.

After the men headed inside, my mother whisked the fat woman into the house, my brothers close behind on her heels, leaving me alone with two cousins about my age.

Their names were Fatima and Angelina.

The older one was taller than me, prettier. She walked over to my chair and perched on the edge, scanning the sidewalks. The neighborhood was Italian, but ritzy; it must have seemed strange.

Bored, Angelina asked to braid my hair.

"Fatima has visions," she said. "The Holy Ghost comes in her room at night and tells her things. Dirty things."

Fatima was fizzy-headed, slow; her eyelids drooped half-closed.

Perching in the corner of the porch, she took me in. After a while, she smiled, saying things that didn't seem to go together: "My mother doesn't speak English. You're short, aren't you? The Holy Ghost is really a dove. We're not allowed to go out after dark. When Angelina turns sixteen, no one will let her drive."

In no time, my father came out to usher Fatima into his office off the far end of the kitchen hall. It was a small room with one red leather chair, hunting rifles, and a stethoscope.

As the porch door snapped closed, my mother's voice came through the crack with a lingering smell of coffee. "A quick examination."

My grandmother drove over and made rabbit with tiny parsley potatoes and string beans from my grandfather's garden. She spoke to the cousins in beautiful Italian, lulling them to stay for dinner. In a thick tongue, they spoke over our heads about diagnoses, doctors, priests.

Fatima's father had coffee-colored skin, his fingers tapped nervously, his mustache twitched. He never seemed to look anybody in the eye, least of all his daughters. "May all your sons become doctors," he told my father.

"I want to be a doctor," Angelina said to no one in particular, to me, maybe.

In the silence, her father lit a cigar and gave it to my father.

She was about to say it again, when her mother reached across the table and clamped her elbow. The smile on my own mother's face faded, returning only when the men stepped into my father's office to continue the consultation.

All I could do was focus on the pile of fragile rabbit bones on the edge of my plate. I clung to my grandmother's scent—olive oil and garlic—as she moved swiftly around the kitchen, stopping occasionally to give me a hug.

That night before bed, I asked my mother.

"*Petit mal* seizures," she said carefully.

"Who says?" I asked

"Your father examined her."

"What is it?"

"Like epilepsy," she said. "She thinks she sees things."

"Like the Holy Ghost standing over her bed at night?"

My mother nodded.

Long ago, I had stopped believing in the Holy Ghost, but the Father and the Son, I knew, came in living color. I understood that Fatima didn't have epilepsy; the man standing over her bed at night was her father.

I couldn't have said how I knew, and I worked, most of my childhood, to forget.

Eventually, the memory of my father rose like the Erie Canal stench of 1977: I am small, almost five, with my father hovering over my bed. There is no possibility of a mistake or religious symbol: the image I see at thirty-one is frozen in black and orange, a clue only my body can decode. My body does the difficult work of remembering what my brain is slow to release. The door, his face, my pain, flesh that goes hot and then dead come together over time, like sluggish sheep in the herding.

Even now, memory is a mystery to me, trapped in the skin like Braille, in the muscle like pleasure, in the bone like an ache.

Pushed against the wall of the faithful, the summer I turned eleven, I considered my options. "What if I become a nun?" I asked my mother.

"A nun?" she said. "Really?"

I shrugged. "Would you be mad?"

"Mad?" She spoke carefully. "If it makes you happy, I wouldn't be mad. Do you think you have a calling?"

"I don't know."

"Did you ask Him?"

I took my mother's God quite seriously, though I didn't really like Him. Jesus was more my speed, like a nice brother, who might take you to the park.

"I don't talk to God," I told her. "I'll ask Jesus. Later."

She looked alarmed. "Everyone's a child of God, you know."

I didn't want to be anyone's child. "I'd rather not."

She looked at me, puzzled.

"Bride of Christ," I said.

By the time adolescence rolled around, she persuaded me that cheerleader was a more viable solution. In a way she was right.

Eventually, I had to choose a boyfriend, so I picked someone not very threatening, who wouldn't pressure me in any way about anything, a boy sweet and slow and patient. Still, all things sexual continued to confound me, forming like pebbles in my shoe.

I told a woman in my college freshman English class that if I didn't end up marrying my childhood sweetheart, I was heading for the nunnery. I could see I'd said the wrong thing by the look in her eyes—a flash of Charlene and Louise.

"I must be gay," I told my college roommate before I'd kissed the woman I was in love with, lain by her side, or held her hand. It was the late eighties; you could make bold statements that were true in metaphor, if not yet in fact.

It didn't take me long to figure it out; I didn't need the convent, after all.

Even so, It's hard for me to feel sufficiently "out," no matter how often or public I make my identity. I still walk around my life as if there's someone left who doesn't know. Maybe it's impossible ever to feel completely out. Or maybe this is the legacy of secret-keeping, a twenty-year-old hangover without a cure.

The private ways of coming out are still more difficult. The Christmas I broke up with my childhood sweetheart—no longer a boy, but a man—my mother took matters into her own hands, "What's going on here? What are you hiding from me?"

I can still picture her, cornering me in the kitchen, her nightgown thin as a tissue, my tea getting cold on the counter top.

I'm not sure how she knew. "What are you? A lesbian?"

I nodded my head.

"I wanted to be the only woman you loved," she said and turned away.

Lately, things have gotten better.

My mother no longer cries at the very sight of me, at the loss of the white wedding, the squelched possibility of my being anyone's bride. She no longer bristles at the females in my life, even the friends. She seems to love my partner, who was Catholic before Castro swiped religion from Cuba, perhaps because she's a lawyer, respectable. Still, though, my mother insists enlightenment will come only after the seventh angel breaks the seventh seal. Book of Revelation.

"Words are our friends," I tell her.

"A good long chat is in order," she says, optimistically, "but not today."

I picture Judgment Day like this: a cup of coffee, the kitchen table, my mother seated across from me.

"What if I'm a lesbian in the next life, too?"

She shrugs. "Everyone's a child of God." She knows what my father did to me. "Lesbian or not," she says, "next time things will be different."

I hold the sentence in my mouth, pressing it against my tongue until it dissolves. Sweeter than a secret: a wish.

THE COMING OUT OF
A GAY PRIDE CHILD

Elizabeth Lorde-Rollins

I had a taste for pretty young men with stiletto smiles and silent eyes when I met Lucy. I was fifteen. My boyfriend was a beautiful mama's boy—he did turn me on—but we hadn't done anything yet. We were both scared, he a lot more than I. I should have known Jay would turn out to be gay, too.

Everything about Lucy made me think of sex. It just oozed out of every pore—she didn't have to try to be sexy, she just was. This ran contrary to everything people say about big women. But the way Lucy moved— deliberately, hips up on one side, then the other; the way her hands, dimples for knuckles, looked on anything: tapping a backgammon piece, cradling a joint and then holding it up to those baby-bow lips—absolutely everything made me think about how it would feel to kiss her. Or have her hair in my face. Or her hips moving under me, steady and insistent.

Both my parents were gay—or rather, all three of them. My mother and her long-term lover, Frances, were the parents my brother and I lived with, and my father had us every other weekend and for a month in the summer. This arrangement, ten years old the fall I met Lucy, was wearing thin: my brother had problems with my dad and didn't want to come on the weekends, but would still acquiesce to Friday night dinner.

My mother had "come out" to us when I was six and Jonathan five. We had been curious about why she and Frances slept together with the door closed the same way she and Daddy did. My mother, never one to shy away from controversial topics, sat down with my brother and me in the living room and told us in plain language that sex was an expression of love, and that sometimes men and women loved each other, sometimes women loved each other, and sometimes men loved each other. She and Frances slept in the same bed because they were grownups who loved each other. She explained this in such a logical, matter-of-fact fashion that my only reaction was to wonder if this meant that Frances and Daddy loved each other, too. Were all three of them going to sleep in the same bed when summer was over and we returned to New York from Providence?

My father was a harder nut to crack. Supported by what I considered overwhelming evidence, my brother and I asked him if he was gay. I was twelve, Jonathan eleven. He told us that he wouldn't answer the question. It was not a child's place to be involved with the particulars of his or her parents' sexual lives. Jonathan and I looked at each other. That clinched it, we agreed. He's definitely gay.

I'd been asked if I was gay on a fairly regular basis since I was eleven and my family had appeared on a TV show about lesbian-headed households. I didn't say I was gay, ever—my stock answer was that I "hadn't yet determined my sexual orientation," and that answer from the mouth of a preadolescent was enough to make most folks back way the hell off—but I was pretty sure that I was straight. I'd had a fevered crush on my math teacher since seventh grade, and a couple of crushes on boys. When I fantasized, I thought about men— naked guys that I liked, in a locker room, taking a shower. I was never with them. I was way too self-conscious for the thought of myself being sexual to turn me on. Sometimes I thought about women to see if that would get to me, but it didn't. I had no visceral reaction when I thought about Diana Ross or Bette Midler or Donna Summer the way I did when I thought about Andy Gibb taking a shower.

My reaction to men scared me—on one hand, I was relieved, because that meant that I must be normal, destined to be straight when I grew up. On the other hand, I wondered if that meant I was going to be alone my whole life. I was already aware that I felt a lot freer to be myself around girls and women than around men. I was also aware that I was no big draw in the romance department—all the boys I had ever liked either (1) didn't know I was alive, or (2) considered me their best friend and confidante in their quest for other girls, usually my best friends. Early on, I figured that there was no way I was ever going to have a boyfriend of my own, even if the thought of certain men made me feel . . . warm. Wet. In sophomore year, when Jay and I started hanging out together, I realized that he made me feel that way. But all we had ever done was kiss. Once, he had let me run my fingertips over his chest, but when he got hard and I wanted to touch him, he wouldn't let me. I hadn't ever thought a woman could make me feel like that. Then I met Lucy.

My mother had breast cancer the fall I started my sophomore year of high school, and asked her friend Diane if she would hire me at the Bakery. Diane ran the Bakery; Connie, her lover, financed it with her psychotherapy earnings. Together they'd created the Bakery, a lesbian salon that could only have existed in the late seventies. Where else could you empty your head and fill your mouth with delicious things all in the same place?

Clients would come to the East Village townhouse right after work, one or two hours before their session with Connie, have a joint or two (remember the days when we thought that drugs *enhanced* therapy?), and play some backgammon or dance. Every once in a while, Connie might ask to have the music turned down, but the therapy room (as we affectionately called it) was right off the cavernous living room/kitchen/dining area, and the doors were double-insulated with dark brown cork for precisely that reason. Most of the time, the sounds of Frankie Crocker spinning on WBLS after work, women laughing and smoking, backgammon pieces being shuffled around, pans clanking, mixers whining, and Diane throwing more logs onto the fireplace were just a soft background to women pouring out their life's dramas (or creating them) behind those heavy oak, corked-up doors.

Diane and Connie were family friends of ours; I'd been behind the cork doors myself once, a single session after which Connie had referred me to a therapist I didn't know personally, with whom I could discuss my growing teenage angst. It was a smart move, referring me—but for the adults, that comfortable, clear space between hang-out buddy and therapist didn't always exist. Diane kept a maternal eye on me—she'd lost her own daughter in a custody battle and had a lot of mother energy just kind of loose and on the run. She didn't rein it in that often, either. She was forever broaching *topics* with me; it was tough just to have a laid-back conversation. So when she asked me if I wanted to work at the Bakery, I figured she was (1) trying to help my parents out by keeping me occupied and (2) probably going to engage me in many a conversation to find out how I was handling my mother's breast cancer. Her motivations ceased to concern me, however, when she told me I'd be paid $5 an hour Wednesdays and Fridays after school, a total of ten hours a week. Hot damn.

So three to eight it was, Wednesdays and Fridays. The first Friday began quietly enough. Diane was all alone in the kitchen and showed me around. My first job would be making chocolate chip cookies. Like all Diane's recipes, this one had a secret ingredient—a mixture of Bosco, half-and-half, and Crème de Cacao—carefully titrated to the flour/butter mixture to produce the desired result. This should be easy, I thought, looking the recipe over, and got started.

The smell of the place intoxicated me and everyone else who walked in. Lemon squares perched on flaky shortbread, dark chocolate madeleines sprinkled with a doily pattern of powdered sugar threatened to float out of French baking molds, Grand Marnier cheesecakes overflowed gingersnap crusts, and apple pies came out of the ovens spitting their juice all over the drop pans. All this culinary activity was accompanied by characteristic fragrances, and sometimes, it was good enough to make you melt. Holy cow. I was going to learn to *make* all this stuff?!

It was exactly four o' clock when Lucy walked in. I had just taken my first batch of cookies out of the oven. Diane looked them over.

"Now's where we begin some quality control," Diane said slowly, after taking a couple of deep breaths and trying to get her face under control. She started to pick at a few cookies.

Lucy came over, her heels striking the hardwood at a clip that belied her size. "Too flat," she pronounced unemotionally. "Diane, just chuck 'em." Then she smiled at me, extending her hand. "Hi, I'm Lucy. How ya doin'?" A greeting, not a question. Brooklyn, maybe Bensonhurst. "Diane told me you were starting today."

"Uh, yeah. It's really nice here. My name's Beth. Nice to meet you."

"Don't worry about the cookies. We'll do a few smaller batches until you get the hang of it." She tossed her purse onto the couch, then her key collection, which was heavy enough to make a warden stand aside. "Here, put this on for me, willya?" She handed me a standard deli apron identical to the one Diane had given me to put on. I took it, still having a hard time not staring at her, which I knew to be impolite. She just had so much . . . energy. She was electric in the spacious, warm and cozy room.

"Put it . . . on you?"

"Yeah—like Diane has hers," she said, turning her back to me expectantly.

After a quick glance at Diane, I let the bib with the neck loop drop, holding the apron taut by the waist strings, and passed it around her so that the fold came to the level of her cleavage. I was about six inches taller than Lucy, and as I made sure the front was in the right spot, I inhaled. Wow. Her perfume was sweet but slightly bitter, like dry wine. There was a faint woodiness to it. All of a sudden, I felt like I had to sit down.

The rest of that afternoon went by very quickly. By five-thirty, the place was packed with women: five or six clustered around the backgammon game in session at the dining table; four on the plushy futon couch built for three in front of the fireplace; two women seated on the floor in front of the couch, happy recipients of a couple of first-class neck rubs; two women dancing. A group with eight partici-pants had started at five in the therapy room. Lucy, Diane, and I stayed in the kitchen, close to the festivities. Diane was making praline cheesecakes that day, and had begun mixing the praline powder to coat the top of each of them. Lucy took on the task of showing me how to make the perfect Bakery chocolate chip cookie, since my first efforts were obviously not even close to what was required. At seven, we took a break to make deliveries. Lucy stayed in the car, and I took the silver parachute bag filled with boxes into first Balducci's and then Rumbul's. On the way back, Lucy really made time. Her silver Toyota zipped in and out of lanes that I hadn't even realized were there. I guessed she'd been a little ginger on the way over to our deliveries so as not to disturb the baked goods. At eight, she asked me to untie her apron and let me know that she would take me to the ferry. I spent the whole trip to Staten Island thinking about her.

By October, Lucy and I were friends. I was flattered that she treated me like a real person, not just a kid. When she was smoking a joint, she'd always hold it out to me and then just pass it to the next person when I declined as if it were no big deal. I would just hold up my hand ultra-cool, as if to say, "That's okay, I just had one at the office," while inside I was saying to myself, "They're offering me *the joint??!!*"

On our delivery trips, Lucy would tell me stuff that she couldn't tell Diane about her frustration with the business and how she felt that neither Diane nor Connie really listened to her, even though they were financial partners. Diane had been Lucy's junior high school teacher. As a teenager, Lucy had been babysitter to Diane's little girl, Karen. Now that Lucy was grown (twenty-eight, to be exact) the fundamentals that had been established early in the relationship served as a ceiling to Lucy—she could only go so far with Diane and feel that she was being heard. Ironically, this dynamic would repeat itself in my relationship with Lucy. Also by October, it was apparent to anyone who hung out at the Bakery that I was smitten with Lucy Cohen.

Diane approached me first. One afternoon, before Lucy got there, Diane opened the conversation.

"You and Lucy seem to get along pretty well."

"She's a nice lady," I answered with what I hoped was a noncommittal tone.

"Well, it's pretty clear that you think she's a very special lady . . ." Diane was looking right at me, I could feel it. And I also knew that there was no way I could look back—not right then, anyway.

"You just want a single batch today, right?" I asked, ducking behind the kitchen island to fetch some cookie sheets.

"Yes, single. You know Beth, we've *all* been through this. It's kind of sweet to see how much you like her. We just don't want you to get hurt, honey."

Gag. Now I was really going to be sick. What a thought! All of these people who had seen me grow up now knew that I had a wicked crush on this straight lady. And they didn't have to worry about me, either. I could take care of myself. On the other hand, Diane was my boss. And I guess I could see how she would be concerned and all. She was always in everyone's business anyway. In fact, everyone was in everyone's business at the Bakery, right or wrong.

"Well, I appreciate you looking out for me, Diane, but honest, Lucy and I are just friends." Four cups of flour, three, four . . . "And I know she's straight. I mean, half the time she leaves here . . ." Sugar, one, two . . . "she's going to meet some boyfriend of hers, all dressed up." I still couldn't look at Diane, but I could feel those cat eyes on every corner of my face.

"Whether she's straight or not doesn't stop you from feeling your feelings, Beth. And sometimes those feelings can be very hard to deal with."

For the first time, I looked up. This needed to be nipped in the bud. "Well, I'm not having any trouble dealing with mine. Honest, Diane. I would tell you."

"Just as long as you know I'm here for you, honey. And so is Connie."

"Thanks Diane, I appreciate it." I hugged her back. Ugh. Why was my love life, or lack thereof, such a topic of interest to these ladies?

Of course, everything I had said was a lie. And of course, it was abundantly clear to all that I was in love with Lucy, especially to Lucy, who was by turns titillated and horrified. In late October, I was sitting next to the gang at around eight-thirty, watching a game of backgammon. I never played; I wasn't good at it, and I didn't like to lose. Lucy was, of course, winning. She always won. Her good humor and her generosity with a joint kept all of her adversaries from getting ticked off at the regularity of her victories. Just in a pinch, always when she needed them, Lucy rolled double fives or double sixes. She had just placed Martha's piece up on the bar when she gave me her glass. "Beth, do me a solid and get me some Coke, please."

"Can I get you anything else?" I asked as I went to the refrigerator.

"How about a flaming hoop?" snickered Martha. Laughs all around. Diane gave Martha a warning look, but said nothing.

Later that night, Lucy went out to the stoop to have a cigarette. No one was allowed to smoke cigarettes in the house. I went with her; by now, this was a ritual. We could hear Anne Murray's voice coming from inside; work was done for the day.

Oh, I just fall in love again.
Just one touch and then it happens ev'ry time. . . .

"So how's Jay?" Lucy asked. This was her favorite line of inquiry. I guess it made her feel that all was not lost if I had a boyfriend.

"He's fine. I'm going over to his house tomorrow night for dinner."

"Oh yeah? And after the doctor-to-be meets his mother's approval, is he going to give you some?"

"Lucy!" I playfully pushed her, laughing. "Who said I wanted any?"

She squinched up against me again, cold in the October night. Without any warning or permission—she knew she didn't need any—

she put her ice-cold free hand between my down jacket and my shirt, where it came to rest on my waist. And I got a major chill that had nothing to do with the weather.

"Of course you want some!" she continued, as if she hadn't touched me, as if it didn't mean anything, as if my head weren't about to split into a thousand love-lost pieces. "It's only natural. He's adorable, that kid."

"Yeah, he's cute. Now you, you're adorable."

"Beth. You must be blind."

"I'm not blind. You must think I'm kidding around or something."

"I don't think you're kidding around. And I know how you feel about me. I even had a dream about you. But I'm telling you, forget it. It's never going to happen."

"Why not? What did you dream about me?" Now I was really intrigued.

"There is no way I'm telling you. Suffice it to say, it was lewd and lascivious."

My vocabulary was decent, but I hadn't come across "lascivious" in my travels yet. It didn't take a Brainiac to figure out, though, when it was preceded by "lewd." I knew what that meant. I was in!

"Lucy, you can't say things are never going to happen. Life is strange. Weird things happen every day."

Lucy allowed herself an ironic look that plainly shouted, Get a load of this fifteen-year-old telling me about how weird life is. Fuhgeddaboudit. She was silent, thinking. "Beth, weird things do happen. But I'm like a champion tennis player who you're asking to go out and play a game of soccer."

Give me a break. Did straight people really think that sleeping with people of the same sex was akin to playing a completely different sport?

"Lucy, if you're great at sleeping with men, you'll be great at sleeping with women. It's still tennis. It's just that the balls are a little different."

"Yeah, right. I don't believe I'm having this conversation with a fifteen-year-old."

"I'm an old fifteen."

"You got that right. But put it out of your head, 'cause it's still not going to happen. If you want to sleep with a woman that badly, find someone else. I wouldn't know what to do."

"I'll show you. And besides, I don't want to sleep with just any woman. I didn't even think I liked girls that way until I met you."

"Oh, great, so I'm responsible for this. Do me a favor. Sleep with Jay, and do it soon. 'You'll show me.' What makes you think *you* know what to do?"

Now it was my turn to think a little. I didn't know how I knew. But I did know that if I ever had the chance to make love to Lucy, I wouldn't need to refer to an instruction booklet for my next move.

I worked at the Bakery all that winter and into the spring. Lucy and I started to spend time together outside of work. I met her brother, Harry, who was hospitalized that spring at NYU Medical Center with a Hodgkin's flare, and her mother, Otti, an extremely attractive older woman who caressed Lucy's name every time she said it. She pronounced it "Luby." Lucy, Connie, and Diane were invited to our house for Christmas and came, definitely making the day more enjoyable for me. At one point, I caught my mother watching me watching Lucy. She just acted as if she'd been glancing my way incidentally, but I knew that she knew something was up.

It was about two weeks later that my mother said something to me about Lucy. As was her way, she waited until we were having a really good time together. We had just gone shopping for something and were on the way home, my mother singing offtune to one of her favorite oldies, Frankie Lymon's "Goody Goody":

*So you found someone who knocked you back off your heels
Goody goody!
So you found someone and now you know how it feels
Goody goody!*

I always had to laugh when I heard my mother sing that song. She took such pleasure in that last line and sang, "You rascal, you," with such gusto that it really was great. After I collapsed in a heap of laughter in the passenger seat, my mother got reflective.

"You know, Beth, loving is never easy." I waited. I could tell this was going to get serious, but where on earth was she going with this? "There are very real power dynamics in any relationship."

"Hmmm," I said, trying to convey the impression that I was listening closely. Nothing ticked my mother off more than the feeling she was being taken less than seriously, and I didn't want to spoil this good time we were having. That year, they were few and far between.

"I know that you care about Lucy, and I really believe she cares for you, too. But be careful. When a person your age gets involved with an older person, the power dynamics always favor the older person. I know Lucy is a good woman, but just be careful, because she may hurt you without meaning to."

Boy, all this concern for my mental health and well-being. I wish these people would keep their advice to themselves and just throw money! "Mom, don't worry about me so much. I'm not involved with Lucy. I mean, she knows I have a crush on her and all, but it's not going anywhere. We're just friends. She's the straightest of the straight; she has boyfriends coming out of her ears."

We'd come to a red light. My mother looked at me over her glasses. That's the look she saved for when she really wanted to get her message across. "Straight, but curious, my girl. They're the worst kind."

The following spring went great, on wings. In mid-March, I turned sixteen. Lucy told me sixteen made no difference; that was still too young to go to bed with. Jay and I spent a lot of time together when we weren't in school, and we'd graduated to a couple of activities that felt really good. I was in no hurry to have intercourse with him, since I was terrified of getting pregnant, and what we were doing felt fine. Lucy asked me what I was up to, and I told her. She seemed to consider it her responsibility to tell me about the ways of men and how to please them, and since I felt woefully underprepared for that aspect of life, I thoroughly enjoyed her candor. There was nothing she wouldn't—and didn't—tell me.

Right after Lucy's birthday, at the beginning of April, I went to Florida for spring break. When I got back, Diane and Connie were away on vacation. Lucy called to tell me she wouldn't be at the Bakery until three-thirty, so not to hurry there from school. It was so quiet in there without all the people; it was even a little eerie. I made a batch of brownies and Lucy whipped through four apple cakes before we even took a breath. But there she was, at the dining table, her back to me, with the afternoon light coming in the cathedral windows, and she was breathtaking. I walked up to her.

"Beth. What are you doing?" she asked without turning around.

"Getting ready to kiss you," I breathed. And she didn't move. I swept the brown hair from her neck, lightly, and then bent to kiss her soft, fragrant skin the same way I'd dreamed of doing a hundred times or more.

"Stop it, Beth."

"Why?" I murmured into her hair.

"You know something? That's a good question." Lucy pushed her chair back, nearly knocking me over, and looked me dead in the eye. "I've been thinking about this, and I've come to the conclusion that if you want to sleep with me that badly, you must be ready for it."

I didn't say anything—I couldn't. Breathing was a challenge. I leaned forward, closed my eyes, and tasted her lips. We spent the rest of the afternoon into the evening on the couch in the therapy room. I wasn't worried about knowing what to do; I just wanted to experience her, to taste her everywhere, to hear her moan. I kissed her soft, silky thighs all the way up to where she ran wet and warm like a spring.

We didn't get out of there until nine-thirty, the time I usually walked in the front door on Wednesday nights. Lucy said she'd drive me to Staten Island. I appreciated it, but said she could just drop me off at the ferry—after all, she lived in the Bronx. Lucy looked at me. "Do you honestly think I would just drop you off at the ferry?"

If we'd known what was waiting for us at my house, maybe she would have. Lucy insisted on coming in with me, don't ask me why. We'd cooked up our story on the way: (1) we were baking late because the workload was heavier without Diane; (2) Lucy drove me home because we'd gone late and ferries were only running once an hour; (3) we'd run into traffic on the BQE going toward the Verrazzano-Narrows Bridge. As I entered the front door, I called out, "Hi! I'm home."

"We're in here, Elizabeth," came my mother's voice, an octave lower than usual, from the dining room. Uh-oh, trouble. My mother only called me Elizabeth when she was pissed. We walked into the dining room.

"Hello, Frances . . . Audre," Lucy greeted my parents, kissing each one on the cheek as if it were such a nice surprise to see them. Damn, she's good, I thought admiringly. She sounds completely natural.

"Hello, Lucy," said my mother, a little coolly considering they'd shared a joint together at their last meeting.

"You all will excuse me, I've got some work to take care of upstairs," said Frances as she practically ran out of the room. "Good night, Lucy," she waved. "On a school night," she murmured to me as she made her exit. "We'll talk about this tomorrow."

Lucy sat down in the chair Frances had vacated, next to my mother.

"So Audre, how ya doin'?"

"Just fine. I presume you two have had an eventful evening?" my mother queried, her eyes on me, still standing at the dining room entrance.

While we went through our explanation, my mother calmly took out her stash and rolled a joint. "That still doesn't explain why you didn't call me," she noted, looking over her glasses in my direction. "Lucy?" as she passed the joint to her right. I just couldn't stand all this normalcy. It was really an effort. Lucy was holding the joint with the same fingers that had been inside of me, making me feel things I'd never felt before, just over an hour ago.

I tried to clear my throat, but I had no air, let alone spit. "Well, I'm really tired. Think I'll go up to bed. Have a good night, you guys." I kissed both my mother and Lucy on the cheek. Lucy ran her finger down my side when I bent over her; my mother couldn't see it from where she was sitting, but she did not miss the quick intake of breath that accompanied that move.

"Good night, Elizabeth," said my mother. "Sleep well."

My mother did not discuss that night with me until many years later. Frances must have had a discussion with Mom about it, because, though I'd clearly violated the rules by staying out late on a school night—and Frances was big on rules, but fair—she never brought it up, either. I guess they figured I was going to suffer enough when I got my heart broken. And they were right.

I didn't come out to my father until almost two years later. We'd just had dinner with Jay, whom my father clearly adored, and gone back to my father's apartment after dropping Jay at the train.

"Jay's a really nice boy . . ." my father began tentatively. I gave him a look with just enough smile to let him know that he sounded a little ridiculous. We were seventeen, after all, and Jay was taller than my father. ". . . young man. It seems that you two are pretty serious about each other."

"Define serious." I could tell my dad was starting to feel tortured, and I was enjoying every minute of it.

"Well," my dad began slowly, starting to sound like a lawyer, which was how he always sounded when he was stressed, "one can tell that you're quite fond of each other, and that there's a mutual respect . . ."

Okay. This was starting to get even better. But I really couldn't laugh, or I would make him mad. Or sad. With my dad, those two emotions usually weren't far behind each other.

"Sure I respect Jay. He's one of my best friends. We've done a lot of growing up together, you know what I mean?"

"I'm trying to. Do you know what colleges he's applied to?"

"I think he really wants to go to Hopkins, and after he got that Westinghouse, I'd be really surprised if they didn't take him."

"But you haven't even applied to Hopkins!" My father sounded absolutely panicked. What was up?

"Yes, I have, Dad. But I don't think I'll go there, even if they accept me. Jay and I love each other, but if we go to the same school, we might keep each other from . . . I don't know, doing different things from what we did in high school. Growing. Besides, I want to go to Harvard. It makes it easier to get into medical school if you have a Harvard degree."

"Well, my dear, Hopkins is no slouch in that department, either. And keep in mind what you might be throwing away. Jay might not be there waiting for you when the two of you graduate your respective universities."

Now not laughing really was a struggle. My poor dad. He really had no idea, even though any fool ought to be able to tell—Jay was way too pretty to be straight.

"Dad—don't you think it's a little early to be thinking about marriage?"

"I think it's too early for you to get married, but I don't think it's too early to think about being with someone you really care about. You and Jay have been together for three years now."

"Dad. I really do love Jay, and we have been a lot of things to each other. But Jay is not completely straight—he sees men, although nobody steady. And I'm not straight, either. I've been in love with Lucy for years."

My father looked as if he'd been punched. This wasn't funny anymore. Suddenly, I felt very, very tired. He was the last person I'd have expected to react like this.

"Lucy? You've been having an affair with Lucy? She's almost twice your age!"

"She's only thirteen years older than me, Dad. And we haven't been having an affair. She only slept with me a couple of times"—don't tell him it was two years ago, that wouldn't be smart, I realized in a rare moment of clarity—"Mostly, we're just friends. But I'm still in love with her. I think I might be a lesbian."

Now he really looked whipped. "I certainly hope for your sake that you're not, Elizabeth. I certainly hope that you're not."

"Dad, how can you say that? You know that gay people are

normal, with interesting lives and families who love them. You of all people should know—I mean, I know that you haven't really come out to us or anything, but—"

"I've told you before that my sexual life is none of your concern. I am your father. But *your* life *is* my concern. And I would like it to be as easy for you as possible. And that is why I say, I hope to God that you are not a lesbian."

"But Dad, Mom and Frances and their friends have great lives, and a lot of fun. They do interesting things. Lesbians think that other lesbians are sexy when they get older; straight women just try to look younger all the time because men think that older women aren't sexy anymore. I mean, there's a lot of great things about being gay. And nobody cares if you're gay anymore. I mean, probably a fifth of my graduating class is gay, and nobody says anything about it."

"Elizabeth, you are woefully ignorant of the historical context that informs our discussion. First of all, if you think that all men find older women unattractive, you've been watching entirely too much television. Second, when it comes to matters of sexual orientation, it is very much not the case that 'nobody cares anymore.' It was less than four decades ago that homosexuals were carted off to concentration camps by Nazis; it was less than two decades ago that homosexuals were killed in Cuba in an effort to rid the Cuban population of homosexuality. Gays are beaten in the streets all over the world to this day." My dad was on a roll now. He'd gotten up out of his chair and was striding about the living room as if addressing a jury, with each point pounding his fist into his other hand. "Third, I don't think you understand how difficult it has been for your mother to maintain ties with her family in the face of her sexual orientation. The relationship your mother enjoys with your grandmother is very hard-won, as is her relationship with both her sisters."

I was crying. I didn't know why. I mean, I wasn't weeping or anything, but my eyes just kept tearing up, and I couldn't stop them. When my dad saw me, he stopped talking and came over to the couch.

"I didn't mean to upset you," he said in a much softer voice, sitting down and putting his arm around me. "You know that I only want what's best for you. You're my special girl, you know that."

"Dad, if I am gay, I can't go around hiding my whole life. What kind of life would that be?"

He looked at me with a rueful half-smile. "Before you ask yourself that question, Elizabeth, be sure that you are gay. You're young.

Almost everyone has a crush at one point or another on a close friend of the same sex. It's really much too early to tell. Leave yourself open."

As I sat on the couch, crying onto his shoulder, still shocked at his reaction—I had expected him to kind of smile bemusedly, to say that history has a funny way of repeating itself—I was pretty sure that I'd hit upon a truth. I was a lesbian. Being attracted to men didn't change that, loving Jay didn't change that. And, like baking the perfect cookie, it wasn't going to be as easy as I'd figured.

Audre Lorde

At the dinner table, 1978

EASTER WEEKEND

Minnie Bruce Pratt

Fayetteville, North Carolina, 1980

I didn't say anything, not for a long time, not for years. Or not much. What *do* you say to your children when they know that the other children live with their mothers, but they don't live with you? What do you say when the teacher tells you that your second-grader broke down and sobbed over the construction paper and crayons and the assignment to make a card for Mother's Day? When your youngest one is still too little to tie his own shoes, and he asks why their father is moving them to another state?

I told them that I wanted them, and their father wanted them too, and the law had given them to him. So they had to live with their father. The oldest asked, "Is the law the sheriff?" I said, "Sort of." He understood not going against the sheriff, who has guns.

I didn't tell him that people in our family, both of his grandmothers, and some of our neighbors, and lawyers and judges, were using another idea of law, "God's law," to keep him and me apart. He knew I didn't believe in God. We'd already talked about that when he was three or four and asking questions about where he came from and where he was going. I'd told him then that I believed there was something without a name, an energy, like electricity, that came and went through everything, and we all held a bit of it. When we died, then our energy went to be part of everything. I said nature was big enough. I didn't say the God on the cards his grandmother sent was too small. He had already seen how his family divided up in that argument. When he was three and his brother not yet talking, we ate dinner on a patio in Florida with his father's parents. Each of us adults had our own TV table, steak, baked potato, salad. No conversation. Suddenly into the silence, he says, "Mama, Grandma says you're a liar because you don't believe in God." What did I answer? I was twenty-five. I didn't know I could make a reality by speaking steadily into that silence. I didn't know the consequences, yet.

But today I've decided to talk to him and his brother. I've decided to "come out to them as a lesbian." We are sitting at the top of the cool, slightly damp, wood steps that lead down from my porch. Odd to make a formal statement, to notify them of what they already know. When they were five and six, sometimes I took them with me to the bookstore where my lover worked. I was "coming out" with her, though into what remained to be seen. When I looked at her, she was surrounded with golden shimmering light. My face must have reflected that bliss. In the car one summer afternoon, as we left the parking lot of that otherwise barren strip mall, the oldest asked, "Are you in love with her?" And I said, "Yes." But very soon I was afraid to tell them more.

I never told them I thought of running away with them, just the three of us. It wasn't that I wanted to be a Madonna with children and a halo around my head. Or a tragic figure, a Pietà, me clutching my lost babies to my breast. I just wanted to be able to hold them in my lap every morning, to have their bodies shift against me, unselfconscious weight, for a few minutes at night.

But when I imagined our existence, the fiction of names, the stories made up to satisfy strangers—and what kind of work would I get?—I couldn't do it. I wanted them to have the rest of their family, to feel how history had tied us to a particular place and time, how history had moved us away. To see my mama and my aunts, to travel half-asleep in the warm fragrant dark to the house on the last piece of the farm, where all the grandchildren had gone in the summer. To see their father, his sister, those grandparents, to run with their girl cousins on a burnt sugar sand beach by the Gulf.

Maybe someday to see, like I had, the ones on the edge of the family, the ones outside. The baby, less than immaculately conceived, given away. The shadow color of cousins on the other side, never acknowledged.

Maybe someday to understand that our separation had come because I was put out of the family, declared not a real mother by the law and their father.

So from the time they were five and six, and I'd moved out, and the divorce papers were signed, they'd lived with their father in Kentucky, a fourteen-hour trip by car. I got to see them by driving there or by taking them to my mother's house, another ten-hour drive. With my friends, I joked that I had gotten "father's visiting rights," but that wasn't true. The terms were much harsher on me, the lesbian mother, than on any errant father. No visits with them out-of-state unless in the presence of my mother or a maternal aunt. No having them in my home if I lived with any other adult. Alternate major holidays (Thanksgiving one year, Easter the next, but never Christmas Day), and some time in the summers. No official child support, but mandated payments into a college fund. Always the threat that if I told the children "too much" about my life, I would lose my scant time with them. I would lose them.

Of course I didn't tell them these details, and today, as we sit on the steps, I wonder what they've thought of our strange travels. The New Year's that we were all crammed into my VW bug, them and our suitcases and my holiday presents for them, including a cage with a gerbil that kept escaping. That was the time we raced up and down two-lane highways, south and north, so we could have three days of winter holiday together. Lately my youngest reminded me that I'd stashed some Oreos on the back floorboard near the heater. At midnight, his brother asleep, he found them and ate them, hot cookies, and I laughed, "I baked them just for you." But I don't remember this. I remember other times, driving through snowstorms and rainstorms and mountains to get to them, starting at night and sleeping for an hour in a gas station parking lot halfway, and then driving some more. No radio in the car. I went in silence, trying to understand what had happened, trying to figure out what to do. I remember all the things I tried that didn't work, like the tomato plants we set out by the fence in their new backyard that wouldn't grow. Not enough sun.

Today is a long time after that. They are eleven and ten, and it's spring break. We've just gotten back from the beach. Our skin is toasted browner, and we sit languidly at the edge of the porch. For a few moments there is nothing important left to do after having been riders of the waves in the glory of the sun.

This is the first time in five years that I could afford an apartment alone, without a roommate to share the expense, and so this is the first time in five years they've slept over at a place I call home. I only have one bed. I'm putting them to sleep on a big pallet of covers on the floor, in their sleeping bags. A makeshift hideout. Their roof is my desktop, an old door stretched across two sawhorses. It reminds me of how I used to sleep on quilts on the floor in the dining room when I was little, every other weekend when my unmarried aunt came home to us from her job in the city. I loved how the house got turned topsy-turvy to make room for her in the family. It only lasted a weekend, but I knew she'd be back in two weeks. For five years I haven't known from one meeting to the next if I would see my children again.

I didn't even have time to buy folding cots for them because this visit was a surprise, unprecedented since the divorce went through. Their father called me on the Wednesday before Easter weekend—he was driving to see friends in the state—did I want to have them for a visit? It wasn't the scheduled holiday, but—

When I was little, my favorite holiday was Easter. Not for any religious reason, though every year I sang with exhilaration "Up from the grave he arose." But it was the life in *up*, in *arose*, the green-white blossoms of the dogwood trees dancing slant again in the skeletal woods, and the silly miraculous stories. I knew a rabbit couldn't carry anything, much less flower-colored eggs. I was a country girl who had eaten rabbit, spit out the buckshot. I had gotten eggs still warm from the hens' straw nests, walked barefoot through the shit-stained dirt of the chickenyard. But I believed the fertile logic in the holiday, though I didn't know it was older than my Bible verses. When I grew up, I found the goddess Eostre in a book, the one who came as a pregnant moon when the sun began its spring. She brought presents of red-dyed eggs, and had a game where she threw death in whatever water was around. So what if she only appeared nowadays as a pre-scription drug, in birth control pills, or menopausal ointments? When the children were little, the two springs they were old enough before they were taken away, I hid the eggs outside in the gray light just before sunup, and put their baskets on the doorstep. Later, they raced with serious faces toward the blue, yellow, purple, red eggs that seemed to have been nested by an unknown wild animal in the dewy grass of our yard.

Maybe because it had been our innocent holiday, maybe that's why I wasn't frightened by him this time. "I have plans," I said, "I have a house rented at the beach with the woman I'm seeing now and her son, for Easter weekend. Of course I'd love to have the boys," I said, "if they can come with us." He hemmed and hawed. He said, "Perhaps you can make other arrangements." I said, "No." I said, silently, *Why are you so eager to give them to me now, after you took them away? Are you meeting a lover?* I said to myself, *I've had to make a life. I can't cancel it at his whim, not even to see them.*

The ramshackle house was on the coast south of the Cape Fear River, right on the beach, facing east. The first morning the five of us ran out on the wooden deck above the water. The light was the golden light of a morning that had never before seen the world. A flight of pelicans swept past us, heading down coast. The wingbeat of each segued, on the beat, into the next behind, until all settled into a silent glide. All day we ran and played in the ocean and the sand, and at night we dyed eggs as we fried fish for supper.

That night my lover and I put the three boys to bed in one room. We sat up for awhile reading and talking while they squirmed and wrestled and argued and slept. Then she and I went into the other room, and closed the door. We stretched worn white sheets over the sagging, musty mattress, and we lay down and held each other and slept.

The next morning the boys got baskets with green cellophane grass and lots of jelly beans and chocolate bunnies. Once I had given them yellow plush chickens that walked when you wound them up. Once I had gotten a spun sugar candy egg, like milk glass with blue and pink roses, with a window cut into one end. I looked through it and saw another world inside, almost too small for me to make out, a place to hide if the one I lived in got too hard.

We ran barefoot on the beach once more, the spring tides, the high old time, splashing cold up to our knees. Then we said good-bye to my lover and her boy, and drove to my house. And the morning became this afternoon.

Now in a long slope of silence we sit together on the steps. I never want this day to end. For a minute this could be any late Sunday afternoon of my childhood. Are they thinking about tomorrow? To-morrow they will go back to their father. Now is my chance to begin to talk to them, to explain the reason why we live like we do. What do you say to your children when, for all they know, you are the only ones who live this way?

But the words are lifeless in my mouth, what has never been said between us. Because I thought they would share any conversation about "lesbian" with their father, and I didn't trust that he would let them be with me if I spoke. Because I never wanted to tell them something and then say, "Don't tell your father." Because I did not want my life to be a dirty buried secret that I told my sons to lie about.

Now a little crack has opened, a way to escape. I never thought he'd let me have them overnight with my lover. But now I have to explain what surely must be a mystery to them. Why would two women and three boys suddenly set up house for a weekend, as if we were kin, as if we were a family? And then just as suddenly have to leave each other, with no promise of reunion? That morning we had faced the sun as it rode over the water and touched us, standing all together on that spit of land like the first time and the last time. I have to explain how this day can be ours forever, and how I don't know what will happen next.

The afternoon is passing, the light is fading. So I say, "There is something I want to talk to you about." They sit through my rapid explanation, the reason I went there with the other woman, that we are lesbians. Do they know what that means? No? Well, we love each other, two women together who love each other are lesbians, two men who love each other are gay. Some people think this is wrong, the laws are against it, that's why the two of them can't live with me. But I don't think it's wrong, it's about love.

There is another silence after this. Finally, the oldest says, "So Jesus was a lesbian?" I can't help it, I laugh. Who's been teaching him about Jesus? Enough religious information so that he even knows about all those male disciples. I say, "Well, he might have been gay. He certainly did love those other men. We just don't know."

Tomorrow they go back to their father. Tomorrow I could get an angry, denouncing phone call and hear that I'll be forbidden to see them for six months, a year, forever. This is my chance to talk to them. The youngest keeps getting up and down, fidgeting. All he wants to do is play tether ball. All three of us know what I am saying: that I am their mother, and I have defied the laws of God and man, and I have been punished for it, and so have they. And we may be again. I sit and hold my oldest boy's hand, and I say, "Is there anything else you want to know? Is there anything else you want to ask me?" They look at me, hesitant, anxious. All three of us know what I am saying: that the universe they live in every day is not the only one, that I have just cracked it like an egg and whispered to them to look through the opening, to where I stand, with others, outside.

Eno River, N.C., 1980

Cris South

POT LUCK

Cynthia Bond

TIME bubbles like a pot of gumbo. Circles of oil skimming the top; peach-red crab claws, slick okra, plum tomatoes, and Galveston shrimp peeking beneath the surface; the weight and girth of flesh—slices of stuffed turkey sausage, chicken slipping from the bones, and all but the hoofs of a cow steeping near the bottom; the foundation of roux—onions, garlic, celery, and thyme giddy and leaping with the rolling boil; the gumbo filé, salt, and white pepper embracing and binding the mixture; and the wooden spoon dipping and stirring like an oar in a green sea. Getting older is adding more garlic and filé for flavoring. It's taking risks and not following the recipe. It's adding Louisiana hot sauce and hot chili peppers and getting your tongue burned. It's learning to dilute the brew with chicken stock. It's the settling of ingredients and relishing the steaming taste. Gumbo, like time, is the flavor of all that was and all that will be. All happening at once.

So when I tell this story, it won't be the entire truth. I'll pour a bit of it into a bowl and close my eyes and slip the curve of spoon into my mouth. I'll feel the broth swirl in the well of my tongue. I'll hold it there and try to isolate one moment, one ingredient: thyme? onion? a string of chicken? And if I'm lucky, I may do it for a second . . . and taste the ripe fear and cantaloupe of Sarah with her panties knotted about one knee. Or I'll smell the Epsom salt and alcohol we burned to keep the ghosts out of our room at the Roger Williams Hotel. The scent of Mom cooking cornbread in the cast-iron skillet at Thanksgiving. And the way Sarah's breath dusted the back of my throat like powdered sugar before we kissed. . . .

I'll recall the innocent seasoning of being twenty-one and not remembering any of the abuse. The prying open of cotton elastic and what Uncle Carl called "my special candy," the weight of his pecan-thick fingers clamping the curve of my head. My jaw dislocating in surrender as my childhood was torn into and sold like chewing tobacco. I'll remember the pain that seared me in two before I had the strength to give it a name. But still it lay there like gristle in the corners of the pot, an unnamed aftertaste I was not to discover for nearly a decade—still one that in singular moments I could almost discern.

But then all of those near memories, tastes, particles, and seconds will blend, I'll give in and relish the tang of the whole. I'll bite and chew and savor and swallow. I'll turn up the bowl and lick the bottom. Then I'll stir the pot, fill the ladle, and serve myself again.

My mother dreamt my first kiss with Sarah. I come from a family like that. We all dream each other's lives. Telephone each other at 5:31 A.M., 12:15 A.M., 3:00 P.M., from Kansas City, Champaign, Chicago, L.A., telling each other in groggy crackling voices, "I dreamt you were trying to unscrew that mason jar and . . ." or "Last night you rode a giant wave of chocolate pudding when . . ." and "So Mom was a snake and her skin kept shedding . . ."

My father's family are "siddity Negroes" from Louisville, Kentucky—educators and doctors. Life-long members of the elite Jack & Jill Club, where all well-heeled Negroes gathered, provided their skin was lighter than a paper grocery bag. My dad couldn't join. The joke when my dad was born was that my grandmother looked at him for the first time through the maternity window and exclaimed, "But he's so daaaaark!" This story was retold every Christmas.

My mother, Zelema, grew up in East Texas farm land. She slept at the end of cotton fields and sucked on the stalks of sugar cane. She learned to fight because she was beat up every day after school because her skin was fair—a tone referred to as "yella." One day, her mother told her that if she came home beaten again, she would whip her. Shortly after that my mother became famous for scratching a "Z" into the flesh of one of her attackers a few weeks after the film *Zorro* showed at a nearby town. By the time she was ten, high school girls traveled to fight her. She was legendary. She learned to frighten girls five times her size with her acidic speech and her scathing tongue. After a time, she rarely had to fight—her foes defeated themselves. She used her verbal acumen to become the only member of her family to attend college, which is where she met my dad. He was a fine arts professor.

My father was set with the unspoken pledge to "lighten" his offspring. My mother, who never wanted her children to be called "yellow" in the schoolyard, was determined to darken the family line. They were a perfect match. My sister and I could, in the dead of winter, pass the "paper bag" test. Our hair could *just* hold a pencil. In a way they had both succeeded.

Still, Dad wanted for me to marry "bright"; Mom, "dark." Never in their wildest imaginings did they envision me with a white person . . . much less a woman.

So my mother dreamt the night that Sarah and I couldn't find an open bar and went to a corner liquor store and bought a six-pack. We cracked a beer open and lay back flat against the grass hill and kissed. I'd only kissed college boys, disco boys, and gay boys who loved the fact I had no breasts . . . So I shoved my tongue all the way down her throat several times, until she pushed me back and said that she'd like to try and kiss me if I could stop "kissing like a boy." She parted my lips with her tongue and I tasted her breath, and my temples started sweating, and my heart curled into the roof of my mouth. This was the summer and the spring and the winter and the fall before Sarah and I moved to the Y.M.C.A. on 34th Street in Manhattan on New Year's Eve 1983.

I was twenty-one and living with Noel Deacon when I met her. I'd just temporarily sort of, only for one quarter, then two, then three, dropped out of Northwestern University after the summer of my sophomore year. Instead of saving my share of the tuition, I'd spent the entire summer working as a waitress at what my friends called the "base of the cock" (the bottom of the John Hancock building), going to the Paradise every night doing group orgy pantomimes to "Tainted Love," and spending the little money left after drinks and makeup on pot and cherries, which were my entire diet for the summer. After searching for me for a month, my mother dragged me back home— then threw me out because men in pickup trucks regularly dropped me off at 6:00 A.M. in front of the house on Olive. Because my mascara was always smeared into my temples and my lipstick had slipped to my chin and cheek. Because there was usually vomit on some article of clothing and the stench of alcohol in the amassing oil of my pores.

I bounced around until I saved enough to get my own place. Noel was the thirty-eight-year-old G.M.D.D. (gay-man-in-deep-denial) who moved in with me after he discovered God. Shortly after that I began to support him. And then he became my boyfriend.

I'd just gotten a job at the Submarine on Main Street in Kansas City, right next door to the John Casablanca School of Modeling where blond Kansas City modeling hopefuls collected and shared lip gloss. The Art Institute was up the street and drew in the matted-hair, chain-smoking, paint-under-the-fingernails crowd. It was also right off of the snobby rich la-de-da Plaza, which brought in its share of suit-and-tie-wearing tie salesmen. The place was always filled.

At the time, I went through two packs of Marlboro Reds a day, if I was lucky. So although I don't remember it exactly, I was probably smoking when I met Sarah. She made the submarines. She wore boys' clothes, wrinkled and big, and she smoked almost as much as me.

I thought that she was the most beautiful woman I had ever seen. Her clipped hair was sifted cork and sand. Her cheeks held a constant blush. She was exactly my height, five eight and a half. Her lips were full and stayed chapped and worn from practicing her trumpet. She had bullet-black eyes and a graceful lean swagger. She wore cowboy boots.

Although all of my friends were gay men, I had never consciously known a "lezzzzbian." As a Midwestern kid, the closest I'd ever gotten to the abstract theory of "female homosexuality" was, at fifteen, calling a number I'd scrawled in my notebook that a friend had given me. It was for the Blue Orchid Studios. I would call from the dining room phone (the only one in a two-story house) and cross my legs and squeeze and grind as a woman's badly recorded voice trembled and purred, "Hello . . . you've reached Blue Orchid Studios. I'm soooo happy you called. Do you know what I'm wearing? Absolutely nothing. And I'm waiting to hear from you. Please leave your message at the beeeep." I would call her again and again and again until I came. Sometimes an actual woman would answer the phone and I would frantically hang up. It was the Blue Orchid in the dining room during the day and pressing into a pair of rolled-up socks under the covers in my bedroom at night while thinking about the Blue Orchid lady that got me going.

Needless to say that at twenty-one I could not fully appreciate the utter majesty of a young, handsome twenty-year-old lesbian trumpet player staring into me while spreading mustard for a triple salami on wheat with provolone. This woman who caught my eyes and held them before looking down into the ashtray. Who, with great concentration, trained me on the sandwich board and discussed tips after the lunch rush. Who I pressed past each morning in the crunched kitchen to get butter and half-and-half from the refrigerator. Wrists, forearms, calves, fingers touching in the effort. This woman who spoke in mumbled low tones, smoke curling from her lips as if she were burning inside.

I later learned that Sarah was from an all-white suburban town. Her father worked on airplane engines, her mother had a part-time job as a receptionist at a nearby factory. Her sister Kira was a trumpet player, too. Kira was straight and blond and played in a rock band named Gilligan. Sarah played jazz. She had since she was a little girl when her parents let her take classes at the Charlie Parker Foundation on Troost.

After a while Sarah started taking me to Kansas City jazz clubs. Dark clinking rooms wrapped in tobacco blankets. Old-timers rising to pitch and wail "Cherokee" and "A-Train" and a bit of Miles. Brown and gray men with wrinkled suits and damp collars screaming, punching, fucking the ether with their music. Sarah would unfasten her case and take her horn out and blow soundlessly through the mouthpiece. Then she'd finger the pedals, the tiny mother-of-pearl circles that said "ssssssss" when she pressed them without breath. We would order drinks. Vodka and grapefruit for me. She was still underage and everyone knew it. She'd been showing up to play in clubs in Kansas City's segregated East Side since she was thirteen. A skinny white girl who could pass for a boy, toting a horn. These were places where pimps and prostitutes met to count cash under tables, swap stories, and order shots of bourbon and beer. Places my sister and I had never even driven by. When Sarah was fourteen, she asked the musicians if she could play. They said yes, glancing at each other with smiles burning their cheeks. She played. She wasn't good. She wasn't bad. But every once and a while she hit a lick that said she might have something. They laughed and let her stay.

She told me this much later. But that night I sipped my drink and listened. I didn't understand the music. I was a Helen Reddy "Angie Baby," Casey Casum's Top Forty, *Chorus Line*, *Showboat*, *Porgy & Bess*, Stephen Sondheim girl. There were no vocals. Only the plucking thumping grind.

This was the music my father would shake his head and get drunk to, cursing Joe Cocker and Mick Jagger for stealing their truth, then cashing in. The music my father wanted to make his life before his family insisted that it be kept as a hobby. The hobby he practiced with four friends while he wrote his master's thesis. The hobby he still lifted his voice to before falling asleep on the living room rug, his head propped upon the base of the couch. The music that would blend into his snoring and then fade as I shook him so that he wouldn't awaken on the floor again. This was his sound . . . these were his smells. These were the rhythms I grew up with—all that I rejected.

And here was this white girl completely transfixed by the sound, mumbling to me now and again about the set, about people like Dizzy and Basie and other names I can't remember. She would wait until she received a nod, then she would go up. She'd pause a beat with her mouth inches from the brass circle. Then she would take a deep breath, purse her lips, and push air through the curving metal.

I would go home to Noel with smoke and music in the weave of my shirt. Soon, I could not abide his antiseptic piney scent and asked him to leave.

I knew I wanted to be near her all the time. I carried her with me everywhere, like a present or a house-warming gift. She met my family, who courteously accepted her as only those of "noble lineage" can do—with great condescension. We started drinking every night. We hung out at the Basement, where her sister played, on Westport. We leaned into each other with a liquored ease and whispered wet and heavy about the music, the men watching us from across the room, and work. We laughed into each other's collars and danced holding the leather of each other's belts to keep from falling. One night Sarah picked up a boy pretty and soft as a girl. His hair was blond and his torso long. She told him to meet her at her apartment. She drove me home. I wouldn't get out of the car.

"You okay?" she asked.

I felt my heart pressing a boulder into my throat. "I don't want you to sleep with him," I squeaked out.

"Him? He's cool. I'll just fuck him until I come, then I'll send him home."

"Before he comes?"

"Of course. I don't care about that."

"I still. Don't. Want. You to sleep with him."

"Why?"

"Cause . . . I like you."

She started laughing. "I like you too, girl." And she shoved me gently toward the door.

"No. I like you like I love you."

She stared at me, then said, "You're drunk."

"Yeah?"

"You're just horny and drunk."

"No . . . no . . . I love you. I want to kiss you and make love to you and . . ."

"Come *on* now . . . ! I just don't feel that way about you, you know? We can talk about it later when you're not so fucked up."

So I cried. She patted me on the arm and sent me away. I cried all night long and wrote fatalistic entries in my journal about lost love and the "shutters" of the soul.

A week later, she picked me up from work and kissed me against a rise of earth and grass.

She came to see me a few days after that. In my studio with no kitchen on J.C. Nichols Road, where I used a hot plate, washed my dishes in the bathtub, and made macaroni and cheese in a plug-in tea maker and let it sit for weeks. She came with her bicycle, and I pushed my clothes out of the way. She lay on her side on the hardwood floor, propping her head in her sturdy arm and hand. She was moist with filmy sweat. She laughed at me behind her smile.

She let me kiss her again. Her breath so sweet and doughy, tongue rising to the tip of my open lips. My heart almost exploding. So watery wet I thought I'd urinated. I wanted to take her shorts off. I remember seeing the outline of her feather breast pressing the cotton of her shirt. An arc of saliva shot out of my mouth barely missing her. She kept quietly laughing.

We moved in together. We lied to everyone. The landlord, my parents, her parents. The small hard day bed in the living room was our linty, water-stained "beard." The first night we moved in . . . I remember that there was hard balled carpet. The ingrown hair carpet. Mustard Brown. We had only moved in boxes. Just a few. It had just become night. The sun room had no curtains and we lit a candle . . . two, three. She hadn't let me make love to her. She was the one who'd been with a woman before—when she was sixteen, when she had run away from home to Los Angeles and lived with a lesbian drug dealer. But she didn't tell me that in the beginning.

That night she let me make love to her. And so I pushed her onto the ingrown carpet and I pulled off her panties and I slowly planted my head between her thighs. They spread like butter. Crinkly and folded and thick. I was frightened by the taste and the slickery elm wet, but I put my tongue inside of her, propelling my head deeper. My tongue felt sandpaper rough. I moved in circles and felt the gulp of discovering her hooded clit. I didn't know what to do. I felt her hand on the curve of my head. She lifted into me. I was scared. Later, she would say that I was brave. I felt the corn silk of her hair on my lips, my nose, my cheek. I was anxious and clumsy as she came into my mouth. Then she lifted me against her collarbone and I watched her like a child. She laughed inside still. I was learning her silence.

She taught me how to make fried apples later that night. We stood barefoot and naked. I lit the gas stove while she gathered the sparse ingredients. She talked me through it. As she scooped a spoonful of butter into the sauce pan, she gave me the apple to wash. She held a paring knife and cut the apple into asymmetrical slices over the bubbling butter, sneaking pieces into her mouth and mine. The kitchen was still bare. And we stirred and tasted with a wooden spoon. No sugar, no cinnamon or nutmeg. Just steaming soft apples being turned into a clean bowl. We ate them as soon as our mouths could hold the heat. Then I tumbled and tripped into her. I kept tasting the sweet apple warmth in the corners of my mouth. We wrestled each other all night long, like bear or tiger cubs. Bruising in our desperation to become one.

The movie *Yentl* had come out. It was my anthem for a new life. Barbra Streisand kissed Amy Irving. And even though Kansas City audiences screamed "Grooooosssss! Leeezzzzzzbos!" during their love scene, I saw the movie eight times.

Sarah and I went and bought a vibrator from the only XXX shop we knew of—or dared enter—in Kansas City. We plugged it in and ground ourselves into it. We took turns slipping it into our bodies as it shuddered and hummed. I watched her bathe to the light of a candle. Dipping under soapy water and rising, hair flat, smiling. Told her she looked like an otter. She dipped and splashed again. The warm water slipped about her breasts, buoyed by the curve of her back. I sat on the toilet seat looking past the dim shadowed light into her black eyes.

A few months later we decided to take Sarah's special apples to my mother's house for a family dinner. Everyone was to bring a dish. I was going to meet Sarah there after her softball game. As I sat the apples down and removed their saran-wrap covering, they looked flat and greasy beside the swell of corn bread, yams, chicken drumsticks crispy fried, and the fresh pot of gumbo. It was Sunday afternoon around 3:00 P.M., and the doorbell rang every twenty minutes or so, ushering in deep rolling laughter and the slip of silk slacks and corduroy jackets. I was in a dress I knew my mother liked. Cream-and-gray linen from the Limited. I felt pretty and warmed by her approval.

Sarah arrived wearing a cut-up T-shirt and dirty jeans. She was the only white person there. And the most disheveled. I began noticing things about her I had never seen before. The way her hair jutted out stupidly behind her ears. And how she never seemed to be able to speak in full sentences. And the ripe low scent I had loved about her became a stench when I saw my mom sniff slightly when she passed us. I went into the downstairs bathroom, and then I started leaving the rooms that Sarah entered. She found me in the kitchen. Her face open and shining. The people in the kitchen quieted a bit as she entered. She was oblivious. "Gosh, something smells so great!" she said, and lifted the lid on the pot of gumbo. That's when I felt a prickly shame for the fawn chestnut hair under her arms. It seemed that the room slowed to a stop as Mom's face twisted in disgust. Like lightning I was at the stove, taking the lid out of Sarah's hands.

"Yeah, Mom . . . this looks great. I can't wait to taste it!" And I flashed my smile for the rest of the evening like a strobe light—like an ambulance warning—as we ate the spicy gumbo and drank mint iced tea. No one ate the apples on the table except Sarah. They congealed and flattened, and I saw Mom secretly throw them away while she was stacking the dishes.

When we got home that evening, Sarah still didn't notice my punishing silence. I ended it by asking her where she'd gotten her shirt. She *answered* the question. How stupid could she be?

I tried to tangle her into an argument all night. Finally, at two in the morning, she tripped. I cannot remember what it was we fought about—because, of course, it did not matter, because whatever it was was *completely* her fault. I do, however, recollect exploding into the kitchen in a mad fit and breaking all of our plates—her plates, really—one after the other until the floor was shards and jagged crunchy edges of white ceramic. To punctuate my disfavor, I threw a plate of spaghetti I hadn't finished at lunch against the wall. It stayed there for over a week where it collected mold and flies, both of us vowing not to clean it.

Sarah stayed out every night that week with her trumpet, long after the clubs closed. Later, she told me she'd been practicing in Thompkins gully right beside the Plaza. How the cops let her play and would sometimes stop and listen. How the echo of the horn bounced against her heart and helped it not to hurt so.

I called my mom after a week. I'd had a dream. Sarah and I were walking on a beach ball in Galveston, Texas, and it was slowly deflating. My family was in the distance having a picnic. I didn't have a chance to tell it.

"How have you been?" my mom started.

"Okay. Mom . . . are you . . . you seem like you're mad at me or something, and—"

"No, I'm not. Not at you."

"But you sort of—"

"I suppose it's your *relationship*."

Silence.

"What do you mean?"

"The fact that you are a—that you are involved. I suppose that is difficult for me at times."

"But we're not—but—I didn't know you knew . . . anything."

"I dreamt, three months ago, two days after Charles Dixon's birthday, that you and she had . . . kissed."

I did the backwards counting, and she was right, to the day. I started crying.

She continued, "It's just that it's difficult enough being a black woman. I don't want you to have to contend with this life." And she began crying. "I want for you to be happy."

"But Mom, I am happy. Mommy, I'm in love. I've never never been in love like this . . . ever ever."

"I have to go," she said and softly hung up the phone.

Sarah came into the apartment as if on cue. I was sobbing and gulping to catch my breath. She asked me what was wrong, and I told her that Mom knew everything. She held me. The phone rang again. I picked it up.

My mom said, "I want you to know that I love you."

"I love you too, Mom."

"And that I will support you no matter what, even though I may not understand."

"I support you too, Mom," I jumbled out. "I love you so much, Mom."

"I love you, too. Now I'm going to go."

"Okay . . . me too."

And we hung up the phone. Sarah and I decided that night to move. We didn't want to lie anymore. We chose New York. We didn't pay our rent for a month. Eviction became part of our savings plan. We got our tickets. As a final statement we wanted to leave our dildo in the hands of a statue on the snooty Plaza. Instead we simply left it on the closet floor of our apartment. We were out.

1980s Kansas City NAACP convention. Larger-than-life hair, padded bra—
often mistaken for a drag queen.

A LETTER TO SOME LESBIANS WHO'VE BEEN OUT FOR A LONG TIME

Mariana Romo-Carmona

THIS is a story about love. It's about my son and about coming out, but not to him or to myself—that happened long before. Though it has been long in coming, it is very hard to tell. I deliberately linger along its shores, dipping a foot in, gathering up and sitting on the rocks.

I know this is a story about love because I love my son; that is simple enough. But a little of what I've learned over all these years is that loving is never enough when it ought to be, and we know this, you and I, lesbians for a long, long time.

I have been sitting on the shore of Lake Superior, inside now because the wind is cold this September day, and I'm letting the early afternoon sun warm my back while the sound of the waves roiling up and crashing lulls me into a sort of quiet. I'm forty-six years old. The waves are crystal clear sometimes, deep, glassy, almost aquamarine.

My hands are lined and veined, the kind of hands I wanted when I was twenty and thought it would be romantic to be the kind of

195

woman who had these hands. It isn't. What do I do with all that I hold in my hands?

When my son was nineteen he finally got himself free, and he decided to live with me for the first time in seventeen years. What I want to do more than anything is give what I hold to my son so that he will understand. That time passes. That waves wear the rocks along the shore. That the short time we spent together is still as long as a lifetime, and that hands get old, that his will, too.

In 1993, my lover and I were living in Manhattan, on the north-west side of Central Park, where we still live now. The previous summer we had gone with my mother and father to my son's high school graduation in a small town in Massachusetts. We were not invited but had been given notice by my son's stepmother. My lover, my parents, and I sat on bleachers across a football field watching a graduation of hundreds of unknown adolescents, waiting for a glimpse of my son, who is my parents' only grandchild.

We saw him as he wound around the field in line with the rest of his classmates. We waved, called out his name, smiled, were cheerful for his sake. When he saw us, he smiled back—I don't think he waved—and kept talking with his classmates. We understood, he was still being held hostage by his father and stepmother, but how the coldness and nonchalance of an eighteen-year-old hurt. After the grad-uation, our family waited timidly, hoping the boy would come looking for us; he knew that we would not simply go and mingle with the "other parents," and especially not his father's family. His stepmother had written me a letter in which she specified, "We will be having a reception for family and friends. You are not invited."

But my son didn't come. My father went to find him and came back reporting that he'd given his grandson a graduation card and told him we'd be waiting to see him in the parking lot. My mother and I were quiet. My lover stood stoically by me, quiet also, but as always in good spirits. "Let's just go see him," she said. With all our courage together, we went.

I found my son in a knot of young friends, and the rest was blurry. I hugged him, he hugged me back, and my parents, and my lover. As if all was well, as if we hadn't made a long pilgrimage just to see him for a few minutes. We weren't allowed much space in the midst of all the activity caving in around us: blue graduation gowns, smiling faces, cameras, flowers, balloons. I felt bitter. I wanted to leave, to drink something sweet like honey, or to know what it feels like to have a child to embrace and talk with in peace. I asked for space.

I took hold of my son's arm; he was so tall now, big, with long eyelashes, his chin bearing the same dimple I wear, his eyebrows dark and straight like mine; he looked just a little like me in his cap and gown, just barely; he was still my son.

We took photographs. My lover took most of them, still steady, whole, dignified, as we all tried to be in that ridiculous situation of vile homophobia. In a little while, we left, embracing one last time, promising to write, to call, to arrange the next visit in Boston. Time passed.

I wrote letters as usual, which went unanswered because teenagers seldom write to their parents, and months later I was informed that my son's family would be moving away and that the next visit was postponed indefinitely. I anguished before and after the few phone calls when I found my son at home or available to talk. On one of these occasions, I was sitting by the phone wringing my hands, crying as usual, thinking about what I could have done differently to make things better. My lover told me I had had enough bad times for one lifetime. She held me, as she usually did when I made these calls, letting me be until I was ready to talk or laugh or move on. This time she said, "You've had enough sadness. No more sadness for you."

But in February of 1993 all the sadness dissipated when my son called. I'd called first, it's true. I'd found him through the student register at Tulane, where I knew he'd be going to school. The thing is, he called a few weeks later, on his own. I hadn't seen him since the previous summer, I'd barely heard him in our brief phone calls in the intervening months. Now, we could talk uninterrupted for half an hour. We could discuss things. My son was free, and I loved hearing how his mind worked, getting to know the young man with his own ideas, his own views of the world. This was my son, a fine human being I had missed so much! And he was coming to see me, hitching a ride from New Orleans to Rochester, New York, on his spring break. I would get him a ticket on Greyhound and be at the station to meet him. He would stay for the weekend.

Nothing had prepared me for the joy of this moment, not all the years of imagining that one day my son would hitch a ride just to see me and show up at my door, ten years, twelve years, fifteen years after we were separated. The pain was gone; I didn't think of it once. We talked so much. I showed him photos, gave him things, reminded him of what he was like when he was little. We sang songs together, told jokes. He saw his grandparents. He promised to come back soon. And in fact, by the spring, since his father would no longer cosign his loans, the boy decided to leave the university and come to live with me and my lover in New York. This was when, eighteen years after realizing I was a lesbian and saying so, I found myself in a nether zone and coming out all over again.

The lake is gray now, the cover of clouds soothes the chill of the lake air but prevents the sun from warming the rocks and lighting the edges of the lapping water afire. It's another day; the waves are noisier. Did I say this is a story about love? It is also about the hopelessness, the absolute, foolish faith of it. I find the words and I lose them. I've walked out twice to smoke a cigarette and ponder why any of us write about coming out, why we have to reveal something to the straight world, as though it deserved or cared to know something about us. Right now, it feels as though every time we come out we lose something of ourselves, by giving something up to the world out there, by agreeing to define and constrain something about us that otherwise would live within us unimpeded. When we define, we chisel away our emotions, carve away at the muscle of our makeup, in order to still it, embalm it, show the inoffensiveness of our nature, this part of our essence. "See?" we say. "We are lesbians, that's all." Not something huge, all-powerful and soaring, but something small. Gay women—just like the boys, only women. Women who love women, who can sit quietly on a talk show and beam into a living room without threatening anybody.

In 1975 when I was twenty-three and my son was a year and a half, I put the final pieces of the puzzle of myself together and realized I was a lesbian. I had always known and I had never known. I matured, that's all. I became a full-grown woman and I understood. At that point, I could also talk about the parts of me that integrated me, that were just as indivisible: a Latina, an immigrant, a feminist, a leftist, an activist, a person who danced and sang, who was a new mother and exuded joy, a woman, a writer, more and more. When I realized I was a lesbian, my world expanded and split open. Of course, you know about this. You have lived it, felt it in your marrow.

Soon after, in May of 1976, I lost custody of my son, when he was two years old. We were separated then, and though I moved heaven and earth in the courts of Connecticut and Massachusetts to see him as much as possible, the next seventeen years transpired in brief visits, isolated weekends, phone calls, letters that disappeared, photographs taken in shopping malls, outside restaurants, next to rented cars, in parks—photographs measuring the years and the changing features of my son: his height, the color of his hair, the dimple

on the chin that comes from my mother's side of the family, and that
smile that almost makes him look like me.

It is late in the year. The streets of New York have that November
look. It's not terribly cold on the sunny side of Broadway in midafter-
noon, but the forecast is guarded and people walk briskly, not at
summer pace. Sidewalk vendors have already brought out this year's
scarves, sheepskin hats, fleece gloves. Just last week they put away the
silver jewelry, the three-for-five-dollars socks, and the batik dresses.
Some guy from Minnesota is looking at the flowers and the eucalyptus;
he is wearing hiking shorts, wool socks, and sandals. My son and I
smile at each other and walk east, toward the park.

It feels good to be a mother again, a mother who can talk to her
son about important and inconsequential things. Racism in American
film. Faulkner, whom he loves and I haven't read. Will he do his
laundry today, or do I have to take it down myself?

At home, the middle room is his and has been decorated anew
with posters, publicity shots from Sam Goody, subway poetry ripped
off from the C train—there's one by T. S. Eliot and one by Audre
Lorde from "Coal." We have both memorized the line "Love is a
word, another kind of open." I pick up the mail and begin to look
through it while making tea. I'm off from work at the youth center
and my lover is still at the lab. My son and I have this afternoon to
spend time together, do errands.

In the mail is a notice from Tulane. A mess with his transcripts,
a problem with his grades, a long drawn-out obstacle that has prevented him from enrolling in another school full time, a story that
took all semester to get straightened out. I've done my best as a parent
to get all the facts, fill out all the forms, and pay all the fees to get
him back in school. What I haven't quite grasped is that the boy hates
to deal with obstacles, paperwork, forms of any kind. A little like me,
in a way. I've always submitted things on the deadline, but it's gotten
easier only as I've gotten older.

"Son," I call. "Here's the letter from school. Let's get this ironed
out today, okay?"

"Uhm," comes the response behind the door.

"Son?"

"In a minute, I'm on the phone!"

I drink my tea, attend to the bills, water the plants. After all, I'm
an enlightened parent, I remember adolescent angst only too well, and
I'm not going to nag. My son is an adult, I'm an adult. I'm going to

stop taking time off from work to run down to the admissions office to check on the status of transcripts because he is working at a music shop and can't get there on time. I laugh at myself. I know I'm spoiling this kid rotten, making up for all those years, and I might as well admit it. Eventually, he comes out of his room and we begin to go over the papers while he plays a Sega game. The news is not so encouraging.

During the time that my son has been home, I've been amazed at the way his character is unveiling. I'm proud of him, of his talent for music, his ability to discuss ideas, the way he gets along with everyone. Sitting on the carpet, with the papers spread out over the coffee table, I glance at him and take in his boyish face still acquiring steadiness, gradually moving into manhood. He can sing *a cappella,* play the sax, remember the songs I taught him when he was little and sing harmony with me. He reads Sarah Schulman and Ruth Rendell, plays basketball, fakes pretty good blues on the piano, charms his grandparents, carries on an amicable video game with my lover— in fact, their personalities match exceptionally well, and I sense real camaraderie between them. At times, I think I'm the only somber one, worrying about details, laundry, deadlines, school, the past.

"Look, Mom." He nudges me away from the forms. He's beaten my lover's score from last night. In my heart I loosen another memory from years past when his father told him I wasn't his real mother, that I was just a friend who came to visit. He was four years old then. Now, he's almost twenty, and he's happy. The past is gone.

But the university will not release the transcript and my son will not be able to get into another school without it. He has to write a letter to the dean and to the professor and make a hardship case so they will agree to let him drop a course he didn't officially drop. I have to insist. I will fill out all the forms, I tell him. I will send everything out express mail first thing tomorrow, but he has to write these letters. I nag him, and he goes back in his room. The lighthearted afternoon is over.

By leaning over and way to the left, I can see the tops of the trees in Central Park from our window. I am so contented in our apartment; it is really my first home in this country after wandering, much of my twenties, from town to town, job to job, without a son, waiting for the time when we might be able to talk freely again. I waited without dreaming, because dreams such as this were nearly impossible. My home with my lover is a solid place, one that is called warm, that is filled with love, the energy of many friends, visitors, meetings, and rousing discussions about literature, the arts, the movement, politics, planning. It's been the birthplace of dreams, of lesbian and gay projects, people-of-color projects, Latina projects, Asian lesbian projects, and it contains happiness, gossip, laughter, tears, all of it. On the walls are posters of Chile, lesbian posters, my mother's paintings, my lover's guitar, and beautiful things we like, things we have collected along the way on our trips to conferences, to rallies for human rights, poetry readings, marches, vigils, and crafts fairs.

Now, our home is also a place of respite for my son. In the months that he has been with us, I have witnessed the effects of his former life. He has been a boy always watched, controlled, monitored. He hasn't felt free or actually trusted until now, hasn't felt free to discuss what he really feels. And what I suspected all those years is in fact true: he didn't feel as though he had a mother; he was told terrible things about me. He has felt orphaned.

For all these things I want to atone, as if I could have changed things somehow, and I think I still can, by being the best mother I can to my son, who is now a young man. I am grateful to let go of all the pain of losing him, the only emotion that was familiar all those years because it was always so tightly connected to my love as a mother. As a mother, I had to learn to give up the child I loved, and still know how to love that way.

Late that night, my son finishes the letters and brings them to me to put in the envelopes. If he can get a response by the following week, he'll just make the admissions deadline at City College.

"Thanks," he tells me, in his gentle way. "I couldn't have done all this without you. Here, read the letter."

The letter is brief, but clear enough. It is persuasive, and my son's argument is sure to make the dean and the professor change the transcript. The letter says that he was unable to drop the course properly due to the chaotic circumstances in his family at the time and all the pressure put upon him by his parents in Kentucky. The reason for the family fights, he has told these two educators, was about his mother in New York being a lesbian, and this created all the turmoil for him during his semester at the university.

In effect, he has lied. Or he has stretched the truth to fit his circumstances. And then, there is a third possibility. I look at my son, who is eagerly inspecting the large bowl of pasta for extra chunks of mozzarella among the sun-dried tomatoes. He's a funny kid; he dutifully places all his dishes in the dishwasher, but he leaves cartons of milk or Coke bottles in the refrigerator with half an ounce remaining. He can't get up in the morning, but he can stay up all night reading Keri Hulme's *The Bone People*. Or more Faulkner, *The Great Gatsby* for the third time, or John Grisham. I'm digressing, trying to think all of this doesn't mean what I think it means.

The third possibility is that my son has viewed the entire history of our separation in a different way. From his perspective, that his mother is a lesbian simply meant his parents argued, that he had to wait for me to pick him up every other Saturday instead of playing with his friends, that his stepmother was a bitch on wheels because she was always checking up on him to find out if his mother had taken him to some gay event.

The Late Show is on TV, and my son is talking about getting tickets for it. My lover is reading the paper, smiling, unwinding from her long day. I kneel down on the carpet by the coffee table and put the letters in the envelopes with the other forms.

"The letter," I say.

"Yeah. You think it's okay?" He's got one eye on the remote, surfing channels.

"I think it will make them change the transcript. I think I understand why you had to write all that," I tell him. He nods.

"When you were at the university, was there a lot of arguing?"

"Yeah, that's when they were talking about getting a divorce and blaming it on me because I wanted to go to school near my girlfriend in Boston—"

"And then?"

"And they would always bring you up and say it was your influence and that I couldn't go to school anywhere on the East Coast because I'd be too close to you."

"So, here you are," I told him, smiling.

"So, here I am," he agreed.

Sealing the envelopes, I added, "I do feel strange being mentioned this way in these letters, but I know it will be effective."

"Yeah, I know. I'm sorry." My son smiled apologetically. My lover looked up from the paper at me. I would tell her later. No more sadness, she'd said. You should have no more sadness in your life.

I wasn't sad then, not on the surface of my being. I was no longer the mother who was only sometimes a mother, who was so vulnerable she could hardly talk about her son without feeling destroyed. Destroyed, but not giving up. Even if I felt like an empty shell, even if I took a long time, I always called, wrote, sent presents, hired lawyers to preserve our *reasonable visitation rights,* made the journey for the visit and tried to have the best time possible with my son.

Perhaps I had been successful and my boy hadn't been so traumatized after all. He'd had a lousy semester at a school he didn't like, far away from his friends and his girlfriend. His parents had been having trouble, arguing, taking the opportunity to blame it on him and his lesbian mother. Different from some teenagers, but nothing out of this world—just a little more exotic, something you could explain to the dean, if necessary.

Light is returning over the lake on this third day. It's dawn, and the waters are calmer than I have seen them before. It is possible to see the blues shifting and gliding to shore on the mild tide. I stayed awake a long time last night, as I did that night with my son and many other nights, wondering, thinking about what I could have done differently.

I remember thinking what difference did it make to have some dean and some teacher at some college read about me this way, in this coming-out letter. I had come out so many times before, always educating, informing, enlightening, as most activist gay people have done. You and I know about this. We are always hoping that more information about our lives will make things better for the next gener-ation of gay people, for the children of lesbians, the families of lesbians and gay men. And I was aware of the cynicism of the situation, the way this letter was a clear manipulation, designed most capably by a victim of homophobia to obtain a little leeway he probably deserved. It was my son's perception: this was what he went through, and this was how things had affected him.

Knowing homophobia as well as I do, I helped. I was the accomplice.

My son was able to get into school and was very happy to return to his studies. He hoped eventually to graduate from a school in Boston or elsewhere, but on the East Coast. We lived together another year and a half, experiencing the range of emotions that mothers and teenage and young adult sons do, only compressed into a very short time. It was wonderful and, many times, confusing. The boy needed to go live his own life, which he did, and for which I am glad. My lover and I will never forget the time he spent with us, when he came home, and when, for a time, my sadness ended.

What I know now is how deeply alienated my son was by spend-ing seventeen years in a homophobic household. It may take him a long time to get over that, to come to his own knowledge of how homophobia trains us to play with people's lives. I never explained to him, probably couldn't have expressed, how I felt seeing my life splayed out in that letter to the dean of some school, with no control over how it was said, my reality squeezed in between mentions of grades, transcripts, upheaval, chaos, turmoil, parents—all that stuff people expect, that allows normal life to continue to flow uninterrupted by the existence of a lesbian mother. I understand that together my son and I were made to come out over and over, to explain and define and separate parts of ourselves that were not separate.

I know that when my son lived with us there were times when we all were perfectly at ease, growing, becoming whole. But ultimately, damage had been done. The letter was just a sign, merely a symbol, loud as it was, of how alienated the two of us were from one another. It saddens me to think that my son, a sweet person, generous, creative, imaginative, was not strong enough to survive what was done to him by keeping him away from me, to survive and fight against what was done to his own mother. In a way, we are estranged now, at different shores from one another. When we talk, there is a deep well of sadness within us, palpable, lingering there, in the heart. We will have to wait a long time for this feeling to dissolve, though we still love each other very much.

As for me, I waited seventeen years to begin to write. And then, I wrote.

Adriana M. Romo

Mariana and her son, October 1979

WAKING UP

Jacquie Bishop

*The stories they tell you not to tell
are the ones that need to be told.*
DOROTHY ALLISON

"JACQUIE, Jacquie!"

The telephone rings. Drunk with sleep and from vodka, I answer, "Huh?" reach for my watch, notice it's 8:30 A.M., and moan.

The voice is urgent. "Jacquie, it's your aunt. Wake up. I need to talk to you about what's been going on."

When I was five, I lived with my aunt for a year because my mother was sick. "Sick in the head," another aunt whispered to me years later. As I try to wake up, I can hear my aunt's voice from somewhere over the yard where my cousins play on the same spot Ku Klux Klansmen burned a cross, past where my grandmother sits churning an old ice-cream maker, somewhere near the river that runs around the house. The same river that carried off the shoes of young children too "ignant" to remember to take them off before going in. I hear her voice, firm and reassuring, as we sit at the kitchen table where she teaches me chess, and again from across the floor where the pattern for a new dress is laid out waiting for me to make it take shape. I feel safe within her gaze, her voice.

My mother beat me. "I'll kill you. I'll beat your fuckin' Black ass. . . ." She repeated these words as she brought the belt or switch or extension cord down across my back, face, legs, arms. My mother stripped, blind-folded, gagged, and tied me. My sister closest in age to me cried, sometimes pleaded, "Please don't! I'll get her to be good. Just stop!" One aunt denied it was happening. The other, the one on the telephone—*"Jacquie, wake up!"*—knew what was going on, and tried to talk to my mother once her rage had settled.

"She's sick in the head. Always has been, now it's just worse."

Since I was five years old, I've known that my aunt loved me. But I am not five anymore. The days of summer are shortening, college is only weeks and 800 miles away. In the evenings I hang out in gay playgrounds: the Duchess, Ariel's, Peaches and Cream, Paula's, *Déja Vu.* Bars.

"Jacquie? Jacquie, wake up."

My girlfriend's name is Marie. Everyone calls her "Niche." She says her mother nicknamed her. Something to do with how she was always looking for a place to fit in. She hid in closets and behind chairs. A demon—her father—chased her. I call her *Niché*—somehow, the French pronunciation makes her sound less desperate. Niché kissed me first. She kissed me in the back room of the local A&P supermarket. I never expected her to follow me back there.

I am seventeen, she is a year or two older. The gay scene demands cool; we are misfits, geeky, awkward. I unbutton my white deli jacket, take it off and throw it onto a workbench. Stained with meat juice, crusty with cheese shavings, it reeks of fish. I need to change my clothes, wash up, dress, and get a drink. Since I was thirteen, I have had at least one drink at the end of each day. Niché is standing inches away from me. Her hair is uncut; it hangs in her face. Her glasses, smudged, round and small on her face, rest on the tip of her nose. Her innocence is both appealing and shameful. I want room, but she just stands there, directly in front of me, going on about pillows and sheets she bought on sale. I want her to leave so I can dress. I want her to wait for me to be ready. I want to be ready for her. I want to be ready for what I've heard can happen between two women. She just stands there. I have no choice. I lift my shirt over my head, and before I can bring my arms down, she does it. She kisses me full on the mouth. Her tongue slips between my teeth and touches the tip of my tongue. Without moving my lips from hers, I pull my shirt off and kiss her back. My hands, I'm not sure where they go. I want to touch her breasts and legs and ass. I rest one hand in the middle of her back and another just above her ass. I kiss her like I kissed James and Archie and Wayne. I kiss her like I wanted to kiss Lorena a year earlier. Lorena and I were drunk and giddy and lying in my bed, staring at each other, wanting and fearing. I kiss Niché with staccato breaths and whispers and tongues gentle. I kiss her like Lorena would have kissed me if my sister hadn't come into my room unannounced. I pull away from Niché the way Lorena and I pulled away from each other. I realize that someone can walk in. There are no locks to keep them out. I can't scream at them to leave as I do with my sisters. I pull away from her, sweaty and anxious. "Niché, please wait for me in the front of the store."

"Jacquie, this is your aunt. I want to talk with you."

I still think of Archie. I had only recently broken up with James. Last summer I went to the museum with another boy, a young man my mother's friend Ann was fucking. He was twenty-two, lanky and strong, a lot younger than Ann. We walked through the garden to the reconstructed old school house. He leaned me against a door. Lifted my legs around his waist as he held me by my ass. My body went numb. He was hurting me. I stared over his shoulder into the glass-encased schoolroom, thinking of *Little House on the Prairie:* neat rows of wooden seats, a child's chalkboard resting on a desk. I made him stop before he could penetrate me, fuck me. But when Niché kissed me, I wanted her mouth on me. This was different from the forced flirtations with boys. With them I did what was expected. I smiled, I cast my eyes downward. With Niché I was interested. I had no fear. I liked it a lot. My mother must have known this, too.

"Jacquie, wake up."

My mother has gone through my things—again. She has found fliers and newspapers and books and announcements. She has found out that I am curious. A week ago, she came into my bedroom and woke me on a Sunday morning.

Early Sunday mornings involved rituals left over from slavery and Jim Crow. Saturday night, cook your Sunday meal: fried chicken, ham, greens, stewed string beans, macaroni and cheese, cornbread. Wake up Sunday at 6:00 A.M., do the children's hair, spend all day in church, invite the preacher to your house, then eat around 4:00 P.M. Although few in my family went to church anymore, they held onto the rituals. They cooked their meals on Saturday, woke up early Sunday, and started calling each other at 7:30 A.M. One, then the other, then another.

"Girl, whatcha cookin' today?"

"Naw, I finished my meal last night . . ."

Hee, hee, haw, haw.

Long distance, local, even if they'd spoken three, four times during the week, they called each other every Sunday morning.

I was privileged. I never knew what it meant to work in the fields or spend a hot, humid day in a Southern church that didn't have air conditioning. As I got older, I learned how to avoid the hot comb or the jar of relaxer that lay in wait next to a plate of bacon and grits. I woke at 10:00 A.M., spent the morning recovering from a hangover no one seemed to notice, then spent the afternoon watching a ball game with my stepfather, my "daddy." I knew their rituals and tried to avoid them—their voodoo spells: Sunday-morning hair-pressing, the smells of big meals, and the sounds of church music blaring from radios strategically placed in the kitchen, living room, and bedroom.

That Sunday morning, there was no Mahalia, no big Sunday meal. My mother was waiting for me in the living room. She wanted to talk. She reached for a clear glass box with fake gold trim. Inside were her cigarettes, some menthol, some regular. She lit one and took a deep drag, watched the blue and clear smoke circle around her then announced, "This will not be a discussion. Just listen!" I was hung over. Hitting the beginning or end of "happy hour" at five bars will do that to you. Vodka and the latest club music were still pounding in my head. Niché's kisses were like dried, flaking paint on my face and neck and hands. I could barely hold my head up, never mind argue. "Talk if you must, just do it quickly," I thought but didn't have the courage to say.

I had no idea what this meeting was about. The high phone bill? Dishes in the sink? Or another lecture about how since the separation from my stepfather we would all have to do more to help out around the house. Instead, my mother spoke to me with faux Southern charm dripping with contempt. Like the contempt I held for her because she dated men for money.

"Gloria, Gloria," the men would say. "I love your cooking."

When I walked from the kitchen to my room, my mother's bedroom door would be open. I could see her as she sat with him, with them, on her bed—rarely in the chairs. Sometimes they watched television. Sometimes they just sat and talked. She wanted to show me off, her smart daughter. My sisters were pretty, but I was smart. "Jacquie come sit with us. Tell Reginald what you learned at school today. He's interested in Russian history, too. Why don't you speak Spanish with him? Did you know he speaks four languages?" Contempt. My mother loved me, was proud of me, and yet held me in contempt.

"I know you're gay. This mess will stop right now."

"Jacquie, c'mon girl, get it together. We need to talk, now!"

"This is not my fault," my mother told me. "I did all the right things—good schools, exposure to music, tutors for your class work. You will not embarrass me by hanging around those people." She told me, "I have called the family." My heart sank as she went down the list. Aunts in New York, Florida, and Georgia; godparents, cousins, and others around the country. "As soon as your sister returns from music camp, I will tell her too." Stunned sober and silent, I waited and wondered if she'd hit me. I wondered if she thought she could beat the queerness out of me. She told me, "If you do not start acting right, I'll ship you off to your father's people's house in Philadelphia."

"Great," I thought, but could not find the courage to say, "The only words you will have spoken to them since you divorced will be, 'Here's your bulldagger niece. You do something with her.'"

So when my aunt called at 8:30 on a Sunday morning, I knew what it would be about. Still, I wasn't prepared.

"Jacquie?"
"Yes, good morning."
"Jacquie, I spoke with your mother." God, my head hurts. How much did I drink? I turn over. The sun greets me first, then a noise that sounds like something is loose in my head. I kick my blanket off the bed, pull the sheet tight around my nude body and prepare myself for another "I talk, you listen" lecture.

"Jacquie, I told your mother she was wrong for going through your things. I have told her this before. When you lived with me, she asked me to read her your diary. I told her 'No!' But now that she's gone ahead and done what she's done, I want to talk to you about it."

I breathe deeply and wait. I do that when these women talk. I've learned from watching my uncles that it's best not to say anything when the women make up their minds to say something. I wonder if the men who marry into this family get together on their own and talk about this. Somehow, I doubt it.

"Jacquie, I want you to know that it disgusts me to think that you would go down on a woman then eat off my plates, use my forks, and drink from my cups. It disgusts me to know that you would choose to be with a woman instead of a man. When you brought that stupid-looking white boy home, the tall one with the buck teeth, I told you then that your friends were always welcome here—even though to give yourself willingly to a white man, a product of the same people who have been raping us for over four hundred years, was beyond my comprehension. Then you dated that Puerto Rican with the crazy mother who kept calling here . . ."

My aunt's refined, slight Southern accent becomes thicker. Though she's lived in New York for years, Florida is in her voice. My mind wanders, I stop listening. I am submerged in warm water. I hear the words but can no longer make them out. I remain in bed and stare at the phone. I notice dried jelly on the rotary. Soon, I feel the sheet around me, smooth as a snake I once held in my hand. Now, as then, I want to scream, but my memories of the woman on the other end of the phone who once said, "I love you," hold me as the water did, suspended and silent.

I lie in bed and remember the snake, how it moved in my hand, how its tongue acted as a sensor, directed its head and body up my arm. I feel the sheet move on me and across my body. I feel it tighten around my legs.

This aunt has promised that no matter what—she repeats it now, like a line from a movie, over and over again, trying to make it real— "No matter what, you're family. I helped raise you, and I will always love you." She loves me, and now she holds me in contempt.

I no longer hear her proud stories of Florida A&M's Marching One Hundred or her imitations of white Southern belles. I think about another time. I think about the snake, I think about my childhood, and I wonder, who will protect me now?

Roberta Raeburn

BANDITOS

Eileen Myles

I probably love alcohol and poetry much more than women, so the first year I no longer drank and took drugs was really confusing.

Here I was a lesbian poet—and I was terrified of women; I mean, without a beer I couldn't even be near women—I mean, ones I wanted to kiss. I would sit across from a woman in a café and this thing I thought of as "the fantasy kiss" would occur. Some part of me that was not my body would lean forward and kiss whoever I was sitting with and it would really freak me out, because I knew in a moment I might lose control and actually do it, so I obviously couldn't spend time with women I felt attracted to because I had feelings, and though I had been prancing around in bars and having crushes and reading poems about my life as a lesbian, I had really never come out, and now I was enduring the weird feelings of being a dyke.

I made a rule for myself that I would only hang around with women I was not attracted to, and I did that for the first year I didn't drink or take pills. The only thing I have to say about that year was that I didn't take into account anyone's interest in me, so I found myself in a lot of bizarre situations, being easily manipulated by someone else's crush. Finally I knew it was time to act. If I didn't do something, I would be no one at all. No one lesbian.

To begin I threatened God. I said, if you don't send me a woman quick, I'm going to drink. And God did his part.

I was introduced to a woman one day, a blonde, about twenty-five and clearly straight. She suggested that since she also didn't drink, we could exchange phone numbers, and maybe have coffee. I remember thinking, oh no, a really gorgeous straight woman wants to hang out with me. My next thought was that this would be good, since I could deal with my own feelings of attraction, but since she, being straight, was unavailable, I could not act, I could just learn to be comfortable with being attracted to a woman. That would be my first step. This was in the summer, and instantly I fell in love.

We would take long walks down to the river and talk about our stuff, and I remember loving her Southern accent and her blond hair, and she was really into Madonna, and I knew she thought she was Madonna, and I thought she was Madonna, too. It was like 1983, so these feelings made sense. She was an East Village girl. It was a feeling and a look. One day we were lying in the grass in a ballfield, and I could see boats passing, and the grass was burned, almost yellow, in the bright July sun, and she was telling me things she had never told anyone else before, and I was just yearning, and thinking if only I could have a girlfriend like this, so sweet and so young and so open to me. I was thirty-three, or I guess thirty-four. I wasn't that old.

One night around then she asked me if I would come over to her apartment and help her get rid of some alcohol. I showed up of course, on my bike, and it was late, maybe around 11, and she had this bottle of Pernod, which I liked a lot, and she didn't like it at all, but she shouldn't have it in the house, if she wasn't going to drink. I stood with her in the bathroom as she poured the yellow liquid down the toilet. It was a very serious moment and then we stepped away into the kitchen. Do you want some tea, she asked.

I could hear the toilet flushing. Tea sounded great, but suddenly I became aware of how pretty she was, and I looked at her red kitchen floor and I started to kind of stutter, and I stepped into her front room for a minute and I said, let me think, and I looked at my watch and it was around midnight. I was sweating lightly. I don't know— I've got to go, I should go!

I left really fast, practically hitting the walls as I ran downstairs and headed over to Second Ave really fast on my bike, and my face felt all rearranged, and I didn't know what to do, because I was losing control and now this woman that I liked so much would see me as a strange jerk, an uncomfortable dyke, and I planned to be a comfortable one. I wanted to drink. I had some tea in my apartment and I looked around. I didn't have any furniture, really.

My bed. And a big gray exercise mat. I had thrown out almost all my furniture because it reminded me of drinking. I had a big teevee. I made my herbal tea really sweet with lots of honey and it would be sickening and I wouldn't think of booze. I thought of her, I thought of myself and what a jerk I was, so uncool. I'm a monster, I thought.

I decided since she was a waitress, I would just go find her at work the next day and say hello and try to be normal and see how big a jerk she thought I was. I arrived at this outdoor café on Second Ave and she was taking an order and I stood there and waited until she was free. She served a million margaritas and she looked great doing it. How can she stand it, I wondered.

Hi, she said, putting her pad in her red apron. I started right in. Listen I feel like I was kind of stupid last night. I uh . . . She looked at me. It was not okay, I could tell. She looked me straight in the eye. I have a crush on you, she said. Everything, my ears, Second Avenue grew wider. I didn't even have eyes, legs I was so shocked. When do you get off work, I said. Come over, okay? She nodded and went smiling to her next table. Extra large, I heard her say.

When the buzzer buzzed I almost hit the ceiling. Hi, she said. I am really exhausted, it was a hard shift. Sit down, I said, patting the exercise mat next to me. It was rolled up like a burrito, and that was the only place to sit. We were watching *Columbo*. I remember watching the faces sail across the screen. I put my hand on her arm. Or maybe on her back. It was so slow, we sat there an hour, a half hour I don't know. At some moment she looked at me, she turned her head and made a crooked smirk with her red lips in that adorable way girls have that says oh well. It was a big kiss, a great kiss, a long kiss. What is this, she asked about the exercise mat, and we unrolled it. We were lovers for the next two years.

East Village, 1984

COMING OUT . . .
OR GOING MORE DEEPLY IN?

Margaret Randall

IN the 1960s, when my generation was in its twenties and thirties and some of us thought we could change the world, a clandestine cell of young Nicaraguan revolutionaries met in a Managua safehouse. After the usual discussion of David-vs.-Goliath strategies, they began to talk about dreams. A young man from an impoverished childhood said he'd had a single dream in his life, and that it was in black-and-white. A more fortunate member of the cell—Doris Tijerino, who later told me this story—said she always dreamed in color.

Tijerino was already a long-time Sandinista activist. It was Cuba, mid-seventies, when I recorded her testimony over the course of a year for a book about a woman in a movement still unknown to people outside Central America. At the end of her tale, Tijerino said, "We've got to keep on struggling, so that someday all our people will dream in color."

Barbara, my lifetime companion, is a painter. Years ago, before coming out as a lesbian, all her work was black-and-white: landscape studies mostly, pen-and-ink lines undulating across the picture plane, representing the earth's rises and hollows. When she was able to claim her sexual identity, her work exploded in her own unique and exuberant color: orange prairies beneath purple skies, unmixed acrylics often squeezed directly from the tube.

Asked to write about my coming out, these two stories came to mind. No mystery, when I acknowledge that coming to my lesbian identity at the age of forty-seven had everything to do with revolution—by which I mean devoting one's life to the creation of a more just world—and with finding one's own identity and truth. In my life these devotions remained in conflict for too many years, a struggle of unequal proportions. I understand that in contemporary discourse "coming out" means deciding to live one's sexual identity openly, an identity considered deviant by mainstream America. But for me, naming myself lesbian was no more difficult than identifying as a socialist, a feminist, or a survivor of incest. These labels and others spell risk or shame for many. For me, they are sources of energy, strength and pride. In my experience, learning to claim the time and space and do the hard, necessary work to go deep inside, to discover the woman I am, has been much more difficult.

I was born in 1936, the oldest daughter in an awkwardly assimilated nonreligious Jewish family. When I was ten, our parents moved us west, from New York to the space and light of New Mexico. Behind a mask of openness and good times, my parents were perennially unhappy. Although they thought of themselves as accepting of all peoples, they changed our family surname to hide its Jewishness, traded used clothing to the Indians for silver and turquoise, and refused to rent a spare room to my black college friend from Ghana. Still, they were adventurous for their time and social milieu, supportive of their children, and proud of our accomplishments. My father, especially, was extremely generous of spirit. He believed in me without reservation.

Lesbianism? As I grew up, it wasn't on the list of acceptable possibilities. There was an aunt and her lifetime companion, but my parents never referred to them as lesbians, nor did Janet and Phyllis themselves use the word; it was simply understood that they had a life together. Still, when I was old enough to remember these women and see their relationship in that context, my mother corrected me: "Well, we don't really know they were lesbians." (To her, the label simply meant sex. How could one know what others did in bed?) My aunt and her partner are both many years dead. A few years back, when New York's Lesbian Herstory Archives was campaigning for capital funds, I was moved to buy a shelf in their silenced names.

I had a Middle American childhood, middle-class and firmly aimed at marriage, motherhood, "success." I wanted to be a cheerleader and my high school's homecoming queen. I was neither, but not for lack of trying. I started writing before I was ten—short stories, typically moralistic—but not until my late teens did I fully understand that this was my first identity: I was a writer.

Still, there were a number of obstacles to becoming myself. To escape the contradictions of an outwardly happy but fundamentally dishonest family, I married young. This first marriage seemed healthy but was abusive beneath the surface, more like what I was trying to escape than I could possibly have known. When I told my husband I was leaving, he destroyed what writing I had kept to date. Barely twenty-one and divorced, I gave up (for the moment, at least) ideas of marriage and the middle class and went to New York City. There I began my creative journey.

By then I knew I was a writer, incipient as the work surely was. I began then, too, to sort out my passion for justice and my vision of a world in which people had enough to eat, equal access to work, education, health—and, yes, poetry. The anti-Communist chill of the fifties still heavily shaped the artistic direction of most young writers and artists in the United States. Although progressive in their personal lives, they believed the "art beyond politics" dictum.

But I didn't stay in the United States. With my ten-month-old son (I had given birth in New York, as a single mother), I traveled to Mexico in the summer of 1961. I thought of it as an adventure, like others I'd had before it. Yet I stayed eight years, married a Mexican poet, and had two daughters with him. Together we founded and edited *El Corno Emplumado/The Plumed Horn,* one of the great bilingual literary projects of the sixties. The poets and writers we met through the journal wrote about everything—including issues of social and political struggle.

Veering from my husband's increasing mysticism, I became more involved in the rebellious politics of the times—through my writing, and as an activist. Near the end of my years in Mexico, I was marked equally by my identity as a maturing poet and my participation in the ill-fated Mexican Student Movement of 1968.

The sixties were coming to a close, and young people around the world were clamoring for justice—for ourselves and others. In Berkeley, the American South, New York's Columbia University, Vietnam, Paris, South Africa, and Mexico. The Civil Rights Movement and America's War in Vietnam were turning points for us; so was the Cuban Revolution. We rejected the encroachments of technocracy upon beauty, health, and fairness. Our poetry unashamedly addressed political concerns. In Mexico City, on the evening of October 2, 1968, Special Forces closed in on a peaceful demonstration and killed more than a thousand people. Ten days later, the 1968 Olympics opened as scheduled.

These events sharpened my political commitment. The following year, I was forced underground and had to flee Mexico. I took my family to Cuba. By then I was living with a U.S. poet, had given birth to another daughter, and had discovered feminism. The connection with feminism was crucial: an electrical charge, an explanation, an immense relief. Yet a struggle would rise within me—subtle at first, eventually clearer and more defining—that kept feminist analysis running alongside but never truly engaging my classical Marxist worldview.

And I was loving men, one after another, still hoping for the relationship I had been conditioned to believe I was "made for," the magical coupling in which the other trusted and was worthy of trust. I had close friends who were lesbians, but we rarely talked about their relationships. In Latin America in the late sixties and early seventies, homosexuality as an identity was not a part of our discourse. Occasionally, I envied these friends in a vague, cautious, jumbled, as yet undefined way.

I lived in Cuba for eleven years and in Sandinista Nicaragua for four. My commitment to feminism compelled me to begin gathering women's stories. I became an oral historian: I listened to, transcribed, translated, and presented those stories to the world. Still, my allegiance to the revolutionary movements and organizations I was linked with kept me from asking essential questions. It was clear that we had to fight for women's leadership, demand more of men at home, and advocate educational and economic equality. But the basic issue of power still eluded me—and a great many others.

My children grew. Wars consumed me. I wrote. I worked tirelessly in a variety of arenas. The world was changing more rapidly than most of us imagined. When, exhausted and dangerously close to breaking, I decided the time had come to go home; I yearned for peace. How could I know that my toughest personal struggles were ahead?

In January 1984, after almost a quarter century in Latin America, I left the 110-degree heat of a Managua morning to deplane in the subzero cold of an Albuquerque night. I expected reentry to be complicated: I didn't have credit, had never used a bank machine, thought of plastic as the molded sandals produced by the Cubans to deal with a scarcity of shoes. I knew affluence would overwhelm me, that entering a supermarket and confronting huge numbers of different brands would cause me to ache for the simpler lifestyle I'd left behind.

I didn't expect the personal challenges, however. In the next few years, I completed menopause, retrieved my first memories of sexual abuse at the hands of my maternal grandparents, and was hit with a deportation order giving me twenty-eight days to leave the country where I was born. I also came out as a lesbian.

When the U.S. Immigration and Naturalization Service ordered me deported because of the explicit criticism of U.S. foreign policy in a number of my books, I immediately decided to stay and fight. It was a First Amendment case, and the trials, appeals, decisions and further decisions took almost five years. Each day, I had to rededicate myself to defending my right to express my ideas, to dissent from government policy, to exercise a mind of my own. Even when my opinions were twenty or more years old, even when I might prefer a different discourse now. As a woman, I was several times led to understand that if I'd only say I was sorry. . . . It was important to stand firm, a simple matter of dignity.

A year and a half into the case, I came out—to myself and a few close friends, but not publicly. Allowing my sexual identity to be known would have shifted the case's politics, diluted its impact, and given the government another whole arsenal with which to prosecute me. It was more important to continue fighting for freedom of expression. It was difficult, often painful, to keep this newly recognized part of my identity a secret, and, for Barbara and me as a couple, it was often extremely uncomfortable. I was being prosecuted under the 1952 McCarran-Walter Immigration and Nationality Act. The government had charged me under its ideological exclusion clause, which stipulated that Communists, Socialists, Anarchists, those having meaningful association with Communists, Socialists or Anarchists, or those who, like me, had written literature or nonfiction unflattering to U.S. government policies, could be barred from entering the United States. But McCarran-Walter also harbored a "sexual deviancy" clause among its thirty-four different reasons a person might be denied entrance to the country. If I revealed my sexual identity, it would not only hurt my case but dilute its importance as a forum in the battle for freedom of expression and dissent. I had committed myself to trying to change the country's antiquated immigration policy. Until I won the case, I would not be able to publicly declare myself a lesbian. Finally, in August 1989, coming out publicly was as much a relief as winning the legal battle and knowing I would be permitted to remain in my homeland.

What sparked my recognition of my sexual identity? How did it happen, and what did it mean? I came back to this country a forty-seven-year-old several-times-married-and-divorced seemingly heterosexual mother of four. There were so many lesbians among the women closest to me by this time that I believe I had discarded the last vestiges of inbred homophobia. I also "needed" a male partner less. Yet I still thought of and presented myself to others as sexually attracted to men.

I have often pondered the elements that combined to bring down the final impediments to self-recognition. I must give credit to the U.S. women's community—largely but not exclusively lesbian—that greeted me upon my return and embraced me in a way I had never been embraced before. A particularly insightful and competent psychotherapist helped me to remember the long-blocked abuse and to dissolve the social compartmentalization that kept the various parts of me separate. I also believe that a new distance from male-centered political work allowed me to pay more attention to my own needs.

One evening, a friend and I were driving back from dinner with another friend in Santa Fe. While discussing a variety of topics, suddenly and casually, as if she were talking about something far less intimate and immediate, my friend said, "Well, when you come out . . ." I no longer remember how that sentence ended. All I heard was "When you come out," as if it were only a matter of time.

Less than a week later, I had my first sexual encounter with a woman (not the one who made the comment). It seemed easy and right. It didn't feel like a major shift, just the next step in coming home. Yes, coming home, rather than coming out. Although I do not believe that being a lesbian is only or even primarily about sex, this was a defining moment.

What did I think about my close to half a century of heterosexual life? Of course I wondered, had all the usual conversations with friends. If my class, culture, and time had offered loving women as a viable option, might I have come out earlier? Undoubtedly. Did I love the men with whom I'd had long-term relations? Yes, I did.

I remembered a conversation with a close woman friend, years before in New York City. We had wondered out loud what it would be like to make love to a woman, but neither of us had been ready to move beyond words. What about my pounding heart on the bus in Prague, 1969, when I sat beside the English actress whose name I cannot even recall? Approaching that woman was clearly not something I expected of myself then.

My partner Barbara and other gay women I know feel they were always lesbians; if allowed to consider it an option, they would have come out years before they did. My life, in retrospect, is less clear. Yet coming out was, for me, an immense and tangible piece of my coming home. Never had I felt so whole. When Barbara and I fell in love, I knew I had found the person with whom I would share the rest of my life. Twelve years later, we're still excited about our relationship, still deeply committed to helping one another grow.

It has never been difficult for me to tell the world who I am. In fact, it has seemed a necessity. I hold dear an exchange with my son during the years of my immigration case. He had come to visit, and I was seeing him off at the airport. He suddenly looked at me and said, "I know how hard this must be on you, not being able to be out. When the time comes that you're able to say you're a lesbian, we want you to know that your children will be behind you one hundred percent!"

And they have been. My son and youngest daughter have had the easiest time with their mother's changed sexual identification, perhaps because Gregory and his family lived in Paris at the time, and Ana in New York City. I am deeply moved when my son and his wife take their children to gay pride events, wanting them to understand something of their grandmother's culture. Sarah and Ximena, my two middle daughters who live in Mexico City, have had a somewhat more difficult time; the society in which they live has been slower to offer real respect. But with openness and love, each of us has managed to hold dignity to the test.

My parents, elderly when I claimed my lesbianism, have also embraced it—and Barbara. When I sat across a café table with my mother and said "I have something to tell you," her knuckles went white.

"I'm a lesbian."

She relaxed. "Oh," she said, relieved, "I thought there was some sort of problem, something bad." In the same conversation, Mother said I was lucky to have been born almost three decades after her. I've never been exactly sure what she meant by that.

Until he died in 1994, my father treated Barbara like a daughter— or was it a son? He clearly adored her, tangibly supported her decision to go back to school, went out of his way to make her feel a welcome member of the family. Dad was an old man, and his sense of social order was pretty well set. If I was the daughter, well, Barbara at some level had to be a man. This was apparent when he hugged me but shook her hand, or when he asked if she'd take a look at the worn-out washer on their kitchen faucet.

Having reached midlife by the time I recognized my lesbian identity made it easier for me to demand respect from parents, children, and the world at large. By my late forties, I already knew quite a bit about who I was. I was not about to accept homophobic treatment from anyone, certainly not anyone who claimed to love me.

When I hear the painful stories of young women being committed to mental hospitals or losing their children, I understand my own privilege. I also know that this privilege has been won by generations of brave women, the struggles of each securing a safer harbor for the next.

And so I have been careful to shoulder my small piece of collective responsibility. When I teach on college campuses, I come out to students as well as colleagues. I respect the fact that others—younger women trapped in the race for tenure—may not have the same freedom to name themselves, and I want to provide a model for my students, who need to know lesbian, as well as straight, academics and scholars. In the Left political arena, I insist that sexual difference be respected. In Cuba and Nicaragua, I have made my sexual identity very clear—my way of supporting Cuban and Nicaraguan lesbians who are fighting their own battles.

I am fortunate. I can be out in the fullest sense of the term. Each day I honor the women who have gone before me, their secret lives and courageous revelations, their losses and gains. Quietly I honor the women who, for whatever reason, still cannot be open today. And I continue to believe that in my life "going more deeply in" best defines what a lesbian identity means.

We must speak and act for ourselves: workers, women, people of different races and ethnicities, lesbians, gay men, bisexuals, the transsexual and transgendered, children, people with disabilities, the elderly and old.

Who defines power? Who uses it? To what ends is it wielded? Only when all of us have the power to define our own needs and to construct our own future will we have achieved victory. Then we will all be able to dream in color.

Meanwhile, I keep searching for the whole me. I continue to be out as I go more deeply in.

Marvin Collins

SEQUINS IN THE MUD:
A COVER GIRL COMES OUT

Karin Cook

I confess to converting. Not in a blinding flash of light. Not all at once upon the altar of a woman's breast. But more haltingly, I'm afraid, my identity shifting slowly, over time.

It was on campus in the late eighties in the wake of AIDS activism and the expanding discourse around multiculturalism and identity politics. Silence Equaled Death. Identity was fixed. One thing seemed clear: there was a right way to be a lesbian.

I was nineteen, still used a blow dryer and, on occasion, aerosol hair spray. Everything I ate, it seemed, violated an international boycott. I slept on floral print sheets. And though I managed to grow the hair on my legs, I used Joleen leg creme to die it blond. I had been manager of the men's soccer team and the only woman on an all-male crew at the local bar. With a slew of boyfriends and a career as a cover girl behind me, I was practically the poster child for heterosexuality.

The early years of my adolescence were marked by dozens of

magazine covers, commercials, and subway posters. At fifteen, I won *young miss* magazine's makeover contest and was signed with the Ford modeling agency. I became Miss YM, the Clearasil girl, a PhisoFace. Aren't you hungry? I asked from under a Burger King visor. Do You Jou Jou? from under my "boyfriend" as we rolled on a grassy hill in tight jeans and brightly colored sweatshirts.

I had freckles and big hair, not long and permed, but poofed in an eighties way. I was shot doing things I would never do in life: cheerleading, ice skating and playing tug-of-war. My niche was romance book covers and I appeared on shelves-worth, embraced by various boys on such classics as *Marry Me Tomorrow, Super Couple, I've Got Two Hearts,* and—my favorite—*Kisses That Miss,* an etiquette book on how to avoid awkward and embarrassing moments.

By the time I came out, there was so much in my closet, there wasn't room for me. With only a semester of women's studies behind me, I knew I had no choice but to keep my past buried and come out with a vengeance.

It all started my sophomore year in a Philosophy class on ethics and AIDS. It was among the first of its kind, but I remember the room more than the syllabus—forty wooden seats bathed in sunlight and arched around a lectern. One day, I came to class late and sat on what was clearly the gay side of the room. When I realized what I had done, I got this zinging in my ears, a busy churning that felt like change. I stayed as still as I could. To calm myself, I stared at a senior in front of me with wire-rimmed glasses and a brown bob. Everything M.B. said was smart.

Our first date was to the Spring Formal. This event coincided with a protest against the conservative newspaper. The controversial editors had invited William F. Buckley to speak on campus at a private dinner amidst a firestorm of criticism. M.B. had been involved in organizing a progressive response.

"Can we go to the protest before the formal?" she asked.

"Sure," I said. "Why not?"

I wore my mermaid iridescent sequin dress and white pumps. It rained. Not a drizzle, but a downpour. My fellow marchers, jeans-clad with workboots and leather jackets, wore a circular muddy path in front of the building. I hobbled along with an umbrella in one hand, my sign, a truncated version of the first amendment, in the other.

I pretended to know the chants, mouthing along erratically like a grade-schooler reciting the Pledge, while the voices of the activists around me drowned out the conservative dialogue inside. By the end,

I was drenched, with mascara running down my face and my stockings so soaked you could see my leg hair, the roots grown black.

At the end of the evening, M.B. made me an offer. She was willing to sleep with me if I was interested in having a lesbian experience, but I should know that she was involved with somebody else. I felt hurt. I didn't want an experience, I wanted her. We kissed in her bedroom. I couldn't get over her velvet cheeks, that tough and springy mouth. Everything was soft and hard at the same time. I could only handle her from the neck up. Her scalp was so hot; she had a scar at her hairline. I remember thinking: Shouldn't you be more freaked out? It all felt weirdly normal.

When she got up to go to the bathroom, I sat at her desk. I thought about all the smart things I'd heard her say. I ran my hand over her books; I sniffed her keyboard. Somehow, I wasn't lesbian enough. I left early the next morning, skulking across campus with a borrowed tee-shirt pulled over my dress. There was no one to tell. And nothing to speak of. As I walked home, nickel-sized sequins littered the path.

M.B. told me that when she first came out the more seasoned queers around her threw a party, serving quiche and showing movies. She was initiated into a community, given the right books and buttons, even advised about her wardrobe. I received no such welcome. The first woman I slept with called me her "straight girlfriend." I was repeatedly asked to justify my past relationships with men, my lip liner, even my ruffled bedspread. Was I real? the community wanted to know. One day a friend inadvertently offered up an answer, referring to me casually as a *femme*. It was one of those first-crocus-of-the-spring moments. I no longer had to be *straight*. I could be femme. Rather than feeling like an impostor, I suddenly had language to describe the strange intersection of who I'd been and who I was becoming.

When my mother arrived to retrieve me from my second year at college, I was waiting with a new set of political beliefs emblazoned on my tee-shirt. My knapsack was covered in buttons. I slapped an empowerment sticker on her bumper. I had just registered for a minor in women's studies. My sentences were peppered with the words *hegemony* and *patriarchy*. It was a two-hour drive home. My mother did not say much as we wound down the Taconic Parkway. At the exit ramp of the Long Island Expressway, she took her eyes off the road to look at me.

"I'm worried you'll be lonely."

"But I have lots of friends."

I felt her stiffen. "It's a very hard route."

In 1991, I signed up for the Reproductive Freedom Ride, a three-month, 4,000-mile bicycle political speaking tour for women's health. There were eleven of us, each focused on a different aspect of women's health, scheduled to speak at rallies and press conferences in over 100 towns across the northern United States. I selected lesbian rights as my issue and gave myself a title. In fundraising for this venture, I borrowed my parents' address books and sent a letter to each of the names listed there. My parents' friends and acquaintances lived mainly in the suburbs. Most were people I didn't really know, but their names sounded vaguely familiar, ones I'd heard as backdrop my whole life. In the letter, I described the project in great detail, offered my assessment of the issues, and shamelessly signed all 130 of them with my name, a bold and angular signature positioned over the words "Lesbian Rights Advocate."

Despite the slow return rate, I got right to work. I asked my father to tune into a morning radio program on which I was scheduled to speak about the ride. Three of my fellow participants and I took turns giving a general overview of the issues. It was a call-in show, and after fielding some challenging questions related to choice, child sexual abuse, and parental consent, I announced that, in my remarks across the country, I planned to address invisibility and homophobia as a health crisis for lesbians.

The next time I saw my father, he asked me if I wanted to go for a boat ride in his Whaler. "Q.T.," my sister mouthed, our code word for quality time. And before I knew it my father and I were motoring out past the moorings and the markers, beyond the buoys and the breakwater. Though I did not grow up with him, there is a certain formality I've come to count on. He is an airline pilot by profession and often looks as if he's in uniform even when he's not. As you might imagine, conversation does not come easily. When we reached the middle of the Connecticut Sound, he cut the engine and leaned forward.

"I've been meaning to ask you about your social life," he said. "We haven't talked much and . . . I am just trying to get a sense of how you spend your time. You know . . . romantically."

His face looked flushed and weary. I glanced at the life preserver, then the float cushions. I still remember that stale foamy smell of the sea. "I go out with women," I said.

"I thought so." We drifted in silence for a few minutes. By this point I was counting gulls and looking around for land. My father cleared his throat. He told me about Uncle Bubber, his favorite relative, who he knew was gay, but to his credit never talked about it. "It never got in the way of us being close," he said.

I looked right at him, our eyes meeting briefly.

"How do you know?" I asked.

The Reproductive Freedom Ride departed from New York City, boarding the Staten Island Ferry with ten bikes and a van full of condoms, speculum, and educational materials. President Bush had been busy welcoming home soldiers from the Gulf War. There were yellow ribbons lining the streets. Clinics everywhere were under siege and the "gag rule" had prohibited federally funded clinics from mentioning the word *abortion* to their patients. At each stop, from Altoona, Pennsylvania, and Crawfordsville, Indiana, to Peoria, Illinois, and Fargo, North Dakota, in front of supporters and protesters, at press conferences and picnics, I came out as a lesbian.

Two hundred miles into the trip, Andrea, the main organizer, who had never been with a woman, made it known that she wanted to be with me. I had never been with a woman who had never been with a woman. We flirted as we biked into Youngstown, Ohio. There was a sudden status associated with being perceived as a seasoned lesbian and, as much as I longed to be considered one, I was terrified of the responsibility.

That afternoon, we were escorted through a group of protesters to the Mahoning Women's clinic for a press conference and then on to Youngstown State University where twenty Zeta Tau Alpha sisters were gathered on the lawn outside the sorority house. They were carrying pocketbooks and their clothes were pressed; we were covered in body hair and bike grease. Andrea opened the discussion with what she thought was a simple question.

"How do we as women feel about our vaginas?"

One woman got up and left.

Another shouted, "What does this have to do with the ride?"

"If we can't talk about our bodies, how can we expect to advocate for our reproductive rights?" Andrea explained.

A red-faced woman challenged our platform on religious grounds. Still another said we were pornographic. It was a difficult way to begin. Somehow we persevered, each of us trusting enough to stay and enter into a conversation. As the discussion wore on, we returned to where we'd begun—with the importance of understanding one's body. In the end, seven women followed Andrea into the house to view, first, her cervix, and then their own.

Andrea and I had been assigned separate rooms in the sorority house. Midway through the night, I snuck into her room at the far end of the ZTA house and slipped into her single bed. All around us we could hear the sounds of sorority girls turning to their beds. After some initial shyness and awkward maneuvering, Andrea and I made love. The sex was sweet and sweaty. At one particularly heightened moment, I sat up to throw off my tank top and out of the corner of my eye saw the silhouette of a man standing on the roof outside our window. He was naked and masturbating. Without even thinking, I hit the deck, dragging Andrea to the floor alongside me. We crawled to the edge of the room and out the door, where we leaned against the wall—panicked and out of breath.

Andrea's immediate impulse was to get angry. She wanted to dump water on him from the bathroom window. I talked her out of it. Did we want the Zeta Tau Alphas to know that after all that talk of vaginas, we were having lesbian sex in the sorority house?

"Why not?" Andrea asked.

It wasn't long before shame crept in. Here I was, the Lesbian Rights Advocate, crawling around on the floor, afraid to confront some frat-boy pervert. Worse still, I had brought fear and humiliation into Andrea's first sexual experience with a woman. I had not been a good ambassador. How could I stand up in public and proclaim my pride?

Two weeks later, at Gay Pride in Indianapolis, we were surrounded by a group of seventy anti-gay protesters carrying signs that said "Burn fags, not flags" and "Sodomites killed Ryan White." The cops allowed the protesters to take over the steps of the monument for more than twenty minutes. It was not until the choir, a sea of gay men in green shirts, filed across the top step that cops closed in and removed the hateful mass of bigots. Just before we got up to speak, someone ran across the stage and pulled down the building-sized Pride banner. It lay in a heap at the edge of the stage.

Their hatred incited my anger. It felt powerful to stand on the stage— to take a public stance. Even though my hands were trembling, my voice remained strong. I recounted the stories of the women we'd met, the lesbians we'd stayed with in every town across America. As my words ecohed back at me through the speakers, it became clear that making speeches was not the same as having conversations. And that coming out en masse to strangers was not nearly as challenging as coming out to the people I know. There was something distant about signing my name to all those fundraising letters and dropping them at the post office. Just as there was a certain comfort in speaking alongside ten women in a strange town and then getting on our bikes and peddling away. For all the strength and experience I gained that summer, when the ride was over and my biker tan had faded, I realized that after 3,832 miles, I still had a lot of ground to cover.

"Miss *YM* 1984"

Patrick Demarchelier

MIND AND BODY

Wendy W. Fairey

i

ON my list of embarrassing secrets, only having been arrested for shoplifting at the age of twenty-eight used to rank higher than being gay. I wonder if it was even called being gay yet. I would have been the last to know, caught as I was in my secret swirl of conflict, desire, and shame. My mother used to speak of "lezzies," which for me had an unfortunate tonal association with lizards. Years later, it was my mother who made her startling attempt at consolation. "Well, of course you feel bad. It takes much longer to get over an affair with a woman than with a man."

"Why do you say that?" I asked her.

"Because women are more alike and for that reason can be so much closer," was her reply.

The question I ought to have asked was, "How do you know that?" She's dead now, and I'm left wondering. She had so many men as lovers. Why not at least one woman? "But she was so heterosexual," I tell myself, just as is my daughter Emma. If truth be told, I welcome some buffer of inter-generational discretion. My friends say it's great that Emma, now in her twenties, feels free to share with me the details of her sexual misadventures. Meanwhile, I feel pulled by her confidences onto the wrong side of a drawn curtain. I don't want to know about the hinted-at "close call" with the Rastafarian in the park, or about the more than close call with the man, at first so nice, who then "frogmarched" her into his bedroom.

"What's frogmarched?" I asked.

"He grabbed me by the ear and marched me along," explained Emma.

"Oh, Emma," I said. "Couldn't you have stopped it? I take it he didn't rape you."

"No," she replied, "he didn't. But Mom, if I get pregnant . . . would you help me take care of the baby?"

Guardedly I said I would—how could I do otherwise? I added, though, that Emma should also put the question to her father. "Isn't he," I ventured, "the better candidate?"

My ex-husband Richard long aspired to be a house-husband. During the years that the children were small and we lived on a farm in Maine, the years they look back to as the time of family happiness, not only did he chop all the wood for our efficient Yodel stove and cheerfully join me each Saturday on our weekly supermarket expedition, but I never even took the children to the doctor—always it was Richard who drove Emma or Matthew down the long dirt road to the pediatrician's backwoods office that doubled as headquarters for a summer campground. Then later, in New York, it was Richard, not I, who became the leading spirit of the Choir Parents' Association when Emma sang as a chorister at St. John the Divine. Predictably, also, it was he who attended not just the concerts but even the afternoon rehearsals of the Bank Street School Brass Band to hear Matt blare his notes as one of four ungifted Middle School trombonists.

And this was the man I was said to have left for "that woman." I hadn't conceived of it as departure. Rather, I'd had in mind an understanding like Vita Sackville West's with Harold Nicholson, though I think I underestimated the role of Sissinghurst and Vita's separate tower there, not to mention Harold's own homosexual proclivities, all of which must have helped make feasible their tolerance. We, on the other hand, were cooped up, coupled up—mother, father, two children—in a five-and-a-half room New York West Side apartment, where, while Richard in the living room dozed over the NBC late-evening news, I would surreptitiously pick up the phone in the bedroom to murmur goodnight to my lover, "that woman."

"Matt is going to wake up one morning and say, 'My mother is a lesbian,' " raged Richard, in furious male alliance, when he found out. The circumstances of discovery had been so banal—a love letter not yet mailed, the envelope peeping from my unfastened pocketbook.

Richard's anger shocked me and seemed unfair. He didn't want passion anymore. Yet he had wept—hard convulsed sounds—the day I said I wanted us to sleep in separate rooms. "I don't know that's what I am," I answered him, numb in the face of his misery and accusations.

I felt no more a lesbian than I had thirteen years before in 1970. When wandering into a lesbian workshop at an early Second Wave feminist conference, it was I who had spoken as an apologist for married love. I had gone to that conference, held at my graduate school, Columbia, with my two best friends from college. Two of us had new babies and had left our husbands taking care of them at home. What an exhilarating extrication! We wanted to hear Kate Millet give the keynote address. I didn't yet realize that reading *Sexual Politics* would make it impossible ever to feel the same about D. H. Lawrence. Norman Mailer and Henry Miller I didn't care about, but I would mourn the loss of Lawrence. *The Rainbow* and *Women in Love* had seemed so thrillingly to capture the rhythms of life and love.

In a spirit of almost idle curiosity, tinged with barely repressed fear and fascination, I had made my way into the lesbian workshop, while my friends opted respectively for "Women and Finance" and "Women's Consciousness Raising." But there was I, among women in blue jeans who were decrying the crudeness of male sexuality. Women, they said, could express sexuality in so many subtle, gentle ways. With men, it was just ramming and rape.

This seemed so wrong to me that I rose to speak. "I'm married," I said, "and I want to tell you—it's an extension of sexuality when my husband and I cook together. Or when we do our grocery shopping. Or when we travel, just sitting side by side in the car, and I see his burly hands on the wheel."

Quizzical glances fell on me; no one smiled. Intensely ill at ease, I stayed only a little while longer, then did my best to move unobtrusively to and out the door. Later, at the Viennese pastry shop on Amsterdam and 116th Street, at least I could repeat what I had said to my two friends as we lingered together at day's end.

My choosing the lesbian workshop wasn't meant as a personal venture or statement. At that point—1970—what I called "that stuff" seemed blessedly behind me. It had always been painful, a history of confused longings. To my ninth grade diary I had poured out my hope to be worthy of friendship with my idol, Piper Farrell, who was a grade ahead. In college, I had yearned for some ill-defined response from Jane Sperling, who acted with me in college theater—Gertrude to my Ophelia in *Hamlet,* Rosalind to my Princess of France in *Love's Labours Lost.* Finally, I had taken the plunge with an inchoate, partial adventure at the age of twenty-five, but even that I considered "romantic" rather than sexual. And certainly, I didn't believe it disqualified me for men and marriage.

That it was Lucy who had suggested I marry Richard only served to underscore this. "What about Richard?" she had said as I was complaining to her about the men in my life. "He's witty and fun and sophisticated." Did she tell me to marry him or just to take him more seriously? I can't remember. Nor can I remember if this advice was given before or after she put an end to what was happening between us.

Lucy and I had become friends in the graduate seminar on Dickens and Trollope, and even closer friends when I got involved in her abortion. At that time she was living in style off her short-term but generous alimony from her Texas oil-millionaire second husband and not quite sure what to do next. In an aimless kind of way she had slept with a good friend's spouse; meanwhile someone had given me a phone number, reassuringly connected with a church, in case I should ever need it. Next, we were standing on her street corner, I with $500 in my pocket, waiting in the cool damp air of an early March afternoon for a green Oldsmobile sedan. We seemed caught up in the script of a grade-B movie when the metallic dark-green car pulled up at the curb and we peered through its window at a man with slick gray hair behind the wheel. "Get in," said the man, who then drove us in silence to 136th Street, a block or two off Riverside Drive. We were directed to a doctor's office and told to wait.

It was a relief to us that the doctor seemed to be a real gynecologist. The pregnant Latina women filling the waiting room went in to him one by one until only we two remained. Finally, a nurse came and pulled down the blinds to the windows facing the street. Later, I remember the sight of Lucy on the table when I was allowed to go to her, and then the driver, who had reappeared, telling us where the car was parked and explaining how the three of us should leave the office, one at a time, at five-minute intervals.

That evening, while Lucy rested in the king-sized bed with the carved headboard that had been her grandmother's, I cooked dinner for her six-year-old daughter, the child from her first marriage to a college sweetheart. I was happy to be with Lucy in her house and to be useful. Two weeks later, when she went down to Mexico to finalize her divorce from the oil millionaire, she started hemorrhaging in her south-of-the-border motel room. The sheets and all the towels, she later told me, were soaked with blood.

That was the spring of 1968. A few weeks after Lucy's abortion, Columbia went on strike. Buildings were occupied, classes suspended, and I found myself spending most of my afternoons at Lucy's apartment, where, sitting together on her sofa, we drank Johnny Walker Black, listened to her Mabel Mercer record, and talked about families, friends, boyfriends, and campus politics. We both supported the students, never mind Lucy's capitalist splendor.

At a party Lucy gave in early May, her current boyfriend and I were the last guests to linger; all three of us were quite drunk. Suddenly, I was on the couch kissing Lucy, and it felt so soft. "Yes," said Lucy, "you can see why men like us." Then she said, "Let's go to bed." I don't remember where Malcolm was when we were kissing on the couch. Was he there, kissing us too? I only remember Lucy. But he was there with us in bed, doing the man's part and talking about the fulfillment of fantasy, to be in bed at once with two women. I remember his blond mustache and the smoothness of his white shoulders. Even more vividly, I remember Lucy's softness as I kissed her mouth and touched her skin, hesitant, though, to touch her breasts.

In the morning, I woke up on the right edge of the bed, realized where I was, and wanted to bolt. Lucy and Malcolm cajoled me to stay for breakfast. Then Lucy said Malcolm and I should go out on a date, that we needed to get to know one another. Compliant, Malcolm later that week took me to the apartment of some friends of his, where he played a bit of poker, and I was supposed to be entertained by just sitting around and watching. That was it for me and Malcolm. Still, when Lucy and I had lunch with our friend Susan and told her what had happened, we all agreed it was okay because a man had been involved.

I'm not sure why Lucy ended things between us, whether she was scared of what might happen next or disappointed that more didn't. There were a couple of enchanted weeks in which we used to lie together on a sofa, hers or mine, kiss one another, and feel all that longing. Then I spent one more night, just one, in her bed, this time without Malcolm. We were kissing as usual when she started to touch inside my thigh. I think if she had continued without speaking, I would not have stopped her. But since she asked, "Should I do this?" I gently said no. Somehow I couldn't be the one to choose it. It was shortly after that night that Lucy dropped me for Ralph, a homely, vital friend of mine whom she had met in my apartment. Ralph would shortly espouse Marxism, abandon his dissertation on Sir Thomas Browne, and go off to work in a factory. In perfect sync with the expiration of her alimony, Lucy took to wearing chamois shirts and oxfords. No more charging at Bergdorf's.

A couple of years later, when I was safely married and pregnant with my first child, I heard that Lucy had ditched Ralph and was living with a woman on a horse farm in Vermont. Years later still, when we were both again in New York—I with two growing children and she with a different woman lover—we had lunch together at the Bank Street Cafeteria but found little to say to one another. By then I was eager to talk about the past, in search of clues to help me through the maze of present confusions. Lucy, however, had no taste for looking back.

I never told Richard about what had happened—we just didn't talk about such things—though most of my close friends knew. In 1973, I brought it up in my women's therapy group. Someone was talking about homosexuals, and I confessed to having had an experience with a woman before my marriage. To my surprise, the others praised my courage and openness. I didn't tell the group about having shoplifted the nine-dollar belt.

I liked being married; it settled and anchored me. I was happy every time Richard walked in the door. So who knows what might have happened—or not happened—if Richard had remained faithful. It was after his affair, four years into our marriage, with the administrative assistant in his office—betrayal I called it at the time—that I resumed falling in love with my women friends. That was also after I had read *Portrait of a Marriage* and been thrilled at the thought that maybe one could have both—the love of a man and the love of a woman. When I thought about being with a man, it always seemed partial and incomplete. When I thought of exclusively being with a woman, it seemed suffocating, overwhelming. I began to think that maybe one could come out right by putting the two together.

Well, I waited another ten years before acting, all the time falling in love with one woman friend or another, someone invariably married or divorced and always heterosexual, telling myself I could make do with these circumscribed, romantic friendships. My desire to be with a woman sexually grew within me. Increasingly, I woke from portentous dreams, full of strangely refracted fear and longing. Meanwhile, Richard and I made love once or twice a month and learned to sidestep the fights that might have troubled our low-keyed, understated companionship.

ii

And then I could tell that Julia Michaelson liked me. Her communication of this was subtle, though later she told me that she used to sit in my office—I was then an associate dean as well as a junior professor—gazing at the top of my breasts in the V opening of my silk shirt. To tell the truth, I was a bit afraid of her. She seemed so smart, so ironic, so superior, smoking her cigarettes in a holder, never tolerating fools. I remember with what trepidation I asked the dean if she could serve on a committee that I chaired. Colleagues had said Julia was a lesbian, and I was excited that she might become my lover, even if her age—fifty-nine to my forty, with her hair dyed red—gave me pause. But then she wrote me a letter saying what a help I had been to the Classics Department, asking what she could do to thank me. Could she knit me a cap? Or invite me to her house on Long Island? There was a main house and a guest cottage. I could have the main house and give elegant little dinner parties and wouldn't even know she was there in the cottage. She wants me, I exulted to myself. She wants me.

There was to be a dinner party at the dean's house, and we had both been invited. "Will you be going?" I asked her on the phone.

"Tell you what," she said. "I'll go if you go."

"Yes," I said, "let's both go." I sat next to her at the party, aware that her leg seemed to press against mine under the table. At the end of the evening we shared a taxi—whose idea was that? As she dropped me off, I leaned over to kiss her on the cheek. Upstairs in my apartment, I realized I was in a state of intense desire.

We arranged to go out for a drink one day after I got off from work. "This is our first date," Julia remarked in the bar of Butler Hall, not gazing out the window at the panorama of the city (as, later, she would gaze out windows with a vengeance), but with her subtly mocking blue eyes looking wryly at me. Maybe it was this evening, after all, that I was brimming with desire in the taxi home. Whichever, it seemed strange that so little actual contact—our sitting side by side, the fleeting good-bye kiss on the cheek—could have such erotic power.

A month later I was in thrall, slipping out of my house to take the Broadway bus the twenty blocks to Julia's. I felt vibrant with conspiratorial anticipation, knowing how we would kiss hello at the beginning of Julia's book-lined long hallway, then sit in the living room to have a drink or two, perhaps accompanied by peanuts—I loved the texture of these details—and then either make love, have dinner, and again make love, or simply have dinner and make love afterwards. "Time for a little siesta?" she had said the first time. We had walked around the corner from her living room into her little bedroom, each room with a splendid river view. And I had put myself into her hands

Her hands. Waking up in my own bed after leaving hers the night before, I would remember their touch. Richard, always an early riser, would be up and about, so the bed remained my own preserve for fantasy. Eyes unopened, I would slowly inhale and try to catch back into my mouth the aftertaste of Julia's body. Burrowing into my pillow, I would pretend that I could still feel her cheek and her brow, and the hollow where her neck curved into her shoulder. I marveled that our affair had such a sureness of touch. When we first went to bed, I was always overwhelmed by the desire simply to touch her, to feel the peace that came with the delicacy of breasts touching and legs entwined, and the security of her reassuring arms and shoulders reaching round me. No man's body had ever been to me so poignantly familiar—perhaps because the focus was always so much more on the distraction of erection. And stilled by her, finding my resting place, I would think, "This is all I want. This is utter peace." Even the effort of lust seemed unwarranted. Desire would well up. I would feel its pressure in us both. But even at the most sexually extended moments, I would feel the sureness of our shared gender, knowing Julia's responses as intimately as my own, almost as if they were my own.

Or so it seemed. Later Julia would tell me that sex for her was best at its most impersonal. *Her* fantasies were of waterfalls and abstract paintings. She asked me to talk to her during sex to keep her more focused.

I, though, at least for those first few months, was swept away, and felt Julia swept along with me. At home I sometimes told the truth about where I was going and sometimes I lied. It was convenient that Julia was a woman—one could visit a woman friend of an evening without suspicion, particularly with a husband who got sleepy early and liked to be left alone to doze in front of the television. Worried, nonetheless, that I might be invoking Julia's name too often, I used to alternate it with that of other friends. I didn't like the duplicity (not that that stopped me) and wasn't used to it either. Julia later told me that she had believed me to be a woman used to managing such complexities, but that she had been wrong. She also remembered that she had warned me. "You're a married woman, darling, with two children," she had said, right at the beginning. "Can you handle this?"

"Oh, yes," I had answered, without missing a beat. My working mother had taught me to say yes to challenges: "Step into the tennis ball, don't back away from it." I was all breeziness and sophistication, hiding, even from myself, that I was less experienced, more naïve, and more serious than I seemed.

I had had the odd extramarital encounter with men, but these in a sense didn't count. They were little times-out from married life— passing trysts at academic conferences or on quick research trips abroad alone. Counting only a little more was my dalliance with a married lover. I had met and resisted him when I was single, able too well to envision the dreariness of watching him rise from his bed to catch the last train home to his wife and children in New Jersey. Later, married myself and living in Maine, I started seeing him on my infrequent trips to New York. I think I was both getting back at Richard—I never forgot that it was he who had broken our trust—and enjoying myself in the role of a sexual adventurer. Once I moved back to New York, though, the liaison fizzled. Neither of us wanted it to be more central in our lives.

So Julia was unprecedented—my first serious adulterous affair. I didn't think of it as adultery. It was too personal for that construction—the release of the pent-up longing of a lifetime. I wandered around in a sensual haze and felt liberated from all my shame about homosexuality. This wasn't homosexuality. Or if it was, who cared? That Julia was a woman seemed at once central and incidental. Richard cursed her as an aging hag, and I felt he understood nothing.

I tried to persuade myself that I was basically a truthful person by proving myself a bad liar. Richard would have to have been blind not to grow suspicious. He was still gracious and easy when I went off for a weekend to Julia's house on Long Island, driving me to Penn Station, urging me to profit from this nice little rest from the children. "Thanks," I said, as I lifted my suitcase from the backseat of our car; then, on the train, I could only think that I would be spending two whole nights in Julia's bed. Already, though, I also felt the strain. When I got to Julia's house and she was showing me round her garden, pointing out all the varieties of yews and junipers and perennials, I experienced a sharp wave of homesickness for my family. The pang then passed as I entered Julia's world of mind and body.

Richard, when he knew, would lambaste Julia as irresponsible. Of course, he said, she offered excitement. She wasn't caring for two children. He saw her as a feckless immoralist—what audacity to call herself a student of ancient philosophy—and me as her impressionable prey.

It felt bizarre to be cast as the innocent. But perhaps that's what I was—what else do you call a forty-year-old wife and mother harboring a fantasy that she has found perfect bliss? I didn't want to make Julia my whole life, but neither could I imagine giving her up. Sitting next to her on her bed before leaving to go back home, discreetly holding her hand in the dark of the movies, dialing her phone number and feeling my heart beat as I anticipated her picking up the receiver, most likely on the third ring, I lived to be in contact with Julia and moved through life like a sleepwalker when I was not.

We were on our family vacation in Maine when Richard found the love letter in my purse. I reminded him that ten years earlier I had been the one to snoop and find the letter stashed in his wallet inviting him to go off to a magic land. He had gone for a while— November to February—while I tended the two babies. I can't attest to the magic for him; for me those were three searing months. Then he came back and I was glad of it. But I never felt quite the same about him again.

Richard said the comparison was ridiculous. What he had done was in no way like this. He ranted. I withdrew. And so began our time of great family unhappiness.

iii

What followed was the end of the marriage, the end of the love affair, and, when the shock of it all subsided, the residual sense of some insight gained, though the "gain" seemed at a terrible cost. An analogy I then found fortifying, though now it seems grandiose, was to the end of a Shakespeare tragedy, that moment that is both denouement and threshold, when passion is spent, the bodies lie strewn about the stage, and the always unspectacular survivors pull themselves together to carry on.

Julia, that fall that Richard first knew, happened to be away on a fellowship in Cambridge to do her research on the mind-body problem in Plato's dialogues. Refusing to give her up, I made a tenacious once-a-month weekend pilgrimage to Boston, where Julia and I would make love in her cozy Story Street sublet and go about to museums, restaurants, and movies. I clung to her and to our affair. When the moment came for me to go home, it always seemed like falling off the face of the earth. I'm not sure which I dreaded more: leaving the magic circle of warm excitement and comfort that seemed generated by Julia, or once again having to face Richard. He was drinking heavily and watching more television than ever. Turning the key in the lock to our apartment, I knew that there he would be, at the end of the long hallway that led from the front door, sitting in his living room armchair, not even looking up from the TV set when I stuck in my head to say a guilty hello. What I always underestimated was how glad I would be to see the children. "Hi, Mom," they would say, as if I'd simply been out to buy milk at the corner store.

They knew what was going on. I had begged him not to, but Richard had told them. He told them right after my first trip to Boston—and in a way, who can blame him? I didn't want them burdened, but he said it was my action that was causing the burden. He told Emma in the morning, before school, and then Matthew after school that same afternoon. The children were thirteen and eleven. What he said, I gather, to each child, was, "Mommy doesn't love Daddy anymore. She loves Julia Michaelson." Emma came to me after Richard had spoken to her. "Both you and Daddy are too proud," she said. "Neither of you can say you're sorry."

It's strange, I thought; of all the negative things I would say about myself, or for that matter about Richard, being proud would not be one of them. We think we understand so much, and then find we know so little about how we are perceived, especially by our children. Later Emma would ask me, "Who is going to take care of Daddy when Matt and I grow up and go to college?" That question shocked me too.

Matt sought me out after school, and he was crying. "It's not true that I don't love Daddy," I said. "One can love a lot of different people. I hope you know that I love you and Emma very much."

Emma hated Julia Michaelson. She hated her so intensely that the next year when Julia developed breast cancer, Emma believed her hatred was the cause. I didn't know this at the time. After Richard told the children about Julia, Emma grew pointedly distant toward me and aloof toward every one else. Looking at photographs of her from that time, I wonder how I failed to recognize her plight. Perhaps because it was as hidden as it was blatant. Emma did well in school, took ballet lessons twice a week, fancied herself at once a ballerina, a potter, a karate blackbelt, and a writer, and pushed down her anger and her pain. "I hated you too," she told me years later. "I believed you had destroyed the family."

I felt as committed as ever to the family—whatever web of love, loyalties and accommodations that term for me then signified—and clung to the hope that the children on some level knew this. At least Matt, after his initial tears, seemed undaunted, but then clearly I wasn't the best judge. He was playing forward on the junior high school lacrosse team, and either Richard or I—rarely both of us, as might have been the case in the old days—would drive him to the practice or the games. "How's Julia Michaelson's cancer?" he asked once with seeming nonchalance as he dashed off with helmet in hand. It only got visibly hard for him when, finally, Richard moved out. "You were lucky," Matt said to me as I helped him pack his bag for a weekend with his father. "At least you knew who to hate." He was referring to my childhood in which I had a detested stepfather.

Then Emma broke down. She stopped eating and marked her forehead with a razor blade. The following week, when she took a razor lightly to her wrist, she landed in the hospital. Richard carried on that it was all my fault, our shell-shocked "family" went into therapy, and my mother made the only reference she was ever to make to the affair, except for her astonishing consolatory comment when it was over. She told me she thought I should stop seeing Julia for the sake of the children.

Guilty and worn out, I lived for months with a taste in my mouth that I identified as the taste of panic—it lodged at the back of my throat and spread from there. I felt as if I had taken a sledge hammer and smashed up life and loved ones. But all the more I fixed on Julia. Nothing and no one, I vowed, could pressure me into giving her up.

As for Julia, this had become clearly not the light-hearted caper that she, to use one of her favorite expressions, had "signed up for." I'm not saying that Julia was fickle. On the contrary, she was a loyal friend in times of trouble. But Julia was also a woman with an admirably precise sense of her own limitations. She had never lived with anyone, man or woman. She had never had a pet, unless you consider the six-foot cactus in her home on Long Island which she had tended from its humble three-inch beginnings. And even that she eventually got rid of. "People stay with me for a while," she said, "often when they are in trouble. Then when they get stronger, they move on."

Julia's trouble—her breast cancer—came a year and a half into our involvement. During the preceding few months, though still committed to the rhetoric of lovers, we were increasingly tense and testy. Julia was making herself less available to me. Nor when we did get together was there the same spontaneous rushing off to bed. In her living room Julia had a swivel chair, in which she liked to sit and talk, cigarette holder in hand, gazing out the window with the river view. "Why am I here?" I would find myself wondering. Both of us looked forward to a little trip we were about to take, hoping it might restore us. The dean was sending me to London and Paris to review our study-abroad programs, and Julia had agreed to join me for the Paris segment. We had found a furnished apartment in the Marais to sublet for a week. I was elated to think that I could be with Julia and do my work at the same time. We would have to be discreet, but that seemed something we could manage.

And then Julia phoned me. "There's a little problem, darling," she said. "They've found a lump in my breast. I have to have surgery the day after tomorrow."

"Oh my God," I murmured in a surge of terror and love.

I was able to bring Julia home from the hospital before I had to leave on the trip abroad. She was so happy to get back to her own place, and I remember, as she eased herself into the swivel chair, how she joked about the mastectomy, saying she might have the other breast lopped off in the interests of bilateral symmetry. There followed just one bad moment, that evening at bedtime. Julia had gone into the bathroom, and she emerged from it deathly pale. "I just almost threw up," she said. The bandages had been removed before she left the hospital, and in her own bathroom mirror she had looked for the first time at the long red sickle of a scar.

Also, for the first time since I had known her, Julia was wearing a nightgown, the one she had bought for the stay in the hospital. That broke my heart. The Julia I knew slept naked and had taught me to sleep naked as well. "Julia," I said, "you don't need the nightgown."

"Oh, all right, darling, whatever you say."

I took her to bed, carefully removed the nightgown, and then gently, very gently made love to her. "Thank you darling," said Julia. "It's nice to be feeling something pleasant."

The moment in the bathroom was Julia's one visible lapse from fortitude in the whole ordeal of having cancer. Whether by upbringing or nature, Julia was stoical. Also I had a theory about her extraordinary coping that helped me to understand it without lessening my admiration. I think we all have a point in our past that remains the age of our self-image. For Julia, it was ten, the year her father died and she cut her hair short and became a committed tomboy. Maybe for Julia, breasts weren't really part of her core sense of self. Or, at least, so went my theory. I don't know what it has felt like for her to wake up every day without one.

I missed Julia's breast but was careful not to show it. I had loved to burrow my face between her large soft breasts, wrapping them around me like earmuffs. Now I lavished on the survivor the attention that had been given to the pair. It seemed, though, a touch strange and lonely. The six months of chemotherapy were dreary, but Julia soldiered on. She lost most though not all of her hair and continued to dye red the little that remained. She tried smoking marijuana to combat the nausea. She taught her classes, chaired her department, and complained about her lack of energy. Work on the mind-body problem did not advance.

We soldiered on too—I pressing and Julia withdrawing—and then ended the affair at more or less the same time as the chemo ended. Julia had a grant to go to England. We talked vaguely about my visiting her, but both knew that I wouldn't. On the family front, Richard had rented a small apartment nearby to us, while I maintained a home for the children. Emma had recovered from her crisis and gone off to boarding school. Matt, living at home, had become a truculent teenager, doing his schoolwork in a grudging though mini- mally adequate way and needing a parent's vigilance. He was angry with me for having "messed up." Without apologizing, I did my best not to mess up further.

Julia was away, and without hope or even desire for our future, I missed her. On the alternate weekends that Matt spent with Richard, I used to go to her country house to tend her shrubs and flowers. Sometimes I browsed through the box of her childhood photos which she had shown me in our early love-struck days. There was little Julia, aged nine, with her blond ringlets, sitting with her beloved father who would die within the year. He had been gassed in World War I and never fully recovered. There was Julia, aged ten, her hair cut short, standing with her two brothers. Then there was Julia as a buoyant, sexy young woman. And her boyfriends and lovers: the German Jew- ish immigrant violinist, touted to me as her first love; the professional mentor, so much older than Julia, who had wanted to marry her but then died; the key woman lover, a brilliant but tragic alcoholic, whom Julia had always looked out for, though the passion, she said, had waned long ago. "Tell me about the past," I had so often urged her. And she had spun the tales of old love affairs. Is it, I wonder, just an extension of possessiveness to wish to have known the person younger? Photos of Richard young had inspired in me the same wistful pressure of feeling. With Julia, though, I think I shifted from wanting to be with her to wanting to be her. Or at least, to be more like her. I admired her life. Julia and her sixty-year-old friends were impressive—they had done their jobs, bought their country houses and were independent women. Julia seemed the least trammeled of the lot—no parents, no children, no pets, no abiding partners. I came to feel a little sorry for her, but at the same time she inspired me.

iv

July 1996. I am sitting with seven other women at a dinner party in Noyac, Long Island. One of these is my lover, though I do not call her my partner. The remaining six are three lesbian couples. We are all about the same age—late forties, early fifties—and all, except my lover, who is my guest—own country houses in the area.

Only one other woman has children as I do, and she and I trade stories. The woman tells how her son at first hated her lover. He was fifteen then and had been rude as only a fifteen-year-old boy can be. That night she said to him, "I'll always love you best, but don't you want to have your own life?" After that, she says, he was fine. He and the lover are now great friends. I, in turn, tell her about my daughter, how a couple of years back I said to Emma, when she was complaining about one of her boyfriends—the one who had wanted to do S & M but, thank God, she wasn't interested—"You're thoroughly heterosexual, aren't you?" I tell the woman what Emma said in response; it gladdened me so at the time and still does. Emma said, "At least until some woman tempts me." That seemed such a wonderful untroubled statement after all we had been through. I tell her, too, about Matt, when he was in college, calling me up in great excitement to tell me that Julia Michaelson's article on the mind-body problem was on the syllabus in his "Principles of Knowledge" course. "She's a really well-known scholar, Mom," he eagerly instructed me, as if I didn't know. Not to be misleading, I add that it also was Matt who said to Emma after Julia had come over once to have a drink in our apartment, "I know it's not right, but I'll always think of her as the villain."

The women at the table start talking about when they knew about themselves. "I always knew," say several. "I just didn't act on it until . . ." Eighteen or twenty-seven or thirty—as one would expect, the age varies. "I always knew," says another. When they were both students at Vassar, she went with her lover to spend the night at the Plaza Hotel in New York. "Did you really?" I exclaim. "How wonderful! What boldness!"

"And what about you?" this same woman, now a successful money fund manager, asks me.

"I'm not sure I know now," I say. "But I took the plunge at forty after fourteen years of marriage."

The word "bisexual" is on my lips. It seems as good a term as any, but I hesitate to invoke it. Not that "bisexual" doesn't fit best, given my history and abiding illusions. I still imagine making love to men, and I do believe I could love a man again, even though I'm totally out of practice. It's just that labels seem so limiting and encoding, so remote from what actually happens. They leave too much out, though I suppose I'm willing to call myself an English teacher, a mother, or a woman, with far less need to equivocate.

I smile at my dinner-table neighbor, conveying my semiapology for a difference in certainty that I hope won't estrange us. She smiles back, and I sense her effort to be tolerant. If I knew her a little better, I think I would tell her my love stories.

ALWAYS COMING

Letta Neely

FOUNDATION

QUEER patron saints shepherded me into the "family" with as much grace and as few scars as possible in the midwest. My coming out, while nothing near as glorious as a debutante's ball, was relatively easy compared to some stories I've heard. I was way, way out before I was reeled in. I didn't know that our brand of love was so scary and so powerful to heterosexuals that it had to be hidden. I didn't learn that until I was nine years old. And then I resorted to doing what my people do in slavery times. I developed masks to wear for the oppressors and learned to switch pronouns with the swiftness of women wiping rouge over bruises. Doing that led to a severe case of multiple persona syndrome—a putting on of faces not fully one's own until habit overcomes bone structure and one is unlinked from one's self. This is a sickness easy to catch in america, particularly if you're Black, queer, and not sure there are other options for survival/

living. I've been studying photographs of my childhood and more recent pictures. I've decided the basic difference is that now I've got one face for most pictures, whereas back then, on any given day after age nine—depending upon whom I was trying to please—my different faces were candy for easy consumption. Still, growing up in Indiana, I'm surprised that I didn't inherit the homophobic mucous that folks regularly pull up from their throats into their mouths and gargle before spitting.

There's often a dichotomy between what people say and what people do. In many ways, my house shouldn't have been a safe haven, but it was the place where I learned to be multilingual. My Black Nationalist father loved Black people passionately and hated queers. He would talk about "gay faggots" and "bulldaggers" with anger. He would say that homosexuality was an illness of white people that we had to stay away from. "That illness," he'd pontificate, "brings down blackfolks, makes us weaker." But my father never said a word against Ron. Ron, who always dressed to the nines. Ron, with his swooshy, elegant walk and scarf forever around his neck, was a friend of my father. Ron never said he was gay, but he radiated queerness like a sunflower in a field of snap peas. Ron was a fairly constant fixture in the lives of my siblings and me. I think he was the first fairy godmother sent my way to let me know it was possible to be "different" and alive at the same time. I'm sure he and I spoke without words, since I had no vocabulary that would mark him as a gay man, and yet years later when I meet him on a random street in a strange city, we recognize each other instantly and he asks, "Are you out yet?"

Above all else—above all the lectures, beliefs, arguments, lessons, and pushes—my parents both gave me a strong will toward independence. Once, in college, when I had not relied on my parents' permission for two years, I asked my father if I could travel around the world. When answered "No," I was astounded. Mostly because I couldn't believe I'd asked. Then he continued with what I still consider the most important thing he's ever said to me: "When you don't have to ask, you can do anything you want."

Most of my earliest friendships with girls walked a thick line between love and love. They were like sisters, and yet there was something more—something impossible, at that age, to put a finger on. When we had arguments, the soil and pavement underneath my feet caved in until there was resolution. As my life happened, I didn't think about specific markers. Now, looking back on my travels, there are places where I would've stuck map pins.

- Ki and I sit in the arm of an oak tree in the back of the play-ground. The conversation between us is serious. Our focus is miles away from the freeze tag game beneath us. We are deciding that we will share Melvin "crooked leg" for a boyfriend. We'd tell him, "You have to take both of us. We have to be together." We are eight years old.

- In third grade, I traipse into the kitchen, my arm comfortably draped around Shaney's shoulder, and announce, "Shaney's my girlfriend!" Mama looks up briefly from the dishes and, without missing a beat, says, "Think about that," and smiles.

- Daddy stands in the doorway watching Shaney and me "clothesburn." We giggle, then jump up in fright when we suddenly glimpse his staring. He orders us to change into our pajamas and go to sleep. ("Clothesburnin'" is Indiana vernacu-lar. My friends tell me that a more universal term is "dry humping.")

- When I graduate from T-ball to softball, Shelly becomes the ulti-mate object of my affections because she hits homers in every game and teaches me to raise my right eyebrow. She earns the right to have BOOM on the back of her uniform in those iron-on felt letters that were so cool then. At her high school volleyball games, she clasps her hands together, moves into place and waits—with a yogi's patience—for the ball to come to her. Shelly lifts her right eyebrow sometimes, uses it as downbeat to fill the pause of a sentence. *God, I love to watch her do that.* I lie in bed at night, willing my eyebrow to move. I plan on marrying her when I grow up.

- Up the street, on the corner of 30th and Broadway, two girls throw bricks at each other at least once a week. Their fights are so fierce and the names they call each other so ferocious. In between the fights, they walk close together on their way to the corner store. I say to a friend, "They fight like they *together.*"

- The boys at T's slumber party have to be home at 12:30. At 9 o'clock, we begin to play "Three Minutes in the Closet." The closet is actually a spare bedroom and the three minutes feels closer to twenty. When it's my turn, Frog chases me around the room, his dick swollen and bulging out of his pants. I hear T's mother on the stairs and breathe a sigh of relief, thinking she's come to stop this madness. She goes back up-stairs to her gin after slurring to T, "Is everything all right, honey?" I'm crying when I phone my best friend, Jemna. Be-fore I can tell her what's going on, she whispers that her family is moving out of town right then. She wasn't allowed to call me so she's glad I called. This first major good-bye hurts more than Frog's insistent dick trying to push its ugly way into my dry vagina.

- My first year of college, Shelly encloses a picture of the groom-to-be. The pain in my chest could sink a ship. I don't go to the wedding. Instead I burn our team picture over the sink and cry.

EATING ENEMY LANGUAGE IN FRIENDLY TERRITORY

Busing in Indianapolis began in the early eighties. When I entered fifth grade, the bus picked us up on the corner of 33rd and Park before the sun woke up. Many of us slept; some of us hastily com-pleted homework in the forty-five-minute ride to Decatur Township. By the time I reached high school, I was one of the few black students still being tracked for college. Most of my neighborhood peers were brilliant. But I, already schooled in the ways of wearing faces and inserting new tongues, was one up on them.

There were only one or two black people in most of my classes, hence, I was cut off from my people in seemingly irreparable ways. Getting lost from home started there—in spaces where I became un-wanted by some of my own people who felt that my necessary lan-guage shifts back and forth made me a "white girl."

At Decatur, there was a virtual cornucopia of young gay people. For many of the white teenagers in the queer underground of my high school, the thought of being discovered was the most dangerous thing *they* had ever faced. *They* wanted to move away as soon as possible. And *they* had someplace else to go—the whole world.

We called ourselves different, acknowledged that we weren't like our peers. Those who passed through the halls without garnering extra attention were lucky. But I was the college-prep black girl who rarely wore a dress and gagged at the thought of a Fashion Fair makeover.

I was the black girl who wore her father's old suit jackets with the sleeves rolled up, two braids back with bangs to school and maroon-framed glasses with lenses thick as nycity fog. I was the nerd hurdler who chased after cute, popular girls who wanted me too—only just for a best friend.

Those of us who couldn't pass for anything but nerds or queers or thespians formed a deep bond. We were bound together by circumstance. There were others like us who could pass, but even the slightest gaydar claimed the blond star boy swimmer, several girls on the softball and basketball team, a few wrestlers, various members of the track team, and some academic heads into its gaze. All of us knew our connection made us a tenuous family. But even then, the use of words to describe each other was sparse. So, in some ways, I nibbled at the corners of life. Afraid that the rest wasn't meant for me.

I first learned that stock expression "You can't go home again" from white high school peers. At the time, I felt cramped. I felt like all my identities contradicted and sought to murder each other. Even with the usual gym-teacher rumors, I didn't know any adult out lesbians. And all the current black role models were part of that "New African" time of speaking Swahili and preserving the sanctity of Black Manhood and Black Womanhood. At the time, I didn't even know who Audre Lorde was. The only thing I knew was that being openly attracted to women was considered peculiar. I remember being mortified when the school's most popular girl (and one of my friends—yeah, that kind) put a huge sign-up sheet in the cafeteria as a prank. People were supposed to sign up if they wanted to be my prom date. She signed the first name, John Holmes. I was offended because he'd already died of AIDS and was rumored to be bisexual. I felt guilty by association and wore a dress to school for the next three days.

My saving grace in high school came when Seana, a brown, muscular senior basketball player when I was a sophomore, leaned her tall self over my way and said, "Always be yourself—it's worth it." Somewhere in the back of my mind, I must have held that advice, because just when I stood on the precipice of losing my self, I remembered it and walked back into my cells.

EL HAJ MALIK SHABAZZ INTERCEDES

This memory is clear and visceral. Even writing about it now, I get chills. I could have been committed to a mental institution. Here is a fractured still life of me at nineteen:

I am living in Bloomington, Indiana, and working at McDonald's. I am not enrolled at Indiana University this semester, but I attend classes and purchase books with money from my plasma, which I sell twice a week. Oddly enough, I am in charge of scholarships and financial aide for the Black Student Union. I attend a white church, Emmanuel Baptist, where I help teach Sunday School to the children. Even though I'm left-handed, I play second base on the church softball team. I am one of the only black members of Campus Crusade for Christ and being groomed to teach Bible Study to the incoming freshmen. Sometimes, I attend black Pentecostal services where I hear my friends—baptized by the Holy Spirit with evidence of speaking in tongues—foam at the mouth in Spanish and/or French gibberish. I protest the imminent war in Iraq. I smoke weed and eat marijuana brownies with my housemates on Saturday mornings. I go dancing at Bullwinkle's, a queer bar, with my white roommates who are hetero-sexual, because it's the best place to dance. I am falling in love with one of my housemates. I have been telling lies for years about every-thing from lineage to cable bills. I am a fairly good thief. I write poetry about injustice. I make a great loaf of beer bread. I have started to lie in my own journal and be legitimately confused of as to truth's whereabouts.

Malcolm X—not Pat Parker, not Audre Lorde, not Ferron or the Indigo Girls—brought me out. I experienced metamorphosis as I read his autobiography for the umpteenth time, surrounded by piles of dirty clothes.

It's that place where he talks about conks. Permed hair is what he means. The chemical process of straightening your hair. He's recalling all the lye burns, the scabs and danger of getting his hair conked. All to fit in with the dominant culture. I hear him loud and clear.

I creep around the house looking for scissors. Upon finding them, I go in the bathroom and put on Tracy Chapman's *Talkin' 'bout a Revolution* tape. I cut off all my processed hair bit by bit, staring at myself in the mirror. I laugh at the fear I see staring back at my courage. I make myself smile and keep cutting, and I wonder what people will say about all the other changes I'm about to let loose. At last, in the mirror, I see my own coarse black hair standing on my head as raggedy and as spirited as freedom. I'm gonna shake all those personas away till I get back to my marrow.

On National Coming Out day, I bind all my newest poems at Kinko's for my mother. I find the prettiest, daintiest card and spend all day thinking of how to say "I'm queer, get used to it" respectfully. Finally, I write:

Dear E-ma, I think I'm a lesbian, but maybe I'm bisexual. I'm ok with it. If it's a sin, it's no more or less a sin than smoking cigarettes. You didn't do anything wrong. I hope you still love me.

When she arrives to pick me up from IU, my clothes are already soaked with sweat. All the way home, she's begging me to read the new poems to her and my brother. Out of thirty-two poems, each one is about women loving women, black women coming out, me being a dyke. I adamantly refuse to recite anything; finally saying, "Please, Ma, read them when you get home." The rest of the ride home is abnormally quiet.

That night, I pretend to be asleep. I pull the covers up over my head and rigidly steel myself for the preparation for rejection. Plus, I'm kicking myself for falling off the truthteller's bandwagon. I have written "I think I'm a lesbian, but maybe I'm bisexual" to make it easier for her to deal with, give her something to hope for.

A few hours later when my mother knocks on the door, I turn away from the door, fake a loud snore. She comes in and wraps her arms around me. She's crying, but she tells me she loves me. In the morning, I find a poem underneath my door. It reads. "Would it have mattered if . . ." Several things follow, until it ends with, "But since we can never really know, does it really matter?"

When I came out to my father a few months later, it was again through a letter. He called and told me to come home alone. Which I did. When I arrived, he was laid out on the floor in a drunkard's sleep. I shook him awake. He turned over once, looked at me and said, "Slim, this shit was predicted in a Michigan University Study. As more black men go to jail or marry white women, more black women are going to be gay. Concentrate on studying, Slim. You don't have to settle for this. Concentrate on your books." He turned back over and went to sleep before I could respond.

HOME COMING

The few times I'd been back home to Indiana were quick jaunts to check in, to make sure I wasn't totally estranged from my family. I'd rush into town with a current lover, try to make everyone comfortable with me, then jet back to Brooklyn when it didn't work.

When *Juba,* my first book, was finished, my father called one night to say that he thought the last poem—which is the title poem—shouldn't have been included. It's a poem about spiritual epiphany between my lover and myself. Needless to say, I was hot under the collar. So hot, I told him it was already being considered for a book award—just to shut him down.

So, when my brother was murdered a few months later, I went home—to my block—unprepared. I was afraid of going home, afraid that my lover wouldn't be treated the same as my brothers' and sisters' partners. Mad that I had to think about that. Wondering what it would be like to be in my father's house and if I would be able to stand it.

There were definitely some awkward moments, but what surprised me was that everyone on the block, from the eldest to the youngest, seemed to know that I was a writer. Not only that, but all my old babysitters and most of the neighbors had read both chapbooks and had bought a copy of *Juba* from Daddy. The first chapbook, *gawd and alluh huh sistahs,* had come out four years earlier, which meant that all the time that I'd been afraid to come home (because I didn't know if I could be myself, because I thought Daddy would think I was embarrassing him) were for nothing. My homophobic father had already proudly outed me to the neighborhood and his coworkers.

It's a trip to hear your seventy-year-old neighbor say, "Sorry about your brother. Is this your girlfriend? Where y'all stay now?" I feel finally like there won't be any more hard doors to open. I'm out at home. Everything else should be a piece of cake.

Finals week

THIS GIRL IS DIFFERENT

Tristan Taormino

1.   I learned what it was like to be queer even before I was queer in the summer streets of Provincetown from my gay father and Marilyn Monroe.

A typical child of divorced parents, I lived with my mom and saw my dad on holidays and school vacations. When I was fifteen, I got to spend the whole summer living at my dad's, and my dad happened to live in Provincetown. I got my first job that summer working at a leather shop, and spent my free time hanging out with drag queens and being crushed out on a dyke bike messenger named Nina. I remember grinning a lot whenever she made deliveries to our store. She had jet-black hair, muscles, looked like a tough tomboy all grown up. It never occurred to me that all my friends back home on Long Island weren't having a summer like I was having. The summer when I wore perfume for the first time, and a transvestite named Lola helped me choose it—it was her scent and I loved the way she smelled. Like spiced apples and vanilla. A summer of lesbian potluck dinners and five o'clock tea dances at the Boatslip. A summer of watching my dad cruise other men on Commercial Street. A summer to remember.

My father was close friends with a performer named Jimmy James, who impersonated Marilyn Monroe. They called it "female imperson-ation," but it was really more than that. He was the most exciting, most glamorous person I knew. Unlike the tired queens with cheap shiny dresses who couldn't even lip-sync very well, Jimmy sang Mari-lyn's songs and talked to the audience in Marilyn's voice. And his nightly transformation was magical. When I saw him during the day, he was always cute and perky and witty. When he got himself in that peach-pink sequined dress and blond wig and diamond bracelets, he embodied her. She was gorgeous and sexy and naughty and brash, and I wanted to be her. Not the Marilyn I'd seen in *All About Eve* with my dad, not the Marilyn on posters and T-shirts everywhere. I wanted to be the Marilyn Jimmy was.

2.   I learned what it was like to be a lesbian in ivy-covered brick buildings from a girljock and a rabble-rouser named Jen. I learned what it was like to be a dyke from 100% pre-shrunk cotton T-shirts that said Read My Lips, I Like Girls, Clitlicker: I'll Be Dammed, Buttfucker: Total Condom Nation, and fluorescent crack 'n' peel stickers that read Fuck Your Gender, Suck My Lesbian Cock, Queer Anytime, Anywhere, Assimilate My Fist. I learned what it was like to be a femme from *Mother Camp* and Joan Nestle and girls who look like boys.

During the first week of college freshman orientation, I met Jessie, a shy soccer player from a small town in upstate New York who lived in my dorm. We sat together in calculus class. Neither of us under-stood our crazy professor's handwriting on the blackboard, but we understood the scribbled notes we passed back and forth, like best friends in high school. She was sensitive, funny, easygoing, and she had the most amazing blue eyes. After one of our weekly dorm meet-ings, Jessie came out to the entire group as a lesbian. When she told us, we all huddled around her, kissing and hugging and encouraging her. I remember returning to my room that night and thinking that she was one of the bravest women I knew. That year, she had a beautiful girlfriend who looked like young Elizabeth Taylor and I loved seeing them together.

All first-year students had to attend a series of awareness seminars, and the Bisexual Lesbian and Gay Awareness Workshop was run by queer students. In the workshop, everyone had to go around the room and say we were gay or lesbian and then talk in the first person about what it was like to be gay or lesbian.

"If you aren't gay or lesbian, we encourage you to consider personal experiences when you felt different or ostracized and relate them to the group," said one of the facilitators, a well-dressed senior with tortoise-shell glasses and chunky black shoes. Some people's stories about being gay were true, but you didn't always know which ones. I knew that Jessie was telling the truth.

It seemed like everyone at Wesleyan was queer or at least wanted to be. Everywhere I looked, there were pink triangle buttons, posters for one of several gay student groups, and same-sex couples holding hands. When the gay-lesbian-bisexual alliance threw a party, it was an event not to be missed. The best music, the best outfits, and by the end of the night, shirtless boys and topless girls bumping-and-grinding til dawn.

Jessie and I flirted for a year, and by the time we were sophomores, I told her that I was through flirting and I kissed her. Just like that. Well, I wanted to, so I did. I was terrified once I did it, and scared about what would happen next. What happens when two girls kiss? She became my first girlfriend. Jessie was the first girlfriend of a lot of girls, actually. She was a one-woman recruiting agent, but so genuine and unassuming no one suspected their daughters wouldn't be safe around her. Coming to terms with my sexual identity for myself and acting on my feelings got all squished together. I guess I didn't have tremendous self-doubt because I had the luxury of being in a place where it was okay, even great, to be queer. Once Jessie and I became a couple, I was holding her hand around campus just like anyone else I had dated. So I slipped out of the closet, telling everyone I was bisexual. A lot of my friends were queer, so they said, "Yippee! Welcome to the family!"

The way I told my mom was less than ideal. I was home on a school break and talking to Jessie for about an hour on the telephone. My mom kept knocking on my bedroom door, telling me to get off the phone. I was totally frustrated and came storming into the living room.

She said something snide like, "I don't know who this Jessie is and why you have to be on the phone with her for so long."

"She's my girlfriend! And I'm bisexual!" I shouted angrily.

I don't actually remember what she said after that.

Telling my gay father was a lot less dramatic. He just said something like, "That's great—whatever makes you happy." Interestingly, he wasn't jumping for joy over me joining the team or anything.

Jessie and I didn't last very long; we really were better off as friends. I don't think people, including me, realized how serious I was—this wasn't an experiment or whimsy—until I met Jen. Jen was the Big Dyke On Campus. She was a senior, super intelligent, opinionated, really out. Everyone knew who she was because she was a big-time activist, very outspoken about things like sex, SM, and porn. She also went to class dressed in men's shirts and ties. This was no friendly, sporty lesbian that everyone found charming. She was a butch dyke, brazen in her gender and style, and I was drawn to her. She was frantically finishing her honors thesis when we first met, and so our early encounters were at the library. I remember kissing her for the first time on the library steps and feeling such intense desire that I thought I would explode and shatter into tiny bits of flesh at her feet. She was a brilliant flirt, so self-assured, so deliberate and generous with her words, so powerful at casting a spell on me. Consumed by her, I wanted to surrender, to give her everything. She was the smartest, fiercest lesbian I knew. And then she was my girlfriend.

Jen used to read *On Our Backs* and *Susie Bright's Lesbian Sex World* to me at bedtime every night. (She was even in charge of bringing Susie Bright to speak on campus that spring.) We were so connected, so engaged in the relationship. Every single day, there was something new to learn, share, discover. I did so many things for the first time with Jen. Jen was the first girl I ever lived with. I experienced the tremors of my first earthquake in bed with Jen and her yellow lab. I had my first taste of what now is my favorite all-time food at the hands of Jen: sushi. Jen was the first woman to fuck me with a dildo. Jen was the first woman to tie me up. The first woman to spank me. To fuck my ass. She topped me for the first time, I bottomed to her for the first time, and we switched. We watched fag porn together. She was the first girl I ever fucked with a strap-on. She was the first girl I ever stripped for. Jen was the first girl I ever bought a tie for. Jen brought me to buy my first pair of Doc Martens. She was so articulate about her desires and her politics, so sex positive, that I felt like I could tell her anything. She was my lover, my mentor, my dyke teacher, and so much of who I am today came from her.

Before her, I felt closeted not only about my desire for women, but my desire to explore the myriad possibilities of sex. Coming out finally gave me the freedom to do so. I was never tortured or miserable with all the boys I'd been with; in fact, physically, they were pretty satisfying. I couldn't always connect with them on an intellectual or emotional level, so I always felt like something was missing. While I was sexually precocious with men, I never tried new things, experimented, voiced fantasies—being a dyke totally coincided with my overall sexual liberation, and the two awakenings became intrinsically linked.

My mom met Jen for the first time over brunch, when we also broke the news that I was going to Hollywood with her when she graduated. Between bites of her BLT, my mother said, "Jen has a reason to go—to start her career. You are running away from home."

3. I am learning what it's like to be me: to be a queer fag's daughter, to be a lesbian smarty pants, to be a dyke activist, to be a femme fag fetishist, to be a pervy porn-watching feminist, to be a boy-fucking drama queen, to be a backdoor betty, to be a butch-loving girl, to be me.

That was the summer I became a dyke. In L.A., I was immersed in queer culture and finally felt like I'd come home, found my tribe, and myself. We became friends with Radical Faeries who lived in vegan households. We marched at Gay Pride in San Francisco and L.A. We joined ACT UP and Queer Nation. It was a swirl of actions and demos, protesting everything from homophobic Governor Pete Wilson to a photo lab at the Beverly Center that wouldn't develop pictures of same-sex couples kissing. I marched down Santa Monica Boulevard in West Hollywood in my Doc Martens hundreds of times, hand-in-hand with pierced and tattooed perverts; on my way to fetish clubs and gay cafés; carrying brightly colored stickers and propaganda for distribution. I stayed all night at Kinko's on Highland making those stickers with Cory, who was copying his zine, *Infected Faggot,* with a bright yellow cover. Cory was a shaved-head-pierced-septum-dress-wearing-civil-but-disobedient-citizen. His anger his rage his spirit and his infected body knew no bounds, and I loved him. When I returned from L.A., I had such a clearer sense of myself, my identity, my purpose.

It was only after I came out as a dyke that, for the first time in my life, I felt ready to celebrate being a girl, and I did. Actually, I overdid. Armed with Esther Newton's *Mother Camp,* Judith Butler's *Gender Trouble,* and Joan Nestle's *A Restricted Country,* I embraced femme. I dressed up in short flowery dresses, pushup bras, satin panties, and lacy stockings. I paid great attention to my long, curly, perfectly-coiffed hair, my glamorous makeup, and especially my pouty lips. I spritzed Lola's smell on my skin—Estee Lauder's Private Collection—and painted my nails. I wore all of it with black combat boots and a brilliant sense of irony. I reveled in my girliness, went over the top, learned how to tweeze my eyebrows and line my lips with a lip pencil.

My gender presentation was unmistakable: blatant female sexuality. I was a proud, in-your-face, take-no-prisoners, uppity, don't-assume-I'm-straight-because-I-wear-lipstick-and-dresses femme dyke. Because femmes are always assumed to be straight or sleeping with men, and I do sleep with men, I made sure to always have a butch on my arm so I'd be read as femme. Even though I was sure I'd be mistaken for straight, the boys took one look at me and steered clear. It was as if I was too much of a woman for them to handle, like I was a handful, and I was. But butch girls love a handful—a handful of tits, a handful of ass, a girl who needs to be handled, a girl who can handle herself.

How I figured out I was a femme had a lot to do with the women I was attracted to and the dynamic between us. When I was in junior high, I used to mess around with a friend of mine named Angela. Angela was one of those girls who developed early; I remember she had big breasts in like sixth grade. We mostly kissed and touched over clothes, and we played out various boy-girl scenarios. I was always the girl—my early femme roots. My favorite of all our little scenes was the one where she was my male boss and I was the secretary. The boss made me have sex with him and told me if I didn't I would get fired. Now this was all before Clarence Thomas, Anita Hill and the media awareness/obsession with sexual harassment. I remember she'd tell me to suck her dick and push my face unmercifully into her crotch, which smelled amazing. The drama of it all—the force, the degradation, the power games—really got me off. After that, there was no going back to simplicity. I was hooked on the power.

Jen really epitomized all the girls I was attracted to then and still am. Being with a butch girl, I was valued for my combination of strength and vulnerability, for dressing up, for wanting an arm to hold onto, hips to wrap my legs around, being able to give my body over to her and say, I trust you, I'm yours. My butch loved me in low-cut dresses, appreciated my sexual voraciousness, worshipped my inner slut. I reveled in the fact that I could be strong and submissive all at once. Surrender and still be a feminist. Being a dyke is not just about who I fuck and love, it's about being a girl who doesn't play by the rules.

Butch girls don't play by the rules either, and I love butch girls. Girls with hair so short you can barely slide it between two fingers to hold on. Girls with slick, shiny, barbershop haircuts and shirts that button the other way. Girls that swagger. Girls who have dicks made of flesh and silicone and latex and magic. Girls who get stared at in the ladies room, girls who shop in the boy's department, girls who live every moment looking like they weren't supposed to. Girls with hands that touch me like they have been touching my body their entire lives. Girls who have big cocks, love blow-jobs, and like to fuck girls hard. Every day, it is the girls that get called Sir that make me catch my breath, the girls with strong jaws that buckle my knees, the girls who are a different gender that make me want to lie down for them.

Someone else said it about me recently and it's right on target: "She gets off on all different sorts of people sexually, but she falls for butches." Like the poet who bought her first strap-on with me and then wanted to sleep with it on. The shrink-in-training who got harassed every time she drove down South. She did look so much like a fifteen-year-old boy: blue button-down shirts, neatly-combed blond hair. The ad exec who had names for her dildos and used to love for me to spit-shine her wingtips. The photographer whose face was so mannish she could pass almost anywhere. The writer who wanted a body like Loren Cameron's. The telephone repairwoman who drove a truck. The cook who had a boy's name. The academic who got cruised by gay men on Castro Street. The cornfed farmboy from the Heartland with arms so hard and strong you swear they've been working the land, not the iron at the gym.

And there's the one who's got the James Dean stare down, and dresses like a clean-cut fag, and looks at me like she could look at me forever and never blink or grow tired or move from the spot she's in. She's a girl who loves girls like me—girls in velvet bras, girls who want to surrender to her mouth. She's a girl who isn't afraid to throw a femme down on the bed and fuck her. Possess her. My kind of girl. This girl is different.

Paul J. D'Arcy

PICTURE THIS

Cecilia Tan

OCTOBER 1985: One worry line punctuates the space between my mother's eyebrows like an exclamation point, as she listens to me tell her what I am pretty sure she already knows. . . . Unaware of her expression, she is holding that most necessary suburban device to her ear: the kitchen phone, the illuminated buttons-in-the-handset kind with fourteen-foot cord that reaches all the way from refrigerator to TV room. She sits on a stool in a New Jersey kitchen newly redone in Southwestern-style turquoise and salmon. She holds the receiver close to her head with both hands, the slight frown of her eyes reflected in her lips as she opens them to say those proverbial words: "Are you sure?"

Actually, I don't know what my mother looked like when I told her I was interested in women. I don't even know what room of the house she was in. But that was the scene as I imagined it when I called her on the phone, six or eight weeks into my first semester at college, and said something like, "It never really occurred to me to tell you this before, and I wasn't even really that sure about it myself until recently, but I think you probably know already, so this is really just to double-check, to make sure you were clear on this . . ."

My coming-out phone call to her came at a strange time—strange in its lack of any particular precipitating event. I did not tell her I was bisexual because I'd just discovered the fact myself; I'd known for some time in the back of my mind. I did not tell her then because I had a girlfriend or even a wild fling. (At the time, I hadn't even had sex with a woman.) I was not worried about being outed or of outing myself through my writing yet—this was many years before I was published. I told her simply because I thought she ought to know. I remember spending most of the conversation trying to convince her that bisexuality was not a "new thing" with me. What was new was the concept of telling her about it, of "coming out" itself.

I was used to being an "invisible minority." As half-Asian, I have always passed for Caucasian. As a tomboy growing up, I often passed as a boy. I was used to being things that were counter to people's assumptions. What had never occurred to me before was that I should *announce* that I was different. I felt rather secure in my self-knowledge and in my identity, and yet, once I was introduced to the concept of "coming out," by osmosis through the Lesbian Gay Student Alliance, I began to worry that, by not formally declaring the pieces of my identity, I was, oh god, in the closet. I was very uncomfortable with the notion that allegiance to a label was necessary in order to be myself. (You should have seen how I battled the Asian-American label that Asian-American student groups continually fought to stick me with.)

And yet I made the phone call. I don't know if the phone was the wisest choice, or if my timing was well-considered. My mom was suffering some degree of separation anxiety at that point, of course, and I'm sure my news exacerbated any paranoid thoughts she'd been having about all the wild and terrible changes that college was sure to wreak on her daughter. But it was my own sense of the sudden gulf between us, of the distance that collegiate nest-leaving creates, that gave me a sense of urgency. I needed to do it sooner, rather than later—by phone, if necessary. She needed to know this fundamental thing about me *now*, before her image of me got too gilded by memory, before the intimacy of eighteen years' living together was lost. I could not live with the idea that if I waited to tell her a year later, she'd decide that she had never really known me—that a stranger had lived in her house all her life.

Besides, I figured I was giving her fair warning, in case I brought someone home at Thanksgiving. As it turned out, I brought a boy home with me, a platonic, good-friend kind of boy, who was actually falling for me really hard, and I was in denial about that . . . but that is a story for a different essay.

September 1985: I'm wearing socks of two different colors, and a hat. A black fedora, I think, though maybe it was a beret. I am a college freshman, and prone to unreadable fashion statements. This time, I am hoping I look weird enough to fit in. I am standing outside the door to a meeting room on the Brown Campus, feeling like a character in a canonical coming-out play, going through what feel like obligatory motions of fear, thrill, second thoughts, and despondency. I'm supposed to be at my first meeting of the LGSA, and I'm there, but the room is empty, and I don't know what to do. I pace and wring my hands, as that's what seems called for.

First, I've had to get up the courage to go. I've had to go through all the rationalizations, beat down my own anti-label, anti-joining attitudes, toss out the bits of random internalized homophobia that will creep into even the most independent mind, and overcome the habitual lameness that could have kept me in my room reading, or sitting in the hallway gossiping, or taking part in whatever other default activities for a weekday evening take up a new student's time. Then I have to assemble the outfit: eclectic without being dorky, cutting-edge without being faddish. This is hard to do. Then the walk to the place through the underground tunnels between dorms and then across an open space to the entrance. As I walk across the quad, I feel that every person I pass must be able to tell where I'm going. Surely gay bashers have taken note of the flyers and posters, too. My heart pounds as I wonder what people are thinking. Paranoia is an entirely novel emotion for me, and I revel in it a teensy bit.

I arrive at the room with no plan of action, but as I come within sight of the entrance I decide to pass casually by the door rather than walk right in. I can perhaps feign discovery: "Oh, what's this? Well, maybe I'll stay." Can't do that with not a soul here. I climb the stairs into the dorm and look for a bulletin board, find a flyer confirming the time and place. Tonight, now, here. I fret for some thirty more minutes, wandering the halls trying to look exceedingly casual (and discovering some startling things, like a room full of pianos in the basement), until at last some people carrying boxes of munchies and soda arrive, and I help them tote stuff in. So much for pretending to "happen upon" the meeting. In that moment, bags of Doritos in my arms, paranoia is left behind like a costume that didn't fit. I've done my first deed—albeit a really, really minor one—as a gay community activist, and have learned my first real piece of gay culture: Gay Standard Time.

November 1985: Rain spatters the car window as the vehicle inches through holiday traffic, the sky winter-dark and gray. My mother grips the steering wheel with both hands, her worry line etching her brow. The windshield wipers blur the red taillights of the car ahead and the reflections from the glistening wet highway. Mom has decided to make one last try to convince me it's just a natural rebellion/growth phase I'm going through, and not to make any decisions now that might ruin my life later. She wouldn't be a mom if she didn't.

This is the first time the two of us are alone on my visit, and it's a gutsy time for her to broach the subject. Stuck in traffic as we are, we risk having a misunderstanding and lapsing into a damaging silence. Fortunately, both Mom and I are deft enough with thorny language and honest enough with our emotions that we negotiate the rocky waters of Coming-Out Conversation #2 unscathed. The exact words are not important and follow the basic script of Coming-Out Conversation #1, the phone call: "Are you sure?" "Yes."

Flip back to some old images: me, age sixteen, clutching the kitchen phone to my own ear, as I dial the phone number of a girl I like a *whole lot* again and again and anxiously wait for her line to get unbusy; me, age seventeen, writing a part for myself in a play for our AP English class in which I am the bisexual Hamlet, unable to choose between Ahab and Tess of the D'Urbervilles. Me, age ten, glued to a television documentary about David Bowie; me, age fifteen, glued to a late-night cable TV showing of the movie *The Hunger,* starring David Bowie and Catherine Deneuve as bisexual vampires. Me, age five, learning to masturbate and getting off on Catwoman as much as Batman; me, age six, playing "Batman and Catwoman" with the daughter of some hippie friends. Bisexuality, fantasy, bondage, erotic surrender, imagination—it's all there from the earliest signposts. I pick and choose some to remind or tell Mom of, as I try to convince her, again, that my bisexuality is not a new thing. And to reaffirm the fact that, no, really, she knows it, too.

By that point in time, I settle into thinking that only secrets should upset people or startle them. If it isn't a secret, how can anyone be shocked? By the time we get out of the car, Mom and I are on the same page once again. She seems to appreciate my openness, realizing that it is truly better to be honest and know one another than to live a lie and the worse messes that can lead to. I appreciate that I have one of the most rational, well-adjusted moms on the planet.

February 1986: Fifty freshmen, three resident counselors, and one head counselor are jammed into the lounge that is the designated meeting space for our floor. The room is a cinderblock rectangle edged with low orange institutional furniture—not quite "couches." We fifty are one "unit," sort of like a "bunk" at summer camp except that we will share the same dorm floor for the whole academic year. Many faces are red and angry, or red and embarrassed, or red and passionate. The Northeast Gay and Lesbian Student Union Conference is coming to Brown soon, and our head counselor has approved our lounge as a sleepover place for conference attendees. Two stereotypical jocks, in khaki shorts and backward baseball caps, are on their feet and demanding that the H.C. acted inappropriately by doing so. They demand a vote.

One of *us,* by which I mean one of us five who are queer, stands up too, and points out that we didn't take a vote on whether the Princeton Marching Band could be housed here, which they were. I don't remember now if I was the one who said it, or Nils, or Ellen, or who. What I do remember is that although we were all out to each other prior to the crisis, we weren't out to everyone else.

The jocks finally make their stand: *they're afraid of AIDS.* They've grabbed on to this thing which is barely a buzzword to them, as some kind of long-awaited justification for all the homophobic shit they would have kicked up anyway. They are practically high-fiving each other for thinking of it, because, after all, what self-respecting, intelligent person would share a bathroom with "that"?

And one of us, Scott or me or someone, finally says that if they think that by keeping the NELGSU Conference out of the lounge they're keeping themselves separated from gay people, they're wrong. That if they think they don't already share a bathroom with gay people, they're wrong. And, by the way, that if they think gay people cause AIDS, they're wrong. But the issue of AIDS seems minor compared to the fact that we have just outed ourselves to the group. We have declared "We are everywhere"—and here we are.

The result of the debate was a "visitor bathroom" policy (people agreed to mark their bathroom doors "okay" for visitors to use or not), and many lacrosse balls winged blindly down the hallways at us from unseen attackers—as if we couldn't guess who'd thrown them. By the time the conference actually arrived, the furor had died down, and we had a very festive gay pride week. Openly gay Congressman Gerry Studds gave the keynote address, and I still remember the climax of his speech. He said that if the message of Harvey Milk to the previous generation had been "Come to San Francisco and be gay," his message to the current generation was "Stay where you are and be gay." It was the second "We are everywhere" for me, and one that convinced me I should stick with the Lesbian Gay Student Alliance, even though I seemed to be the only bisexual on the campus (or the only one admitting it). Stay where you are and be yourself.

I picked "bisexual" as one label I didn't vehemently resist, partly because I liked that the definition of it was so nebulous. I had to "invent" bisexuality, I felt, which fit nicely with my antilabel attitude. It was a word everyone knew, and yet I had no bisexual culture to read about or participate in, no bisexual role models—unless you counted the old celebrity chameleon David Bowie himself. That suited me fine.

July 1991: My mother, my sixteen-year-old brother, and I are seated at a Formica table, four paper placemats and place settings in front of us. We are in a family restaurant in Orlando, Florida, waiting to order breakfast. Our heads are bent toward our laminated menus, bright with photographs of eggs, bacon strips, shiny buttered toast, stacks of pancakes with rivers of syrup. The restaurant is crowded with people, the air full of clatter and sizzle and conversational buzz.

I am trying to judge whether any of the clientele are locals, or truck drivers, or militant Nazi types, or right-wing fundamentalists, or anything other than tourist families minding their own business. I have never been gay bashed (unless you count the lacrosse balls of my freshman year) and I don't relish the thought of inviting an incident now. However, I am wearing a black T-shirt with interlocking pink and blue triangles on it, emblazoned with the slogan "Bisexual Pride." We're going to hit Disneyworld as soon as Dad returns from a game of golf. (The shirt seemed like a good idea at the time.)

Not three days earlier we had been on a cruise ship together, and my father had expounded on the good sense of wearing T-shirts that announce one's interests. "Look at that couple over there," he had said, pointing to a married pair wearing matching shirts that said "We (heart) Our Basenji" or Pomeranian, or whatever variety of dog it was. "They probably meet other people right away who are also into those dogs." He went on to posit that my brother wore a lot of tie-dye so he could meet other fans of the Grateful Dead. What more perfect setup could there be for making sure Dad knew and remembered my sexual orientation? This is, of course, many years after my original coming-out conversations with my mother. I'm not really sure that he was ever fully informed, and, even if he was, that he remembers. After all this time, there haven't been any significant reminders. I've still never brought a woman home for Thanksgiving.

As I'm putting the shirt on that morning, my brother says, "Dad's going to have a conniption when he sees that shirt." My reply: "Why? Doesn't he know?" Shrug. We meet my mom in the lobby. She says, "Dad's going to have a conniption when he sees that shirt." Me again: "Why? Doesn't he know?" Shrugs all around.

In the restaurant, no one appears to bat an eye. When we arrive at Disneyworld, I get many knowing looks and winks from the staff. Dad either never notices the shirt or, as I hoped, he has not in fact forgotten and is not fazed. This is a very good thing, considering the two major comings-out I have yet to spring on the family, simultaneously, the following year.

December 1992: Fire flickers in the fireplace, colored lights circle the Christmas tree, a Charlie Brown Christmas soundtrack plays from the corner stereo. Mom, Dad, Julian, and my very significant other, corwin, are seated on couches and loveseats, piles of wrapping and bows at our feet, piles of gifts in our laps. Mom is holding one of my gifts to her in her hands and reading what it says on the back. It is a slim gray book, barely bigger than a pamphlet, really, bearing the title *Telepaths Don't Need Safewords.*

This little chapbook is my first significant work of fiction, I feel. It is three erotic short stories, all with themes of bondage and SM, which I have collected and self-published under the new company, founded that March, Circlet Press. This has been a year of change, as drastic perhaps as the year I moved out of the house and went to college. This year I quit my job in publishing and entered a graduate writing program, founded a press, and made my first professional fiction sales. I've sold one story to the *Herotica 3* anthology, one to *Penthouse.* My mom knows this, I've told her everything, and yet . . . it has taken me eight months to give her a copy of the book.

It's Christmas Eve, and corwin sits in our family circle, looking over his gifts, laughing at my father's jokes, joking with my brother. No one mentions, or notices perhaps, that he wears a leather collar around his neck.

May 1993: I picture my mother in the same position with the same expression, on stool, phone held to head with two hands, worry line and so on, as she leaves me a tense-sounding answering machine message. Nothing in the words themselves says that anything is wrong, and yet there's an unmistakable edge there, not heard since a rainy car ride in 1985. I know, with an unnatural surety, that she has finally read the book.

I call her back. She has clearly been rehearsing what to say to me. No sooner does she mention that she has read it than she produces a very tough monologue about how she didn't spend her youth fighting for civil rights in the South to have me grow up to glorify slavery. Once this piece is said, she relaxes, and, since I can't think of an adequate response, our conversation goes on to be like most of our phone conversations. We talk politics and pop culture, she catches me up on hometown gossip.

Then she begins to complain about my father. Mother's Day has just passed, and they've had a fight—Mom wishes she'd had certain issues out with him when they were newlyweds. She has almost thirty years of stored-up resentments over things she didn't mention then, and so is unable to mention now. Our commiseration somehow leads me to describe the principle of negotiation, this being the basis of all loving SM relationships. I point out that the purpose of negotiation is to overcome the sad fact that partners, no matter how much they love one another, can *not* read each other's minds. Each one is obligated to tell the other what they feel, otherwise consent has no meaning. I end with a leap of logic along the lines of, "So that's why I feel that my eroticization of SM has to do with trust and respect for a special bond between two individuals, and nothing to do with the subjugation of one race of people by another for economic reasons." Mom—who is, remember, extremely rational and well-adjusted—replies, "Oh. I get it now." We've never argued about it since.

July 1994: My mother is a fairly tall woman, stylish and poised. Picture a cross between Princess Diana and Hillary Clinton, disguised as a suburban housewife. This is a woman who was P.T.A. president, taught cooking to Girl Scouts, and attended every performance of the Scotch Plains Fanwood High School Marching Band. She parks her minivan on the sidewalk outside the local downtown "corner" store. This is the place where I bought comic books and baseball cards as a kid, where they have a soda fountain counter and sell magazines. Mom marches up to the counter and demands multiple copies of the new issue of *Penthouse*. The clerk looks at her like she's a little nuts. She proudly informs him that her daughter's first published fiction in a national magazine is in that issue.

I'm exaggerating the scene a bit, I'm sure, but isn't that all the fun of being a fiction writer? Here is one part I did not make up:

when Mom ran out of copies of *Penthouse* to give away, she began photocopying my story and mailing it to friends and relatives. She informed me on the phone (why are so many of these episodes tied to the phone?) that she had even given copies of it to my old English teachers at the high school, and that they had liked it. "Mrs. Perka said she always knew you'd make it."

"Mom, it's *Penthouse,* it's porn, it's smut," I replied. I inquired, with a bit of a gulp, if Mom had read the story before spreading it all around. Mom, a former English teacher herself, replied that not only had she read it, she thought the dream sequence near the beginning lent a certain ambiguity and richness to the ending. Mom thus becomes the first literary critic to analyze my smut.

November 1996: This one I did not make up. There's a huge Barnes & Noble Superstore on a highway in New Jersey that my mother frequents. Cappuccino bar, places to sit and read the latest Terry McMillan or Isabel Allende. She goes in to pick up five copies of *Ms.* magazine, which has a story of mine in it. At last, I thought, a national magazine Mom can really, truly, be proud of buying. Mom was a charter subscriber when I was an infant, so I am absolutely beaming to have a piece in there. While browsing, she picks up some other books: *Herotica 4* (which I am also in), the latest from Amy Tan. She goes to the cash register, and the clerk remarks that she is buying quite a few copies of the magazine. "Of course," my mom says. "My daughter has a story in it." She hands over her VISA card to pay for the purchases, and the clerk, seeing the name on the card, gasps out, "Are you Amy Tan's mother?"

June 1998: There's a yellow-and-white striped tent in my mother's backyard waiting for me and my brother and my father to erect it. Tables and chairs to seat 100 people are stacked next to it. Summer cicadas whirr in the humid air, and we are praying for no thunderstorm this evening. Mom has hired a jazz band and caterers and mailed countless invitations to friends, family, my godparents, old high school English teachers. This party has all the trappings of the classic suburban high school graduation party, only this coming-out occasion is for the publication of a book. This is my fiction-writer debutante party.

Five years' worth of erotic short stories are finally collected into one volume and, more importantly, published by a big, reputable New York publishing house. The fact that the press is reputable, that the book was published as literature and not as mass market smut, does not change the fact that every story in the book is graphically sexual and that many of them contain bondage and SM. The fact that the press is reputable does not help when, hours later, as relatives and neighbors sit under the tent in a citronella haze, my mother whispers to me, "Everyone's waiting to hear you read." I page through the table of contents, looking for a story that's funny, short, not too auto-biographical, not too graphic, no bloodletting or piercing—I'd had a woman faint a few days previous at a gay bookstore during one of those. . . . I realized as I stood there cataloging my work that, once again, total and completely honest disclosure was the only possible tactic. Only secrets should upset people or startle them. Still, I decide against reading the gay male vampire story and go with the final story in the book, a futuristic lesbian motorcycle encounter. They love it.

Every now and then, I have one of these Star Trek "alternate universe" moments, where I get a flash of what my life would be like if I kept my sexuality a secret. Rain lashes me as I return alone from the bookstore to my basement hovel. A single bulb hangs over my desk as I stare at the blank screen, nervously tapping out a word or two. I look in the mirror but can't decide what to change. My cat is aloof and ignores me. Every day is a strain, the sword hangs over my head by an unseen thread. My relationships don't last, my creative output is low because of damaged self-esteem, I have nightmares where everything is out of control. . . . How can anyone love me?

I shake myself and snap out of it. I have never regretted my policy against secrecy.

August 1998: In Florida, my mom is in another Barnes & Noble having another interaction with a clerk. This one is not going so well. Mom has gone in there to try to find a copy of my book. She has already bought dozens of copies of the book to give to friends, and needs another one for an old friend from high school she is visiting. She is puzzled that a book that is so prominently displayed at her local B&N seems to be missing from the shelf. She asks for the book at the counter, and the clerk, upon hearing the topic, scolds her. "Lady, this is the Bible Belt."

Now I'm the one clutching the phone to my head with two hands, as I sit in my home office, surrounded by heaps of paperwork and manuscripts and unread books, my tornado nest of creative work, listening to my mom suffer the abuse that no one dares heap upon me directly. "She treated me like I was some kind of sicko, can you believe that?"

"Yeah, Mom," I croak. "Some people."

Brown University orientation week, 1985

LAYERS OF THE ONION, SPOKES OF THE WHEEL

Pat Califia

COMING out is such a hard process that it's no wonder most lesbians and gay men can only manage it once in a lifetime. Coming out begins when we recognize, in a stigmatized Other, something of ourselves. Something disturbing we feel we must bring forward—at first into our own consciousness, then to a community of like-minded people where we hope to find welcome, and finally to outsiders. Coming out transmutes what is loathsome or unimaginable into something valuable and nourishing—garbage into gold, sickness into bread. This is an inherently terrifying experience because it means disobeying the voices of social disapproval (and often, self-hatred as well) to risk becoming a more honest, but not necessarily happier or safer or more loved, person.

Coming out is a normal developmental process of differentiation, in the context of our culture's sex-negative pathology. It also encompasses other stages of adult life which vanilla, gender-congruent, heterosexual people are able to take more for granted—autonomy from

276

the family of origin, sexual initiation, learning courtship skills and other social skills, relationship formation, consolidation of ties to a friendship network and a community, and (sometimes) clarification of political, moral, and spiritual values that impel us to take action.

Although coming out does not necessarily involve all three stages (coming out to self, subculture, and society at large), the individual who cannot move through the entire process usually is not fully able to separate from the judgments and distorted thinking of the surrounding culture and develop his or her own self-validating, stable identity as a member of a sexual minority. One of the most crucial tasks of coming out is to defeat the shaming voices of self-obliteration and reject the temptation to live for others' gratification and approval rather than our own. By coming out to ourselves, we free up the energy we spent keeping a part of ourselves hidden. By coming out to our kindred spirits, we acquire allies and rewards for integration and openness. We strengthen our little corner of the world, the walled gardens where some of our secrets may be told. By coming out to outsiders, we serve the health of the entire social body. We shut down, or at least contest, the omnipotence of the institutions that foster stigma; we replace ignorance and invisibility with the faces and lives of real people. We widen and clear the path for others to come out as well.

None of this is meant to imply that the power to come out lies only with the individual. The dangers that greet sexual nonconformity are quite real and at times life-threatening. There are few situations more painful than needing to come out when it is too unsafe to manage it and survive the process. This is a loneliness like no other; it generates a level of stress that can also be life-threatening. Those of us who have come to any sort of sexual sanctuary, however narrow or beleaguered, must never forget those who are prevented from joining us, and we must never stop trying to extend them practical as well as psychic aide. The work of coming out is rescue work. It is a prayer for the freedom of everyone who cannot escape—political prisoners, hostages to fundamentalism.

We cannot complete the last phase of coming out, witnessing to outsiders, unless we are very strong (or desperate). If our private lives have been revealed without our consent, we must gather whatever dignity and courage we can scrape together and put the best face on things we can muster. Whether willingly or no, stage three of coming out involves service to the body politic. It is at its core an attempt to ease human suffering. And so it has inherent spiritual value. To the extent that the first phase of coming out can be seen as the individual becoming more and more willing to mirror the self as a gift of our creator, to understand and love the self we were given by that creator, it too is a spiritual quest. And the attempt to foster kinship, love, and mutual care in the face of hatred and violence is also, I believe, an activity that brings us closer to the divine. Perhaps awareness of this aspect of our lives as queer people, the compassion we must learn to apply to our own wounds and the wounds of others, can help us to resist burnout as activists and breakdown as perpetual outsiders. We do not need to believe in deities or heaven and hell in order to recognize the healing power of bearing witness when evil is done, and encouraging the growth of kindness and justice.

The notion of heaven is, at any rate, only useful when people ask themselves what they could do to create a heaven on this planet, during this lifetime. The notion of God is only helpful when we worry over the problem of what constitutes goodness and attempt to make our best qualities manifest in every mundane interaction with other living creatures. I do not know how many more thousands of years the savior archetype will have to persist in our myths, legends, and catechisms before we realize that the only effective saviors we could possibly have are one another. Cruelty and evil are human problems, not defects of God, and we have it within our own power to banish them. No supernatural intercession is necessary. When people who suffer refuse to do so in silence, and instead make a public spectacle of their persecution, it is one more push against the stubborn resistance our species displays toward growing a collective conscience that will no longer tolerate such things as genocide, poverty, and discrimination. By coming out we establish the edges of a nation that as yet has no territorial boundaries, as cartographers understand such things. Still, those boundaries must be defended, often with our lives.

But there is another side of this, our grim combat with those who hate us. There is a powerful temptation to split and view everything bad as associated with the Enemy, everything good as within our camp. But that is distorted thinking, at best, self-righteousness at worst. We cannot hope to grow as a lesbian and gay community if we punish other people for speaking their sexual truth. Coming out is made more difficult because of the shortcomings of our own community. Some of these defects are not our fault; we may be so marginalized that we have few resources left to comfort one another. But as our resources permit, we are responsible for doing better than our opposition, even if the only victory we want to achieve is on the battlefield of public relations.

We tend to avoid these responsibilities because they seem tedious rather than a source of power. Getting into martyr mode encourages a lazy attitude toward our own clutter. Or we can become scavengers, unable to stop attacking, even if we are simply ganging up on someone who is weaker than ourselves rather than storming the Bastille. I think, for activists, the paradigm of the farmer or the mason is much more useful than the paradigm of the warrior.

What does all this have to do with my own coming-out story? I feel, on one level, that I've told this tale so many times it must lack all interest for me and the reader. Yet perhaps it's never been told in quite this way, with the power of forty-four years of self-reflection and hindsight to color it. Be patient with me, if you can, as I try to connect this skein of theory to the fabric of my life. When I try to sum up what I know about coming out, I find myself thinking about several key shifts in my identity—coming out as a lesbian, coming out into S/M, coming out as a grateful addict in recovery, a pagan, a disabled person with a chronic illness that affects my immune system and causes persistent severe pain, coming out as bisexual, and coming out as transgendered. I've given these in roughly chronological order. Some people would no doubt believe that some of these items don't count as "real" comings-out, or that it isn't possible for one person to hold all of these different identities in the same being. I have only my own experience to go on here, and that experience is that each of these transitions had a profound effect on my sexuality and was accompanied by a dramatic shift in who was willing to be in my chosen family. Each was a wall of fire I had to walk toward and through; each involved confronting stigma and my own self-loathing. And from each I have drawn a great deal of solace on both physical and extraphysical planes.

What I remember about coming out as a lesbian in 1971, at the age of seventeen, in Salt Lake City, Utah, is how very harsh the times and that place were. I was part of a generation of young people who protested the war in Vietnam, experimented heavily with drugs, worked for social change and justice, and tried to free sex and love from the strictures of the heterosexual nuclear family. Certainly there was joy in that work, but it was more often either boring or frightening. It was only a decade after all of our marching and protesting that we found out how badly we had frightened the authorities and how powerful we were. At the time we were mostly aware of our fights with each other, burnout, the hostility we encountered from the media and from older people who were not politically involved, the violence that met our calls for peace and eventually seduced some of us into taking up violent means ourselves.

Friends of mine got killed in Vietnam. Other friends went to Canada, went underground, went to prison. Hippies were universally hated, frequently the target of abuse just as queers are today. I was a hippie, but hippies didn't necessarily like queers or feminists. There was one dyke bar in town, and it was working-class, hostile to antiwar work and the women's movement. I knew maybe three other dykes who were feminists, and they all had such serious personal problems of their own that they weren't much help to a kid who was trying to come out into a community that did not necessarily want my underaged, long-haired, dope-smoking, bra-burning self. Older dykes would not sleep with me because they thought it was "cradle-rob-bing." It was assumed to be a terrible thing to do to another woman, to "make her be that way." When I tried to join a lesbian choral group, because it did not require ID like the bar, I was told I could not come back because I did not look like a lesbian. If I had not accidentally run into another eighteen-year-old who also needed someone to bring her out, I would probably have had to wait years to connect with an out-of-town trick who did not know I had been placed off limits. Nevertheless, I spoke about being gay at college classes, I came out to straight friends, and I took an enormous amount of crap in the dorm rooms at school for being the only visible gay woman at the University of Utah. Jocks used to threaten to beat their girlfriends if they were ever seen talking to me, and do even worse to me.

Coming out was very lonely. I had very few friends. Most of the adult lesbians I knew were alcoholics, chronically unemployed, prone to violence, self-hating, apolitical, closeted, cliquish. Lesbians hated each other. If you found a lover you stopped going to the bar because you could not trust other lesbians; they would try to break up your relationship. My first woman lover went into the military, where she turned in other lesbians so she would not be exposed. One of my dyke friends got a job as a supervisor in a cabinet-making company and refused to hire lesbians because, she said, they were unreliable employees who were disliked by the other workers. The only thing that seemed worse to me than the apolitical lesbian community I came out in was the strangulation of pretending to be straight. I came out only because I could not go back; there was no place for me to stand in the het world. I was driven out.

Moving to San Francisco improved things somewhat. There was more public lesbian space there—six bars instead of one. But it did not alleviate the loathing with which my family viewed me. Nor was San Francisco in the early seventies any sort of gay utopia. We had no gay-rights law, queer bashing was a frequent event, and everyone had lost at least one job or been denied a place to live. It was a relief to be surrounded by other lesbian feminists, but only to a point. Bar dykes and feminists still had contempt for one another. Feminism rapidly became a way to reconstitute sexual prudery, to the point that it seemed to me that bar dykes were actually more accepting of and knowledgeable about the range of behavior that constituted lesbianism. In the bars or in the women's movement, separatism was pretty much mandatory, if you didn't want to get your ass kicked or be shunned. Separatism deteriorated into a rationalization for witch hunts in the lesbian community rather than a way for women to bond with one another and become more powerful activists. The lesbian community of that decade did terrible things to bi women, transgender people, butch/femme lesbians, bar dykes, dykes who were not antiporn, bisexual and lesbian sex workers, fag hags, and dykes who were perceived as being perverts rather than über-feminists. We were so guilty about being queer that only a rigid adherence to a puritanical party line could redeem us from the hateful stereotypes of mental illness and sexual debauchery.

What did I gain? I came a little closer to making my insides match my outsides, and that was no small blessing. The first time I met other dykes I recognized a part of myself in them, and knew I would have to let it out so I could see who I was. For a time, being a lesbian quieted my gender dysphoria because it made it possible for me to be a different kind of woman. That was an enormous relief. For a long time, I hoped that by being strong, sexually adventurous, and sharpening my feminist consciousness, I could achieve a better fit between my body and the rest of me. Lesbianism was a platform from which I could develop a different sort of feminism, one that included a demand for sexual freedom and had room for women of all different erotic proclivities. I had a little good sex and discovered that I was not a cold person, I could love other people. It was as a lesbian that I began to find my voice as a writer, because in the early days of the women's movement, we valued every woman's experience. There was a powerful ethic around making it possible for every woman to speak out, to testify, to have her say. But there were always these other big pieces of my internal reality that lesbianism left no room for.

The first big piece of cognitive dissonance I had to deal with, in my second coming out, was S/M. I date my coming out as a leather dyke from two different decisions. One was a decision to write down one of my sexual fantasies, the short story that eventually became "Jessie." At the time I wrote the rough draft of that story, I had never tied anybody up or done anything else kinky. I was terribly blocked as a writer. I kept beginning stories and poems that I would destroy. I have no idea if they were any good or not. My self-loathing was so intense, my inner critic so strong, that I could not evaluate my own work. So I decided to write this one piece, under the condition that I never had to publish it or show it to another person. I just wanted to tell the truth about one thing. And I was badly in need of connecting with my own sexuality since I was in the middle of what would be a five-year relationship with a woman who insisted we be monogamous, but refused to have sex with me.

So I wrote about dominance and submission, the things I fantasized about when I masturbated that upset me so much I became nauseated. Lightning did not strike. As I read and reread my own words, I thought some of them were beautiful. I dared show this story to a few other people. Some of them hated it. Some of them were titillated. Nobody had ever seen anything like it before. The story began to circulate in Xerox form, lesbian samizdat. I found the strength to defend my story when I was told it was unspeakable or wildly improbable.

In October of 1976, I attended a lesbian health conference in Los Angeles and went to a workshop there about S/M. In order to go to a workshop, you had to sign a registration sheet. I was harassed by dykes who were monitoring this space to see who dared sign up for that filthy workshop. On my way, I had to walk through a gauntlet of women who were booing and hissing, calling names, demanding that the workshop be canceled, threatening to storm the room and kick us all out of the conference. The body language and self-calming techniques I had learned when I had to deal with antigay harassment on the street came in very handy, but how odd it was to be using those defenses against the antagonism of other dykes. Their hatred felt like my mother's hatred. I am so glad I did not let it stop me.

When I got home from that workshop, I knew that I was not the only one. Not only were there other lesbians who fantasized about sadomasochism, there were women who had done these things with each other. I decided to come out again. If there were other leather dykes in San Francisco, they had to be able to find me, so I had to make myself visible. This meant that I often did not get service at lesbian bars, or I was asked to leave women-only clubs and restaurants. I was called names, threatened, spit at. I got hate mail and crank calls. But I also found my tribe. And because I had already experienced my first coming out, I knew we were not going to be an ideal, happy family. I could be more patient with our dysfunctions, and see them as the result of being scared, marginalized, kicked around. Being a leather dyke took me another step closer to dealing with my gender issues. I could experiment with extreme femme and extreme butch drag; take on a male persona during sex play. I gave up separatism because I needed to take support from any place where it was available. Gay men already had a thriving leather culture, and I wanted to learn from them. I also wanted to have sex with them. It still wasn't okay as far as lesbian feminism was concerned to be bisexual, to be transgendered, but I could bring those folks into my life and make alliances with them. I could defend them in print. There was even more good sex, and people who loved me and received my love despite the fact that it was dangerous for us to show ourselves to one another. I faced my sexual shadow, and she bowed to me and then danced beautifully in profile against the white walls of my consciousness. My writer's voice was unlocked.

I don't know how I would have gotten through any of those changes without drugs and alcohol. I came out of high school with poor social skills, partly because I was such a weird kid people were put off by me, and partly because my mother's religious fanaticism and my dad's alcoholism isolated our family. Drugs were a way for me to make friends, connect with other people, have a role at social occasions, begin conversations, get people into bed. When I was depressed or frightened, they helped me to make it through the night. I also occasionally got a glimpse of some larger love beyond the pangs of longing I felt for my fellow creatures, a love that was like an ocean of bliss. I felt as if that was the place where I had come from, the place where I would return, but I had no idea what that meant about how I should live my life. When I came out as gay and rejected the Mormon religion that had been forced on me as a child, I became alienated from spirituality as well as religion. I always had an altar on top of my dresser, and I was constantly reading about goddess worship, but I didn't reach out to others in the Wiccan community. It would have been the one thing too many, and women-only Wiccan circles were rabidly antiporn and anti-S/M in those days.

Coming out as a clean-and-sober person and as a spiritual being happened simultaneously for me, in 1991. Like any other coming out, cleaning up was a matter of "choosing" the lesser of two evils, at least in the beginning. I had briefly experimented with heroin in the company of a lover who was a long-term junkie. Smack felt like the experience I had been looking for my whole life. It was like being bathed in a cold sea of uncaring euphoria. I liked it better than sex. When I thought about that, and when I saw what it had done to my lover, I got scared enough to decide it was time to make another big change. Once again, I lost friends and sex partners. People told me I wasn't an addict, I didn't have to do this, why didn't I just abstain from heroin and do everything else? The problem was, using other drugs just made me homesick for heroin, and they no longer got me high enough. What I discovered in recovery was that being an addict is linked to being dishonest, and if you want to stay sober, you have to give up your secrets. The secret I chose to give up first was my paganism, my love for the goddess and my belief in Her love and goodness. I went looking for other people I could celebrate and worship with. The only thing that upsets people more than my being a sadomasochist is the fact that I'm a Goddess-worshipper.

No, twelve-step adherents and pagans are not perfect people (and usually they are not the same people). But by this time I was giving up on even wanting that. All I wanted was to get relief from the constant craving to escape reality with a chemical infusion so I could stick around for the rest of my life. And if I was going to live that long, I needed to know why I was here, who had put me here, and what I was supposed to be doing.

I'm really grateful that spirituality came into my life before I developed fibromyalgia. I've always loathed saccharine homilies that link disease with spiritual growth. When people paint verbal cherub's wings on somebody with a terminal illness, it makes me want to gag. You shouldn't have to get cancer or AIDS to be able to think about the greater meaning of your life. Stereotyping the ill as being closer to the angels is just one more way to ignore the grittier aspects of our reality, a way that the [temporarily] well or able-bodied put distance between themselves and us. But the truth is that many people don't face such questions until we are in pain, or know that our lives are coming to a close. Being disabled certainly gives you a reason to look beyond your suffering body for a source of contentment and meaning. I know there are crips who force themselves to go on just because they are so pissed off about being sick or hurt. I can't run on anger alone. Maybe I'm too old, or maybe it's just the ulcers.

Another leather dyke once told me, at a play party which I attended with my broken leg in a cast, "I see you finally got what you deserve." As far as I know, this woman wasn't my enemy. But she seemed to take it for granted that because I was a top, the universe would of course turn around and zap me, even though my "hurting" people was all about making them happy. How, then, could I hope for a compassionate reception outside of the leather community? It's still hard for me to talk about being disabled, in either venue. For the first two years I walked with a cane I frequently encountered women who would tell me how unattractive it was. That's petered out, at least in San Francisco, but I still encounter enough other unpleasant bullshit. I get challenged, verbally or physically, by leather dykes who think that my disabled status disqualifies me as a top. Or I am simply erased as a sexual being. In large public events, people frequently crash into me. They literally don't want to see anybody in leather who is also walking with a cane, or in a wheelchair. And, of course, both pervs and nonpervs are poorly educated about autoimmune conditions and prefer to see them as psychosomatic. This is all about well people being afraid that something mysterious will strike them down and put them in pain. And, Goddess forgive me, I have terrible days when I sorta wish they could have that experience, if only briefly, to teach them a little more empathy. Most of the physical help I've gotten coping with my illness has come from other disabled people, who can ill afford it, and I think that's pretty shameful.

At San Francisco Sex Information, after a moving lecture about the limitations that a deteriorating central nervous system had placed on her sexuality, a disabled woman was asked if there were compensations for being disabled. She was understandably outraged. "Well, the back of my neck has gotten really sensitive," she said bitterly, "but that hardly makes up for everything else." People are in such a hurry to dismiss, downplay, and overlook physical challenges that I hesitate to dredge up some of the positive aspects of living with hampered mobility, chronic pain, and cognitive problems. Certainly I have had to learn patience with myself and with others. I've had to become more assertive, to cope with medical people and with ignorant non-crips. When I become resentful or despondent, I've learned to focus on my gratitude. There are many things in my life which exist outside of my pain and give me joy. I'm especially grateful for the fact that I am able to continue to work, since many people with this illness cannot. Clear-seeing has become very important, since I need to know more than ever what I can and cannot do, and divine others' intentions toward me.

The fact that my body has become a source of at least as much misery as pleasure has paradoxically made it easier for me to stop calling myself a lesbian and use the term bisexual instead. I just don't have the energy any more to hold up facades. Back in 1971, I initially told people I was bisexual, but discovered this meant that straight people saw me as a heterosexual who occasionally dabbled in not-very-serious sex with "other girls," while gay people saw me as a dyke who hadn't come all the way out of the closet yet. Nobody trusted me, and nobody would dance with me. In 1980, when *Sapphistry* was about to be published and my first article about lesbian S/M appeared in *The Advocate,* I said in that article that if I had a choice between being marooned on a desert island with a vanilla dyke or a leather boy, I would take the boy. I got an extremely irate phone call from Barbara Grier, owner of Naiad, the company that was going to publish *Sapphistry,* informing me that they did not publish books by bisexual women, and if that was what I was, she would yank the book. Already in the midst of a firestorm about being public as a sadomasochist, I acquiesced, and delayed this coming out by another twenty years. I became "a lesbian who sometimes has sex with men."

I still think this is a valid category, and remain unconvinced that the most important thing you can know about someone's sexuality is the preferred gender of their partner. But today I'd rather not argue about it. I need to keep things as simple as possible. Bisexual people are still being excluded from the gay community's cultural and political life. And I find myself being personally affected by that exclusion. It hurts me and makes me angry in a way that it would not, I think, if I were not on some level affiliated with bisexuals. I would rather stand with a group of people who don't expect me to turn myself into a pretzel to explain what makes my dick get hard. This doesn't mean I think it's wrong or passé to be a Kinsey 6. But I do think a quest for purity of any sort is almost always morally dangerous.

Being more open about having sex with men has brought my own gender dysphoria to the fore. When I put my body up against a male body, what I notice is how hard it is for me to feel connected to my own flesh. Even more important has been the experience of loving someone who is a female-to-male transsexual (FTM), my domestic partner, Matt Rice. I knew Matt before he transitioned, and it has been such a positive change for him. By taking testosterone and getting chest surgery, he not only allowed himself to become and live as a man, he became a much better person—kinder, more patient, happier, sexier, sweeter. (Although he still won't suffer fools gladly.) The fact that Matt has managed his transition with this degree of success gives me hope that I might be able to find a less distressing place for myself. I expect, like any other coming out, this will have its shitty aspects. But I think it will also create a greater sense of freedom and comfort.

It's hard to write about coming out as a transgendered person because I don't know, as I type this, how that will get expressed in my public life. I haven't begun taking hormones yet, much less had any surgery. I'm still in the place of talking to my therapist, talking to friends, reaching out to people in the FTM community, getting more information about what it means to transition. Perhaps I am one of those people who can never fully identify as male or female. If so, being read publicly as a guy might be as unsatisfying for me as being perceived as female.

What I do know is that I can't continue the way that I have been for the first forty-four years of my life. I'm tired of being unhappy with my body. Tired of pushing people away from my breasts and cunt, feeling angry about the fact that my self-perceptions don't match what other people see, worn out by the laborious process I have to go through if I'm going to perform sexually as a woman. My body feels like the biggest and most inconvenient piece of drag anybody ever had to lug around. While living as a man would certainly involve being cut off from some aspects of my history, my experience, and my self, living the way I am now cuts me off from equally valid personas and desires. I am afraid to change, very afraid, and yet I think I do not really have a choice.

One day in therapy I was trying to tell my therapist why this had all come to a head for me. Suddenly I could not speak because internal events were too intense to express for a little while. It was as if a tunnel of light had opened up from my chest that ran back into my past and connected me with the self I was as a child. That little person was so angry about being told "she" was a girl, and shoehorned into that narrow role. How can I separate sexism from gender dysphoria? I'm not sure anybody can. All I can tell you is, I've done all the things I was told that girls couldn't and shouldn't do, and I've been a female sexual outlaw for a really long time, and it hasn't fixed things for me. It hasn't made me feel at home in my body. The child who cried every night about not being a boy needs to be heard, and it is my job to be a strong lesbian mother and parent that child with unconditional love.

Why do I feel this way? I don't know. It feels crazy. My body is pretty girly. The obvious explanation is that I am, like everyone else in this sexist culture, a misogynist. But I love female bodies. I love breasts and cunts. I just happen to intensely dislike mine, most of the time. Yes, I grew up in a culture that was intensely sex-negative. No, that's not all that is going on here. I can't think of one more thing I could do to liberate myself from the voices of erotic shame, and I still find myself thinking, my body should look more male. I feel more like a guy than a woman. Ironically, even though most of my lesbian partners have encouraged me to be as masculine as possible and reacted with dismay or outrage when I femmed it up, very few of my lesbian friends or exes will support me if I do transition. I think this has to do with their fear of their own latent bisexuality.

One of the ways I have to talk with my gods is to use divining tools to ask them what they want me to do. When I draw a rune to ask Freya why this is happening, I get the same rune over and over: Gyfu, the Gift. For most of human history, people who have walked between genders were revered since it was thought that they might be able to intercede between heaven and earth as well, unite other polarities to the benefit of their people. Our society has no such sacred caste. But I believe my goddess wants me to do this, made me this way for a reason. Perhaps it is my spiritual vocation in this life to experience virtually every aspect of sexual oppression and speak out about the suffering it causes. Or maybe I'm just reaching for grand explanations because I don't want to be perceived as delusional. I'm a therapist, and I know what therapists have to say about people like me.

When I first came out as a lesbian in 1971, identity politics were so pervasive that this modality didn't even have a name; it was simply the sea in which every queer sank or swam. One of the key assumptions of identity politics is that we can reveal in one grand social drama of coming out the absolute inner core of truth that makes up one's "real self." Coming out is seen as a process like peeling away the layers of an onion or the petals of an artichoke. Identity politics also assumes that your political allies will have to be people who share your identity because nobody else could understand your oppression or really be committed to fighting it; that people who share some aspects of your sexuality but not others are either afraid to come out or traitors to the cause; that it's not possible for someone to change the way they label themselves without being dishonest or cowardly.

Now I see queer politics quite differently. I know from personal experience that I can't trust somebody just because their sexual preferences or their gender identity resembles my own. I know we can make allies who are indignant about injustice even if it does not impinge directly upon their own lives. I see coming out as a lifelong process that proceeds as I become ready to understand and accept aspects of myself which bear lessons I need to learn at different points in my life. Each new coming out does not recreate me as a whole new person; I think some people view it this way, but this is crazy-making and too compartmentalized for me. It's more like being able to see each and every spoke of the wheel that makes up my being, or like opening up and furnishing another new room of my soul.

I wonder what coming out would be like if we were not forced into these defensive positions of tribal loyalty and us–them thinking. What if we could say to a friend who was embarking on a new coming out, "I love you, and so I must also love this new aspect of yourself. Because I care about you I want to know more about it. Let's both learn from this." Instead, what usually happens is a great deal of indignation, betrayal, and rejection. I think this is because a person who is coming out threatens the identities of former acquaintances, partners, and coworkers. If someone else's identity can be fluid or change radically, it threatens the boundaries around our own sense of self. And if someone can flout group norms enough to apply for membership in another group, we often feel so devalued that we hurry to excommunicate that person. This speaks to our own discomfort with the group rules. The message is: I have put up with this crap for the sake of group membership, and if you won't continue to do the same thing, you have to be punished.

We seem to have forgotten that the coming-out process is brought into being by stigma. Without sexual oppression, coming out would be an entirely different process. In its present form, coming out is reactive. While it is brave and good to say "No" to the Judeo-Christian "Thou Shalt Nots," we have allowed our imaginations to be drawn and quartered by puritans. I believe that most of the divisions between human sexual preferences and gender identities are artificial. We will never know how diverse or complex our needs in these realms might be until we are free of the threat of the thrown rock, prison cell, lost job, name-calling, shunning, and forced psychiatric "treatment."

I do not think human beings were meant to live in hostile, fragmented enemy camps, forever divided by suspicion and prejudice. If coming out has not taught us enough compassion to see past these divisions, and at least catch a vague glimpse of a more unified world, what is the use of coming out at all? I have told this story, not to say that anybody else should follow me or imitate me, but to encourage everyone to keep an open mind and an open heart when change occurs. The person who needs tolerance and compassion during a major transformation may be your best friend, your lover, or your very self. Bright blessings to you on the difficult and amazing path of life.

Phyllis Christopher

FREEDOM RINGS

Kanani Kauka

THE first time I came out to another person I was stoned.

Actually, that's not true. It would be more accurate to say I was about to become stoned, but the question, so unexpected, forced the air—or what air there was amid the hashish smoke—from my lungs as I coughed out a perfectly good toke.

I was twenty. She—the questioner—was my professor. We were in a hotel room in the middle of somewhere in southern France, one day into a two-day art history field trip, a few weeks into a three-month French foreign study program. The other students on the trip were elsewhere, playing cards in their rooms, drinking at the bar. I was in the room I was sharing with two other students and the professor, except none of my bunkies were there. Just the professor.

I can't remember exactly how I came to retrieve the stash and the pipe, can't remember how I came to load the pipe, can't remember what would have prompted me to do so in her presence. I do remember that she lit the pipe and breathed deep. I watched her release the smoke, pass me the pipe. My turn. I relit the sticky ball of hash in the bowl. I took as full a breath as I could.

So, she said. You think you're a lesbian?

(She didn't, exactly, speak those words. She asked me the question in French. I replied in French. My entire first time coming out to another human being took place in a language I can barely read now, let alone speak. This amazes me more than the fact that I was having it with my professor while smoking hashish.)

What else could I do? I coughed. My eyes watered. Umm, I said. Well, umm, yes, I think so. Yes.

Oui.

No one has asked me that question since, and I can't remember the last time I volunteered the information. Well, no. Untrue. Standing in my mother's kitchen, six months after coming out to my professor, sleep-deprived after end-of-term finals, I said, Mom, I'm a lesbian.

I don't remember much of that conversation either, except that it went okay and I don't think she was terribly surprised.

Since then, though, I don't think I've said those words to another person, at least not as a way of telling them that I am a lesbian. Show, don't tell, right? It was easier to just start going out with girls, and let everyone else figure it out. I dropped the word "girlfriend," casually, into any conversation where it was remotely appropriate. When possible, I would start sentences with "Well, as a dyke, I . . ." For a while I wore T-shirts ("Dyke" in rainbow colors was my favorite) and freedom rings. I put Queer Nation stickers—blaze orange, black type— on my jackets.

But for years now it hasn't really been necessary. I mean, how do you come out when almost everyone you know is queer? I feel bad on National Coming Out Day because I don't know who else to come out to—the bank teller? The guy with the dog who lives across the street? The bus driver?

Now there's an idea. I've lived in Takoma Park, Maryland, for five years. Takoma Park has been called the Berkeley—or the Cambridge, depending on what coast you're from—of the South. It's liberal. It's nuclear-free (really). The city council recently voted to censure Burma. You're not allowed to cut down a tree on your property without permission from the town. Domestic partners can register as such at city hall. Naturally, it's a dyke-fest.

My girlfriend (I'll call her Rachel) and I have been riding the same bus to the Metro station together nearly every weekday morning for the last two years. After a few weeks, all the commuters on the bus start to look familiar. You begin to notice who travels with whom. You start to give people secret nicknames (Franklin Planner Guy, Park Service Guy, Beautiful Woman, Vancouver Boy). Pretty soon you start noticing each other around town, start saying hi at the farmers' market. You don't know each other's names, but if someone disappears from their regular bus for more than a few days, you begin to wonder if they're okay, if they've moved or changed jobs. It's an odd sort of community.

Rachel and I wondered sometimes if our fellow workers had nicknames for us, too. What would we call ourselves? Dress Alike Girls? We've committed the Ultimate Lesbian Sin—dressing alike—on more than one occasion. We have totally dissimilar clothing tastes, but an unfortunate affinity for the same colors, so we've been known to show up at each other's houses in the morning to find one of us wearing tailored silk khakis, black pumps, and a dark blouse—that would be Rachel—and the other (that would be me) in khaki shorts, black sneakers, and a dark blue T-shirt. Embarrassing. We finally decided that our bus gang would call us Joined at the Hip Girls. We'd sit at the back of the bus, hold hands sometimes, whisper. We didn't need to wear T-shirts that said "Dyke."

But we didn't actually think about it very much either. We felt safe enough in our little bus world to be "straight acting" (ha ha).

And one morning, when we were standing on the platform at the Metro station, one of our bus buddies approached. She's a tall, light-skinned African-American woman with a penchant for outfits that Rachel admires, and we had wondered if she were family; she had that look about her. She apologized for interrupting and said, I just wanted to tell you guys that it's so nice to see you in the mornings. I looked at Rachel, a little puzzled. I mean, the woman continued, You both just look really happy when you're together, you sort of glow.

I started to blush. My ears got very, very hot.

Umm, I umm, I said.

Rachel was more composed (although she was blushing too). She thanked the woman graciously, and asked her name. Kara, she told us. I actually ran into Kara the other day at the grocery store, and we rode the bus home together. I found out that she's a poet and a sculptor, and she lives three blocks from me. I told her I was writing about her in an essay I was doing for an anthology. She laughed and said, Oh, because of that thing I did that morning?, and chatted for a few more minutes. I don't remember the rest of that conversation either, really. After all this time, is it possible that I'm still traumatized at the thought of coming out?

My girlfriend and I hold hands at the farmers' market. We have dinner (breakfast, lunch, tea, whatever) at Mark's Kitchen, a little restaurant in downtown Takoma, where we always sit at the same table and where, if one of us appears without the other, we are asked by the dyke waitress, Trish, where our other half is. It seems normal. I never think about it anymore. What was once so raw and conscious, overwhelming everything (for years, it seems, every breath, every step, was echoed by an internal chant: I am a lesbian), is quieter now, almost dormant. Every so often, it flares to life. I can never predict what will set it alight, but I'll feel it, that blaze of power that is nearly physical: I *love* being a dyke. Everything takes on an unnatural clarity. Colors are brighter; women are more beautiful. I felt that way a lot when I first came out. I miss it.

It's exhausting, of course, to live that way. And there's something about acting as if everyone knows I'm a lesbian that provides its own moments of fun. Like when Rachel and I are at the supermarket and the checkout person looks at us very carefully and says, Are you sisters? (Rachel looks really Irish. I really don't.) We giggle. Yes, Rachel said once. Twins.

National Coming Out Day is a couple of weeks away. Maybe I'll dig out my old T-shirt, borrow a set of freedom rings from someone (the colors have long since worn off my set), dig out my old sticker-covered denim jacket.

Or maybe I'll just ride the bus with my girlfriend, where we'll sit at the back, holding hands and whispering.

TOGETHER ALONE

Eva Kollisch

I am in a hotel in Washington, D.C., for the gathering of the KTA—
the *Kindertransport* Association. My two brothers and their wives are
here too. From 1938 to 1939, ten thousand Jewish children were sent
on "Children Transports" out of Germany, Austria, and Czechoslova-
kia to England—to safety. The parents were left behind. Most of the
parents were killed in concentration camps. My brothers and I were
among the lucky ones. Our parents got out.

Until recently, the *Kinder* who eventually wound up in all parts
of the world, just led their separate private lives. What was there to
talk about? Witnessing and story-telling in public gatherings belonged
to the victims and survivors of the camps. We were appropriately
modest about our experience. In 1990, however, the first KTA meting
was held in the United States. Then the words came, and sometimes
the tears: we discovered that we had a "story" too.

That first large KTA meeting had been held in a well-known
hotel in the Catskills. In the thirties, forties, and fifties, the hotel had

been a popular vacation spot for New York Jews. Singles came, and families and old people. They consumed enormous amounts of food—gefilte fish, herring in sour cream, latkes. . . . Singles paired off, old people played cards, children tumbled on the lawn and ate in their own dining hall. There was badminton, shuffleboard, tennis, and swimming. In the evenings, entertainers told Jewish jokes and the big bands played music to which everybody sang and danced.

I wondered about those times. Were there really happy Jews in America then? Those who were able to put a distance between themselves and Europe, I speculate. The rest must have felt guilty, at least some of the time, for not having been touched by persecution.

That's how we feel too, we *Kinder*. Guilty for having survived. . . .

This hotel in Washington is modern and impersonal. I check into my room, my brothers and their wives check into theirs. I have a single. Naomi, my companion of many years, was unable to come.

Would it be easier for me with Naomi here? I conjure up her high cheekbones and her hooded eyes. That keen intelligence, augmenting mine, would have helped me see things in their full complexity. Those arms would have cradled me at night. . . . If Naomi were here, would we be recognized as lesbians? Or would we just be taken for two old lady-friends? I picture us together, two gray-haired women with fine features and a certain Greenwich Village look. It would have been easier. . . . Nothing to explain, let people think what they want. Yet it's becoming clear to me that I will be able to give myself more fully to this experience alone.

About 150 people have come from all over the United States. Most are couples; there are some single women and a few single men. So many of the faces are familiar. It's not that I know them personally. Oh, maybe two or three whom I recognize from an earlier gathering. But we're all around seventy, give or take a little—that makes a tribe of sorts; in addition, people have that familiar look that is produced by a shared crucial experience. I always think that I can recognize Communists, Trotskyists, antiwar protesters, feminists, gays and lesbians. Then why not these *Kinder?* Survivors. Aren't they, of all my different associations, most truly my people?

Once again we tell our stories. This is my brothers' and mine:

In July, 1939, we came on a *Kindertransport* to England to live with different families. My brothers were happy with their family—the M.'s who lived in Bristol. I hated my family—the P.'s from Southport. I was barely fourteen. They made me scrub floors and be a nursemaid to two snotty little boys. No pay; no school; not enough to eat. No one to talk to. I had to share a bed with the old grand-mother, though there were plenty of rooms in that house.

But all those troubles were minor compared with my biggest worry: Mutti—our mother. It was already September 1939, then Oc-tober—and she was still stuck in Austria. Our father had been able to get out. Confused and feeling guilty, he was on his way to America.

All of us, my father, my brothers, and I, were trembling over my mother's fate. Fear for her life was all that mattered; everything else was put on hold. But when the breath-restoring news arrived that my mother was safe—at the very last moment she had been able to flee and join my father in New York—I became a self-pitying child again. I sent out heartrending letters describing my life with the P.'s and pleading for rescue. It worked. The Refugee Committee and my uncle, a refugee who had also settled in Bristol, found me a home in that city with Mrs. B. (sister of Mrs. M.) and her two little girls. Mrs. B.'s husband was away in the navy; Mrs. B. was glad, as she told me later, of another human presence in the house. She was a warm and generous woman who stuffed me with food, corrected my English, and gave me the keys to my own room. The little girls and I adored each other. I was able to see my brothers often.

Eventually we got our visas and affidavits—the war was already well under way—and, crossing an ocean full of torpedoes, we left to join our parents in America. A happy story, compared with those of many of the other *Kinder* here, my brothers and I hasten to say.

Three times a day the *Kinder* eat, sitting around large round tables, hardly paying attention to the food. They always sit with different people and exchange basic information. From where? What school? Left at what age? How long in England? When to America? Your parents? . . . if one dared to ask.

Whatever has happened since that time is wrapped up in a sen-tence or two. Most of these people here have led successful lives: they are professionals or in business. They are married or widowed, with children, grandchildren—they've been model citizens. . . . But all those long years of safety in America still seem a little unreal—as the discussion will bear out.

Anyway, we've come not to talk about what happened later, but about those few crucial years during the war which bound us in a common fate; "our story" is etched deep inside us.

When they put us on a train in Vienna or Berlin, there were tears and laughter; handkerchiefs waved, children craned their necks to see their parents; some of us were excited, some cried; we ate lunches packed by our mothers and played games to pass the time. At the border were the SS with their dogs; everybody, the children as well as their adult guides, was stiff with fear. Then over to Holland— Holland was still free—orange juice and smiles.

In the boat crossing the Channel, many were seasick. In London, the children had numbers tacked to their coats for identification. The Rescue Committee (made up of Jewish organizations and Quakers) took charge. We were sent to various places in England—to families who had requested a refugee out of compassion or because they wanted free domestic help; or to farms or boarding schools or temporary hostels; or eventually to the Isle of Man, where if you were a male over sixteen after 1940, you might be interned as an enemy alien.

Some of the boys went into the army if they were old enough— that was after 1941. There were Jewish refugee soldiers who were sent on the most dangerous missions behind enemy lines because they knew German; there were Jewish refugees serving in resistance units, like the Free Czechs stationed in Britain. The Free Czechs flew dangerous bombing missions. They would accept Jews. But anti-Semitism was not unknown even among these courageous, seemingly enlightened anti-Nazis: one of the *Kinder* reported that he had been asked to drop his pants during a medical exam, then was told, sorry, he had a "minor disability" that kept him from becoming a pilot.

Did the men have more interesting stories than the women? I wondered. Or do they simply talk more readily?

All day there are panel discussions and large and small group meetings. My brothers and I mix easily with the other *Kinder*. My brothers perhaps a little more easily. They are so clearly likable and respectable, with their gray hair, their warm smiles, their devoted wives, their stories told without self-consciousness. I am a little more self-conscious. People smile to see us three siblings together. They take pleasure witnessing our survival.

I feel so young that I'm sometimes startled to realize I'm the same age as most of the others here. Then it strikes me again with new force that these old *Kinder,* who look and talk the way I do, also feel defined by their early experience of rupture and exile. I've always felt a little rootless, in spite of my close family, my beloved partner, and my friends. But now I hear that many of these substantial men and women have also felt all their lives vulnerable and alone, in spite of their successes in the world. "Alienated" is the word they most often use. It stands for being there yet being simultaneously outside; a way of impersonating "normalcy"—a balancing act in which I'm at home. (Am I doing it even here? Yes, at times even here.)

A tiny old woman, a grandmother, says: It's a feeling that at any moment the ground could shift under you and swallow you up. Another *Kind,* a bearded, distinguished-looking professor, explains: "I've lived in a large comfortable house for many years, I have a family, good friends, and tenure at my university—but in my mind my suitcase is always packed."

I feel a tenderness for these *Kinder* so much like myself; they are my brothers and sisters. And this pink-cheeked youthful seventy-five-year-old from Vienna who sits next to me at lunch: he had spent a year in Buchenwald right after the Anschluss, not for being a Jew but for being a socialist; and he is *still* a socialist and internationalist, he doesn't hate all Germans, he doesn't believe in flag-waving, American, Israeli, or any other. I could have kissed him. For a moment I think he should have been my husband—I who for many years have shared my life with women.

One panel discussion is on the subject "Identity: Who Are We?" A poised, sensitive-looking woman describes herself as a rape and incest survivor. She stands tall and proud; she tells the large audience that she had been sexually abused in the family she lived with as a *Kind* in England. And when she was finally reunited with her own parents, her mother had a breakdown and her father beat her and abused her sexually as well.

You could tell that this woman had had many years of therapy. She said it had taken her until now to speak of these matters publicly. If not here, where? she asked. She was tense, defiant, barely controlling her anger; she was speaking on the verge of tears.

When it was over, I wanted to rush up and take her in my arms, I was so moved by her and so impressed by her courage. At the same time I felt shy. I haven't suffered like that. And also, I haven't talked about my "identity."

Later during the discussion a man says that one of the most precious things we have lost is continuity with our childhood friends— you can never make friends like that again. I think of the girls of my Jewish boarding school whom I have loved—killed or scattered all over the world. Now I feel like embracing him. How well he understands.

The thought that strikes me periodically and then gets pushed aside again, is how "straight" these people are. It's a thought that hadn't even occurred to me at the first KTA meeting I attended where the discovery of what we had in common was all that mattered. If there is even one gay person in the room, I say to myself now, he or she is well-hidden. And I too am well-hidden. I wear lipstick and earrings, I'm often seen with my brothers; on occasion I speak of my son, my grandchild, the college where I taught for many years. Clearly I too am a "respectable" person in the eyes of these others. Would they look at me differently if they knew?

One or two men have paid courteous attention to me. I enjoyed that. "Passing" seems like the most natural thing in the world, especially in a group like this where we're all survivors and the Holocaust overshadows everything. Yet I can't hide from myself any longer that even here, where I think I feel at home, there are moments when I'm overcome by a sense of not belonging.

One man, an artist, speaks of the years he spent on a farm in Northern Ireland during the war, together with twenty other boys and girls. They learned to milk the cows and mow the fields; they had to build their own cabins; at night, when they went to sleep and it was cold, they held each other close—also because they missed their parents. They were an intense community—many were already Zionists and dreamt of going to Palestine after the war. The man concludes: "I have never felt so at home anywhere as during those years with those boys and girls. They were my family."

I can well imagine his feelings; I envy him. Just then I learn from a newspaper clipping on the display table that during the time I was so unhappy in Southport, a group of Jewish refugee girls from Vienna were living in Southport too, in a boarding school; they kept a collective journal of which I read some excerpts. What they all said was how they had nurtured each other and how much fun they'd had, apart from the endless worry about their parents. If I had only met them in the park where they went to play badminton every day, if I had only been able to join them, how happy I would have been. I imagine them taking me home with them and refusing to yield me up to the horrible P.'s when they come to claim me. ("*Our* little refugee girl," Mr. or Mrs. P. would say when they introduced me to their visitors. "Oh, aren't you generous, my dear . . ." the visitors would reply.) One feels guilty speaking ill of those who give you shelter, however poorly—but I wouldn't have felt guilty telling my story to *those* girls; they would have understood and truly sheltered me.

More stories are told, more than I can absorb. So much heartache. So much strength in survival.

One story touches me particularly. A waiflike woman in her sixties—young compared to the rest of us—says that she was only six when she was sent to England. Her mother had left for England earlier—she had gone there as a domestic. The grandmother had sewn the mother's address inside the child's coat. In England, the girl was sent to a family who wanted to adopt her. They spoke no German, and the little girl spoke no English. All she could do was point to the address sewn inside the coat. Finally, it dawned on her hosts to write a letter. "We have a little girl here with your address sewn inside her coat. Who are you?" The reply came instantly. "I am her mother." (The relationship had been so self-evident to the grandmother that she had sewn in the address with no name.) The mother arrived in tears. Mother and child were reunited.

There is quite a lot of awareness in this group that we are not the only refugees. What we have suffered—separation from parents, running for our lives, the murder of loved ones—is the story of millions of others. In recognition of this, the KTA has a charitable fund to help other refugee children, no matter what their religion or from what afflicted country they come.

Once during the discussion about "identity" and belonging or not belonging, I quote Virginia Woolf: "As a woman I have no country; as a woman I want no country; as a woman my country is the entire world"; but for the word "woman," I substitute the word "Jew."

But even as I say this I wonder: Can you really feel closeness and love for the entire world? I cannot even summon up those emotions for most of my neighbors. But it is true: Every refugee is, for that infinitesimal amount of time I can bear to identify with her or his suffering, my sister, my brother.

Some people come to congratulate me on what I have said. Even if it is rhetoric, I think, it is also true. The fact that some of my fellow *Kinder* have been moved by the quote makes me feel good; I have spoken for them too.

The conference comes to an end. On the last evening there is klezmer music and folk dancing. A young Israeli woman has been hired by the organizers of the conference to demonstrate the steps. True, most of the people here would feel more at home with the fox-trot and the waltz. But for communal dancing there is nothing like klezmer. The rhythm gets into your blood. And many of us are moved by the Yiddish or Hebrew we don't know how to speak.

The young Israeli woman leads the couples; she shows them when to form circles or pass under each others' arms. Some of these old people show remarkable agility. My two brothers and their wives, too, are skilled dancers; they get up on the floor and join in. But you don't have to be a member of a couple or even graceful; anyone and everyone is invited to go up to the dance floor, though more than half of the people remain seated at their tables.

My feet itch, they beat out the rhythm. After these intense two days of remembrance and shared suffering, dancing is a welcome relief. No, it's more than that, it's a celebration. After all, we have come through—we're alive!

I would have loved to go up and dance with the others, but something holds me back. Shyness? Knowing that I'm not a good dancer? I still remember getting yelled at in my school in Austria for bowing instead of curtsying, for crossing over into the wrong row.

I go upstairs to my room. Suddenly I feel like an utter failure. Coward, I berate myself. And it isn't just the dancing. I should have had the courage to say that I am a lesbian. I've been "out" many years to my family and at the college where I was teaching. But how do you come out to a hundred and fifty people; strangers? They have just become strangers. . . .

I vow that I will do it the next time, starting with the small KTA meeting that is planned for New York. I will say: "My partner is a woman." Or I will use the "L" word. If they don't feel easy with that pronouncement, I won't come back. I can hear my brothers saying good-naturedly: "Was this really necessary? Everybody accepts you as you are. . . ."

"It's not true that everybody accepts me as I am," I argue mentally with my brothers: "Even for you, dear ones, I may constitute a bit of a problem in public. . . . No? So much the better. Thanks. Then you'll stand by me . . . ?"

It's not true, I argue with myself, that I can just walk out on these people—my fellow *Kinder*. And now I'm getting angry. How dare they reject me? Force me to break the bonds that connect me to them? They of all people should understand. . . . Bitterness rises in my throat. So, to hell with them, I say. But it's not so easy. They haven't rejected me *yet*. I'm going to fight. Yes, I'll take them on one by one. They are my people.

And having said that and made my decision to come out but stay in, I experience a sudden euphoria. I practice the steps they are dancing downstairs. Three steps to the left, cross over, three steps to the right. I bow, I curtsy, I turn around. And suddenly I am aware of high cheekbones and hooded eyes. Soft arms embrace me. My partner has come.

In this happy story I'm telling myself, people are dancing. They widen the circle to let me in. They say: "Where have you been? We've been waiting for you to come." "*Out?*" I ask. "*Ja, Ja.*" They nod their heads. They put their arms around me. I put my arms around Naomi. We're all in this together. We sway with the rhythm. We perform the unfamiliar steps. We're all good dancers here. We have no country . . .

May I hold on to these feelings of euphoria and trust as I steel myself for the next meeting of the KTA.

Certificate of Identity, London, 1940

DIARY OF A MAD LESBIAN

Lesléa Newman

I see by the headlines in our local gay newspaper that tomorrow is the start of Coming Out Week. Big deal, I think, trying not to yawn. I couldn't be more out if I tattooed a huge "L" on my forehead. I'm a nationally-known lesbian author. I spend the better part of the year touring the country to lecture on lesbian politics. I've done the talk-show circuit as an out lesbian. I've even heard that my name has become a code word among certain circles: "Have you read Lesléa Newman's books?" asked in a hushed tone of voice can sometimes mean, "Are you a lesbian?" Big deal is right. I am about to learn that, just like everything else, coming out begins at home.

MONDAY

I spend the day in my study, as usual, and when Mary comes home we decide to stroll into town for a bite to eat. We walk closely

304

together, my arm hooked into the crook of Mary's elbow. A dapper-looking man dressed in a beautiful suit smiles and tips his hat as he approaches. "You've got a beautiful daughter," he says to Mary as we pass.

I am speechless. Did he actually say what I thought he just said? Besides the fact that Mary is only twelve years older than I am, I am irate at the fact that our relationship is perceived as anything other than it is. I turn and yell over my shoulder, "She's my lover, not my mother," but the gentleman has rounded the corner, already out of sight and earshot. I shrug, and as we continue our walk, I remind Mary that it's Coming Out Week. She chuckles and reminds me, "You'll have to do better than that."

TUESDAY

After supper, Mary and I go to the mall so she can buy some pants for work. Like many butches, she likes to buy her clothing in the men's department. We particularly like JCPenney because it has an isolated dressing room right near the men's clothing section that is marked neither male nor female. Often when Mary shops for clothes, we have to carry her selections from the men's department over to the ladies' dressing room, which is on the other side of the store. This can be extremely inconvenient, especially because many stores only let each customer take in three items at a time.

Mary picks out various pairs of pants, and we head for our favorite dressing room. It's locked, so I go in search of some help. I return to where Mary is waiting, with a saleswoman around my mother's age in tow. "Do you want to try those on?" she asks Mary, all smiles. Mary nods, and the woman unlocks the door. I wait outside; Mary emerges occasionally to show me how she's faring. We both like one particular pair of pants, but they're a bit too big. I go in search of the saleswoman again, who finds the pants in the appropriate size and brings them back to Mary, who thanks her and continues trying things on.

Our shopping spree is a huge success: Mary has chosen half a dozen pairs of pants. We bring them to the same saleswoman, who rings them up happily. Mary signs the charge slip and the woman hands two enormous shopping bags to her over the counter. "Some-body's husband is going to be very happy tonight," the saleswoman chirps.

Mary and I look at each other. *Coming Out Week,* she mouths to me, silently, her eyebrows raised. Finally I speak up. "Somebody's husband probably will be very happy tonight," I agree, "but it won't be either of ours." Not coming out, exactly, but hopefully making a point.

WEDNESDAY

Mary and I go out to dinner at a local Italian restaurant. We sit at a cozy corner table, order drinks, and look over the menu. I'm not that hungry, so I order soup and salad.

Mary considers the shrimp scampi. "Is it very garlicky?" she asks our waitress.

"Oh yes, it's chock full of garlic," the waitress replies, thinking that's the answer Mary wants to hear.

Mary looks at me; she knows how I feel about garlic. I shrug my shoulders and say, "Go ahead and order it. But," I pause, "don't be surprised if you find yourself sleeping on the couch tonight." There, I think. If that's not coming out, I'll eat a pound of pepperoni.

Our waitress doesn't even blink an eye. "Don't worry," she leans down to Mary and addresses her behind her hand, in a stage whisper loud enough for me to hear. "I've got some breath mints in my pocket, and I'll slip you one with dessert."

I lick my index finger and mark an imaginary scoreboard in the air. Finally, Coming Out Week success story number one.

THURSDAY

The minute I sit down to write, the phone rings. "Is Leslie there?"

Nine times out of ten, anyone who says my name wrong is either a solicitor or someone else I don't want to talk to. "This is Les-lee-uh," I say, pronouncing all three syllables of my name slowly and deliberately.

"Oh, hi, Leslie," the woman says. "My name is Estelle and I'm calling because—this is so funny—I met your mother on a cruise ship last week, and I promised her I'd call you."

"That's nice," I say, because after all, what else can I say?

"My friend and I were talking about living in Northampton, and your mother was sitting right behind us and she leaned forward and said, 'Did you say Northampton? My daughter and her roommate live in Northampton.' "

"My roommate?" I ask.

"Yes, and what's even funnier is that I think I worked with your roommate a long time ago. Isn't her name Mary Vazquez?"

I am still reeling from the fact that my mother refers to my lover of ten years as my roommate, and I take it out on Estelle. "Mary's not my roommate," I snap. "She's my spouse."

"Tell me something I don't know," the woman snaps back, her voice indignant. "Mary was like that back when we worked at the hospital together, twenty-five years ago."

We both burst out laughing. So much for the old roommate ruse.

FRIDAY

It's time for my annual pap smear, which, ironically I get at our local Family Planning Center. I fill out the form, which unexpectedly provides a wonderful opportunity for coming out: a blank space next to the words, Method of Birth Control. I put down "Lesbianism," and then just for fun, add the words, "100% foolproof!" The doctor comes into the room, goes over my chart and chuckles. "I guess there's no chance that you're pregnant," she says, making a note on my chart.

"No," I smile, relieved at her reaction. "No chance at all."

LATER THE SAME DAY

I decide to treat myself to a manicure and stop in at a salon. A woman motions for me to sit down at her station, so I do. She takes my hands and studies them for a minute before she whips out her nail file.

"I like your ring," she says to me, shaping my thumbnail into an oval. "How long have you been married?"

"Ten years," I say proudly.

"Wow," she stops filing for a second and looks up at me, impressed. "What's your secret? It's hard to find a man that will stick around that long."

What do I tell her? In the spirit of Coming Out Week, I opt for the truth. "I'm married to a woman," I say, my voice still full of pride.

"Really?" My manicurist interrupts herself again to stare at me. "You're a lesbian?"

I nod, bracing myself.

"You know, my girlfriend and I were just discussing this," she says, moving on to my index finger. "We wish we could be lesbians.

We do everything together: we go shopping together, we go out to movies together, we have drinks together . . . But I don't know about having sex together." She leans forward and drops her voice to a husky whisper. "How is the sex? I mean really. Is it as good as with a man? Do you use one of those things, you know . . ." She leans forward even further and looks at me expectantly, as if I am about to tell her the most intimate details of my life. I lean forward, too . . . and reach toward the wall for her nail color chart.

EVEN LATER

After my manicure, I stop at a Clinique counter in a local store to pick up some mascara. They are having an "eye clinic," so I allow the Clinique rep to brush various shades of shadow across my eyes.

"Oh, that looks lovely," she says, holding up a mirror so I can see. Personally I think the purple eye shadow I am now wearing makes me look bruised, so she wipes it off and replaces it with a smoky shade of blue. "That's it." She takes a step back to admire her handiwork. "What do you think?"

"I like it," I say, studying my reflection.

"Are you married?" the Clinique woman asks me.

"Yes," I say, since Mary and I did have a commitment ceremony, complete with rabbi, many years ago.

"I bet your husband won't even recognize you, you look so beautiful," the woman says to me.

Unsure if I've just been complimented or insulted, I decide to honor Coming Out Week yet again, and clarify my marital status. "I don't have a husband," I say, still staring into the mirror as if I am addressing my own reflection.

"I thought you said you were married." The woman takes a ball of cotton and dabs at a minuscule smear of eye shadow on my left cheek.

"I'm married to a woman," I tell her matter-of-factly as I give myself a final once-over in the mirror. "I'll take this," I say, "and some mascara, too."

The woman rings up my purchases and tells me to have a nice day. "And don't forget to come back tomorrow and tell me what your husband thinks," she calls as I start to walk away. I turn back around and mouth: *Read my lips: I'm a les-b-i-an,* slowly and with great exaggeration, but my gesture is useless: the woman is already giving her undivided attention to another customer.

SATURDAY

My friend Tim invites me to accompany him downtown to the annual Octoberfest. Along with craft tents and food stands, there is entertainment, including a dunking booth for local celebrities. Tim is to be dunked at one o'clock; he works in a copy shop and knows everybody in town.

Tim takes his seat in a chair above a vat of water. Somebody throws a ball at the target. It misses. Someone else tries. It hits its mark and Tim goes down. He comes up sopping wet and laughing and gets dunked again. A crowd gathers to watch. Tim makes a face at me before hitting the water a third time. I yell encouraging words as he hoists himself back up into the hot seat again. A man standing nearby turns to me and says, "Your boyfriend is really getting it."

I throw him a look. "He's not my boyfriend," I say.

"He's not?" The man is genuinely surprised. "What is he, then, your son?"

I am forty-two and Tim is twenty-eight. While I suppose I could have given birth to him when I was fourteen, there are other options. "No," I say, taking a deep breath. "I'm a lesbian and Tim is a gay man. We're friends."

The man blows a puff of air out the side of his mouth, as if to say, *Just how stupid do you think I really am?* Then he jams his fists into his pockets and, without another word, stomps away.

SUNDAY

After going out for an all-you-can-eat brunch, Mary and I stroll through town, window-shopping. We step into a store that sells cards, clothing and *tchotchkes*. Mary sees something she likes: a tiny, miniature Ouija board on a key chain. "Why don't you wait outside for me," I ask, and as soon as she leaves, I bring the trinket up to the counter.

There is a woman in front of me buying a black-and-green sweater. "What do you think?" she asks the cashier. "Do you think this is too young for my husband?"

The cashier, who sports nose, eyebrow, and chin rings, pushes a lock of magenta hair out of her eyes. "I don't think so," she says. "Unless your husband is, like, seventy-five."

The woman hems and haws, and since I was raised in New York, where everyone's business is everyone else's, I offer my opinion. "I think your husband will love it," I say, as I move to a neighboring cash register. "I mean, my husband's fifty-five. Do you think this is too young for my husband?" I hold up the toy.

Everyone laughs, oblivious to my feelings of guilt. I know that I was being campy, referring to Mary as my "husband" in the same way gay men often refer to each other as "Missy" or "girl," but since no one else knows I was camping it up, I have committed the ultimate crime: I have "passed"—and on the last day of Coming Out Week, too. I should be ashamed of myself. But is it really such an awful thing to want to feel normal for once in my life? To just be one of the crowd?

"That's nine ninety-five." The woman who rang up my order interrupts my thoughts. She is also young, probably a student at Smith or one of the other local colleges. I open up my wallet, and the top part, the part that has a picture of Mary in it, flips open. Whoops, I guess I just outed myself, I think—but guess again. The woman looks right at my smiling Mary tipping her Fedora and asks, "Is that your husband?"

"Yes," I say, for lack of a better answer.

"Oh, he looks like he'll really enjoy this," she says. "He looks like a lot of fun."

I take my purchase outside to where Mary is waiting and tell her the whole story.

"Let me see that picture," she says. I open up my wallet and she looks at the photo. "Am I a handsome cuss or what?" She puts her arm around me and, laughing like the joke's on the rest of the world instead of on us, we walk the long way home.

Lesléa Newman (left) and Mary Vazquez on their wedding day, September 10, 1989

CONTRIBUTORS

Jacquie Bishop is a native New Yorker, free-lance writer, published poet, women's healthcare educator and sex and sexuality trainer. Much of her work concerns the political, the personal, the sexual, the unexamined. Bishop has worked in the area of HIV/AIDS education, prevention, and primary care since 1984. She is a contributor to *LGNY* (a New York City gay biweekly newspaper) and recently delivered a speech at the Lesbian and Gay "Beyond Borders" Pride Rally and a keynote speech at the National Black Gay and Lesbian Leadership Forum. Her writing has appeared in numerous periodicals and anthologies, including *The Arc of Love; Bad Attitude; Black Lace; BLK* magazine; *It's a Black Thang; Leather Woman II: Clash of the Cultures; New Youth Connections; On Our Backs; Tangled Sheets: Lesbian Erotica;* and We Be Women Press. *(Photo credit: Pat O'Brien)*

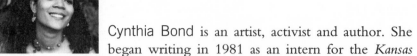

Cynthia Bond is an artist, activist and author. She began writing in 1981 as an intern for the *Kansas City Times,* where she graduated to copy girl and then became a contributing freelance journalist. She then worked for the National Headquarters of the N.A.A.C.P. Bond attended Medill School of Journalism at Northwestern University before transferring to the American Academy of Dramatic Arts in New York City, where she received the Drama League Scholarship. She worked for many years on the New York stage with notable talents, including Pulitzer Prize-winning playwright Charles Fuller and Academy Award-winning director Mike Nichols, and was also a repertory member of the acclaimed Negro Ensemble Company. She has worked extensively in television and has won critical acclaim for her film and stage work. After developing a creative writing workshop for at-risk youth, Bond found a new calling and has worked in social services for the past seven years. As the new director of the Pedro Zamora Youth HIV clinic at the Los Angeles Gay & Lesbian Center, Bond works to improve the lives of gay and lesbian youth through advocacy, empowerment and youth-sensitive health care. She has worked artistically with youth in a variety of venues, including the UCLA Community Based Learning Program, the Los Angeles Cultural Affairs Department Youth Division, and as the Artistic Coordinator for the Youth Services Department at the L.A. Gay & Lesbian Center. She is currently working on her first novel, *Ruby,* an excerpt from which was critically praised when it appeared in the anthology *Afrekete. (Photo credit: Renée Martínez)*

Cheryl Boyce Taylor is a performance poet, activist, and visual artist. Her work has appeared in numerous journals and anthologies, including *The Zenith of Desire, In Defense of Mumia, Catch the Fire, Chelsea #64,* and *Best Lesbian Erotica.* Her first book of poetry, *Raw Air,* was published in 1997 by Fly By Night Press in association with A Gathering of Tribes. Boyce Taylor has presented her work throughout Africa, Europe, and the Caribbean. In 1994 she toured the U.S. as a road poet with Lollapalooza Music Festival and represented New York City at the National Poetry Slam Festival in

Asheville, North Carolina. She has created lyrics for Eve Buglarian and her band Twisted TuTu and has been a collaborating artist in the Thelma Hill Dance Project's production "Toenails of Steel and Ruby Red Text." She appears in *Litany for Survival,* a film on the life of poet/activist Audre Lorde. She is currently working on a book about her travels to Gorée Island, Senegal, West Africa, the largest slave port in Africa. She lives in Fort Greene, Brooklyn, New York. *(Photo credit: D. L. Weber)*

Blanche McCrary Boyd's most recent novel is *Terminal Velocity.* Her previous novel, *The Revolution of Little Girls,* won the Lambda Literary Award for Lesbian Fiction in 1991. Her essays and stories have appeared in the *Village Voice, Esquire,* the *New York Times Sunday Magazine, Vanity Fair,* the *Oxford American,* and many other publications. A collection of her essays from the *Village Voice, The Redneck Way of Knowledge,* was recently reissued by Vintage, with an introduction by Dorothy Allison. Boyd teaches at Connecticut College. *(Photo credit: Marion Ettlinger)*

Rebecca Brown's new fiction, *The Dogs: A Modern Bestiary,* was published in 1998 by City Lights. She is also the author of six other works of fiction, including *The Gifts of the Body, The Terrible Girls, Annie Oakley's Girl, The Haunted House, The Children's Crusade,* and *What Keeps Me Here.* Her work has been awarded the Boston Book Review Award for Fiction, the Lambda Literary Award, the Pacific Northwest Bookseller's Association Award, and a Washington State Governor's Award. It has been widely anthologized, including stories in the *Norton Anthology of Literature by Women* and the *Penguin Book of Lesbian Short Stories.* She has taught at the University of Washington, Extension, Pacific Lutheran University, and The Richard Hugo House, and has recently joined the MFA faculty at Goddard College. In 1998 she coproduced, with Nico Vasilakis, the Stein-a-thon, the first ever twenty-four-hour marathon performance of the work of Gertrude Stein. Her criticism and reviews appear frequently in the arts weekly *The Stranger.* She lives in Seattle, Washington. *(Photo credit: Rick Dahms)*

Pat Califia's fiction and nonfiction writing about the politics of desire have appeared all over the place. S/he has two short story collections in print, *Macho Sluts* and *Melting Point;* a collection of essays entitled *Public Sex; Diesel Fuel,* a collection of poetry; a lesbian sex manual entitled *Sapphistry;* and *Sex Changes,* a book about the politics of transgenderism. Magazines that have featured hir work include *The Advocate, Out,* and *POZ* magazine, among others. Califia's advice column currently appears in *Girlfriends* magazine. S/he is working on a new collection of short erotic fiction for Alyson Publications and a novel for Masquerade Books. Califia lives in San Francisco with two cats, two dogs, a snake, and a pet boy. *(Photo credit: Jesse G. Merril)*

Mary Beth Caschetta is the author of *Lucy on the West Coast and Other Lesbian Short Fiction* (Alyson, 1996), which *Ms.* magazine called "a spectacular collection of women and girls, fugitives and ghosts, invalids and activists . . . a sensitive and telling portrait of contemporary American life—lesbian life." A pharmaceutical copywriter by day, Caschetta also adjuncts variously at Hunter College, Fordham University, New York University, and Vassar College, teaching writing. She is currently finishing her next collection of stories, *Wonderful You,* and working on a first novel, *A Hundred Mothers.* She lives in Brooklyn with her partner and two cats. *(Photo credit: Dixie Sheridan)*

Chrystos is a Menominee poet, author of *Not Vanishing, Dream On, In Her I Am,* and *Fire Power,* available for a short time longer from Press Gang, and of *Fugitive Colors* (Cleveland

State University Press). Some of her work has been translated into a bilingual German edition called *Wilder Reis,* from Orlanda. She is the recipient of many awards, most recently an Audre Lorde grant to complete her novel, *Mon Oncle, Mon Amour.* She has been a proud lesbian since 1964. In the bars of the sixties, the phrase "cherry picker" was a slang term, somewhat derogatory, for butches who preferred one-night stands with women who hadn't been sexual with other women yet. *(Photo credit: Chick Rice)*

Karin Cook's first novel, *What Girls Learn* (Pantheon/ Vintage), was selected as a finalist for the 1997 Barnes & Noble Discover Great New Writers Program, won the 1998 American Library Association/*Booklist* Alex Award, and was the *Booklist* Editors' Choice for Young Adults. Cook graduated from Vassar College and the Creative Writing Program at New York University and has been a fellow at the MacDowell Colony, the Millay Colony, and the Virginia Center for the Creative Arts. Her work has appeared in numerous anthologies and in *Redbook, Condé Nast Women's Sports,* and *Out* magazine. She has taught writing at New York University and was the curator of the In Our Own Write workshop series at the Lesbian and Gay Community Services Center. A youth advocate and health educator, she has coordinated national health education training programs for Condomania, the first chain of U.S. condom stores and the Body Shop's "Protect & Respect" AIDS education campaign. Cook currently works as the Director of Public Relations for The Door, New York City's oldest and largest multiservice youth center. She lives in New York and Provincetown. *(Photo credit: Marion Ettlinger)*

Jane DeLynn is the author of the widely acclaimed novels *Don Juan in the Village, Real Estate, In Thrall,* and *Some Do,* and the recent collection *Bad Sex is Good.* She has been published widely in anthologies in the U.S., Great Britain, and Japan, and has written articles and essays for a number of magazines and newspapers, including *Mademoiselle, Glamour, Harper's Bazaar,* the *New York Times,* the *New York Observer, The Advocate,* and the *Women's Review of Books.* She lived in Dhahran, Saudi Arabia, for two months during the Gulf War as a correspondent for *Mirabella* and *Rolling Stone.* Musicals and theater pieces for which she wrote the libretto have been performed at the Brooklyn Academy of Music, Theater for the New City, and Encompass Music Theater. *(Photo credit: Robert Giard)*

Wendy W. Fairey is Professor of English at Brooklyn College of the City University of New York, where she teaches courses in English literature and creative writing. She is the author of *One of the Family* (W. W. Norton, 1992), a family memoir. In this she writes of her experience growing up in Hollywood as the daughter of gossip columnist Sheilah Graham and, encouraged by her mother as well as the ghost of F. Scott Fitzgerald, learning to love English literature. Her critical essays, short stories, and pieces of creative nonfiction have appeared in the *Virginia Quarterly Review,* the *New England Review, 13th Moon,* the *Journal of English and Germanic Philology,* and *British Vogue.* Her work has also been anthologized in *Season of Adventure: Traveling Tales and Outdoor Journeys of Women Over Fifty* (Seal Press), *Contexts* (Harvard University Press), *Dutiful Daughters* (forthcoming, Seal Press), and *A Jeffersonian Harvest: Selected Essays from 75 Years of the Virginia Quarterly Review, 1925–2000* (forthcoming, University of Virginia Press). Wendy Fairey lives in New York City and East Hampton, Long Island. *(Photo credit: Carmen Luisi)*

Beatrix Gates has published a new collection of poetry, *In the Open,* a Lambda Literary Award finalist from Painted Leaf Press, as well as two previous volumes, *Shooting at Night* and *native tongue.* She edited the anthology *The Wild Good: Lesbian Photography & Writings on Love,* which called on her years of experience as editor and designer of Granite Press. She has been awarded fellowships at the MacDowell Colony and the Millay Colony, and scenes from *The Singing Bridge,* a collaborative opera with composer Anna Dembska, were performed at the Ceres Gallery. Organizer of A Different Light's Poetry Series, she has also served on the Kitchen Table: Women of Color Press Transition Team. She has worked as a freelance editor and taught writing, literature, women's studies, book arts, and literacy in many settings, including Goddard College, the Writer's Voice, NYPL, the New School for Social Research, and NYU. She is currently writing autobiographical prose and working on collaborative translations of poems from the Spanish with Electa Arenal. She lives in Greenport, New York. *(Photo credit: Electa Arenal)*

Judy Grahn's work as legendary poet and independent publisher fueled the explosion of lesbian-feminist writing and publishing that began in the 1970s. She published her first books of poetry with the Women's Press Collective, of which she was a cofounder, in Oakland, California: *The Common Woman, Edward the Dyke and Other Poems,* and A *Woman Is Talking to Death.* Her books of poetry, drama, stories, and essays include *She Who; The Work of a Common Woman: The Collected Poetry of Judy Grahn, 1964–1977; The Queen of Wands; The Queen of Swords;* the ground-breaking gay and lesbian cultural history, *Another Mother Tongue: Gay Words, Gay Worlds;* and *The Highest Apple: Sappho and the Lesbian Poetic Tradition.* Grahn's work centers on reclamation of the values, philosophies, and aesthetics of the Sacred Feminine. Her latest nonfiction work, *Blood, Bread, and Roses,* outlines a new origin theory of culture as flowing from women's blood rituals, especially menstruation. She is engaged in continuing research, most recently in South India. Internationally recognized as a poet, cultural theorist, and lesbian-feminist, Grahn teaches her own work and theory in two MA programs at New College of California. Her many honors and awards include the Publishing Triangle's Lifetime Achievement Award in Lesbian Letters and an American Book Award. *(Photo credit: Jean Weisinger)*

Bertha Harris was born in Fayetteville, North Carolina, and was educated at the Women's College, UNC, Greensboro. She came to New York "to find lesbians," but the South and its voices pervade her writing. She has been called "one of the most stylishly innovative American fiction writers to emerge since Stonewall." Ann Wadsworth says of Harris, "Possessing a fine aesthetic sensibility and a gargantuan sense of fantasy, her experiments with the form of the novel are unlike any other examples of 'new lesbian fiction' that have been published since 1969." Harris' work includes the novels *Catching Saradove* (Harcourt, 1969), *Confessions of Cherubino* (Harcourt, 1972; Daughters, 1978), and *Lover* (Daughters, 1976; New York University Press, 1995). She is currently at work on a new novel, *Really Awful Queers*. *(Photo credit: Camilla Clay)*

Holly Hughes began her thespian career at WOW Café during the dawn of the Reagan era. Her first play, *The Well of Horniness,* was presented at many of the most infamous nightspots of 1980s-New York—the Pyramid Club, Danceteria, and the Limbo Lounge—as well as art spaces such as PS 122, among others. In the years since her debut, Hughes has performed at Dance Theater Workshop, BAM, the Manhattan Theatre Club, La Mama, and Soho Rep, as well as throughout the United States, Canada, Great Britain, and Australia. *Dress Suits to Hire,* written for Lois Weaver and Peggy Shaw, won an OBIE for performance in 1994. Hughes has also received several NEA grants and funding from the Rockefeller, Ford, and Astraea Foundations. A collection of five of her plays with accompanying essays, *Clit Notes: A Sapphic Sampler,* published by Grove Press, was nominated for a Lambda Book Award. She has worked with groups to create theater pieces based on personal narrative, such as *The Talking Cure* at DeMonfort University in England, *The Mystery Spot* at Kalamazoo College, and most recently *Student Bodies* at the University of Iowa. She has taught workshops at Yale, the Graduate Writing Program at Brown, Barnard, New York University, the University of New Mexico, Dartmouth, Harvard, Swarthmore, and the University of Puget Sound, among other schools and performance spaces. *O Solo Homo: The New Queer Performance,* coedited by Hughes and David Roman, was published in June 1998. Hughes is currently at work on a new solo with acclaimed director/designer/performer Dan Hurlin and on a collection of plays from the first ten years of the WOW Café, which she will coedit with Carmelita Tropicana (forthcoming from the University of Michigan Press). *(Photo credit: John Lovett)*

Karla Jay has written, edited, and translated ten books, the most recent of which is *Tales of the Lavender Menace: A Memoir of Liberation.* Her anthology, *Dyke Life,* won the 1996 Lambda Literary Award in the category of Lesbian Studies. She is editor of NYU Press's series, "The Cutting Edge: Lesbian Life and Literature." She has written for many publications, including *Ms.* magazine, the *New York Times Book Review,* the *Village Voice, Lambda Book Report,* and the *Harvard Gay and Lesbian Review.* She is a professor of English and Director of Women's and Gender Studies at Pace University in New York City. *(Photo credit: Jill Posener, 1995)*

Jill Johnston wrote for the *Village Voice* from 1959 to 1980, first as an art and dance critic, then as a columnist writing on her own life and on queer culture in an innovative, unconventional style she made famous. She has contributed critical writing and reviews to *Art News,* the *New York Times Book Review,* and *Art in America.* Johnston is the author of *Marmalade Me; Lesbian Nation: The Feminist Solution; Gullibles Travels; Mother Bound: Autobiography in Search of a Father; Paper Daughter: Autobiography in Search of a Father; Secret Lives in Art: Essays in Art, Literature, Performance; Jasper Johns: Privileged Information; Admission Accomplished: The Lesbian Nation Years; Marmalade Me: Revised and Expanded;* and the forthcoming *Write First, Then Live: The Reclamation of Family and Origins.* Johnston and Ingrid Nyeboe were legally married in Denmark in 1993 (same-gender marriage was legalized by Danish Parliament in 1989). *(Photo credit: Peter Hujar)*

Judith Katz is the author of two novels, *The Escape Artist* (Firebrand Books, 1997) and *Running Fiercely Toward a High Thin Sound* (Firebrand Books, 1992), which won the 1993 Lambda Literary Award for Best Lesbian Fiction. Her work has appeared in numerous anthologies and journals, including *The Penguin Book of Women's Humor* (Penguin, 1996), *Tasting Life Twice: Literary Lesbian Fiction by New American Writers* (Avon, 1995) and *The Original Coming Out Stories* (Crossing, 1990). She has received fellowships for her fiction from the Minnesota State Arts Board (1995 and 1989), the Bush Foundation (1991), and the National Endowment for the Arts (1991), as well as a Loft/McKnight Fellowship (1990). She was a YMCA Writer's Voice resident in 1996. Judith currently teaches in the Hamline University MFA/MALS Program and the University of Minnesota Women's Studies and MLS Programs. *(Photo credit: David Moses Olkon)*

Kanani Kauka has been an editor with the *Lambda Book Report* since 1993. Her work has appeared in the anthologies *Tomboys! Tales of Dyke Derring-do* (edited by Lynne Yamaguchi and Karen Barber) and *Out For Blood* (edited by Victoria Brownworth). Born in Honolulu, she moved with her family to Boston when she was twelve, and still considers New England home. She graduated from Dartmouth College, where she majored in history, activism, and being one of four out dykes on campus. She learned to love books and tell stories from her mother, who died three years ago. *(Photo credit: Sue Noseworthy)*

Eva Kollisch was born in Vienna, Austria, and came to the United States as a Jewish refugee in 1940. She taught German and Comparative Literature at Sarah Lawrence college for over thirty years and is now retired. Eva Kollisch has written stories and memoirs, including a book-length manuscript about her experience as a young Trotskyist during World War II. For much of her life she has been active in the peace and feminist movements. She is a mother and grandmother; her partner is the poet Naomi Replansky.

Joan Larkin's collections of poetry are *Housework, A Long Sound,* and *Cold River.* Twice winner of the Lambda Literary Award for poetry, she coedited the ground-breaking anthologies *Amazon Poetry, Lesbian Poetry,* and *Gay and Lesbian Poetry in Our Time.* Her work includes *The Living,* a play about AIDS; *Sor Juana's Love Poems,* cotranslated with Jaime Manrique; and *Glad Day,* a book of meditations for lesbian, gay and bisexual, and transgender people. She is coeditor of Living Out, a gay and lesbian autobiography series published by the University of Wisconsin Press. She has received fellowships in poetry and playwrighting from the National Endowment for the Arts, the New York Foundation for the Arts, and the Massachusetts Cultural Council. A teacher of writing for many years, she has served on the faculties of Brooklyn, Goddard, and Sarah Lawrence colleges. She lives and writes in Brooklyn, New York. *(Photo credit: Laura Silver)*

Heather Lewis is the author of *House Rules,* which won the Ferro-Grumley Award, the New Voice Award, was a Lambda Book Award finalist, and was optioned for film. She was the guest editor for *Best Lesbian Erotica 1996.* Her work is included in *Living with the Animals, Surface Tension,* and *Best Lesbian Erotica 1997.* Her latest novel is *The Second Suspect.* She lives in New York City. *(Photo credit: Jill Krementz)*

Elizabeth Lorde-Rollins, M.D., was born and raised in New York City by her mother, Audre Lorde, her parent, Frances Clayton, and her father, Edwin Rollins. After graduating from Radcliffe College of Harvard University in psychology, she taught third grade in a Harlem public school for three years. She also taught adult education in English grammar and composition at District Council 37 for four years. She is a 1993 graduate of the Columbia College of Physicians and Surgeons and completed her residency in obstetrics and gynecology at the Sloane Hospital for Women of Columbia-Presbyterian Medical Center in 1997. Currently, she practices obstetrics and gynecology in Pennsylvania. Her poetry has appeared in *The Arc of Love*, edited by Clare Coss. *(Photo credit: Fromex Photos)*

Eileen Myles is a poet who has been living and writing in New York since the mid-seventies. She came out of the East Village poetry scene and worked as assistant to the poet James Schuyler, who was a friend and great influence on her work. From 1984–86 she was the Artistic Director of St. Mark's Poetry Project. Myles is a virtuoso performer who has read her poems at CBGB's, Stanford, and MOMA; toured nationally in 1997 with Sister Spit, San Francisco's all-girl spoken mike; and read her work in Germany, Russia, and Iceland. She coedited (with Liz Kotz) *The New Fuck You: Adventures in Lesbian Reading.* Her articles and reviews have appeared in *The Nation*, the *Village Voice, Art in America, Out,* and *The Stranger.* Her books of poetry and fiction include *School of Fish, Maxfield Parrish, Chelsea Girls,* and *Not Me.* Currently, she's completing a novel called *Cool for You.* *(Photo credit: Amy Steiner)*

Letta Neely is a Blk Dyke, Earthkeeper, Feminist, Writer, and Teacher. She was raised in Indianapolis, Indiana. After a stint in Brooklyn, she now resides in Massachusetts. She is the author of a book of poetry, *Juba,* published by Wildheart Press and nominated for a Lambda Literary Award, and two chapbooks: *gawd and alluh huh sistahs* (collective effort coalition) and *when we were mud* (Lunar Offensive). *(Photo credit: Lynne Mendes)*

Joan Nestle was born in New York City in 1940, a working-class Jew raised by her mother, who worked as a bookkeeper in the garment industry. She came out as a lesbian in Greenwich Village in the 1950s, marched in Selma in 1965, joined the ranks of the feminist movement in 1971, and helped establish the Gay Academic Union in 1972. In 1973, Nestle cofounded the Lesbian Herstory Archives, which now fills a three-story building in Park Slope, Brooklyn. Nestle's most recent book is *A Fragile Union: New and Selected Writings* (Cleis Press). She is the author of *A Restricted Country* and editor of *The Persistent Desire: A Femme-Butch Reader.* She is coeditor (with Naomi Holoch) of *Worlds Unspoken: An Anthology of International Lesbian Fiction* and the *Women on Women* lesbian fiction series. With John Preston, she coedited *Sister and Brother: Lesbians and Gay Men Write About Their Lives Together.* She has received numerous awards, including the Bill Whitehead Award for Lifetime Achievement in Lesbian and Gay Literature, the American Library Association's Gay/Lesbian Book Award, and the Lambda Literary Award for Lesbian Nonfiction. She lives in New York. *(Photo credit: Kathryn Kirk)*

Lesléa Newman is an author and editor whose twenty-seven books include *The Femme Mystique, The Little Butch Book, Still Life with Buddy, Out of the Closet and Nothing to Wear, A Letter to Harvey Milk,* and *Heather Has Two Mommies.* Her literary awards include Creative Writing Fellowships from the Massachusetts Artists Foundation and the National Endowment for the Arts. Four of her books have been Lambda Literary Award Finalists, and her work has been nominated for a Pushcart Prize. Her newest book, *Girls Will Be Girls,* a novella and short stories, has just been published by Alyson Publications. She divides her time between Massachusetts and New York. Her website address is *www. lesleanewman.com (Photo credit: Mary Vazquez)*

Minnie Bruce Pratt came out as a lesbian in Fayetteville, North Carolina, in 1975. Her second book of poetry *Crime Against Nature,* was about her loss of custody of her two sons, and her struggle as a lesbian mother to continue a relationship with them. *Crime Against Nature* was chosen as the 1989 Lamont Poetry Selection by the Academy of American Poets, was nominated for a Pulitzer Prize, and received the American Library Association's Gay and Lesbian Book Award for Literature. She coauthored *Yours in Struggle: Three Feminist Perspectives on Anti-Semitism and Racism* with Elly Bulkin and Barbara Smith. Her other books include W*e Say We Love Each Other—Poems, Rebellion: Essays 1980–1991,* and *S/HE,* stories about gender boundary crossing. Her most recent book is *Walking Back Up Depot Street,* a collection of narrative poems about growing up in, and leaving, the segregated South. She can be reached at *www.mbpratt.org (Photo credit: Doug Lawson)*

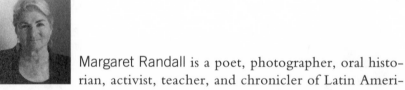

Margaret Randall is a poet, photographer, oral historian, activist, teacher, and chronicler of Latin American progressive movements. Her poetry, essays, short stories, articles, book reviews, and translations have been widely published for more than thirty years. A more detailed version of the anecdote that opens her story can be found in her book *Doris Tijerino: Inside the Nicaraguan Revolution, as told to Margaret Randall* (Vancouver, Canada: New Star Books, 1978). Her books include *This is About Incest, Memory Says Yes, Walking to the Edge: Essays of Resistance, Sandino's Daughters, Sandino's Daughters Revisited,* and, more recently, *The Price You Pay: The Hidden Cost of Women's Relationship to Money* and *Hunger's Table: Women, Food & Politics.* In Holly Near's words, "Margaret Randall is among the most enduring artists who choose/dare to express political sensibility in poetry of the heart." *(Photo credit: David Rae Morris)*

Mariana Romo-Carmona is the author of a lesbian novel, *Living at Night* (Spinsters Ink) and a collection of short stories, *Speaking Like an Immigrant* (LLHP); winner of the Astraea Lesbian Writers Fund Award, 1991; coeditor of *Cuentos: Stories by Latinas* (Kitchen Table Press), *Queer City* (the Portable Lower East Side), *Conditions Feminist Journal,* and *COLORlife!* magazine. She has been published in English and in Spanish in an eclectic variety of anthologies and periodicals, was producer and commentator in the first Latina Lesbian feminist radio program, WHUS FM, 1977–1980. She has been an activist in efforts to create spaces for publication of lesbian and gay people of color, and has been recognized with community awards by MACT/NY, *Las Buenas Amigas,* and the NYC AVP Courage Award. *(Photo credit: June Chan)*

Cecilia Tan is the author of *Black Feathers: Erotic Dreams* (HarperCollins, 1998) and *Telepaths Don't Need SafeWords* (Circlet Press, 1992). She is best known for combining erotica with science fiction and fantasy themes. Her work has appeared in *Best American Erotica* (1996 and 1999), *Best Lesbian Erotica 1997, The Mammoth Book of New Erotica,* and dozens of other magazines and anthologies of erotic SF/F. She is active in the National Leather Association and the National Coalition for Sexual Freedom. Her two cats are not aloof and she and her male life partner are "very queer for each other."

Tristan Taormino is the author of *The Ultimate Guide to Anal Sex for Women* and winner of the 1998 Firecracker Alternative Book Award. She is series editor of *Best Lesbian Erotica* and coeditor of *A Girl's Guide to Taking Over the World: Writing from the*

Girl Zine Revolution. She was publisher and editor-in-chief of *Pucker Up* and is a contributing editor of *On Our Backs.* Her writing has appeared in *Heatwave, Chick-Lit 2, Sex Spoken Here, The Advocate,* the *Boston Phoenix, Paper, Sojourner,* and *XXX Fruit. (Photo credit: Kevin Abosch)*